Word Study That W... for All Learner...

WORDS THEIR WAY™
Online Course for Teachers

//CODiE//
2011 SIIA CODiE FINALIST

This self-paced, interactive, professional development workshop is designed to help teachers, reading specialists, literacy coaches, and staff development trainers master the methodology of the Words Their Way™ word study approach for their students.

The Words Their Way™ Online Course for Teachers provides:

- **Personal training**—self-paced practice on your own time.
  - **Individual instructional path**—tailored path based on your grade level or role in your school.
  - **Interactive practice**—classroom video, student writing samples, assessments, and activities.
  - **Immediate feedback**—assessment that tracks and guides your mastery of the Words Their Way™ approach to word study.

Learn more and view the introduction at www.pearsonlearning solutions.com/online-learning/words-their-way-online-workshop

WORDS THEIR WAY™
Training for Teachers

Words Their Way™ Training for Teachers is a three-day, face-to-face workshop that will help teachers and literacy coaches unlock the potential of word study and enhance learning in phonemic awareness, phonics, vocabulary, spelling, fluency, and comprehension. Key features include:

- High-quality training on the research-based book *Words Their Way™*, developed with the Words Their Way™ author team
- Training focused on characteristics and instruction at each developmental spelling level
- How to effectively implement the Words Their Way™ approach in your classroom

WORDS THEIR WAY™
Virtual Training for Teachers

Pearson's virtual institutes are a travel-free and schedule-friendly way to learn about implementing the Words Their Way™ word study approach. Professional development is provided in 12 sessions over 4 weeks from leading authors and experts, featuring live sessions and self-paced learning.

WORDS THEIR WAY™
Coaching and Modeling

In this job-embedded professional development, a Pearson consultant works directly with teachers and coaches to analyze data, review lessons, and address areas of student need.

Coming soon! MY ONLINE WORKSHOP: WORDS THEIR WAY™

Short self-paced online modules sold in bundles that reflect a range of developmental levels

Learn more about Pearson Professional Development at www.pearsonpd.com

ALWAYS LEARNING

PEARSON

The Words Their Way™ Series

Words Their Way™: Word Study for Phonics, Vocabulary, and Spelling Instruction

The core Words Their Way™ book gives you the tools you need to carry out word study instruction, while complementing the use of any existing phonics, spelling, and vocabulary curricula. New online PDToolkit for *Words Their Way™* now available with the fifth edition.

Words Their Way™ Companion Volumes

These 5 companion volumes are targeted to the word study instruction of an individual stage of spelling development outlined in the core book, and, with reproducible sorting pages and directions, the books provide a plan of action for motivating and engaging your students.

Words Their Way™ with English Learners

Based on the same solid research, the *Words Their Way™ with English Learners* book and companion sort books for Spanish speakers help you determine what your students bring with them from their home languages, where their instruction in English orthography should begin, and how best to move these students through their development and help them master their new language. New online PDToolkit for *Words Their Way™ with English Learners* now available with the second edition.

Newest additions to the Words Their Way™ series!

Vocabulary Their Way™: Word Study with Middle and Secondary Students

With a focus on developing vocabulary with students in intermediate, middle, and secondary grades, this new book offers research-tested ideas for helping students use word patterns to puzzle out meaning to content area vocabulary. It also provides much needed assessment information to help teachers gauge where to begin instruction as well as hands-on opportunities for teachers to keep students' attention and interest as they build vocabulary.

Words Their Way™ with Struggling Readers: Word Study for Reading, Vocabulary, and Spelling Instruction, Grades 4–12

This new resource provides specific guidance, strategies, and tools for helping struggling students catch up with their peers in literacy. The thrust is intervention—specifically, utilizing word study with its hands-on, accessible approach to aid students struggling with the vocabulary, fluency, and comprehension load of middle and secondary classrooms. This book will help you determine student needs, provide you with the strategies to guide each student toward success in content area comprehension, and even outline ideas for fitting these strategies into your crowded schedule.

Learn more at www.allynbaconmerrill.com/wordstheirway

Word Study In Action

Words Their Way
With English Learners

Words Their Way™: Word Study in Action with English Learners
The official companion eases your classroom preparation!

Word Study in Action with English Learners, the classroom-ready companion to **Words Their Way™ with English Learners: Word Study for Phonics, Vocabulary, and Spelling,** is ideal for your students from diverse language backgrounds.

- Use the research-based developmental perspective to guide phonics, vocabulary and spelling instruction for Emergent, Beginning, Transitional, and Intermediate English learners.

- *Words Their Way™ with English Learners* will help you understand what English learners bring with them from their home language and *Word Study in Action* will help you guide students as they progress with literacy in English.

- 15-minute daily lessons integrate easily into literacy blocks.

- Weekly assessments monitor progress and guide instruction.

- Provide hands-on learning experiences by sorting ready-made pictures and words into specific categories such as concepts, letters, syllables, spelling patterns and sounds. Sort in your students' home language and English to tie the languages together and build upon commonalities.

Program Components

Each classroom package (Level 1, 2, 3, and 4) includes: 12 Word Study Notebooks, Teacher Resource Guide, Big Book of Poems and Resource CD-ROM.

- **Student Word Study Notebook**—Includes 36 leveled sorts based on phonics, vocabulary, and spelling.
- **Teacher Resource Guide**—Offers weekly lesson plans to guide and instruct.
- **Big Book of Poems**—Thirty-six poems that correspond to the weekly lesson.
- **Teacher Resource CD-ROM**—Includes games that correspond to the 36 sorts, sorting cards and their translations, and copy of the poems to reproduce.
- **Words Their Way™ Library**—Thirty-six books that provide additional reading and discussion opportunities. Libraries sold separately.

PEARSON

WORDS THEIR WAY™

Word Study in Action Developmental Model

Implement the *Words Their Way*™ Philosophy Today!

Words Their Way™: *Word Study in Action Developmental Model,* the official classroom-ready companion to *Words Their Way*™: *Word Study for Phonics, Vocabulary, and Spelling Instruction,* provides teachers with everything they need to implement *Words Their Way*™ in a ready-to-use format.

Newly Revised with Whiteboard Activities DVD!

By teaching with this program, you can:

- Instruct students at their developmental level while ensuring foundational skills, spelling, and vocabulary standards are being addressed.

- Implement an essential word study curriculum in just 15–20 minutes per day using routines and instructional practices provided.

- Utilize the program components for success. Classroom Starter Packs include 10 stage-specific student books, a comprehensive Teacher Resource Guide, a comprehensive Teacher Resource CD, a Whiteboard Activities DVD, and a Big Book of Rhymes (available at specific levels).

For more information and pricing, please visit **pearsonschool.com/wtw**

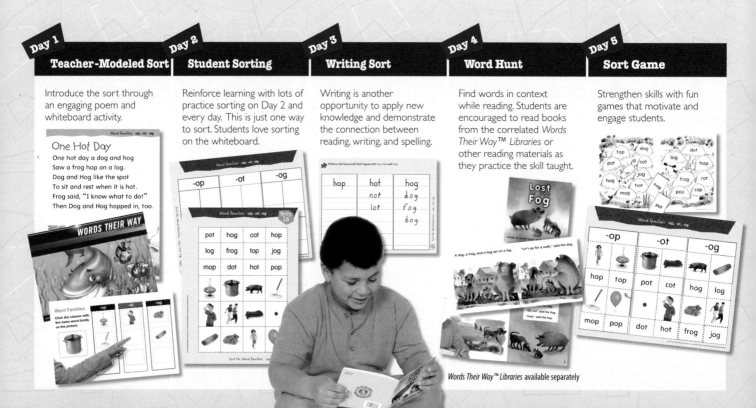

Day 1	Day 2	Day 3	Day 4	Day 5
Teacher-Modeled Sort	**Student Sorting**	**Writing Sort**	**Word Hunt**	**Sort Game**
Introduce the sort through an engaging poem and whiteboard activity.	Reinforce learning with lots of practice sorting on Day 2 and every day. This is just one way to sort. Students love sorting on the whiteboard.	Writing is another opportunity to apply new knowledge and demonstrate the connection between reading, writing, and spelling.	Find words in context while reading. Students are encouraged to read books from the correlated *Words Their Way*™ *Libraries* or other reading materials as they practice the skill taught.	Strengthen skills with fun games that motivate and engage students.

One Hot Day

One hot day a dog and hog
Saw a frog hop on a log.
Dog and Hog like the spot
To sit and rest when it is hot.
Frog said, "I know what to do!"
Then Dog and Hog hopped in, too.

Words Their Way™ *Libraries* available separately

Words Their Way™ with English Learners

Word Study for Phonics, Vocabulary, and Spelling

SECOND EDITION

Lori Helman
University of Minnesota, Twin Cities

Donald R. Bear
University of Nevada, Reno

Shane Templeton
University of Nevada, Reno

Marcia Invernizzi
University of Virginia

Francine Johnston
University of North Carolina at Greensboro

Boston · Columbus · Indianapolis · New York · San Francisco · Upper Saddle River
Amsterdam · Cape Town · Dubai · London · Madrid · Milan · Munich · Paris · Montreal · Toronto
Delhi · Mexico City · Sao Paulo · Sydney · Hong Kong · Seoul · Singapore · Taipei · Tokyo

Vice President, Editor in Chief: Aurora Martínez Ramos
Associate Sponsoring Editor: Barbara Strickland
Editorial Assistant: Meagan French
Executive Marketing Manager: Krista Clark
Marketing Manager: Danae April
Production Editor: Annette Joseph
Editorial Production Service: Omegatype Typography, Inc.
Manufacturing Buyer: Megan Cochran
Electronic Composition: Omegatype Typography, Inc.
Interior Design: Carol Somberg
Cover: Source Stockbyte/Getty Images

Credits and acknowledgments borrowed from other sources and reproduced, with permission, in this textbook appear on appropriate page within text except for images appearing as follows:

Color Insert: C-3, *Left,* Miroslav Georgijevi/Getty Images and *Right,* Stretch Photography/Blend Images/Getty Images; and **C-4,** Gelpi JM/Shutterstock. **Text Pages: p. 56,** *Bread,* Photolinc/ Shutterstock; *Ham,* Photolinc/Shutterstock; *Cheese,* Krzysztof Slusarczyk/Shutterstock; *Apple,* Paul Koomen/Shutterstock; *Milk,* Evgeny Karandaev/Shutterstock; *Blouse,* PzAxe/Shutterstock; *Jacket,* pavia/Shutterstock; *Mittens,* Rusian Kudrin/Shutterstock; *Socks,* Africa Studio/Shutterstock; *Skirt,* Africa Studio/Shutterstock; and **p. 120,** Forster Forest/Fotolia.

Library of Congress Cataloging-in-Publication Data

Words their way with English learners : word study for phonics, vocabulary, and spelling / Lori Helman . . . [et al.]. — 2nd ed.
    p. cm.
  Includes bibliographical references and index.
  ISBN-13: 978-0-13-611902-9 (pbk.)
  ISBN-10: 0-13-611902-6 (pbk.)
  1. English language—Study and teaching—Foreign speakers. 2. English language—Orthography and spelling—Study and teaching (Elementary) 3. Vocabulary—Study and teaching (Elementary) 4. Word recognition. 5. Reading—Phonetic method. I. Helman, Lori.
  PE1128.A2W673 2012
  420'.4261—dc22

2010029145

10 9 8 7 6 5 4

ISBN-10: 0-13-611902-6
ISBN-13: 978-0-13-611902-9

This book is dedicated to the students and teachers who learn from and teach each other in multilingual classrooms. We learn from you in the process.

ABOUT
the AUTHORS

LORI HELMAN

Lori Helman is an associate professor in the Department of Curriculum and Instruction at the University of Minnesota, Twin Cities. Her research focuses on the reading and spelling development of students learning English as a new language. Lori was a bilingual teacher, a district literacy coordinator, and a new teacher leader in her region before coming to higher education. She teaches classes in reading development for diverse students, effective instruction for students with reading difficulties, and leadership skills for reading specialists.

DONALD R. BEAR

Donald R. Bear is director of the E. L. Cord Foundation Center for Learning and Literacy in the Department of Educational Specialties, College of Education at the University of Nevada, Reno, where he and his students teach and assess students who experience difficulties learning to read and write. A former elementary teacher, Donald currently researches literacy development with a special interest in students who speak different languages and he partners with schools and districts to think about how to assess and conduct literacy instruction.

SHANE TEMPLETON

Shane Templeton is Foundation Professor of Literacy Studies in the Department of Educational Specialties at the University of Nevada, Reno. A former classroom teacher at the primary and secondary levels, he has focused his research on the development of orthographic and vocabulary knowledge. He has written several books on the teaching and learning of reading and language arts and is a member of the Usage Panel of the *American Heritage Dictionary*.

MARCIA INVERNIZZI

Marcia Invernizzi is director of the McGuffey Reading Center in the Curry School of Education at the University of Virginia. She and her multilingual doctoral students enjoy exploring developmental universals in non-English orthographies. A former English and reading teacher, Marcia extends her experience working with children who experience difficulties learning to read and write in numerous intervention programs, such as Virginia's Early Intervention Reading Initiative and Book Buddies.

FRANCINE JOHNSTON

Francine Johnston is an associate professor in the School of Education at the University of North Carolina at Greensboro, where she coordinates the reading masters program and directs a reading clinic for struggling readers. Francine is a former first grade teacher and reading specialist, and she continues to work with schools as a consultant and researcher. Her research interests include current spelling practices and materials as well as the relationship between spelling and reading achievement.

BRIEF
CONTENTS

CONTENTS

CHAPTER 3

Organizing for Word Study in Multilingual Classrooms: Principles and Practices   51

CHAPTER 4

Word Study with English Learners in the Emergent Stage   77

CHAPTER 7

Word Study with English Learners in the Syllables and Affixes Stage   193

CHAPTER 8

Word Study with English Learners in the Derivational Relations Stage   225

PREFACE

What Is Word Study?

For teachers, word study is a powerful approach to integrate the teaching of phonics, vocabulary, and spelling to improve students' literacy skills. For students, word study is a meaningful and hands-on way to learn how words work in English—their meanings, spellings, and patterns. In this book you'll find word study activities rooted in the developmental and instructional frameworks presented in *Words Their Way™: Word Study for Phonics, Vocabulary, and Spelling Instruction* (Bear, Invernizzi, Templeton, & Johnston, 2008), but tailored to students learning English as a new language. *Words Their Way™ with English Learners* builds on the same proven framework of assessments and instruction, this time in light of research into the needs and strengths of students with oral and perhaps written skills in a language other than English.

The research and instruction outlined in this book offer a teacher-directed, student-centered plan for systematic word study as an essential component of literacy learning. Teachers learn to assess students and interpret their spelling errors in tandem with other literacy behaviors. Teachers also learn to better understand the linguistic strengths that English learners bring with them to the classroom; from this information teachers identify not only the range of developmental activities that are appropriate for their students, but also the specific linguistic features that may be difficult and require additional support and attention. Throughout this process, *Words Their Way™ with English Learners* serves as an indispensable guide to teach your students the sounds, patterns, and meanings of words in English.

New to This Edition

The major impetus for this second edition of *Words Their Way™ with English Learners* was to add electronic resources to support the printed text. The current book includes an extensive media component on the PDToolkit website, including video clips from four classroom programs that have implemented word study with English learners. The website also includes electronic forms for managing assessments, planning word study groups, and creating your own sorts. It contains hundreds of prepared sorts and games that match the instructional activities described throughout the book; teachers simply go to the website to find the sort most appropriate for their students' developmental levels and either print out copies or have students use the interactive versions. On the website, teachers will also find foreign language spelling assessments for Chinese, Korean, and Spanish speakers. Many additional features have been included in the printed text as well, including instructional ideas based on the most recent research, extensive graphics to show readers how to implement the sorts and other word study activities, a new chapter to address word study for students at the advanced derivational relations level of word study, and a teacher-friendly introduction to the theory and assessment of word knowledge development in English.

New PDToolkit for *Words Their Way™* with English Learners Web Resources

Accompanying *Words Their Way™ with English Learners*, Second Edition, is a new website with supportive media components that, together with the text, provides you with the tools you need to carry out word study instruction that will motivate and engage your students and help them succeed in literacy learning.

The PDToolkit for *Words Their Way™ with English Learners* website is available free for six months using the password that comes with this book. After that, it is available by subscription for a yearly fee. Be sure to explore and download the resources available at the website. Currently, the following resources are available:

- Thirty minutes of video clips outline the development of word knowledge in English and show examples of word study in action with English learners at the kindergarten, second grade, and fourth grade levels. One video clip takes a look into a third grade classroom designed to support the academic and linguistic achievement of students learning English as a new language.
- An assessment tool provides electronic versions of numerous assessments and record-keeping forms and helps teachers administer and score the inventories, evaluate students' development, organize students into instructional groups, and keep track of class progress.
- Resources for conducting spelling assessments in Spanish, Korean, and Chinese, including voice files of the word lists in these languages, are also included.
- Hundreds of sorts, games, and other word study materials are provided to accompany the activities described throughout the printed text. The materials are clear and easy to manage, and they use pictures that will help students learn new vocabulary words.
- An extensive library of illustrations is included so that teachers can create picture sorts and games that teach vocabulary while students examine important conceptual ideas, phonics skills, or spelling patterns. The words depicted are translated into six languages: Spanish, Arabic, Chinese, Hmong, Korean, and Vietnamese.
- A Create Your Own feature allows you to modify and create sorts by importing pictures and words into word sort templates.
- Word sorts provided can be used in conjunction with interactive whiteboards.

In the future, we will continue to add other resources.

Content in the Printed Text

- A new chapter (Chapter 8) explores word study with English learners at the derivational relations stage, in which they examine word roots, cognates, and spelling–meaning connections. A number of instructional activities are presented to engage advanced spellers in meaningful and challenging word learning opportunities.
- Over the past five years a more extensive body of research into the literacy development of English learners has emerged. This research has been included to enhance the theoretical foundation and instructional activities presented throughout the book.
- Hmong translations of all of the pictured words for sorts and games have been added to the five languages already featured (Spanish, Arabic, Chinese, Korean, and Vietnamese) so that teachers can use this vocabulary as a resource for working with students, their families, and community members.
- References to multilingual and language-learning materials and websites help teachers access resources that build on the cultural and linguistic foundations of students from a wide range of backgrounds.

Format in the Printed Text

- Dense chunks of text have been broken up with the use of figures, boxes, and graphic representations for ease of understanding.
- Numerous pictures and sample sorts clarify how to do the instructional activities through each of the developmental levels.
- Developmental sorts and spelling inventories in other languages have been put on the PDToolkit website for easier access.

- The redesign of the book emphasizes coherence between the media and the book. Newly designed marginal icons link the reader to specific videos, sorts, or assessments on the web.
- The media guide in the Appendix summarizes what media has been integrated into each chapter and where to find it in the text and on the Web.

How to Use This Book: An Overview

Words Their Way™ with English Learners describes a process of designing word study that follows a simple progression:

1. Know your students and their language and literacy backgrounds.
2. Identify developmental levels and organize for instruction.
3. Implement word study.

Begin by evaluating your students' language and literacy capabilities, and end by providing developmentally and linguistically appropriate instruction in phonics, vocabulary, and spelling. The overview and instructional chapters in this book will guide you through this process.

Chapters 1 through 3 introduce teachers to the stages of spelling and reading development, the assessments used to determine where students fall along this developmental continuum, how to tailor instruction to support students learning a new language, and the best ways to organize your classroom for word study.

- Chapter 1 presents an overview of the research behind the developmental and instructional models for word study. It describes the way students' knowledge of other oral and written languages affects their learning of English language and literacy.

- Chapter 2 gets teachers started on assessment, explaining guidelines for observation and assessment and showing you how to interpret English learners' spelling in light of the influence of the other oral and written languages they know. As we observe in detail in Chapter 2, like monolingual English spellers, nearly all misspellings by English learners are "interestingly correct." This chapter provides interpretations of students' spelling to show what features to consider when teaching phonics, vocabulary, and spelling to English learners.

- Chapter 3 presents routines for classroom management and organization, as well as support strategies that make instruction understandable to English learners. The schedules introduce students to word sorting, and the routines provide the directed instruction that English learners need to study phonics, vocabulary, and spelling.

Once you've assessed your students' development based on the tools provided in Chapter 2 and have used Chapter 3 to develop routines for word study, the information and materials in Chapters 4 through 8 as well as the Appendix and PDToolkit website will guide your specific instruction. Each of these chapters focuses on a specific stage of spelling, outlining the most appropriate and effective word study instruction for each respective developmental level from the emergent learner through readers and writers in the derivational relations stage. Each of these chapters closes with a rich bank of word study activities that promises to engage your students, motivate them, and improve their oral and written abilities in English.

- Chapters 4 through 8 present word study activities, including concept sorts, word sorts, literature ideas, and games for each developmental level, that fit into a rich literacy curriculum. Each chapter begins with a research-based description of the stage and how the essential literacy activities of Read To, Read With, Write With, Word Study, and Talk With work together to support English learners' language and literacy learning. Principles of instruction germane to each particular stage of spelling development are followed by word study activities that teach and clarify aspects of written English. The activities sections are tabbed for your convenience, creating a user-friendly classroom resource.

- The Appendix at the back of the book contains the English assessment tools; pictures to use in sorts and games; translations of the picture words in English, Spanish, Arabic, Chinese, Hmong, Korean, and Vietnamese; example picture and word sorts; sound boards; and game templates you'll need to get your word study instruction under way. You will also find references for research citations, children's literature connections, sources of multilingual and language development resources, and an index.

- The PDToolkit website for *Words Their Way™ with English Learners* for this second edition text provides all of the reproducible and interactive materials in one place.

  - All of the assessment materials discussed in Chapter 2
  - Concept picture sorts, phonics picture sorts, and word sorts from each of the instructional levels, as outlined in Chapters 4 through 8
  - Templates for sorts, games, and other word study activities, as outlined in Chapters 4 through 8
  - Sound boards with pictures to help students learn letter–sound correspondences
  - Electronic versions of the assessment tools in English
  - Electronic versions of assessment tools in other languages
  - Pictures to use in sorts and games
  - A Create Your Own feature, where you can design sorts that match your students' vocabulary, phonics, and spelling levels

- The website also provides classroom footage of teachers working with English learners at a variety of developmental levels to increase their vocabulary, phonics, and spelling knowledge.

Companion Volumes

We believe you'll find that the hands-on word sorting approach to word study is an invaluable literacy tool for both your English learners and your students whose primary language is English. Broaden your word study understanding and instruction with the variety of additional materials available. Purchase any of the following invaluable professional resources at www.allynbaconmerrill.com/wordstheirway:

Words Their Way™: Emergent Sorts for Spanish-Speaking English Learners, by Lori Helman, Donald R. Bear, Marcia Invernizzi, Shane Templeton, and Francine Johnston [Specially designed to support English learners]

Words Their Way™: Letter Name–Alphabetic Sorts for Spanish-Speaking English Learners, by Lori Helman, Donald R. Bear, Marcia Invernizzi, Shane Templeton, and Francine Johnston [Specially designed to support English learners]

Words Their Way™: Word Study for Phonics, Vocabulary, and Spelling Instruction, Fifth Edition, by Donald R. Bear, Marcia Invernizzi, Shane Templeton, and Francine Johnston

Vocabulary Their Way™: Word Study with Middle and Secondary Students, by Shane Templeton, Donald R. Bear, Marcia Invernizzi, and Francine Johnston

Words Their Way™ with Struggling Readers: Word Study for Reading, Vocabulary, and Spelling Instruction, Grades 4–12, by Kevin Flanigan, Latisha Hayes, Shane Templeton, Donald R. Bear, Marcia Invernizzi, and Francine Johnston

Words Their Way™: Letter and Picture Sorts for Emergent Spellers, by Donald R. Bear, Marcia Invernizzi, and Francine Johnston

Words Their Way™: Word Sorts for Letter Name–Alphabetic Spellers, Second Edition, by Francine Johnston, Donald R. Bear, Marcia Invernizzi, and Shane Templeton

Words Their Way™*: Word Sorts for Within Word Pattern Spellers*, Second Edition, by Marcia Invernizzi, Francine Johnston, Donald R. Bear, and Shane Templeton

Words Their Way™*: Word Sorts for Syllables and Affixes Spellers*, Second Edition, by Francine Johnston, Marcia Invernizzi, Donald R. Bear, and Shane Templeton

Words Their Way™*: Word Sorts for Derivational Relations Spellers*, Second Edition, by Shane Templeton, Francine Johnston, Donald R. Bear, and Marcia Invernizzi

. . . .
Acknowledgments

There are many educators who have guided our way and assisted us in writing this second edition. First off, we thank Amy Frederick, a doctoral student and English learner teacher from Saint Paul Public Schools, who provided feedback, suggestions, and help with the logistics of the videotaping. We are so appreciative of the teachers who opened up their classrooms to model word study and effective strategies in teaching English learners: Linda Woessner, Claire Roberts, Kristen Polanski, and Fawn Nguyen. Thank you for sharing what word study looks like with students learning English! Helen Shen and Minwha Yang have been kind enough to share the spelling inventories and scoring guides they have created and we are very appreciative of their efforts. We are deeply indebted to the people who translated the word and picture sorts: Iman Chahine—Arabic, Qiang Li—Chinese, Joanne Vang—Hmong, Minwha Yang—Korean, and Thuy Ho—Vietnamese. The work in this book builds on the lessons of many experienced teachers, including Tamara Baren, Carol Caserta-Henry, Shari Dunn, Keonghee Tao Han, Wei Xu, and the numerous teachers we visit in classrooms each day. We also thank our colleagues at our respective universities: University of Minnesota, Twin Cities; University of Nevada, Reno; University of Virginia; and University of North Carolina at Greensboro.

We wish to express our appreciation to the reviewers of our manuscript for their insights and comments: Brett Elizabeth Blake, St. John's University; Marsha Riddle Buly, Western Washington University; Julie Coppola, Boston University; Daniel DeLao, Lew Wallace Elementary; and Kristi A. McNeal, California State University, Fresno.

1

Word Study with English Learners and the Development of Orthographic Knowledge

Understanding Word Study with English Learners

The percentage of students from diverse language backgrounds is growing dramatically in U.S. schools. To teach all students effectively, well-prepared professionals must understand the strengths, challenges, and learning paths of students who are becoming proficient in English at the same time they are learning to read and write it. You may be one of the many teachers or educational specialists working to adjust your literacy teaching methods to build on the strengths and meet the needs of English learners in your program. *Words Their Way™ with English Learners* is written for you. Using the word study approach to teaching phonics, vocabulary, and spelling that focuses on students' development, we call this book *Words Their Way*, because teaching their way is to teach developmentally.

> Word study is an approach to teaching phonics, vocabulary, and spelling.

Perhaps in your classroom or program you have just a few English learners who need support with academic language. On the other hand, your classroom might consist primarily of students who do not speak English as a first language. Maybe your English-learning students all come from one language background, such as Spanish. Or perhaps your school works with students from dozens of primary languages. Your students may be the children of immigrants, or they may have themselves just arrived from another country. Some English learners may have a strong language and literacy background in their home language, and they may have studied English before arriving. Some students come to the U.S. classroom with few or no print-related experiences because they have not attended school before, or they may come from a culture that is primarily oral in its use of language. All of these scenarios commonly exist in elementary and secondary schools in the United States.

Whether you work in a self-contained classroom or provide supplemental services to students learning English, this book is designed to guide you as you implement word study instruction and integrate it into other components of language and literacy learning with your students. You will learn about development as well as how to be mindful of the influences of students' primary languages as they learn English. Ralph Waldo Emerson compared language to a city, and in the building of this city, every human being brings a stone (Emerson, 1895). By understanding the language and literacy resources students bring with them, teachers build classroom learning environments that are conducive to learning to read and write in English.

Throughout this book and the accompanying website, you will meet teachers who assess and teach developmentally in light of students' first languages. For example, in Ms. Polanski's kindergarten class, children learn vocabulary by sorting pictures conceptually. Further

PDToolkit

for Words Their Way™ with English Learners

Go to PDToolkit, choose your book, click the Videos tab, and watch the two videos titled "Vocabulary Development and Concept Sorting with Kindergarteners in the Emergent Stage" and "A Week of Sorting with Second Graders in the Early Within Word Pattern Stage."

along the developmental continuum we see how Ms. Woessner, a second grade teacher, helps children sort words and pictures by vowel sounds. All of the teachers we present have a keen sense of what to teach by understanding students' development and their language backgrounds. You will also meet teachers who include students' knowledge of vocabulary in their primary languages as they teach upper-level vocabulary. For example, when Ms. Costa studies *petroglyphs* (rock + carving) with her fifth-graders, Spanish speakers brainstorm the word *piedra* in Spanish because it, like *petro* in Greek, means "rock."

The word study activities in this book expand and deepen students' word knowledge and vocabularies. Many of the examples are from Spanish speakers, who comprise the largest group of English learners in U.S. schools, but we also draw examples from a variety of other language groups learning English. When possible, commonalities and contrasts among the different languages are presented. For example, many consonant sounds like the final /d/ and /t/ sounds may be omitted by English learners from several languages, including Spanish and Thai, as well as many dialects of English. Being aware of these common challenges makes it possible to focus on the same skill with students from different language backgrounds.

You will find activities that support oral and written language development while stimulating vocabulary learning. For example, the pictures in the concept sorts create a way for students to be involved in using new vocabulary. When students read a series of words aloud to check their sorting, they experience and learn ways to pronounce words and sounds that may be new to them. Reading a set of prefixes in English with a partner and looking for meaning connections also teaches them how to pronounce new words. At the upper levels of word study, students learn a more technical, content-oriented vocabulary as they compare Greek–Latin connections in English and their home language.

In this introductory chapter and the next two, you will find information on how to assess development and organize instruction. Then you will find five chapters, each dedicated to one of the five stages of development. The myriad word study activities will serve your students as they study English phonics, vocabulary, and spelling. By mastering the principles taught in these activities, students will advance as readers and writers.

Instruction in Multilingual and Multiliterate Contexts

Students who are learning English grow up in multilingual and multiliterate contexts with two or more languages and literacies. They can experience a variety of learning scenarios in different American schools. Some English learners are able to participate in **bilingual programs** that allow them to develop literacy skills in their home language while learning to speak, read, and write in English. Other programs involve specially tailored instruction to support students as they tackle content in all-English settings. In some schools, "newcomer" programs provide an initial setting for helping English learners transition into the new cultural and academic content of their schools. Recent research findings have pointed out that English learners who do not receive language support in school show much less progress in reading and math achievement when compared to similar students who participate in language support programs such as bilingual education or **sheltered English** (August & Shanahan, 2006; Genesee, Lindholm-Leary, Saunders, & Christian, 2005; Slavin & Cheung, 2005; Thomas & Collier, 2002).

Who Are English Learners in the United States?

Recent U.S. demographic data shows that 10.8 million of the roughly 58 million children ages 5 to 17 speak a language other than English at home; of this group, 2.7 million children speak English with difficulty. Interestingly, the percentage of children having difficulty speaking English has decreased progressively since 2000, from 31 to 25 percent. The ten most prevalent languages are presented in Table 1.1. Of those English learners having difficulty speaking English, 75 percent speak Spanish as their first language, 12 percent (320,000)

▶ **Bilingual Programs**
Bilingual programs encourage literacy development in students' home languages and in English.

▶ **Sheltered English**
Sheltered English is an approach to instruction that provides additional support for students learning English by simplifying language, defining vocabulary, and providing time for students to discuss content area studies.

speak Asian/Pacific Islander languages, and 10 percent (287,000) speak Indo-European languages (Planty et al., 2009). As can be seen in Table 1.1 (based on U.S. Census data from 2000), there are differences between the elementary and secondary grades in the top ten languages spoken by students of limited English proficiency. Interestingly, more children of immigrants are entering school at the secondary than at the elementary level (Capps, Fix, Murray, Ost, Passel, & Herwantoro, 2005).

In elementary grades, six out of seven students with limited English proficiencies live in linguistically isolated homes where they do not hear English. These students' experiences at home may be related to the slower rate at which they learn English (Capps, Fix, Murray, Ost, Passel, Herwantoro, 2005). Students' proficiencies in English vary by demographic subgroups and poverty levels (Planty et al., 2009).

There is a relationship between limited English proficiency and poverty. Of school-age children who are poor or nearly poor, 18 percent are English learners; in contrast, non-poor students account for only 3 percent of English learners (Planty et al., 2009). And most schools with many students of limited English proficiency have large low-income populations (Cosentina de Cohen, Deterding, & Clewell, 2005). More than half the students of immigrants in elementary schools are economically disadvantaged.

Most states show increases in the number of children of immigrants in their schools. For example, between 1990 and 2000, enrollment by children of immigrants increased by 153 percent in North Carolina, 148 percent in Georgia, and 125 percent in Nebraska (Capps et al., 2005). Of the 20 percent of school-age students who are children of immigrants, three-quarters were born in the United States and are U.S. citizens. Nearly 70 percent of children of immigrants live in the six most highly populated states: California, Texas, New York, Florida, Illinois, and New

| TABLE 1.1 | **Top Ten Languages Spoken by Limited English Proficient Children by Grade Level, 2000, from Pre-K to 5th Grade and 6th to 12th Grade** |

LANGUAGE	NUMBER	PERCENT
Pre-K to 5th Grade		
Spanish	1,360,000	76.1
Chinese	46,000	2.6
Vietnamese	44,000	2.5
Korean	25,000	1.4
Hmong/Miao	24,000	1.3
French	20,000	1.1
German	19,000	1.1
Russian	17,000	1.0
French/Haitian Creole	16,000	0.9
Arabic	14,000	0.8
All languages	**1,676,000**	**100.00**
Pre-K to 5th Grade		
Spanish	1,394,000	71.6
French	58,000	3.0
Vietnamese	57,000	3.0
Chinese	53,000	2.7
Korean	31,000	1.6
French/Haitian Creole	27,000	1.4
German	25,000	1.3
Russian	21,000	1.1
Hmong/Miao	21,000	1.1
Tagalog/Filipino	20,000	1.0
All languages	**1,612,000**	**100.00**

Source: Adapted from Capps, R., Fix, M., Murray, J., Ost, J., Passel, J., & Herwantoro, S. (2005). *The New Democracy of America's Schools: Immigration and the No Child Left Behind Act.* Washington, DC: The Urban Institute, p. 17. Retrieved from www.urban.org.

Jersey. California has the largest percentage of these students at 47 percent. Other states that have a higher population than the national average include Nevada, New York, Hawaii, Texas, Florida, Arizona, New Jersey, Rhode Island, and New Mexico (Capps et al., 2005).

Parents of English learners can have quite different views and experiences of schooling given their levels of education. Children of educated parents have a more comprehensive understanding of school tasks than children whose parents did not attend school. According to the census results of 2000, less than half of the parents of young children from Mexico had completed high school, and only 4 percent had completed college. In contrast, 43 percent of young adult immigrants from Asian backgrounds had earned at least a bachelor's degree (Garcia & Cuéllar, 2006; Ruiz-de-Velasco & Fix, 2000).

Languages Spoken by English Learners in the United States

The differences in the sounds and structures of students' primary languages will influence how word study is tailored to their developmental needs. An introductory understanding of the world's languages provides some insight into how to plan for the linguistic differences among English learners. There are approximately 5,000 oral languages around the world (Comrie, Matthews, & Polinsky, 1996), and in schools in the United States, there are over 180 oral languages spoken as home languages (Capps et al., 2005). Spanish is the primary language of approximately 50 percent of the English learners (U.S. Census Bureau, 2007), and as noted, many of these students have difficulty speaking English.

The languages spoken by students can be classified into language families. You can imagine that with 5,000 languages, researchers and linguists would develop different ways to classify languages. Some have described 95 to 170 language families. To provide a sense of the depth of these language families, four of the families are presented in Figures 1.1 through 1.4.

The Indo-European language system, shown in Figure 1.1, includes 46 percent of the world's native language speakers, approximately 3 billion people. All of these languages sprang from a common source, Sanskrit, and spread throughout Europe. Some of the Indo-European languages like Latin and Sanskrit are extinct as spoken languages. A number of the languages are related through their shared cultural and linguistic histories; for example, there are many commonalities among the vocabularies of English, French, Spanish, Italian, and Romanian

FIGURE 1.1 Indo-European Languages

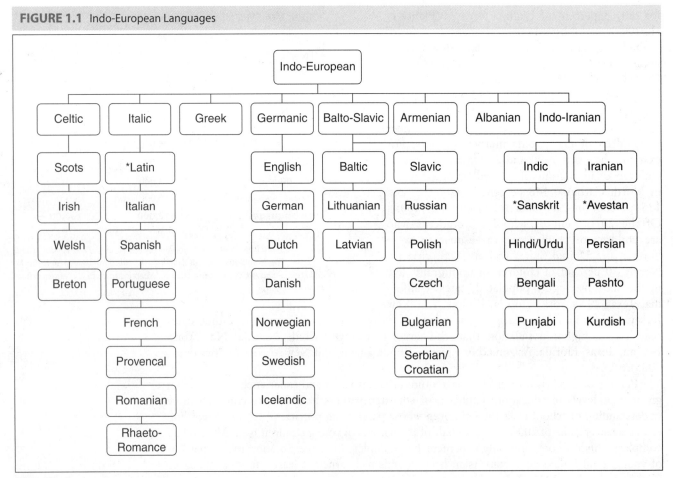

*Extinct language

Source: Adapted from Comrie, Matthews, and Polinsky (1996).

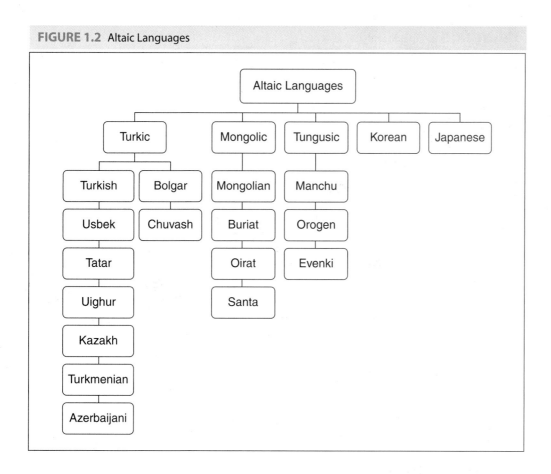

FIGURE 1.2 Altaic Languages

(Comrie, Matthews, & Polinsky, 1996). Therefore, in English vocabulary instruction we help Spanish speakers to see into English through the 10,000 to 15,000 Spanish and English cognates, words that share a common base. You'll see how this is done in word study in Chapters 7 and 8.

The Altaic language family (Figure 1.2) derives its name from the Altai Mountains of Central Asia and stretches from northeast Asia to Eastern Europe, including languages such as Turkish and Azerbaijani. Most of us in the United States are unfamiliar with these languages. It is humbling to realize that 10 million people speak Uighur, mostly in China but also in Uighur-speaking communities throughout the world, even in the United States. Although there is some disagreement, most linguists include Korean and Japanese in this family as well (Crystal, 2003).

Afro-Asiatic languages (Figure 1.3) are found in Northern Africa and the Middle East and include the 200 million speakers of Arabic. Both Hebrew and Arabic share many features, including the way different vowels signal different grammatical functions, like plurals and different tenses, unlike in English where -*ed* forms the past tense.

The fourth language family is the Sino-Tibetan, which includes over 250 oral languages. These languages are spoken in China and Southeast Asia. As shown in Figure 1.4, there are eight dialects of Chinese, including Yue (Cantonese). As the official language, Mandarin is the predominant language spoken by 1 billion Chinese. The dialects of Chinese are quite different from each other and can be as dissimilar as German is from Swedish (Crystal, 2003). Some linguists include the Hmong-Mien languages spoken by approximately 5 million people in southern China, Vietnam, Laos, and Thailand in the Sino-Tibetan family (Comrie et al., 1996).

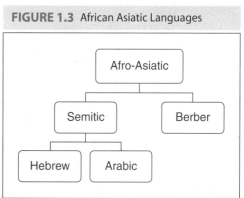

FIGURE 1.3 African Asiatic Languages

FIGURE 1.4 Sino-Tibetan Languages

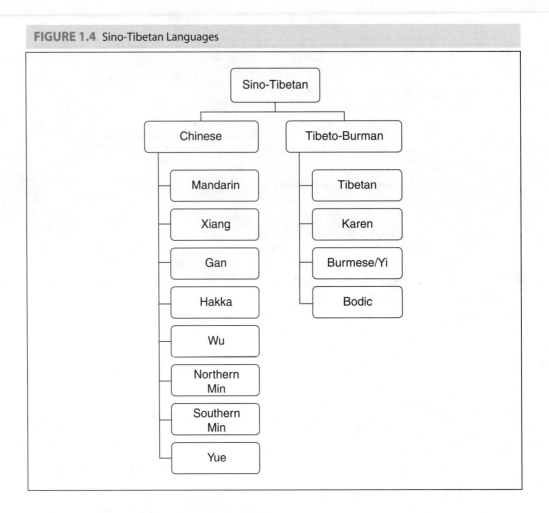

····················
Students' Knowledge of Orthography and the Three Layers of English Spelling

▶ **Orthographic Knowledge**

The knowledge students have about the correct sequence of letters, characters, or symbols in a written language.

Why is it important to understand students' **orthographic knowledge,** their comprehension of how words are spelled? The short answer is that orthographic knowledge and development in the areas of phonics, vocabulary, and spelling are essential to students' reading and writing growth.

There is a reciprocal relationship between reading and writing development. Reading informs writing, and writing makes for better readers and spellers. Great writers are invariably great readers; autobiographies and biographies of many great authors reveal that they are usually voracious readers, particularly in their genres. They learn how to write by reading and imitating others as they develop their own styles (Bear & Templeton, 2000).

There are also powerful and significant relationships between reading and spelling. Spelling is a conservative measure of what students know about words, for if students know how to spell a word, they nearly always know how to read the word. The groundbreaking research of Edmund Henderson (1990) provides a good sense of the relationship between reading and spelling development. Through the study of how students spell, it has been possible to determine what they know about words and, because students' word knowledge governs how they read, to discern the type of instruction that would be useful.

Understanding the Three Layers of English Spelling

All writing systems have three layers: sound, pattern, and meaning (see Figure 1.5). Every language has its unique blend of these layers, and the stages of spelling development follow from understanding these three layers. It will be beneficial to begin with a description of the three layers in English.

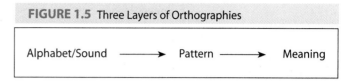

FIGURE 1.5 Three Layers of Orthographies

Alphabet/Sound ⟶ Pattern ⟶ Meaning

The sound layer reflects sound–symbol relationships, and in orthographies or writing systems that use an alphabet, the sound layer is labeled the *alphabet layer*. The English spelling system is at heart an alphabetic orthography because all of the individual sounds or phonemes of the language are represented by letters. For example, the letter *b* represents the consonant /b/ sound. The sounds are organized into two groups—consonants, which usually have a reliable match, and vowels, which are more complex. A handful of letters (*a, e, i, o, u,* and sometimes *y*) represent 15 different vowel sounds. In addition, there are some consonant letter pairs known as *digraphs* that represent unique sounds—for example, *ch, sh, th,* and *wh*. Overall, English has to represent 44 different sounds with only 27 letters, so the system is not as simple as some other alphabetic languages described later in this chapter. Chapters 4 and 5 focus on learning the alphabetic layer.

The second layer of English writing is called the *pattern layer*. Consonant–vowel–consonant (CVC) is the basic pattern (as in *cat*) and describes the common closed syllable that ends with a consonant and usually has a short vowel sound. Long vowel patterns in English include the CVVC (*rain*), CVCe (*time*), and CVV (*pie*) patterns. Many words in English contain silent letters or letter combinations that have no sound but help to signal particular vowel sounds. For example, *light* contains the *igh* pattern that represents a long vowel sound as it does in *right, slight,* and *night*. Without the *gh* these words would be *lit, rit, slit,* and *nit,* which have the short vowel sound. Students learning English must also come to understand that sound alone does not govern spelling. *Pain* cannot be spelled PAN but might be spelled PANE or even PAYNE because it has a long *a* sound. In fact, *ai, a-e,* and *ay* are all long *a* patterns. The study of single-syllable long vowel patterns is discussed in Chapter 6. Two-syllable word patterns are related to how syllables combine, as seen in the contrasts between the sound and patterns in *legal,* an open VCV pattern, and *napkin* and *dinner,* both VCCV pattern words. These patterns are discussed in Chapter 7.

The *morphology* of a language is reflected in what is called the *meaning layer*. There are two morphology types: inflectional and derivational. **Inflectional morphology** involves the addition of suffixes such as *-ed, -ing,* and *-s* to base words to indicate tense and number, such as when *walk* becomes *walked* or *boy* changes to *boys*. Inflectional morphology and two-syllable word patterns are explored in Chapter 7. **Derivational morphology** involves the addition of prefixes and suffixes to base words or Greek and Latin word roots to indicate a change in a part of speech or other differences in meaning that are sometimes quite subtle, at other times quite significant. For example, *pre-* + *approve* = *preapprove, dis-* + *approve* = *disapprove; derive* (a verb) + *-ation* = *derivation* (a noun). Instruction begins with easy morphological features such as prefixes and suffixes (*un-, re-, -ly, -tion*) and inflectional endings (*-es, -ing, -ed*) added to base words. It extends to Greek and Latin word roots, such as *spec* in *spectacle, spectator,* or *speculate* and *therm* in *thermometer, thermal,* or *thermos*. These roots serve as the bases of many technical and specialized vocabularies. Chapter 8 describes activities to teach students about the history and derivations of words.

English is well suited to accommodate new terms and grow its vocabulary. There are probably 300,000 word forms, and nearly a million words including all word forms (*crashed, crashing*). There are nearly 600,000 words in dictionaries and another 400,000 words that are mostly scientific and uncataloged except in specialized references. Speakers do not use anywhere close to the million available English words. In a week, mature readers read 2,000 different words of the 55,000 words they have learned. Specialized vocabulary is acquired at work or in professional studies.

▶ **Inflectional Morphology**

The study of how words change when suffixes are added to words for verb tense (*talk, talked, talking*) or number (*dogs, foxes*).

▶ **Derivational Morphology**

The study of how words change when a prefix or suffix is added to a stem or root (*predictable*).

Stages of Literacy Development in English

In order to become literate in English, learners must orchestrate these three layers through "progressively more complex reciprocal interactions" (Bronfenbrenner & Evans, 2000, p. 117) that are often described as stages or phases of development (Invernizzi & Hayes, 2004). Edmund Henderson and his students (1990) have outlined the five stages of spelling and reading shown in Figure 1.6. As discussed in depth in *Words Their Way*™ (Bear et al., 2008), our research aligns with similar models proposed by Chall (1983), Ehri (1997), and Perfetti (2003). By assessing their spelling, it is possible to determine what stage of spelling students are in; these stages of spelling are highly correlated with their reading development and achievement. For example, we have found significant correlations between students' spelling and their achievement on standardized reading tests.

Here we offer a brief description of these five developmental stages. Table 1.2 at the end of this chapter outlines these stages, and more information about each stage can be found in Chapters 4 through 8. These stages overlap because learning is gradual and learners do not abruptly move from one stage to the next. There is an interaction among the layers; students who have progressed to the meaning level realize that changes in the meaning layer produce changes in the sound of the word. For example, notice the sound and meaning changes from adding a suffix to *compose* to form *composition*. However, at any particular moment in students' development, a specific phase or stage will usually dominate their thinking about words (Rieben, Saada-Robert, & Moro, 1997).

THE EMERGENT STAGE. During the emergent stage students are introduced to the first layer of English—alphabet and sound. Typically students in this stage are preschoolers and kindergarteners, but English learners of any age may be in this stage if they have had little or no formal schooling. Young children first write with letter-like scribbles but transition to letters as they learn the alphabet. However, there may not be any discernable letter–sound matches. Moving from this stage to the next depends on learning the **alphabetic principle:** Letters represent sounds in systematic ways. In order to study the sounds in words learners need to acquire **phonemic awareness,** an understanding that words consist of a series of sounds that can be isolated and examined.

THE LETTER NAME–ALPHABETIC STAGE. During the letter name–alphabetic stage students learn to use letters to represent the sounds of words in a systematic way (i.e., they learn **phonics**), first partially as when very young children write B or BD for *bed*. Consonant sounds are usually mastered first and then vowels, as learners develop skill in isolating medial sounds. *Bed* might be represented as BAD, showing how short vowel correspondences are used but confused even when heard. Students in this stage are typically in kindergarten and first grade but English learners who are first learning to read and spell English will often start off in this stage. Readers in this stage read slowly and word by word, pointing to words to keep their place on the page. They begin to slowly acquire **sight words,** words that they recognize immediately in any context. Sounding out unknown words letter by letter is difficult because they do not have much vowel knowledge. By the end of the letter name–alphabetic stage of spelling (corresponding to the beginning stage of reading), students learn the short vowel CVC pattern, or what is called the *closed syllable pattern*.

THE WITHIN WORD PATTERN STAGE. The name of the next stage of spelling, the within word pattern stage, illustrates how important the idea of pattern is at this time. In the early part of this stage students learn to recognize the common patterns of vowels (V) and consonants (C) as in the CVCe (*late*), CVVC (*train*), CVV (*blue*), and CV (*go*) patterns. Later they learn to spell more complex vowel patterns such as *ought*, *edge*, or *earn*. Single-syllable words are mastered in spelling, and in reading, students are approaching fluency; they have enough power in word recognition to often read fluently and with expression. Because there is so much to learn about the vowel system of English this stage can last for several years, especially

▶ Alphabetic Principle
The knowledge that letters and letter combinations represent the sounds of language.

▶ Phonemic Awareness
The ability to consciously manipulate the individual sounds in a spoken language.

▶ Phonics
The systematic relationship between letters and sounds.

▶ Sight Words
Known words that are recognized and pronounced "at sight."

FIGURE 1.6 Synchrony of Literacy Development in English

	ALPHABET/SOUND				PATTERN				MEANING		

Reading and Writing Stages/Phases:

Emergent	Beginning	Transitional	Intermediate	Advanced
Early Middle Late	Early Middle Late	Early Middle Late	Early Middle Late	Early Middle Late
Pretend read	Read aloud, word-by-word, fingerpoint reading	Approaching fluency, phrasal, some expression in oral reading	Reads fluently, with expression. Develops a variety of reading styles. Vocabulary grows with experience reading.	
Pretend write	Word-by-word writing, writing starts with a few words to paragraph in length	Approaching fluency, more organization, several paragraphs	Writes fluently, builds expression and voice, experiences different writing styles and genre. Writing shows personal problem solving and personal reflection.	

Spelling Stages/Phases:

Emergent → Letter Name–Alphabetic → Within Word Pattern → Syllables and Affixes → Derivational Relations →

Examples of misspellings:

Word	Emergent	Letter Name–Alphabetic	Within Word Pattern	Syllables and Affixes	Derivational Relations
bed	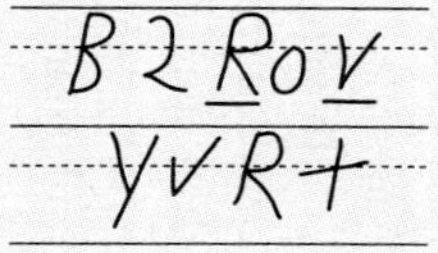 B2RoV YvR+ (handwriting)	b bd bad	_bed_		
ship		s sp sep shep	_ship_		
float		f ft fot flot flott	flote floaut flowt _float_		
train		t trn jran tan chran tran	teran traen trane _train_		
cattle		c kd catl cadol	catel catol cattel	_cattle_	
cellar		s slr salr celr	saler celer seler	celler seller _cellar_	
pleasure		p pjr plasr plager	plejer pleser plesher	pleser plesher plesour	_pleasure_
confident				confadent confednet confedent	confedent _confident_
opposition				opasishan oppasishion oppasistian	opostian oposision _opposition_

for struggling readers and English learners. However, this stage lays important groundwork for the two upper-level stages that follow.

THE SYLLABLES AND AFFIXES STAGE. The syllables and affixes stage begins with the study of how single-syllable patterns (CV or CVCe) combine in multisyllable words (i.e., *relate*). Students are ready to examine different syllable patterns, and they develop the skill of knowing where to look to begin to divide words into syllables. Students continue to draw on their knowledge of sound differences and patterns to understand the rules associated with e-drop and consonant doubling (*tape/taping* and *tap/tapping*), but by the end of this stage the meaning layer of English becomes important in the study of prefixes (the *re-* and *un-* in *redo* or *undo*) and suffixes (the *-ly* or *-er* in *slowly* or *slower*). In upper-level word study, the meaning layer is crucial to vocabulary development.

THE DERIVATIONAL RELATIONS STAGE. Students in the derivational relations stage examine the functions and spellings of meaning-bearing parts of words. Students see that word endings work grammatically (for example, *-ic* as in *frantic* signals an adjective and *-ion* as in *action* turns a verb into a noun), and semantically they study more difficult prefixes and suffixes. As the name of the stage indicates, learners examine how different words can be *derived* from a single base word or word root: From the base word *relate* we can derive the words *relative, relationship, relativity, correlate, correlation, correlative,* and so forth. Notably, students come to understand what is termed the *spelling–meaning connection* (Templeton, 2004): Words that are related in meaning are often related in spelling as well, despite changes in sound. For example, notice how the spelling *deriv* remains constant despite the change in pronunciations of the vowels when different suffixes are added: <u>*derive*</u>–<u>*derivative*</u>–<u>*derivation*</u>.

▶ **Synchrony of Literacy Development**

The ways that students' reading, writing, and spelling develop together.

The Synchrony of Literacy Development. In Figure 1.6, stages of reading are related to stages of spelling development. This is described as the **synchrony of literacy development** because reading, spelling, and writing develop together. Figure 1.6 includes reading behaviors and spelling errors characteristic of each stage. There is such a close relationship in the development between reading and spelling that the spelling assessments we present in Chapter 2 can be used to think about grouping for instruction.

The bands at the top of the figure illustrate how these stages begin with the alphabet layer as students learn the basic sound–symbol correspondences and collect a beginning sight vocabulary. Follow the progression of spelling errors at the bottom of the figure and connect the misspellings to reading levels. For example, at the bottom of the figure, find the misspelling FLOT for *float,* a common error by students in the middle of the letter name–alphabetic stage. Move up the figure to the reading stages (beginning), and notice how students characteristically read in a word-by-word fashion with fingerpointing and no indication of fluency.

The corresponding reading stages in the upper levels are the intermediate and advanced reading stages. Silent reading is the dominant mode of reading, and students find ways to adjust their reading styles to suit different purposes. Intermediate readers acquire these styles and increase their reading rates gradually. Advanced readers are more accomplished and can read rapidly, learning new reading skills as they enter new genres and fields of study. They learn new vocabulary words as they learn new concepts. They can already adjust their reading rates to skim and scan, and they can adjust their rate according to the relative difficulty of the materials.

In parent meetings, teachers often share charts like Figure 1.6 to show the relationship between reading and spelling. Sometimes, parents know more about how their children spell than they do about their reading. Showing the relationships among reading, spelling, and writing places students' literacy behaviors in perspective and provides parents with a better understanding of how their children will progress.

The Slant of Development. Students can typically read many words before they can spell them, so reading achievement will usually look slightly ahead of spelling. For example students may spell *float* as FLOT but read *float* correctly when the word is a part of a text or even when presented in a list. This propensity can be described as the **slant of development** and shows the relationships between students' spelling and reading and how learning in reading and vocabulary reach ahead of spelling. Reading and spelling draw on the same base of orthographic knowledge, but, as a recognition task, reading is a little easier to do correctly compared to a productive task like spelling. This slant is a relationship that makes it possible to use students' spelling to think about their word knowledge and reading development.

Teaching vocabulary and grammar can be a little ahead of students' spelling. For example, after teacher-led, explicit instruction about plurals like -*s*, -*es*, or -*ies*, students may understand plurals at an introductory level; when they use these suffixes correctly in their writing, it is clear that they have mastered the principle of how plurals are formed in English. Once concepts and vocabulary are taught to introduce ideas and principles, we conduct intensive word study to give them experience from which to make generalizations that they can use every day in their reading and writing.

▶ **Slant of Development**
The idea that reading ability is slightly ahead of spelling ability. Reading words accurately comes before spelling them correctly.

What Students Bring to Learning to Read in English

Teachers need to know what languages and background experiences students bring to their learning and show interest in their home languages and cultures. Some helpful questions to gather this information through discussions with students are presented in Chapter 2. At other times, you may ask students to write about what they are learning in English and then discuss one of their key points during a conversation. This will allow you to understand and at the same time document your students' thinking.

Research has helped to capture students' thinking about how they are learning to read and write in English (Jiménez, Garcia, & Pearson, 1996; Kenner, Kress, Al-Khatib, Kam, & Tsai, 2004). Student reports in these studies are probably similar to what you will hear from your students. For example, in one classroom students were asked to write and then talk about what was hard about learning to read and write. A Hmong speaker, Dang, who was born in the United States, wrote, "I think that how to speu [spell] longer words are harder." Dang may have been saying that he was proficient with single-syllable and easy two-syllable words, and his writing reveals this. His **spelling inventory** (see Chapter 2) indicated that he was learning about long vowel patterns in the latter part of the within word pattern stage of spelling (see Chapter 6). In his misspelling of *spell* as SPEU, the lack of the final *ll* may be attributed to his difficulty in pronouncing the /l/ sound.

Mark, another Hmong speaker who was also born in the United States, wrote "Panoss [pronounce] words out." Mark was slightly less proficient than Dang in reading and spelling but near enough in development to be in the same group. Mark did not spell the /r/ sound, reflecting the difficulty he may have been experiencing in grade-level reading and writing. In small groups the study of the /r/ and /l/ sounds helped both students understand more words and improve their vocabularies while refining their pronunciation.

▶ **Spelling Inventory**
A spelling inventory is a carefully designed spelling assessment used to determine what students know about words and their structures. See Chapter 2.

Build on Students' Language and Literacy Experiences

Four steps based on what students bring to the learning environment can be followed to plan word study for phonics, vocabulary, and spelling instruction (see Figure 1.7). Throughout this book, we will help you learn how to put these steps into action.

1. *Compare oral languages.* What languages do students speak? What are the basic characteristics of those languages? What sounds and linguistic structures exist in students' home languages but not in English? English can be compared to other languages in several ways: through phonology, the

FIGURE 1.7 Four Steps to Plan Word Study Instruction with English Learners

1. Compare oral languages.
2. Compare written languages.
3. Know what language and literacy experiences students have had.
4. Plan word study to help students achieve.

sounds of the language and how they are produced; morphology, how words are structured; semantics, meanings of words and vocabularies; and syntax, how words are ordered into sentences. In the instructional chapters of this book, we present word study activities that compare sounds and words to help students contrast languages and learn new words and concepts in English.

Students' languages may be compared with English to find the syntactic differences and similarities. Certain English grammatical structures may be so different that it helps to have students practice the new constructions. For example, in many languages, there are no equivalents for the use of *do, does,* or *did* in verb forms. As a result, students may say, "Do she go?" Therefore, many English learners will need explicit instruction and plenty of practice in when to use *do* or *did* in forming questions or statements.

In the area of phonology, the sound system, there are sounds in English that do not occur in students' primary languages. In such cases, look for the sounds that a student substitutes. In most cases, English learners make substitutions based on a close match. For example, Arabic does not have a /p/ sound and many Arabic speakers substitute a /b/ for /p/ in English, pronouncing *pan* as "ban." Specific phonics and phonemic awareness activities that highlight these comparisons at appropriate times are worthwhile.

2. *Compare written languages.* What is the structure of the students' home writing system? Consider the directionality of the writing: Does the writing run left to right, right to left, top to bottom? Notice how the sounds are spelled: Does the writing system use an alphabet or characters (as in Chinese)? Does the spoken language use the Roman alphabet (as in many African languages like the Cameroon languages or in Asian languages such as Hmong or Vietnamese)? It is helpful for you as a teacher to learn which consonant and vowel sounds are used as well as to know which letters are used to spell different vowel sounds in the most prevalent languages in your classroom. Have conversations with students about their home languages and literacies and, as they become comfortable in the classroom, ask them to share their writing, favorite books, and stories from their home languages. Students who can read characters can pronounce them and describe their meanings. Welcome parents, elders, and community members to share the written languages of students. The Internet is a wonderful source of information about languages, such as the sounds and letters of students' native languages.

Once you have a sense of what sounds and letters exist in students' home languages, compare them with English. How do the letter–sound correspondences in the student's written language compare to the letter–sound correspondences in written English? For example, the letter *a* in Spanish sounds like the short *o* in English, and so students sometimes spell the short *o* sounds with *a* based on their knowledge of Spanish spelling.

3. *Know what language and literacy experiences students have had.* Like three-quarters of the world's population, students learning English are in varying stages of using two or more languages (Crystal, 2006). Many English learners were born in an English-speaking country but have had little literacy-based interaction in English, and this also has an impact on learning at school.

As discussed earlier, English learners have a wide range of experiences with English. In a large demographic study of children with limited English proficiency (LEP), 46 percent had been born in the United States. Of the students born outside the United States, 15 percent had lived in this country for five or more years, 22 percent had been in the United States for one to four years, and close to 20 percent of the English learners had lived in the United States for less than a year (Zehler, Fleischman, Hopstock, Stephenson, Pendzick, & Sapru, 2003). Thus, students come to school with differing strengths and challenges in learning to read and write in English.

Children's success in learning one language is highly related to their learning of another. For example, children with numerous language and literacy experiences have extensive vocabularies when they enter school. For native and second language learners, the amount of language they hear affects their development. In a groundbreaking longitudinal study, Hart and Risley found that some children had heard 30 million more words than other children by the time they entered kindergarten (1995). English learners who already have a strong vocabulary in one language have more to draw on when they learn English. Literacy learning in school builds on the language and literacy experience children have at home, the number of books in the home, the number of opportunities children have to see parents engaged in literate activities, and the amount of conversation they hear and are involved in.

The level of family literacy predicts the achievement of children, regardless of the country in which the parents or grandparents were educated (Reese, Garnier, Gallimore, & Goldenberg, 2000). The more years of schooling among adult family members, the greater children's literacy achievement. What students know in one language or literacy is used to learn oral and written English. Rather than complicate learning, literacy in another language facilitates learning to read and write in English. Informally, get to know the level of education among family members, even grandparents.

4. *Plan word study to help students achieve.* Select activities and strategies for successful learning experiences, develop expectations for learning, and plan for *intensity* and *duration* of instruction for each student. Because of the differences in language and literacy experiences among students, this book includes activities at different levels of oral and written English development. In setting goals, consider where a student should be developmentally at the end of the school year. What progress will be achieved if, for example, a student is involved in small-group instruction an extra hour three times a week at a particular developmental level for 20 weeks?

English learners with little literacy in their home language are often older when they enter particular stages of development and modifications are needed. Instruction is focused on students' development, but given the age of the students, word study and some of the games must be designed to interest older learners. In addition, reading and vocabulary activities need to be adapted for older learners. For example, Chapter 5 includes ideas for creating reading materials that will be of greater interest and relevance for older students in the beginning stage of reading. We have also included suggested accommodations for older students in each of the instructional chapters.

What oral and written language proficiencies do English learners bring to classrooms? Consider four examples of ways in which students' languages and literacies blend:

1. Jesús comes to school proficient in oral and written Spanish. Instruction includes directed comparisons between his home language and English. Home literacies support oral and literacy development in English. Learning a second language enriches students' first languages (Guion, Flege, Liu, & Yeni-Komshian, 2000; Lieberman, 1991; Ransdell, Arecco, & Levy, 2001; Schmitt & McCarthy, 1997).

2. Flora is a fourth-grader who has recently emigrated from China. She is proficient in speaking and reading Mandarin. Bilingual learners negotiate between languages and literacies, and students' first languages will affect the strategies they employ (August & Shanahan, 2006; Tolchinsky & Teberosky, 1998). The more closely two orthographies are aligned, the easier the second writing system is to learn (Bialystok & McBride-Chang, 2005). The differences between English and Chinese are great, and Flora will be involved in intensive English language instruction throughout her elementary and middle school years. Sometimes, it is unrealistic to expect that students, particularly adults, will achieve equal proficiency in the two languages (Grosjean, 2000). A realistic goal for secondary students is to achieve a proficiency in English that is within a grade level of their current placement.

3. Kia is a second grader who speaks Hmong and hears no English at home. In addition, because Hmong has traditionally been a primarily oral form of communication, she has

had very limited experience with reading and writing. She is in the situation of learning to speak English and learning about print at the same time.

4. Omar does not have extensive language development in Spanish, his first language, even as he is being instructed in a new language, English. His parents did not attend much school, and he has few language interactions at home. Omar has much to achieve, and this will be accomplished through intensive and extended experiences in language and literacy in his classroom and in classes with an English language support teacher. As is true in most communities, there are often significant educational, social, and economic differences among English learners. Omar's parents and siblings come to school twice a week in the evenings for English language and parenting classes. As part of these classes, parents are involved in activities that encourage language interaction. Together, parents and children make family books or dictate letters to send to family members; parents learn how to read children's books in Spanish, and the parents and children sort pictures conceptually to learn English vocabulary.

Understanding Word Study in the Classroom

Word study is an umbrella term that includes all aspects of learning about words: how to read them, write them, and what they mean—in other words, phonics, spelling, and vocabulary.

Word Study Instruction

WORD STUDY IS DEVELOPMENTAL. The word study activities in *Words Their Way™ with English Learners* describe the teaching of phonics, vocabulary, and spelling for English learners at various developmental levels. If, for example, you are teaching English learners who are studying short vowels in the letter name–alphabetic stage, you would refer to Chapter 5 in this book for activities that clarify consonants and vowels that are often confused in English. Through all of the teaching activities in this book it is important to help students concentrate on the meanings of the words to develop vocabulary along with phonics and spelling.

When phonics, vocabulary, and spelling are integrated with reading and writing, more instructional time is available to teach in cohesive small groups for differentiated, developmental instruction. In integrated word study instruction, spelling is a means for learning phonics and vocabulary. When students study spelling patterns they also learn about phonics and the sound system; for example, they learn that long vowel words like *lake* and *nail*, *wrote* and *boat* are spelled using predictable patterns that are pronounced in certain ways. In the upper levels of word study, vocabulary is enhanced as students learn how spelling is related to the meanings of words. For example, students learn that prefixes have particular meanings, such as that both *dis-* and *in-* mean *not* as in *disease* or *infrequent*.

VOCABULARY IMPROVES WITH WORD STUDY. Vocabulary instruction should be a part of each word study lesson. Teachers clarify the meanings of the words in the sorts during the lesson even when phonics is the primary focus, and students should be asked to use the words to enhance attention to meaning throughout the activity.

Some word study activities focus exclusively on vocabulary instruction. **Concept sorts** are semantic sorts that grow vocabularies as students sort words and pictures by their relationships in meaning. For example, in a concept sort of actions, English learners may become familiar with many new vocabulary words like *hop*, *skip*, and *jump*. Pictures are particularly effective with older students who do not know much English: They can complete a sort using the pictures and then listen to others use the English terms as they explain how they sorted. A number of concept sorts can be found on the website.

PDToolkit

for Words Their Way™ with English Learners

Go to PDToolkit, choose your book, click the Sorts & Games tab, and select Picture (Concept) Sort or Picture & Word (Concept) Sort from the Type filter.

▶ **Concept Sort**
A concept and vocabulary development activity in which pictures, objects, or words are grouped by shared attributes or meanings.

Vocabulary can be taught with concept sorts in which students categorize key vocabulary words from content areas. Teachers first model how the concepts are related and class charts are developed. Next, students record these sorts into the content sections of their **word study notebooks** and add more words that come up from their reading and study. As a resource students create for themselves, word study notebooks connect reading, writing, and word study. After hunting for related words from their reading and adding them to their notebooks, English learners have a vocabulary reference to use as they write.

▶ **Word Study Notebooks**
Notebooks in which students write word sorts that follow particular spelling patterns, and then add new words from their reading and keep other notes related to word study activities.

WORD STUDY IN THE LAYERS OF ENGLISH SPELLING FOR LEARNERS OF ENGLISH AS A FOREIGN LANGUAGE. English is an international language, and around the world, people of all ages are learning English. Foreign language teachers also use word sorts and related activities to teach secondary and adult students who do not live in English language settings. These English as a foreign language (EFL) learners are similar to English-speaking secondary and postsecondary students in the United States enrolled in foreign language courses.

Students learning English as a foreign language who are highly literate in their primary language progress through the stages of orthographic development in English in the manner we have outlined if there is a sufficient amount of English in their current instructional setting. If the learners' primary language is closely related to English, they may progress through the stages at a faster pace. After an informal spelling assessment chosen from those provided in Chapter 2, teachers guide EFL learners to the word study activities at their developmental levels. Throughout the instructional chapters in this book there are word study activities suitable for EFL students. Teachers can use the lists of words created in sorting to highlight different points about English pronunciation—for example, "Do you hear that all of these words have the same vowel sound in the middle?"

Many benefits are derived from examining words carefully and relationally. By also teaching at students' instructional level, learning is tied to their development.

The Three Layers of Spelling and Stages of Development in Other Written Languages

The sound/alphabet, pattern, and meaning layers are blended uniquely in all writing systems, and students use their knowledge of their primary written and oral languages to learn English. Teachers need to understand what students will bring from their primary languages and literacies as they learn to speak and read English. For example, English learners will be unfamiliar with particular sounds that do not exist in their primary languages (Helman, 2004). For them, acquiring new sounds requires instruction and practice, through activities such as picture sorts for rhyming and beginning sounds, as addressed in Chapter 4. Spelling stages and orthographic development have been studied in many languages including English, Finnish, French, German, Greek, Portuguese, Spanish, Chinese, and Korean (Bear, Templeton, Helman, & Baren, 2003).

Earlier in this chapter, four language families were introduced graphically in Figures 1.1 to 1.4. By knowing a little about these language families, we can make comparisons to English and know which particular features are important to emphasize and clarify in English word study instruction. The following examples show several of the ways that students' first and second languages may interact at each of the three layers: sound/alphabet, pattern, and meaning.

At the sound layer in Spanish, the /sh/ sound is not used and the closest phoneme Spanish speakers have is /ch/, which many Spanish speakers use as a substitute—for example, spelling and pronouncing the word *ship* as CHEP.

At the pattern level in Spanish, many words end with a vowel or an open syllable, a format that is less common in English, in which words are more likely to end in consonant sounds. In English, there are many long vowel patterns with silent vowels and consonants such as the *gh* in *night*. This notion does not apply to Spanish. The silent *e* pattern found in English words like *home*, *same*, or *time* is also not found in Spanish.

At the meaning level, grammar, syntax, and knowledge of semantics influence reading and writing. For example, languages other than English do not use -*ed* inflectional endings. When speakers of other languages read or hear English, they may not detect or understand -*ed* endings on words. As a result, they often omit this ending altogether in their speaking and writing.

Shallow and Deep Orthographies

Alphabetic writing systems that are easy to sound out and are highly regular in their sound–symbol correspondences are called **shallow orthographies** and described as transparent or translucent. In written languages like Albanian, Estonian, Finnish, Italian, Polish, and Spanish, each letter has a consistent, specific sound that makes it easy to decode and spell words. Students do not need to reach deeply in Spanish to spell its 24 sounds. Other orthographies that are less shallow are considered semitranslucent or semitransparent. German, for example, has a combination of transparent and deep features.

French and English are **deep** or **opaque orthographies** in which correspondences between letters and sounds are often complex and indirect. In English spelling, for example, upper-level learners reach deeply into the patterns and meanings of words and word parts to spell proficiently. Although short vowel combinations like the CVC pattern may be relatively transparent because each letter forms a predictable and discernible sound, the long vowel patterns students must examine show the variety of relatively dark or opaque features in English. For example, contrast the single representation of short *e* in CVC words like *met* with the variety of long *e* patterns (CVVC, CVCe, and CVV) in *meat*, *green*, *theme*, and *key*. Deep orthographies are also found in Arabic and Chinese.

SPANISH, A SHALLOW OR TRANSPARENT ORTHOGRAPHY. Compared to English, readers and spellers of Spanish rely on its orthographic transparency and the power of the alphabetic principle to read and spell both single and polysyllabic words for a much longer period of development than in English—through the beginning and transitional stages of literacy development. In English, readers and spellers spend longer in the pattern layer. After the letter name–alphabetic stage in Spanish, when the alphabetic principle is learned, students only have a few ambiguities to master, such as the different hard and soft sounds for *g*, depending on the vowel that comes before, or the need to learn how to use accent marks.

The model of Spanish literacy development in Figure 1.8 illustrates the synchrony of learning. This developmental model shows when to expect particular reading and spelling behaviors. Notice how the stages of reading are beneath the alphabet, pattern, and meaning layers of Spanish orthography. The three layers of orthographies, alphabet–pattern–meaning, govern development. Each language offers its own mix of the onset and overlap of the three layers and the actual features that comprise each layer.

After learning the alphabetic principle during the letter name–alphabetic stage in Spanish, students move to the pattern layer and examine the ambiguities of Spanish spelling. Similar to the within word pattern stage of English spelling, at this stage of reading in Spanish, learners examine the pattern and meaning layers in Spanish writing, as when they move beyond letter–sound regularities and begin to include accent marks to spell easy words. As they learn how to use accent marks, students make links between spelling and meaning.

Let's look at a few examples of how pattern and meaning layers overlap in Spanish:

- Accent marks sometimes determine meaning in Spanish. The *e* is accented in *té* (tea), but not in *te* (you).
- Accent marks can sometimes change the part of speech. For example, when *esta* is used as a pronoun, an accent is added (*Ésta es más bonita—This one is prettier*).
- Adding suffixes to words can require an accent. For example, in adding -*ación*, a suffix like -*ation* in English, an accent mark is added to adjust for the change in stress that is created. In this way the word for *classify* (*clasificar*) becomes *classification* (*clasificación*).

▶ **Shallow Orthography**

A writing system in which each letter makes a consistent sound to form words that are easy to decode.

▶ **Deep or Opaque Orthography**

Orthographies that do not have a fully consistent match between sounds and letter combinations, such as using several different letter combinations to make identical sounds. Arabic, Chinese, and English are examples of deep orthographies.

FIGURE 1.8 Spelling Stages, Focus of Spelling, and Reading Stages in Spanish

	ALPHABET/SOUND		PATTERN		MEANING

Reading and Writing Stages/Phases:

Emergente (Emergent)	Principiante (Beginning)	De transición (Transitional)	Intermedio (Intermediate)	Avanzado (Advanced)
Sonido prominente (Salient sound)	Representación completa de sonidos (Complete sound representation)	Letras mudas y sonidos contrastes (Silent letters or ambiguous sounds)	Sílabas y el uso de afijos (Syllables and use of affixes)	Raíces de palabras (Word roots)

Spelling Stages/Phases:

Emergente → (Emergent)	Nombre de letra/alfabética (Letter Name—Alphabetic)	→ Patrones entre palabras (Within Word Pattern) →	Acentos y afijos → (Syllables and Affixes)	Derivaciones y sus relaciones → (Derivational Relations)
S or U for suma	PAN for pan	quisiera	geometría	herbívoro

The process of studying the meaning layers of both Spanish and English involve the study of word derivations going back to the Latin and Greek. For example, the words *democratica* and *democratic* both come from Greek *demos* (people) and *kratos* (rule), and *cráneo* and *cranium* are both derived from Greek *kranion*. Printed and online Spanish dictionaries and etymologies are important tools for students who are studying words at the derivational relations stage.

CHINESE, A DEEP ORTHOGRAPHY. Chinese writing is not based on an alphabet but instead uses thousands of characters that must be memorized. Though there is a sound or phonetic component, Chinese is sometimes called a *logographic* writing system because it evolved from drawings representing ideas rather than speech sounds. In fact, Chinese characters are used by speakers of other languages such as Japanese and Korean to represent sounds in those languages. Chinese is a deep or opaque orthography, and what might be called words are composites of between one and several characters. For example, nouns are two or three characters in length. Characters are always single syllables with phonetic and meaning components (Spinks, Liu, Perfetti, & Tan, 2000). In daily writing, 3,000 of the 40,000 characters are used.

In elementary schools, children in China learn 2,500 to 3,000 characters. The exact number of characters to be learned at each grade level varies from 160 to 430 (Shen & Bear, 2000). Beginning in kindergarten they are introduced to *pinyin*, an alphabetic system that helps them learn the Mandarin language, but the use of pinyin is brief, ending in second grade. However, having learned pinyin, speakers of Chinese learning English will have some insight into how an alphabetic system is structured.

Stages of development have been described for the character-based orthography of Chinese. In a study of 1,200 children's writing and spelling samples, a developmental sequence following the three layers was observed. For example, 96 percent of first-graders' spelling errors were classified as sound-based phonological errors. These errors decreased as pattern and meaning errors increased (Shen & Bear, 2000).

Chinese writing is different from alphabetic systems even though the same layers of orthography are present. In addition, there are significant differences in grammatical structures between English and Chinese. Some of these differences can be seen in the beginning of a letter excerpted from Chang (2001). A word-for-word transliteration of the letter illustrates the different grammatical structures: *come letter receive, thank you regard not earlier return letter, please forgive*, which would be translated idiomatically as *Thank you for your letter, and thanks for the regards. I'm sorry that I didn't write earlier. Please forgive me!* As you can see, instruction in English syntax will be an important consideration for Chinese speakers.

Knowing about Chinese helps us to know about other languages spoken and written by hundreds of millions of people. Chinese writing began about 1500 B.C.E. and has served as the basis for many other writing systems derived in Asiatic and Indic writing systems. This was true for Korean until the fifteenth century when King Sejong commissioned the creation of a 24-letter phonetic alphabet with 14 consonants and 10 vowels. As a result, the modern Korean alphabet with 19 consonants and 21 vowels is one of the most phonetically transparent orthographies.

The differences in the complexity of orthographies are apparent in the relative difficulties students have in learning to read in different languages. A more regular orthography presents fewer problems for learners. A recent study comparing Italian and English word reading found more reading difficulties among English readers than Italian, a more transparent writing system (Paulesu et al., 2001). This study suggests that word reading difficulties are apparent earlier for students learning a writing system in a deep orthography. In a shallow phonetically based writing system such as Spanish, Italian, or Romanian, students may have fewer difficulties learning to read words because there are fewer vowel sounds, fewer vowel changes, and more regular sound–symbol correspondences. Difficulties in reading and spelling may not appear until later, when polysyllabic word patterns are encountered.

Integration of Word Study into Literacy Instruction

Word study takes place throughout the day in a balanced literacy program that includes five essential literacy components: Read To, Read With, Write With, Word Study, and Talk With activities, summarized as RRWWT (Bear, Caserta-Henry, & Venner, 2004; Bear, Invernizzi, Johnston, & Templeton, 2009). Every effective literacy program involves these five types of activities, which provide a context for integrated instruction to address the language and literacy learning needs of English learners. Although the focus of this book is word study, this aspect can only be effective if it is part of a rich balanced literacy diet that includes the other essential literacy activities.

Essential literacy activities are outlined in Table 1.2 (p. 20). In the first column, we suggest how much time to devote to each activity during the instructional time for literacy. These RRWWT activities belong in every literacy program, and to make progress in reading, students benefit from word study instruction or practice each day, along with additional time dedicated to reading independently.

In this chapter we have outlined the importance of understanding students' language backgrounds and described how word study is related to students' orthographic development. We conclude with Table 1.3 (pp. 21–22), which summarizes the stages of literacy development, the characteristics of readers and spellers at these five stages, and the literacy activities that accompany each stage. Use this summary to match students' characteristics to appropriate word study activities like those presented in the second column of Table 1.2.

The next chapter guides you through an assessment process to more explicitly identify students' progress. Once you understand their developmental stages, you will know the most relevant word study activities for your students and how to connect the essential literacy activities to their word study levels.

TABLE 1.2 **The RRWWT Essential Literacy Activities**

ESSENTIAL LITERACY AND RELATED CURRICULA	PROCEDURES AND ACTIVITIES
Read To	
Language development Motivation Comprehension Vocabulary Narrative structures Social interaction 15–30 minutes of daily explicit instruction	• Read materials from literature that offer rich oral language and involve students in discussions • Use a Directed Listening–Thinking Activities format (Predict-Listen-Confirm) • Read informational texts that support content learning • Read materials that may be too hard for students to read accurately themselves • Discuss and chart new vocabulary in context with examples
Read With	
Comprehension Fluency Concept of word in print Word recognition Vocabulary 10–30 minutes of daily explicit instruction	• Choose materials at students' developmental and instructional levels (good comprehension, accuracy, and fluency) • Use a Directed Reading–Thinking Activities format (Predict-Read-Confirm) and KWLs for content materials • Guide discussions to support comprehension • Support, choral, and repeated reading with beginning readers for fluency and word recognition • Have emergent readers practice rereading memorized one- and two-line rhymes or familiar texts to learn to track text for concept of word in print
Write With	
Writing process Narrative structure Verbal expression Concept and language development Motivation Writing correctness and mechanics 10–30 minutes of daily explicit instruction	• Present strategies for students to use when they write independently • Write with students to create a community of writers • Teach the steps of the writing process • Schedule writing conferences between students and between teachers and students • Create writing groups to explore a common topic or theme or for editing • Accept invented spelling in first draft writing • Writing for emergent and beginning writers that encourages students to analyze the speech stream
Word Study	
Phonics Vocabulary Spelling Concept development Morphological knowledge 10–20 minutes of daily explicit instruction	• Picture sorts for sounds • Concept sorts with pictures and words • Word sorts for consonants, vowels, syllables, prefixes, suffixes, cognates, roots • Word study games • Word hunts • Word study notebooks to record sorts and to add words found in word hunts • Written reflections of why students sorted as they did • Charts of words that share common features like prefixes and suffixes • Examinations of interesting words that students find when they read • Consult reference materials such as dictionaries and etymologies
Talk With	
Language expression Vocabulary Motivation and social interaction Concept development 15–20 minutes of daily explicit instruction	• Encourage students to talk through activities like think-pair-share • Use new vocabulary several times a day • Have students use concept sorts and pictures to support their talking • Support creative dramatics, storytelling, and discussion groups about meaningful topics so that vocabulary, language structures, and thinking mature • Have students use the new vocabulary multiple times in meaningful contexts

TABLE 1.3 **Developmental Stages, Characteristics, Reading and Writing Activities, and Word Study Instruction**

CHARACTERISTICS	READING AND WRITING ACTIVITIES	WORD STUDY FOCUS
I. Emergent Stage with English Learners—Chapter 4		
1. Scribble letters and numbers 2. Developing concept of word, do not point accurately to text that they have memorized 3. Lack letter–sound correspondence or represent most salient sound with single letters 4. Pretend to read and write 5. Learn the sounds, rhythms, syntax, and vocabulary of English	1. Read to students and encourage oral language activities 2. Model writing using dictations and charts, often one or two sentences or lines in length 3. Encourage pretend reading and writing 4. Teach easy poems and ditties in English 5. Develop Personal Reader activities for language expression and to practice pointing to words as they read; Levels A–C 6. Have students draw pictures to support writing	1. Develop oral language and vocabulary with concept sorts of pictures and objects 2. Play with sounds of English to develop phonological awareness 3. Plan activities to learn the alphabet 4. Sort pictures by beginning sound 5. Encourage fingerpoint memory reading of ditties, songs, easy rhymes, dictations, and simple pattern books 6. Encourage invented spelling 7. Sort pictures for same ending sounds
II. Letter Name–Alphabetic Stage with English Learners—Chapter 5		
Early Letter Name–Alphabetic		
1. Represent beginning and ending sounds 2. Use letter names to invent spellings 3. Have rudimentary or firm concept of word 4. Read word by word in beginning reading materials	1. Read to students and encourage oral language activities 2. Help students to develop a firm concept of word by plenty of reading in predictable books, ditties, dictations, and simple rhymes; texts are one and two lines on a page and are highly predictable; Levels C–D 3. Record and reread individual dictations 4. Have students label pictures and write in journals regularly; length of writing is one and two sentences	1. Collect known words for word bank 2. Sort pictures and words by beginning and ending consonant sounds 3. Sort to disambiguate similar sounds between primary language and English (e.g., *d* & *t, p* & *b, b* & *v*) 4. Study word families that share a common vowel 5. Study beginning consonant blends and digraphs 6. Encourage invented spelling
Middle to Late Letter Name–Alphabetic Stage with English Learners		
1. Correctly spell initial and final consonants and some blends and digraphs 2. Use letter names to spell vowel sounds 3. Spell phonetically, representing all salient sounds in a one-to-one, linear fashion 4. Omit most silent letters and preconsonantal nasals in spelling (BOP or BUP for *bump*) 5. Fingerpoint accurately and can self-correct when off track 6. Read aloud slowly in a word-by-word manner	1. Read to students 2. Encourage invented spellings in independent writing, but hold students accountable for features and words they have studied 3. Collect two- to three-paragraph dictations that are placed in Personal Readers that are reread regularly; Levels D–G 4. Encourage more expansive writing and consider some simple editing procedures for punctuation and high-frequency words; length of writing can be several lines, up to a page	1. Sort pictures and words by different short vowel word families 2. Sort pictures and words by short vowel sounds and CVC patterns; begin with a single vowel and compare across vowels 3. Clarify vowel sounds that are in contrast with their primary languages such as the short *o* and *a* with Spanish speakers 4. Sort to examine consonant blends with pictures and words 5. Study preconsonantal nasals and digraphs at the ends of words toward the conclusion of this stage, including *ck, ff, nt, nd, mp* 6. Sort pictures comparing short and long vowel sounds 7. Collect known words for word bank (up to 200)

(continued)

TABLE 1.3 **Continued**

III. Within Word Pattern Stage with English Learners—Chapter 6

1. Spell most single-syllable short vowel words correctly 2. Spell most beginning consonant digraphs and two-letter consonant blends 3. Attempt to use silent long vowel markers 4. Read silently and read orally with more fluency and expression 5. While approaching fluency, comprehension will vary with knowledge of English language 6. Write more fluently and in extended fashion; write enough to make revision and editing useful	1. Continue to read aloud to students 2. Conduct repeated readings for speed, accuracy, and expression with poems or reader's theater, charting reading rate 3. Guide silent reading of simple chapter books, Levels H–L 4. Have students write each day, conduct writer's workshops, conference, and publish	1. Complete daily activities in word study notebook 2. Sort words by long and short vowel sounds and by common long vowel patterns 3. Picture and word sorts to refine perception and pronunciation of the vowels of English 4. Compare words with *r*-influenced vowels 5. Examine triple blends and complex consonant units such as *thr, str, dge, tch, ck* 6. Explore less common vowels, diphthongs (*oi, oy*), and other ambiguous vowels (*ou, au, ow, oo*) 7. Explore homographs and homophones for meaning, pronunciation, and spelling

IV. Syllables and Affixes with English Learners—Chapter 7

1. Spell most single-syllable words correctly 2. Make spelling errors at syllable juncture and in unaccented syllables 3. Read with good fluency and expression 4. Read faster silently than orally; prefer silent reading 5. Write responses that are sophisticated and critical	1. Plan read-alouds 2. Guide silent reading and literature and content reading discussions, Levels M–S 3. Include self-selected or assigned silent reading of novels of different genres 4. Teach simple notetaking and outlining skills, and work with adjusting reading rates for different purposes 5. Have students explore reading and writing styles and genres	1. Examine the meanings and pronunciations of plural endings 2. Study compound words 3. Study consonant doubling 4. Study inflected morphology and the grammar and pronunciation underlying suffixes (plurals, past tense, adjectives) 5. Study open and closed syllables (VCV, VCCV) 6. Explore syllable stress and vowel patterns in the accented syllable, especially ambiguous vowels 7. Focus on unaccented syllables such as *er* and *le* 8. Explore unusual consonant blends and digraphs (*qu, ph, gh, gu*) 9. Study base words and affixes 10. Focus on two-syllable homophones and homographs 11. Join spelling and vocabulary studies; link meaning and spelling with grammar and meaning 12. Explore grammar through word study 13. Sort and study common affixes (prefixes and suffixes) 14. Study stress or accent in two-syllable words

V. Derivational Relations with English Learners—Chapter 8

1. Have mastered high-frequency words 2. Make errors on low-frequency multisyllabic words derived from Latin and Greek 3. Read with good fluency and expression 4. Read faster silently than orally 5. Provide written responses that are sophisticated and critical	1. Provide time for silent reading, exploring various genres, Levels T and up 2. Help students develop study skills, including textbook reading, notetaking, adjusting rates, test taking, report writing, and reference work 3. Have students focus on literary analysis 4. Engage students in writing for various purposes each day	1. Focus on words that students bring to word study from their reading and writing 2. Join spelling and vocabulary studies; link meaning and spelling with grammar and meaning 3. Investigate cognates between English and primary language (e.g., 10,000–15,000 cognates between English and Spanish) 4. Examine common and then less common roots, prefixes, and suffixes (e.g., *ion*) 5. Examine vowel and consonant alternations in derivationally related pairs (e.g., *decide/decision*) 6. Study derivational morphology, including Greek and Latin word roots and stems 7. Focus on abstract Latin suffixes (*ence/ance; ible/able; ent/ant*) 8. Learn about absorbed or assimilated prefixes (e.g., *ir̲responsible, cor̲respond*) 9. Explore etymology, especially in the content areas 10. Examine content-related foreign borrowings

2

Getting Started:
The Assessment of
Orthographic Development

This chapter presents the process and materials required to assess the spelling, word knowledge, and vocabulary of English learners. Along with the supporting materials in the Appendix and on the website, this chapter guides teachers in understanding the developmental approach laid out in the instructional chapters (Chapters 4–8) that follow. Students' spelling in English can be classified by the stages of spelling and the types of errors that are common among English learners. Understanding these errors helps teachers choose which types of word sorts to pursue with their students. Consider how spelling in Mrs. Holmes's second grade class leads her to study students' oral and written languages.

Mrs. Holmes Asks, "Why Does Roberta Spell Bed as Ber?"

Mrs. Holmes observed that Roberta and a few other students spelled the word *bed* as BER; she had seen it enough to sense that this was not a random error. She noticed this pattern because *bed* is the first word of the Elementary Spelling Inventory (see Appendix, page 251). One student spelled *bed* BEDR. This was an unusual misspelling yet also related to Roberta's error, but Mrs. Holmes did not at that time know enough about Spanish to interpret it herself. What is it about Spanish that would lead a Spanish speaker to substitute an *r* for the /d/ sound? She waited to ask the reading specialist or a colleague who knew more about Spanish.

In the meantime, Mrs. Holmes thought about the students who made this spelling error. Mrs. Holmes saw that they were in the letter name–alphabetic stage of spelling; they knew how to spell most beginning and ending consonants and were learning to spell short vowel words. They also read like beginning readers—in a word-by-word manner—just the behavior that one would expect for letter name–alphabetic stage spellers (see Figure 1.6 to check for the synchrony in reading and spelling). For this particular student, Mrs. Holmes turned to Chapter 5, the instructional chapter for letter name–alphabetic spellers, and found the discussion of *r/d* substitution and also the sorts provided to help students contrast these final sounds.

The first section of this chapter, Assessing Spelling Developmentally, walks through the spelling assessment process, beginning with the choice of assessment, administration, interpretation, and subsequent planning for instruction. The model of spelling development presented in Chapter 1 is the foundation of this assessment process. A spelling assessment indicates a student's stage of spelling and, consequently, which chapters to turn to for phonics, vocabulary, and spelling activities suitable for that stage. Specific spelling inventories, scoring guides, and checklists are provided and discussed, along with student spelling examples. Many

of the forms are found on the website for easy access. In addition, you will find on the website a feature analysis for electronic data entry of individual students and whole classes.

In a later section of Chapter 2 we examine the spelling errors characteristic of learners from different writing systems. We present spelling inventories to administer to students from three language backgrounds: Hangul (the name for Korean writing), Chinese, and Spanish. Although this text only addresses inventories in these three additional languages, they illustrate the process of developing spelling assessments in other languages and help you make sense of students' writing and reading in any language. Some school districts use these inventories with newcomers from specific background languages to understand what literacy resources students bring. The final section of this chapter, Oral Language Development and Vocabulary Learning, continues the discussion of assessing oral language development of English learners and how to use assessments to plan Talk With and Read To experiences that can be built into word study activities.

Learning the Sounds of English

The teachers in the video that accompanies this book administer an appropriate spelling inventory three or four times a year to track students' word knowledge. The spelling assessment of a child from the second grade section of the website illustrates some of the special considerations that must be made in teaching English learners.

Yibeltal is seen in the front of the small group in Ms. Woessner's second grade classroom. Yibeltal's primary language is Oromo, a language spoken in Ethiopia. An analysis of Yibeltal's spelling (shown in Figure 2.1) indicates that he is in the early part of the within word pattern

FIGURE 2.1 Yibeltal's Spelling Sample

1.	fane	14.	frite	1.	fan
2.	Pet	15.	Ching	2.	pet
3.	Dig	16.	crle	3.	dig
4.	rige	17.	Wiches	4.	rob
5.	hoPe	18.	trne	5.	hope
6.	Wate	19.	Shitde	6.	wait
7.	gum	20.	sPle	7.	gum
8.	Slade	21.	grawl	8.	sled
9.	Slick	22.	thirty	9.	stick
10.	Shin	23.	Camte	10.	shine
11.	drime	24.	tris	11.	dream
12.	Blade	25.	ClaPing	12.	blade
13.	Kach	26.	writing	13.	coach
				14.	fright
				15.	chewing
				16.	crawl
				17.	wishes
				18.	thorn
				19.	shouted
				20.	spoil
				21.	growl
				22.	third
				23.	camped
				24.	tries
				25.	clapping
				26.	riding

stage of spelling, and in the video, he is involved in a lesson in which the students are examining short and long vowels.

Many of Yibeltal's spellings are correct or make sense as errors, but a number of the misspellings are curious and lead us to think that he would benefit from further study of the vowel sounds of English. As examples, it is unusual for students who can spell so many words correctly to write RIGE for *rob*, or spell the /ewi/ in *chewing* with an *i* (CHING), the long *e* in *dream* as DRIME, or the long *o* with an *a* (KACH). It is also interesting to note the missing vowels in the words that are *r*-influenced or have the *l*-glide: *crawl* (CRLE), *thorn* (TRNE), and *spoil* (SPLE).

Although Yibeltal can read materials at the transitional level, in guided reading levels H to J, it is not clear that he understands the structure of short vowel words and it is likely that he needs to learn more about the pronunciations of English vowels. This can be accomplished through vowel sorts with pictures and words as described in Chapters 5 and 6.

Assessing Spelling Developmentally

In this section we outline the spelling assessment process, beginning with the choice of assessment and its administration and interpretation. The results of a **qualitative spelling inventory** are used to guide a teacher in developmental word study instruction. The spelling assessment results indicate each student's stage of spelling and, consequently, where in this book to find appropriate activities to teach phonics, vocabulary, and spelling at any developmental level. Specific spelling inventories are also provided and discussed, along with student spelling examples.

Qualitative Spelling Inventories

Students' spelling can be analyzed to assess their word knowledge and to plan word study and reading instruction (Invernizzi, Landrum, Howell, & Warley, 2005). A four-step process is used to assess students' spelling:

1. Begin by collecting samples of students' spellings. The qualitative spelling inventories with directions included in the Appendix (page 248) or on the website provide an easy way to do this. As developmental spelling inventories, they include words that assess salient features related to particular stages of spelling (Schlagal, 1992). In these inventories, words on the lists are ordered, in part, by difficulty. Not only do students' spelling errors indicate their stages of spelling but also reveal what students know about word structures, knowledge used for reading as well as spelling (Bear & Templeton, 2000).

2. Next, use a **feature guide** to score and analyze spelling to determine a spelling stage. Make a copy of the feature guide in the Appendix to score each student's spelling, or use the electronic feature guide on the website.

3. Use the classroom composite form or the spelling-by-stage classroom organization form to develop word study groups. These forms are found on the website. Organize differentiated instructional groups and partnerships for word study based on students' development.

4. Monitor progress over the year. Most teachers administer a spelling inventory three or four times through the year to observe progress and identify students who may need a tailored intervention program. The spelling data are also passed on to the next year's teachers to help in their planning. Some school districts and statewide literacy initiatives use the inventories to assess and monitor students' development.

Word study instruction is based in large part on what is learned from these qualitative spelling inventories. Use these assessment results to choose which features to study, and select word sorts and other activities from the scope and sequence and from the collections of activities in the instructional chapters (Chapters 4–8).

▶ **Qualitative Spelling Inventory**

A carefully designed spelling assessment used to determine what students know about words and their structures and to highlight, where possible, their confusions about particular sound, pattern, and meaning relationships in written English.

for Words Their Way™ with English Learners

Go to PDToolkit, choose your book, click the Assessment Tools tab, and select Assessment Materials to see the qualitative spelling inventories, feature guides, classroom composites, and the Spelling-by-Stage Classroom Organization Chart.

▶ **Feature Guide**

A tool used to score students' spelling responses according to a set of features that become progressively more difficult.

Assessment materials are found in the Appendix and on the website.

Choosing a Spelling Inventory

How do you know which spelling inventory to administer? Table 2.1 shows a collection of spelling checklists, inventories, scoring guides, and classroom organization forms to use with a broad range of students in preschool, primary, intermediate, and secondary classrooms and with students from Spanish, Chinese, or Korean writing backgrounds. In the upcoming section, we focus on three of the inventories and one checklist: the Primary Spelling Inventory (PSI), the Elementary Spelling Inventory (ESI), the Picture Spelling Inventory, and the Qualitative Spelling Checklist. As may be seen in Table 2.1, these and other inventories are included on the website that accompanies this book.

Directions for administration are provided at the beginning of each inventory. Administer the inventories to students as you would any spelling test, but do not let students study the words in advance. The spelling errors students make during first-draft, uncorrected writing can also be used to analyze their spelling development as well as to confirm what is observed in the spelling inventories.

Many teachers of English learners often begin with the Primary Spelling Inventory (page 248) to see whether students know how to spell single-syllable words. Review the Primary Spelling Inventory, and if you think students can spell 15 or more of the 26 words correctly, then instead administer the Elementary Spelling Inventory (page 251) that surveys spelling development over all five stages. The following summaries briefly describe the most frequently used inventories.

- *Primary Spelling Inventory (PSI) and Feature Guide.* This 26-word list is used with students in grades K to 3, from emergent to early syllables and affixes spelling. The easiest word is *fan* and the most difficult is *riding*.

- *Elementary Spelling Inventory (ESI) and Feature Guide.* This inventory covers a wider range in 25 words, for students in K to 6, from emergent spelling to derivational relations. The easiest word is *bed* and the most difficult is *opposition*.

- *Picture Spelling Inventory and Feature Guide.* Use the picture inventory in the Appendix and on the website with students who have only a basic understanding of English. The pictures provide extra support and clarity. This 20-word list is designed for grades K to 3 and ranges from emergent to early syllables and affixes spelling. The easiest word is *lip* and the most difficult is *whistle*.

- *Qualitative Spelling Checklist.* This one-page questionnaire found on the website provides a way to analyze the spelling in a student's first-draft writing and determine a general assessment of spelling stage. Examples are given of the types of spelling errors students make across all five stages of spelling. Make a copy of the checklist for each student. The key is to acquire enough misspellings from each student to determine a stage, which means that two or three first-draft writing samples may need to be collected.

This set of spelling inventories satisfies most spelling and word knowledge assessment needs with English learners. The spelling inventories in students' primary languages are discussed later in this chapter.

How to Administer Spelling Inventories to English Learners

Follow the directions provided in the inventories. Note the following points to prepare students to spell the words as you say them:

- *Ease tensions about spelling words students do not already know how to spell.* Although it is important to value correctness, on the spelling inventories and in first-draft writing students should spell words the best they can. Some English learners have attended schools where mistakes in writing were strongly discouraged. Model for students how to spell difficult words: "What letter would I write to spell the first sound that I hear when I say the word _____?"

TABLE 2.1 **Assessments Found in the Appendix or the Website**

ASSESSMENTS	GRADE RANGE	DEVELOPMENTAL RANGE
Kindergarten Spelling Inventory and Scoring Guide (website)	Pre-K–K	Emergent to early letter name–alphabetic
Kindergarten Spanish Spelling Inventory Assessment and Scoring Guide (website)	Pre-K–K	Emergent to early letter name–alphabetic
Emergent Class Record (website)	Pre-K–K	Emergent to letter name–alphabetic

Primary Spelling Inventory
  Inventory (p. 248 & website)
  Feature Guide (p. 250 & website)
  Classroom Composite (website)
	K–3	Emergent to late within word pattern

Picture Spelling Inventory
  Inventory (p. 254 & website)
  Feature Guide (p. 256 & website)
	K–3	Emergent to syllables and affixes

Qualitative Spelling Checklist (website)	K–8	All stages

Elementary Spelling Inventory
  Inventory (p. 251 & website)
  Feature Guide (p. 253 & website)
  Classroom Composite (website)
	1–6	Letter name to early derivational relations

Spelling-by-Stage Classroom Organization Chart (website)	K–6	Emergent to early derivational relations
Intermediate-Level Academic Vocabulary Spelling Inventory (website)	5–12	Within word pattern to derivational relations

Upper-Level Spelling Inventory
  Inventory (website)
  Feature Guide (website)
  Classroom Composite (website)
	5–12	Within word pattern to derivational relations

Content Vocabulary Self-Assessment (website)	5–12	Within word pattern to derivational relations
Matching Greek and Latin Roots with their Meanings (website)	5–12	Syllables and affixes to derivational relations
Assessing Students' Knowledge of Prefixes and Suffixes (website)	5–12	Syllables and affixes to derivational relations

Language and Literacy Survey
  Survey (website)
  Explanatory Material (website)
	K–5	All stages

Assessments of Orthographic Knowledge in Students' Primary Languages (website)	1–12	All stages

Chinese Spelling Inventory and Audio File
  Inventory (website)
  Audio File to Administer Chinese Spelling Inventory (website)
  Guidelines to Interpret Chinese Spelling Inventory Errors (website)
  Feature Guide (website)
  Explanatory Material (website)
	1–6	All stages

Korean Spelling Inventory and Audio File
  Inventory (website)
  Audio File to Administer Korean Spelling Inventory (website)
  Feature Guide (website)
  Explanatory Material (website)
	1–6	All stages

Spanish Spelling Inventory and Audio File
  Inventory (website)
  Audio File to Administer Spanish Spelling Inventory (website)
  Feature Guide (website)
  Classroom Composite (website)
	1–6	All stages

- *Read words in the sentences provided and offer additional support as needed.* Make up an additional sentence, use the word in a phrase, locate pictures, use a movement to clarify meaning (for example, blow a *whistle*), or provide a synonym. Do not sound the word out for the student.

- *Have students say the words as they spell.* Saying the words is supportive to students: It may remind them of letter–sound correspondences or help them notice sound similarities between English and their primary language.

- *An optional step is to ask students to place a question mark or star beside words whose meanings are unclear.* Words flagged with question marks give you insight into students' vocabulary development, particularly those at the third grade level and beyond. You can ask students to spell the starred words a second time to observe other strategies they may have.

Determine a Stage with Power Scores

A power score, which is based simply on the number of words the student spells correctly, will establish a stage of development for each child. Table 2.2 shows how many words students need to spell correctly to be at a specific stage for the three most commonly used inventories, the Primary Spelling Inventory (PSI), Elementary Spelling Inventory (ESI), and Upper-Level Spelling Inventory (USI). Power scores are shown for the three gradations within each stage— Early (E), Middle (M), and Late (L). For example, a student who spells 7 words correctly on the ESI is in the middle of the within word pattern stage of spelling. The power score indicates which chapter in this book to turn to for instructional activities. For the student who spells 7 words correctly on the ESI, the activities in the middle of the sequence in Chapter 6 would be most appropriate.

Feature Guides to Analyze Spelling Development and Features to Study

The website contains feature guides that are used to analyze spelling. The Assessment Application provides an electronic format for scoring, storing the information, and establishing groups.

To focus more precisely on the actual orthographic or spelling features students should study, use a feature guide to examine the quality of students' spelling attempts. For each student, make a copy of the feature guide that accompanies the spelling inventory in the Appendix or use an electronic form found on the website. As shown in Figure 2.7 (page 37) later in this chapter, check the features that students spell correctly and write in the features that students substitute for the correct spellings. Total the errors for each column. *The first column in which the student misses more than one feature is the place to begin word study instruction.*

As shown on the feature guide in Figure 2.7 (page 37) as well as the feature guides in the Appendix, the top two rows indicate the relationship between spelling stages and word study

TABLE 2.2 **Power Scores and Estimated Stages**

INVENTORY	EMERGENT	LETTER NAME			WITHIN WORD PATTERN			SYLLABLES & AFFIXES			DERIVATIONAL RELATIONS		
		E	M	L	E	M	L	E	M	L	E	M	L
PSI	0	0	2	6	8	13	17	22					
ESI			0	2	3	5	7	9	12	15	18	20	22	
USI						2	6	7	9	11	18	21	23	27

features. Look to the top of the column for the stage of spelling development for the student being assessed. In this case, it is determined that the student is in the within word pattern stage.

Look to see if there are patterns in the substitutions your students make. Many of the typical substitutions we have observed in the spelling of English learners are highlighted and discussed in detail throughout the instructional chapters that follow.

Establish an Instructional Level: What Students "Use But Confuse"

PDToolkit
for Words Their Way™
with English Learners

Go to PDToolkit, choose your book, click the Assessment Tools tab, and select Assessment Materials to see the feature guides.

In order to plan meaningful word study teachers need to distinguish their students' instructional levels from their independent and frustration levels, as described in terms of students' knowledge:

1. What students know already, or their independent level
2. What they "use but confuse," their instructional level
3. What they are not attending to or leave absent, their frustration level (Invernizzi, Abouzeid, & Gill, 1994)

With respect to word study, these three levels can be determined by using one of the feature guides to score a student's spelling sample.

Table 2.3 summarizes these three levels with two student cases. The two examples outline what students "use but confuse," or their instructional levels. Mitra and Daniel are at slightly

---

TABLE 2.3 **Finding Students' Instructional Spelling Levels**

INSTRUCTIONAL LEVEL ASSESSMENT GUIDELINES	MITRA EARLY LETTER NAME–ALPHABETIC SPELLER	DANIEL MIDDLE LETTER NAME–ALPHABETIC SPELLER
	BD for bed SP for ship YN for when LP for lump JRF for drive LIN for line WS for whistle	BAD for bed ship—correct WEN for when LOP for lump JRIV for drive LIN for line WISTL for whistle
Independent level • What students know • What students spell correctly • No formal instruction is needed	Spells some beginning and final consonants.	Spells beginning and ending consonants, some blends and digraphs, many short vowel word families
Instructional level → • **What students use but confuse** • **Features misspelled, substitutions** • **The place to focus word study instruction**	**Spells most beginning and final consonants, and an occasional vowel. Uses letter name strategy (Y for *w*) and articulation (JRF for *drive*). Continue to study beginning and ending sounds and easy short vowel families.**	**Includes a vowel in each stressed syllable. Vowel and consonant substitutions based on articulation and letter name strategy. Study short vowels.**
Frustration level • What students leave absent • Deletions, features omitted • Instruction at this level is introductory and brief.	Omits vowels and most blends and digraphs.	Omits long vowel patterns, and some blends and digraphs.

different levels of development: Mitra is an early letter name–alphabetic speller and Daniel is in the middle of the same stage. The implications for instruction need to be reflected in assignments and small-group activities: Mitra begins by studying beginning and ending sounds and Daniel can start with short vowels.

Six Types of Spelling Errors Made by English Learners

Six types of spelling patterns are common among English learners. These patterns, shown in the examples of the feature guides that follow, demonstrate the ways students compare and contrast English with their primary languages and literacies.

1. *Misspellings reflect minimal contrasts between the primary language and English.* Two sounds that are entirely alike except in one way are called *minimal pairs;* for example, in English, /s/ and /z/ make a minimal pair—they are articulated in the same way, except that the /z/ is **voiced.**

   Different languages have different sets of sounds. For example, not all languages have a /z/ sound. If a sound in English does not exist in their primary language, then students are likely to substitute a letter sound from the first language that is similar. For example, Chinese speakers may spell /z/ with an *s,* and Spanish speakers often make the same substitution. Consonant substitutions are common in the letter name–alphabetic stage. A full feature list for consonants and vowels that are likely to be confusing is presented in Chapter 5.

2. *English learners often do more sounding out.* English learners use their knowledge of consonants and vowels in their primary language to spell and analyze words. This is evident in the reading and spelling of students who are accustomed to (1) a transparent writing system such as Spanish, in which the letters make the same sound in all words, or (2) a language with an open syllable structure in which many or most of the syllables end with vowel sounds—for example, consonant–vowel (CV) as in *papa* and *suma.* In Spanish and in many other languages, such as Hmong or Chinese, the syllables are frequently open. As we discussed in Chapter 1, English writing is not transparent; it is opaque because letters combine to make a variety of sounds. In a transparent orthography such as Spanish, *name* would represent a word pronounced "nah-may." Spanish-speaking students expect that each letter will be sounded, and they look for greater consistency in the sound–symbol correspondences, so they do more sounding out than English-speaking students do. For example, to spell *name,* they may extend the /m/ at the end into a separate syllable— "nay-muh."

   Students may add sounds when pronouncing slowly the word they are attempting to spell, thus they may spell DIMENED for *dimmed.* This insertion of sounds may be seen among students whose primary languages do not have **consonant blends** similar to those found in English. For example, students trying to make sense of consonant blends may add a vowel between consonants (FEREND for *friend*) or delete a final sound as in spelling *nest* as NES. In Spanish *s*-blends have a vowel before them, creating a separate syllable, as in *Español* (Spanish) or *escuela* (school).

   Chinese speakers may insert a slight vowel sound or something that sounds like a breath between *s* consonant blends; *smoke* may be spelled SIMOK. Here again, students add vowels between the consonant blends.

   Hangul, the Korean script, clearly represents each vowel sound, and because all syllables are accented in Korean, unaccented syllables and the schwa (/ə/) sound are not perceived clearly by Korean-speaking students (Yang, 2005). At the ends of final syllables, Korean-speaking students often add a sound; for example, they may spell *church* as CHURCHI and *English* as INGLISHI (Keonghee Tao Han, 2005, personal communication).

3. *English learners often substitute whole words.* Students familiar with writing systems that are quite different from English may be less skillful at making sound discriminations and may

▶ **Voiced**

A sound in which the vocal cords vibrate. Place two fingers lightly on your throat and say /s/ and /z/. Can you feel the difference? Other voiced and voiceless contrasts include /b/ to /p/, /d/ to /t/, /g/ to /k/, and /v/ to /f/.

▶ **Consonant Blends**

Two- or three-letter consonant sequences such as *bl* or *str* that still retain the individual sounds of each letter.

therefore substitute whole words more often than students who have learned more transparent orthographies like Spanish. English learners and especially those who are older may substitute a known word for an unknown word because the words share sounds and sometimes functions. For example, students might spell WHILE for *when* or BORDER for *broadcast*. Some students may rely on a relatively small set of known words in English; this strategy prevents them from attending to and recognizing the sounds at the ends of words or syllables.

4. *Greater variability is seen in the spelling of English learners.* English learners may appear inconsistent, spelling more difficult words correctly while misspelling easier words. For example, a student may spell *happy* and *ocean* correctly but misspell *kite* as KIT and *bed* as BEAD. This may be because English learners memorize the spellings of words that are beyond their basic orthographic knowledge. Or they may make substitutions that are unlikely from native speakers, such as POK for *hope*.

5. *Students may omit ending and middle syllables.* Students' knowledge of the easy inflectional endings will have an impact on their spelling. For the less proficient English learner, contextual knowledge does not guide spelling the way it does for students with a complete grasp of the structure and vocabulary of English. For example, when English speakers hear "We camped down by the river last weekend," the past tense indicates that the spelling is *camp* + *ed* even if, for dialectical reasons, the *-ed* is unarticulated. Someone who does not (1) hear the /t/ sound in *camped* and (2) does not automatically know that the sentence is written in the past tense will have less information to support spelling.

   Spelling some polysyllabic words may overload students. The words can be hard to say and spell (words such as *repetition, constitution, separately*). As a result, while students concentrate on spelling the beginning and ending sounds, the middle syllables can escape attention and are omitted. If internal syllables are omitted often, then the student is probably studying words at a frustration level. For instruction, take a step backward and choose easier words that provide practice with the features that the students are ready to understand. Later, with reading experience and word study, learners will also begin to study **morphology,** which will help them attend to and understand parts of words they had been omitting. Their study of morphology will help them understand how words with the same endings are related in spelling and meaning, such as words that end in *-er, -ily, -ies,* or *-ion.* Examining words that end with these suffixes provides an opportunity to study both the meanings of words and their grammatical functions. Through continued examination of these word structures, students have a stronger foundation from which to explore some of the less obvious unaccented ending syllables such as *-le, -el, -ate,* and *-ence/-ance.*

6. *English learners follow the same developmental sequence as native English speakers, but they often need more time and experience.* English learners are usually acquiring the oral language at the same time they are learning about the written language. This often means that they need more time to learn the sounds of English before they can internalize the spelling. For example, many English learners do not discriminate between the short *e* and short *i* sounds. Even so, we see English learners making the same types of spelling errors as native speakers at different stages of development.

▶ **Morphology**
The study of word structure and the meaningful parts of words, including bases, roots, prefixes, and suffixes.

Grouping and Choosing Features and Activities for Word Study

At this point in the assessment process, use the classroom composite and spelling-by-stage classroom organization forms on the website to develop word study groups. The first place on the feature guide where a student misses more than one feature is the place to begin instruction, or you can use power scores to determine the stage. Write students' names under the stage of development on the organization chart. Then divide the class into relatively even

PDToolkit

for Words Their Way™ with English Learners

Go to PDToolkit, choose your book, click the Assessment Tools tab, and select Assessment Materials to see the classroom composite forms and the Spelling-by-Stage Classroom Organization Chart.

groups for word study. Often, classroom teachers have three groups for literacy instruction and word study is included in this small-group instruction. Four or five groups are possible when aides, English language teachers, or special educators come into the classroom for instruction. In Chapter 3, we provide a more comprehensive discussion of how to organize classroom instruction. A sequence of instruction for each developmental stage found in your word study groups is available in the appropriate instructional chapter of this book.

Assessment at Each Spelling Stage

There are special considerations to keep in mind at each stage of development when assessing English learners. The following discussions of each stage include at least one sample of student spelling that brings to life the contrasts English learners experience.

Assessments with English Learners in the Emergent Stage

During the emergent stage, students grow from scribbling in their writing to the ability to spell the key sounds in words. The progression of writing development can be seen in Figure 2.2, viewing clockwise. Students begin with scribbling that mimics cursive writing. The circles and lines of the next sample are a closer approximation to individual letters. The last two examples include letters, and the shape that looks like a 2 may be an attempt at a letter like *s*.

Several related assessments inform the teacher's knowledge of emergent spelling: alphabet knowledge, concept of word in text, and writing. If students do not write in a conventional manner, then it is useful to learn what alphabet knowledge students have and investigate if they have a concept of word in text.

ALPHABET KNOWLEDGE. At the beginning of kindergarten, many students know the names of between 10 and 18 letters. At the end of kindergarten, students on average know the names of 20 uppercase letters. When children know the names of more than 9 letters, they can begin to study letter sounds. To assess the alphabet, ask students to name them in random order using a list or letter cards (both lowercase and capitals). Look for accuracy and speed in naming the letters.

By encouraging students to write in their first languages, teachers observe what letters, strokes, words, or characters students know in their primary languages. Students enjoy sharing alphabets and looking at similarities between their alphabet and the English alphabet. See page 261 in the Appendix for several sample world alphabets. Alphabets are a fascinating topic to students, especially as they speculate about the similarities across languages. Chapter 4 presents several alphabet activities.

CONCEPT OF WORD IN TEXT. The ability to point accurately to text is a crucial part of learning phonics and spelling in the emergent stage (Flanigan, 2007; Morris, Bloodgood, Lomax, & Perney, 2003). Students develop a concept of word in text through lots of experiences with print, including (1) learning letter names, (2) teacher modeling of how print works through shared reading/big book experiences and shared writing, (3) teacher emphasis on student awareness and first attempts to work with beginning consonant sounds, and (4) the students' own efforts at writing. Concept of word

| **FIGURE 2.2** Progression of Emergent Spelling |

Source: Bear, D. R., & Barone, D. (1998). *Developing Literacy: An Integrated Approach to Assessment and Instruction.* Boston: Houghton Mifflin. Used by permission.

in text is important because learners who cannot point accurately to a line or two of memorized or familiar text will not be able to find the words on the page in order to learn them or firm up their knowledge of phonics from their exposure to text.

Concept of word is assessed with easy rhymes or stories and through observing how accurately students can point to memorized text. Students who fingerpoint accurately to *Humpty Dumpty* and recognize most of the words in the rhyme in isolation demonstrate that they have developed a concept of word in print.

Concept of word in English takes slightly longer to acquire than in other languages. In Chinese, each character represents a syllable, and therefore the match between the figure and the recitation is one to one (Lee, 1990). In contrast, English has one-syllable as well as polysyllabic words. Children who do not have a concept of word in text will be saying the second syllable of *Humpty* as they point to *Dumpty*. In a primary language, students acquire concept of word in print toward the end of the emergent stage. However, during the early grades it may be difficult to find familiar text in English for a child who does not know much English. Therefore, there may be a delay in the acquisition of concept of word among English learners in the emergent stage. This means that without extended literacy experiences during kindergarten, English learners may not come to first grade with a stable concept of word in print.

The activities in Chapter 4 and in *Words Their Way*™: *Emergent Sorts for Spanish-Speaking English Learners* (Helman, Bear, Invernizzi, Templeton, & Johnston, 2009a) and *Words Their Way*™: *Letter and Picture Sorts for Emergent Spellers* (Bear, Invernizzi, Johnston, & Templeton, 2009) help students to acquire a concept of word in text. Once they have a concept of word, most students will associate sounds in English with similar sounds in their primary language.

WRITING. Encourage students to write without fear of making spelling errors. Show emergent writers that drawing and writing can perform the same function of communicating; they can talk and write or draw to share the same experience. It will be useful to observe students' spelling in their unedited free writing, excluding words that they may have copied.

Left-to-right directionality in English does not take much time to learn for most students, but students who are used to writing letters from a different direction and with different forms may write slowly at first. Students who have studied character-based writing systems such as Chinese may have learned to look at writing with the expectation that both sound and meaning will be represented, because this is how Chinese characters are constructed. For older English learners unfamiliar with the alphabet, learning to make the letters may be a tedious process. Many activities to learn the alphabet are presented in Chapter 4 and in the supplements for students in the emergent stage.

Assessments with English Learners in the Letter Name–Alphabetic Stage

English learners acquire three strategies during this stage.

THREE STRATEGIES FOR SPELLING FOR LETTER NAME–ALPHABETIC SPELLERS

1. *Students use the letter names of the alphabet to spell.* For most letters, the letter name is a significant clue to spelling. The /b/ sound is part of the letter name, "bee." The letter name strategy is evident when a child spells *when* as YN. What letter name makes the /w/ sound? Not the name for *w* (which comes from the idea of a "double-*u*"); instead, the letter name *y*, "wye," makes the /w/ sound, and thus *when* is spelled YN.

2. *Letter name spellers use how and where sounds are made or articulated in their mouths to analyze and spell words.* For example, in spelling the /dr/ sound, students who do not know the blend of /d/ and /r/ as in *drum* may spell *drum* with a *j*, JRUM, because the /jr/ blend of /j/ and /r/ feels like /dr/ (actually, the /jr/ is a little easier to pronounce than the /dr/).

The same strategy of using articulation and a letter name strategy is seen in the way students spell vowels. The letter name works well for the long vowels, as in PAL for *pail*. The way that students spell short vowels, however, is perhaps the most sophisticated use of the letter name strategy. Students say the word aloud as they spell, and then they use the letter name of the long vowel that *feels closest in the mouth* to the short vowel. The substitutions are systematic and predictable. For example, the short *e* is spelled with the letter name *a* (*bed* is spelled BAD), and the short *i* is spelled with the letter name *e* (*ship* is spelled SHEP). English learners in this stage not only rely on how sounds are articulated in the mouth, they bring their home languages and sound systems to reading and writing. English learners are familiar with a different system of vowels, and they need to identify how English vowels are spelled and pronounced. The letter name strategy is explored in Chapter 5.

3. *The alphabetic principle is foundational during this stage.* Students use what they know about letter names to learn letter–sound correspondences, beginning with high-frequency letters in words (*b, m, r, s* as opposed to *j, k, q, v, w, x*). Students in the letter name–alphabetic stage learn sight words and establish letter–sound correspondences. There is a reciprocal relationship between the growth of phonics knowledge and the number of sight words students acquire.

As with Mitra's spelling in Table 2.3, students attend first to beginning and then ending consonants to spell and read words. Then, like Daniel, they turn their attention to sounds in the middle. English learners follow a similar path: They first learn beginning sounds, then focus on final sounds, and finally on medial vowel sounds. Many languages have a greater number of open syllables, syllables that end in a vowel sound (like *vida, mucho,* or *primero* in Spanish). In those languages, more final vowels are represented in students' spelling and fewer final consonant sounds.

During the letter name–alphabetic stage, students learn about consonant blends, **consonant digraphs,** and short vowels. In the next stage, they will turn their attention to long vowels and continue to study consonant blends and digraphs, but the letter name–alphabetic stage is all about **phonological awareness** (Ehri, 2006).

The Primary Spelling Inventory (PSI) is probably the best inventory to use with letter name spellers because it has seven single-syllable short-vowel words (p. 248). The Elementary Spelling Inventory (ESI) is best used for students who are mastering or have mastered the spelling of short vowels (page 251). The way students spell the first ten words is a clear indication of their knowledge of the alphabetic principle and long vowel patterns. The Picture Spelling Inventory and the accompanying feature guide found in the Appendix (p. 254) and on the website contains ten short vowels to assess letter name stage spelling.

EXAMPLES OF STUDENTS' SPELLING DURING THE LETTER NAME–ALPHABETIC STAGE. The first example for this stage (see Figure 2.3) is by a Korean-speaking kindergartener, Hyun, who is an early letter name–alphabetic speller. The first word, *top*, is spelled TO. Although the omission of sounds is common among students at this stage, the final /p/ sound is problematic for many Korean-speaking students because no final /p/ sound exists in Korean.

Hyun spelled the first and last sounds of lid (LD) and bet (BT). The spelling of wag as WC is unusual for English speakers. As will be seen in greater detail in Chapter 5, /g/ and /k/ differ only in voicing: The voiced /g/ sound may be substituted by the /k/ because Korean speakers do not make this distinction between voiced

PDToolkit

for Words Their Way™ with English Learners

Go to PDToolkit, choose your book, click the Assessment Tools tab, and select Assessment Materials to see the Picture Spelling Inventory and the feature guide for the Picture Spelling Inventory.

▶ **Consonant Digraphs**

Two consonants that represent one sound, such as *ch* or *th*.

▶ **Phonological Awareness**

An awareness of speech sounds such as syllables, rhyme, and individual syllables.

FIGURE 2.3 Early Letter Name–Alphabetic Spelling by Hyun, a Korean Speaker

Word	Student's Spelling
top	TO
lid	LD
wag	WC
bet	BT
run	R

(/g/) and unvoiced (/k/) sounds. Thus, *c* represents the /k/ substitution for /g/. Even though it may be unclear why students spell the way they do, the crucial part of the assessment is to determine what students do correctly, and with which orthographic features they are experimenting. Once this is determined, instruction begins with easy contrasts like final /k/ with final /t/. As students become ready, the finer contrasts (/k/ to /g/) are introduced. As an early letter name speller, Hyun continued with beginning sound word study and discrimination of final sounds in phonemic awareness activities. Phonemic awareness of older learners can be facilitated if they have extensive sight vocabularies.

The next spelling sample (Figure 2.4) is from Reyna, a 6-year-old Spanish speaker in the middle letter name–alphabetic stage. Her most prominent error is inserting final vowels at the ends of the first two words, which are short vowels and closed syllables, as well as at the end of *chase*, spelled HESU. The *b* for *p* substitution in *ship* is a common misspelling among English learners. The letter name strategy is evident in the spelling of digraphs and blends. The *dr* blend is often spelled as *jr*. Other blends and digraphs are omitted, which is common among letter name–alphabetic spellers.

Reyna makes reasonable substitutions for the vowels. The long vowel substitution of *e* for *a-e* in *chase* is common given how close the *e* sound in Spanish is to the long *a* in English.

Reyna's instructional level is at the letter name stage. Many of the error types discussed for this stage are evident in her spelling. Reyna's spelling of *train* as HRIN is related to the similarity in sound between /tr/ and /ch/. When pronouncing the *tr* in *train* slowly, the /ch/ can be felt in the mouth just before the /r/. In addition, the letter name for *h* in Spanish is "ah-chay," and she may use the letter name for *h* to spell /ch/. In spelling *closet*, Reyna has represented the unstressed final syllable but has not included the final /t/ sound. This ending matches syllabically but not phonologically in the last word, BIJID for *beaches*. Note also how Reyna has spelled the /ch/ sound with a *j*, a sound that is close in articulation to the /ch/.

The next spelling sample makes the bridge between the letter name and the next spelling stage, the within word pattern stage. This sample demonstrates how students sound out unfamiliar vowels at the same time as they learn more sight words and something about long vowels. Benjamín's sample (Figure 2.5) is from the primary inventory. He knows beginning consonants, blends, and digraphs: *ch, dr, sh, bl, fr, ch,* and *ck*. He spells just one short vowel correctly though the misspellings are common for middle letter name spellers: DREM for *dream*, DEG for *dig*, GOM for *gum*. It is also interesting to see that Benjamín has learned to spell two common long vowel words: *hope* and *wait*. He will, however, benefit from a careful study of short vowels before he goes on to study long vowels.

At first, some spelling errors by English learners look like within word pattern spelling errors in which students are using but confusing long vowel patterns, such as VCVe (NALE for *nail*), VCCV (CAIK for *cake*), or CVV (SAI for *say*). Benjamín has several spelling errors that involve two vowels: SHAIN for *shine*, BLEAD for *blade*, COUCH for *coach*, and FRAIT for *fright*. As noted earlier, English learners do more sounding out and may represent more sounds as they elongate the vowels. In this case the two vowel sounds that can be heard in long *i* (/ah/ and /ee/) and long *a* (/ay/ and /ee/) are spelled out.

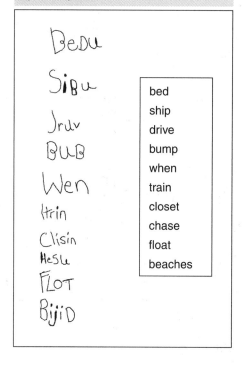

FIGURE 2.4 Middle Letter Name–Alphabetic Spelling by Reyna, a Spanish Speaker

BeDu
SiBu
Jruv
BUB
Wen
Hrin
Clisin
HeSu
FLoT
BiJiD

| bed |
| ship |
| drive |
| bump |
| when |
| train |
| closet |
| chase |
| float |
| beaches |

FIGURE 2.5 Middle Letter Name–Alphabetic Spelling, by Benjamín, a Spanish Speaker

1 fean
2 pet
3 deg
4 roop
5 hope
6 Wait
7 gom
8 Sleid
9 Steck
10 Shain
11 drem
12 blead
13 couch
14 frait
15 choint

| fan |
| pet |
| dig |
| rob |
| hope |
| |
| wait |
| gum |
| sled |
| stick |
| shine |
| |
| dream |
| blade |
| coach |
| fright |
| chewing |

It is a positive development to see final sounds represented correctly in all of Benjamín's single-syllable words. When it comes to two-syllable words, he has perhaps confused an *-ing* with *-int*, spelling *chewing* as CHOINT.

FIGURE 2.6 Within Word Pattern Spelling by Soo, a Korean Speaker

Word	Student's Spelling
fan	fean
pet	pet
dig	dig
rob	rob
hope	hope
wait	wate
gum	gum
sled	sled
stick	stick
shine	shine
dream	dreme
blade	blad
coach	coch
fright	frite
chewing	chuin
crawl	cran
wishes	wises
thorn	drn
shouted	shout
spoil	spoy
growl	Joun
third	serd
camped	campte
tries	chride
clapping	clapn
riding	riding

Assessments with English Learners in the Within Word Pattern Stage

Learning during this stage calls for a balance in studying long vowel patterns and continuing to learn about vowel sounds. For many English learners the distinctions between long and short vowels do not exist in their primary languages. In Spanish, for example, there are strong and weak vowels, and in tonal languages, vowels are tuned or differentiated by changes in pitch (high, mid, low, rise, fall, rise-fall, etc.). Many English learners will experience confusion among vowels that are close in articulation, such as long *e* and short *i* (*sheep/ship*, *eat/it*, *bean/bin*).

SECOND ATTEMPTS IN SPELLING. When administering the inventory to students in this stage, you may ask them to make additional attempts at spelling words they think they have misspelled. Ask students not to cross through previous attempts: "Write your new tries to the side. Make a few guesses if you like." These attempts are interesting diagnostically and show you the depth of their knowledge.

EXAMPLE OF SPELLING DURING THE WITHIN WORD PATTERN STAGE. Soo is a Korean-speaking student whose spelling reflects the development of English learners (Figure 2.6). Soo spelled 9 out of 26 words correctly. She has some understanding of long vowel patterns as she adds a silent *e* in DREME for *dream* and FRITE for *fright*, but she omits other silent vowels in patterns, for example, in BLAD for *blade* or COCH for *coach*. Soo shows inconsistency with the /sh/ sound, spelling it correctly in *shine* but representing it with an *s* in WISES for *wishes*.

These difficulties are apparent in the scoring of Soo's feature guide in Figure 2.7. Looking across the bottom row shows what she has mastered and what needs attention. Soo first misses more than one on the consonants digraph feature (scoring 4 out of 7) so this feature needs some review. She knows her blends but her score of only two on long vowels indicates that this should be the main area of instruction.

Soo's spelling reflects contrasts between Korean and English. For Korean-speaking students, the /r/ and /l/ sounds may be indistinguishable. Notice also that *spoil* does not have an ending *l* and the *r* in *growl* is omitted. Throughout, the *r*'s and *l*'s were difficult for her to represent. Soo's speech reflects these confusions between /r/ and /l/. She spelled only two of the inflectional endings (*riding* and WISES for *wishes* compared to SHOUT for *shouted* and CAMPTE for *camped*). Again, Soo does not enunciate these sounds in speaking. Her study of morphology in later stages will reveal some of the grammatical relations to consider in spelling and reading.

Assessments with English Learners in the Syllables and Affixes Stage

The upper level is composed of two spelling stages, the syllables and affixes stage (Chapter 7) and the derivational relations stage (Chapter 8). By the time students are in the later part of the syllables and affixes stage,

FIGURE 2.7 Soo's Feature Guide for the Primary Spelling Inventory

Student's Name: Soo Teacher: Rignak Grade: 3 Date: October 10

Words Spelled Correctly: 9/26 Feature Points: 35/56 Total: 44/82 Spelling Stage: Within Word Pattern

SPELLING STAGES →	EMERGENT	LETTER NAME—ALPHABET			WITHIN WORD PATTERN			SYLLABLE AFFIXES		
	Late	Early / Middle	Late		Early / Middle	Late		Early		
Features →	Consonants		Short Vowels	Digraphs	Blends	Long Vowel Patterns	Other Vowels	Inflected Endings	Feature Points	Words Spelled Correctly
	Initial	Final								
1. fan	f ✓	n ✓	a ea						2	0
2. pet	p ✓	t ✓	e ✓						3	1
3. dig	d ✓	g ✓	i ✓						3	1
4. rob	r ✓	b ✓	o ✓						3	1
5. hope	h ✓	p ✓				o-e ✓			3	1
6. wait	w ✓	t ✓				ai a-e			2	0
7. gum	g ✓	m ✓	u ✓						3	1
8. sled			e ✓		sl ✓				2	1
9. stick			i ✓		st ✓				2	1
10. shine				sh ✓		i-e ✓			2	1
11. dream					dr ✓	ea e-e			1	0
12. blade					bl ✓	a-e a			1	0
13. coach				ch ✓		oa o			1	0
14. fright					fr ✓	igh i-e			1	0
15. chewing				ch ✓			ew ui	ing in	1	0
16. crawl					cr ✓		aw a		1	0
17. wishes				sh s				es ✓	1	0
18. thorn				th t			or —		0	0
19. shouted				sh ✓			ou —	ed —	2	0
20. spoil							oi oy		0	0
21. growl							ow ow		0	0
22. third				th s			ir er		0	0
23. camped								ed te	0	0
24. tries					tr chr			ies ide	0	0
25. clapping								pping pn	0	0
26. riding								ding ✓	1	1
Totals	7/7	7/7	6/7	4/7	6/7	2/7	1/7	2/7	35/56	9/26

Word Study for Phonics, Vocabulary, and Spelling Instruction © 2008 by Pearson Education, Inc.

Word study with students in the last two stages is focused on vocabulary and making meaning connections among affixes and roots.

they participate in classroom word study without much accommodation. English learners in these upper levels bring a richness to the group when they share the spelling and meaning patterns in their primary oral and written languages. You will see that the emphasis for word study from the late syllables and affixes stage onward makes links between the derivations and word parts that are shared across languages.

Assessment of syllables and affixes spelling begins with a look at how students combine syllables and how they spell unaccented syllables in two-syllable words. Students are also beginning to understand inflectional morphology, which includes the principle of consonant doubling (*hop/hopping* compared to *hope/hoping*). Easy prefixes and suffixes are learned during this stage, and students study how to spell different endings, such as *-ed*, *-es*, *-ies*, and *-ment*. Many English learners are also figuring out how these suffixes function grammatically. Their knowledge of English grammar and syntax will begin to support their spelling efforts during this stage. Therefore, in Chapters 7 and 8 you will find a variety of word study activities that combine grammar and spelling instruction.

The syllables and affixes stage is a time to study pronunciation of one- and two-syllable words, vowel sounds in two-syllable words, and endings—for example, the three sounds of *-ed*: /t/, /d/, /ed/. Therefore, in the assessments, teachers listen for how students pronounce these final sounds (for example, *locked* /t/, *waved* /d/, *painted* /ed/).

Spelling two-syllable words illustrates how word study incorporates English grammar and inflectional morphology. In the syllables and affixes stage, spelling is closely linked to the study of past tense, verb forms, and gerunds (words that end in *-ing*). Students study some of the spelling patterns of two-syllable words, like consonant doubling, at the same time as they look at gerunds. Students examine words that end with *-s* and *-es* at the same time as they study plurals while also noticing pronunciation differences in endings with /s/ sounds compared to those with /z/ sounds.

EXAMPLES OF SPELLING DURING THE SYLLABLES AND AFFIXES STAGE. Gustavo, whose primary language is Spanish, began school in the United States in kindergarten, and as an end-of-year fourth-grader, he is in the early part of the syllables and affixes stages of spelling (Figure 2.8). Gustavo has learned to spell long and short vowel patterns as well as consonant blends and digraphs.

The first word Gustavo misspells is *spoil*, which he writes as SPOYLLED. That Gustavo includes an *-ed* means that he is listening for this ending. He is still learning some of the complex vowel patterns as seen in his spellings of *chewed* and *shower*. For *ripen*, the *b* in RIBEN makes sense as a substitution of /b/ for /p/. What are most noticeable about his spellings are the ending syllables. He is experimenting with the apostrophe to spell inflectional endings as in CARY'S for *carries* and MARCH'T for *marched*. He will benefit from instruction focusing on simple affixes and how spellings change when they are added.

With polysyllabic words, Gustavo does not use meaningful units in the base words such as *please* in *pleasure* or *tion* in *opposition*. Systematic study of

FIGURE 2.8 Syllables and Affixes Spelling by Gustavo, a Spanish Speaker

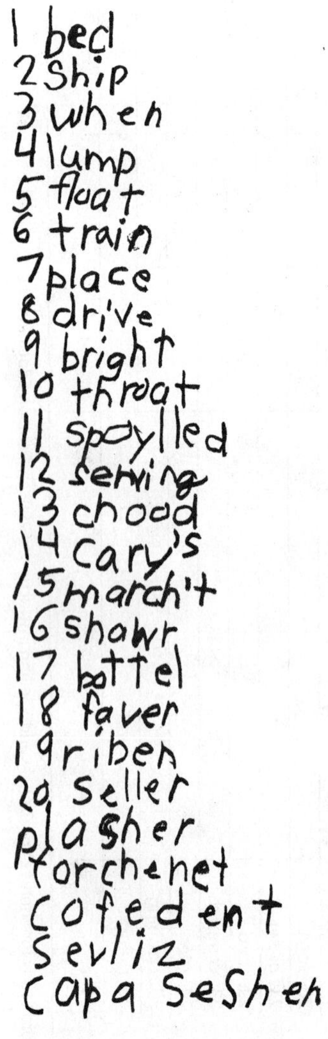

Gustavo's spelling list:
1. bed
2. Ship
3. when
4. lump
5. float
6. train
7. place
8. drive
9. bright
10. throat
11. spoylled
12. serving
13. chood
14. cary's
15. march't
16. shawr
17. bottel
18. faver
19. riben
20. seller
pl asher
torchenet
Cofedent
Sevliz
Capa Sesheh

Elementary List

bed
ship
when
lump
float
train
place
drive
bright
throat
spoil
serving
chewed
carries
marched
shower
bottle
favor
ripen
cellar
pleasure
fortunate
confident
civilize
opposition

inflectional suffixes, beginning with the easiest ones, will be important for him to understand grammatical relations. As a fourth-grader, vocabulary study will be important to support his learning in the content areas. There will be many polysyllabic words that he cannot spell and may not be able to read or understand. When he studies science or social studies it will be useful to scaffold his understanding of content words. This is addressed in Chapter 8.

Assessments with English Learners in the Derivational Relations Stage

To assess derivational relations stage spelling, students' knowledge of more complex prefixes (*com-, a-, ad-*) and suffixes (*-ance, -ent, -ious*) is assessed, as is their knowledge of words derived from roots: *credible* from the root *cred* ("believe") and *spectacles* from the root *spec* ("look"). In word study activities, English learners in this final stage make comparisons of roots across languages. They use knowledge of their home language to enrich the study of word families and word histories.

An assessment of orthographic knowledge indicates what vocabulary needs to be taught. Students in the derivational relations stage are learning the specialized vocabulary of the content areas through reading and content lessons. Students benefit from direct instruction of vocabulary that they have not acquired informally through reading. Students who are in the secondary grades and have just reached the syllables and affixes stage will benefit from a vocabulary program that encompasses the academic, procedural, and content vocabulary that students need for success in school. This means that students need to learn a core academic vocabulary—words that stretch across all content areas, such as *analyze, thesis, procedure,* and *attribute,* along with content-specific academic vocabulary such as *respiratory, autocracy,* and *sonnet.* The elementary inventory and the upper-level inventory are used to assess English learners in these last two spelling stages. In addition, the vocabulary assessments we present in part three of this chapter provide insight into word study instruction for students in these last two stages.

Students in the derivational relations stage are also advanced readers. They use reading academically, and they know how to be flexible in their reading rates depending on the materials and purpose for reading. Derivational spellers learn most new vocabulary from reading.

EXAMPLE OF SPELLING DURING THE DERIVATIONAL RELATIONS STAGE. The next sample, Figure 2.9, is from Mai, a student born in the United States who speaks Vietnamese in her family and among her friends. Mai is in the derivational relations stage, and she demonstrates a thorough knowledge of many of the principles that students learn in the syllables and affixes stage of spelling: most inflectional suffixes, consonant doubling, and patterns for unaccented syllables (*bottle, ripen*). Mai does confuse CARRIED for *carries.* Her spelling of the last five words is telling. She has learned inflectional suffixes like *-ate* in *fortunate* (PHORTENNATE), the *-ent* in *confident* (CONPHONDENT), the *-ize* in *civilize* (SIVELIZE), and the *-tion* in *opposition* (OPPISITION). The *ph* for the /f/ sound comes from using *ph* in her spelling of Vietnamese. Although

FIGURE 2.9 Early Derivational Relations Stage Spelling by Mai, a Vietnamese Speaker

Mai's spelling	Target word
I bed	bed
II ship	ship
III when	when
IV lump	lump
V float	float
VI train	train
VII place	place
VIII drive	drive
XI bright	bright
X throat	throat
11 spoil	spoil
12 serving	serving
13 chewed	chewed
14 carried	carries
15 marched	marched
16 shower	shower
17 bottle	bottle
18 favor	favor
19 ripen	ripen
20 celler	cellar
21 pleaser	pleasure
22 Phortennate	fortunate
23 Conphondent	confident
24 Sivelize	civilize
25 oppisition	opposition

Mai still needs to concentrate on prefixes and suffixes, with support from her teacher and classmates, she is ready to begin to study roots and related words (*confide/confident, oppose/opposition*). Because Vietnamese is her primary language, she will not be able to draw on cognates and will need to study the meaning connections among words in dictionaries and the etymological references presented in Chapter 8.

The Role of Dialect in Spelling Assessment

The continuum of language variations can range from minor differences in regional accents and the pronunciations of a few vowels to extensive differences in pronunciation, vocabulary, and sentence structure or grammar. Students who speak a **dialect** or **creole** of English that differs from the standarized academic version benefit from word study that clarifies the sound contrasts between "school" English and their speech. They do not speak another language, but a version of English that is influenced by other languages. Listen for the variations of English you hear among students. In your area, you may meet students who, along with their families and friends, speak in a dialect created out of the interactions among languages, cultures, and speakers of different ages.

Here are four questions to consider as you listen for English-based dialects and creoles:

▶ **Dialect**
A variation of a language used by a group of people, usually in a certain region.

▶ **Creole**
A language that originated from a combination of two or more languages.

* Do you know of a specific language that influences the student's speech in English? Is there a Spanish, African, or Asian language influence? For example, Spanish influences Tagalog, spoken in the Philippines. Similarly, French, African languages, Spanish, and English all influence Haitian Creole, spoken by thousands of children in Florida.
* How do the ways students pronounce words vary from what you expect to hear?
* What do you notice grammatically? Is there a particular part of speech that is omitted or said in a different order? Are verbs or pronouns omitted or in a different order?
* What phrasing illustrates what you hear in the student's speech or writing? Consider the student's use of these language forms and standard English in the classroom. Are there times when students use one form of English and not another?

English learners will speak with a dialect that combines the regional English where they live with the influence of their primary language. If you teach children in specific geographic areas, there is an opportunity to learn the dialect's vocabulary, pronunciation, and grammar, such as Gullah in South Carolina and Georgia, Jamaican Creole, or Hawaiian English.

Students who speak English-based dialects do not need to change their pronunciation to learn to read and spell. Just like English learners, speakers of dialects benefit from word study that shows them how their speech is related to the alphabetic, pattern, and meaning layers of English spelling. This word study can include picture and word sorts that focus on particular features.

Assessment of Spelling in Students' Primary Languages

We know that the more students know about literacy in their primary language, the more they have to bring to learning English. Students who understand a good deal about the orthography of their primary languages are going to make swifter progress in learning English than students who are unfamiliar with any writing system (August & Shanahan, 2006; Genesee et al., 2005). For this reason it is useful to learn about students' orthographic knowledge in their primary languages. Analyzing spelling errors in students' primary languages provides a window to their orthographic knowledge and literacy development. In the following section, spelling inventories to assess students' orthographic knowledge in Spanish, Chinese, and Korean are presented. School districts in the United States are using these inventories with newcomers who are beginning readers in English. For educators who want to develop inventories in other languages, these examples are presented as models.

Assessments function best when a fluent reader administers the inventory to the student. English language teachers who speak the language being assessed can administer, analyze, and interpret the students' spelling. Parents and other teachers may be able to administer the inventory or provide some interpretation. A recorded version is quite useful when there is no opportunity to bring in a native speaker. For the three foreign language inventories presented here, recordings in those languages can be found on the website. In most communities there will be someone literate in the language of interest who can help interpret any confusions at the base of the misspellings. The analyses of students' spelling in their home languages illustrate what they know about words and written language, which can help in planning word study in English.

Using Spelling Assessments and Sorts with Students Learning Foreign Languages

Teachers who teach English as a foreign language can use the English spelling assessments discussed in the previous section to understand the word knowledge of students learning English as a foreign language. Likewise, foreign language teachers in the United States use the Spanish, Chinese, and Korean spelling inventories discussed in this section to assess students' word and orthographic knowledge in these foreign languages.

Once teachers know where their students are developmentally, they involve students in word study activities in the foreign language students are studying. For example, English foreign language teachers in China and Japan have begun to use the word sorts presented here to teach students about the three layers of English. In the United States, teachers are developing sorts as an active way for students to learn the sounds and characters of Chinese and Japanese.

Inventories and Spelling Development in Spanish, Chinese, and Korean

Three inventories are presented here with analyses of students' spelling in Spanish, Chinese, and Korean. These inventories are based on the development of spelling we have observed in those languages and describe a hierarchy in the acquisition of features. These inventories have been administered to many students: several thousand in Spanish, 2,200 in Chinese, and 1,200 in Korean (Bear, Han, Wei, & DeMartini, 2010; Helman, 2005; Shen & Bear, 2000; Yang, 2005). Directions and scoring guides may be found in the assessment section of the website.

SPANISH SPELLING INVENTORY. The Spanish Spelling Inventory on the website assesses features across the developmental continuum in a similar way to that of the English inventories. As discussed in the presentation of Spanish stages in Chapter 1 (page 16), the names of the stages are different and in some cases represent slightly different features. For example, in Spanish, as in English, an emergent speller is likely to hear and encode a highly prominent sound in the word; however, in Spanish this sound is as likely to be a vowel sound as a consonant sound. This is because Spanish has fewer CVC words; its most common word structure is CVCV, so the vowels are more prominent.

Because Spanish is a much more transparent orthography than English, the within word pattern, or *patrones*, stage is less complex. In the early part of this stage, learners begin to understand silent letters such as *h*, the use of *u* to create the hard sound of *g* as in *guisante* or

el	el
suma	suma
pan	pan
red	red
campos	campos
plancha	plancha
brincar	brincar
fresa	fresa
aprieto	aprieto
guisante	guisante
Quiciera	quisiera
guigante	gigante
actristes	actrices
voy	voy
LLiero	hierro
bilingue	bilingüe
Lapizes	lápices
estraño	extraño
altobus	autobús
halla	haya
Jeolmativa	geometría
caimal	caimán
intalgime	intangible
elviboro	herbívoro
cicologo	psicólogo

with *q* in *qu*, and contrasting letters that have the same sound such as *v-b*, *s-c-z*, *y-ll*, or *g-j*. Later in the *patrones* stage more complex vowel patterns are assessed.

At the syllables and affixes level, the Spanish spelling inventory focuses on accents and affixes. Finally, the derivational relations stage looks at the correct encoding of Latin or Greek elements in words based on meaning, when phonetic options are ambiguous, such as the inclusion of *p* in *psicólogo*.

The sample shown in Figure 2.10 is from Julisa, a third-grader, in October of the school year. Julisa is in the early within word pattern, or *patrones*, level of spelling development—as can be seen in her spelling in Figure 2.10 and in the feature guide scoring in Figure 2.11. She has mastered all of the features in this inventory at the emergent and alphabetic levels involving the representation of sounds in words, including digraphs, blends, and preconsonantal nasals. She begins to use but confuses letters that can represent the same sound, such as using a *c* for *s* in QUICIERA and *ll* for the beginning sound in *hierro*. She also overgeneralizes the *gui* as she attempts to spell *gigante*. The place to begin word study with Julisa is in the area of silent letters and those with interchangeable sounds (*contrastes*). She scored 4 out of 7 features at the early within word pattern level and 3 out of 5 features at the late within word pattern level. Although she did write one accent mark on her spelling words, this generally seems to be a feature she is not regularly using yet, so the *acentos y afijos* level of study is currently above her instructional level.

Given the transparency of the Spanish orthographic system, Julisa will likely be able to decode just about any text at this point in her literacy development. Her need to consider pronunciation of unfamiliar, multisyllabic, accented words may break up the fluency and expressiveness of her reading in some cases. Most likely, the limits of her academic word knowledge and background experiences would be the greatest constraint on her reading level at this point.

In English, Julisa quickly learned the alphabetic layer, and with some confusions, was mastering the spelling of short vowel words. She is learning about long vowel patterns in English and is able to read in English at roughly a second grade level. Word study instruction for Julisa focuses on learning the vocabulary and grammar of English through plenty of experience in reading and oral language activities.

CHINESE SPELLING INVENTORY. Approximately 88,000 school-age students with Chinese language backgrounds in the United States speak English with difficulty (Planty et al., 2009). Students who are literate in Mandarin will find it easier to learn English than students who have little experience with any written language. With the 1.3 billion Mandarin language speakers in China, as well as the many students learning Chinese as a foreign language, this Chinese spelling inventory may have great utility in understanding the orthographic development of children learning to read and write in Chinese. The Chinese Spelling Inventory with directions, feature guide, and case study is found in the assessment section of the website. This inventory assesses three types of spelling errors and two stages of orthographic development of elementary Chinese students from first through sixth grades. The spelling errors in this inventory assess students' orthographic knowledge in the first two stages. The first stage is referred to as the *phonological correspondence* stage (Shen & Bear, 2000). The second stage is titled *parallel growth of graphic patterns and semantic components*. Chinese is a deep orthography that provides no obvious sound–script correspondences. Despite this lack of sound–script correspondence, first and second graders rely heavily on sounding out strategies to write Chinese characters.

KOREAN SPELLING INVENTORY. About 44,000 Korean Americans have difficulty speaking English (Planty et al., 2009), and many of these students can read Korean. This inventory can give teachers a sense of the level of literacy that they bring to learning English. One study found that students' spelling is related to their reading comprehension in

FIGURE 2.11 Feature Guide to the Spanish Spelling Inventory for Julisa's Spelling

Directions: Check the features that are present in each student's spelling. In the bottom row, total the features used correctly. Check the spelling stage that summarizes the student's development. Begin instruction at that stage with a focus on the types of features where the student missed more than one feature in a column.

Student's Name: Julisa Teacher: Brisley Grade: 3 Date: October 15

ETAPAS DE LA ESCRITURA →	EMERGENTE		ALFABÉTICA			PATRONES			DERIVACIONES Y SUS RELACIONES		
	Tardía		Temprana	Media	Tardía	Temprana	Tardía	Acentos y Afijos			
Características →	Vocal Prominente	Consonante Prominente	Vocalas/ Consonantes	Representación de Sonidos	Dígrafos, Sílabas Cerradas	Contrastes, Letras Mudas	Diptongos Homófonos	Tildes, Plurales, Afijos	Raíces	Puntos	Palabra
1. el	e ✓	l ✓								2	1
2. suma	u ✓	s ✓								2	1
3. pan	a ✓	p ✓								2	1
4. red			re ✓	d ✓						2	1
5. campos				os ✓	mp ✓					2	1
6. plancha				pl ✓	ch ✓					2	1
7. brincar			c (k) ✓	ar ✓	n ✓					3	1
8. fresa			sa ✓	fr ✓						2	1
9. aprieto			o ✓	ie ✓						2	1
10. guisante				ante ✓		gui ✓				2	1
11. quisiera				iera ✓		qui ✓				2	1
12. gigante			ga ✓		nt ✓	gi gui				2	
13. actrices				tr ✓	ac ✓			ces tes		2	
14. voy						v ✓	oy ✓			2	
15. hierro						h ll	ie ✓			1	
16. bilingüe						b ✓	üe ue			1	
17. lápices						c g		á a			
18. extraño				ñ ✓				ex es		1	
19. autobús								ú u	auto alto		
20. haya							h-y ll				
21. geometría								ía ıa	metr mati		
22. caimán							ai ✓	án al		1	
23. intangible								ible ıme	tang tal		
24. herbívoro								í ı	herb elu		
25. psicólogo								có co	psi ci		
Totales	3 (3)	3 (3)	5 (5)	10 (10)	5 (5)	4 (7)	3 (5)	0 (9)	0 (5)	33 (52)	11 (25)

SPELLING STAGES:

☑ TEMPRANA ☐ MEDIA ☐ TARDÍA

☐ EMERGENTE
☐ ALFABÉTICA
☑ PATRONES
☐ ACENTOS Y AFIJOS
☐ DERIVACIONES Y SUS RELACIONES

Words Spelled Correctly: 11/25
Feature Points: 33/52
Total: 44/77

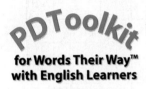

Korean (Bear et al., 2010). Furthermore, there are nearly 70 million Korean speakers, and this inventory provides some insight into their literacy development. The Korean Spelling Inventory found on the website assesses four stages of Korean spelling development (Yang, 2005).

Only three languages have been discussed, but there may be a dozen or more languages represented in your school. Guidelines to assess development at each spelling stage in other languages are presented in a PDF file on the website titled Assessments of Orthographic Knowledge in Students' Primary Languages. This discussion will assist educators who want to create spelling inventories in other languages.

Oral Language Development and Vocabulary Learning

Assessments to understand students' oral language learning are presented in this section. In the first part of this section, we discuss the oral language development of students in English, including ways to think about students' oral language proficiencies. In the second part of this section, we focus on the vocabulary that English learners acquire through literacy. Several vocabulary assessments address written English and are designed for students who are aiming to learn content vocabulary and the morphology of English. These assessments are most useful for students of intermediate language proficiency in the intermediate and secondary grades. The materials for all of these assessments are found on the website. The chapter closes with a brief discussion about talking with parents on language and literacy learning.

Learning about Students' Oral Language Development

Students who have well-developed oral language and vocabulary in a home language have a strong base to build on when learning to read and write in English. In the area of word study, consider three reasons why the study of students' languages is important for effective word study:

1. Teachers who learn about languages learn about their students. Languages are fascinating! Languages are complex, they are ever changing, and they interact. Each language tells a story about its users (McCabe & Bliss, 2003).
2. There are similarities among languages. Languages share roots and sounds, and this can be seen in their common histories. These similarities can be helpful and can guide instructional conversations.
3. There are differences among languages. Languages have different sounds, words, and ways of saying things. These differences may be examined and clarified in word study activities.

Studying students' home languages is a way to learn about other people in other cultures and countries. To get to know the English-language development of students, listen to their language use in their home languages.

Critical Questions about Students' Languages and Learning

To survey students' language use and to plan Talk With language activities, consider the questions and areas of inquiry presented in Figure 2.12. Key concepts in these questions are highlighted for emphasis. These questions can help open up discussions among teams of teachers serving a common group of students. The questions can also be adapted to encourage sharing

FIGURE 2.12 Questions to Explore Students' Language and Literacy

1. What *language* or languages other than English does the student *speak*?
2. *How often* does the student use the primary language? What *percentage* of the time is this primary language spoken?
3. How common is the language in *this school?*
4. What is the student's preferred language in which to view *television?*
5. *How long* has the student been *learning English?*
6. How would you describe the student's willingness to *start a conversation?* (Dickinson, McCabe, & Sprague, 2003, p. 558)
7. Is he or she *understandable* when speaking in English? (Dickinson, McCabe, & Sprague, 2003, p. 558)
8. How often does the student use *varied vocabulary* or try out new words (words heard in stories or from teacher)? (Dickinson, McCabe, & Sprague, 2003, p. 558)
9. Does the student speak in *connected phrases?*
10. Is the student *expressive* in his or her speech?
11. Are there sounds in English that you notice are difficult for the student to *pronounce?*
12. How many years did the student receive *formal education* in the home language?
13. What is the level of *literacy development* of the student in the home language?
14. Does the student *read text* in the *home language* with accuracy, fluency, and expression?
15. Does the student use the *home language* for *writing* in classroom activities?
16. In writing, does the student *blend* the home language with English?

among students. The focus of these questions is students' language experiences in their home language and can be used with peers and parents. To expand on these questions with a more detailed survey of students' language and literacy development see the Language and Literacy Survey on the website.

A few of the 16 questions in Figure 2.12 survey students' educational experiences. The students who have had educational experiences in any language bring academic vocabularies, knowledge of school processes, and information to the literacy table about how and why people read and study words.

Levels of Proficiency and Formal Tests of Oral Language

In most school districts, students' language development is assessed. For example, using the levels of oral proficiency described in Figure 2.13, students in the first two levels would receive support services (Zehler, Fleischman, Hopstock, Stephenson, Pendzick, & Sapru, 2003, p. 40).

Several formal and standardized tests of oral language are available in English and Spanish, and most districts have a common assessment they use with English learners. Some of these tests are scored to give an indication of how a student's performance compares with a national sample. Additional tests are presented in students' primary languages, although few have been standardized. This is a growing area of study and development, and new tests should become available each year.

A number of professional resources review these tests including the SIOP materials (Echevarría, Vogt, & Short, 2010), the *Handbook of English Language Proficiency Tests* (Del Vecchio, 1995), *Handbook of Spanish Language Proficiency Tests* (Guerrero & Del Vecchio, 1996), *Resources about Assessment and Accountability for ELLs* (National Clearinghouse for English Language Acquisition, 2006), and *State Assessment Policy and Practice for English Language Learners* (Rivera & Collum, 2006).

PDToolkit

for Words Their Way™ with English Learners

Go to PDToolkit, choose your book, click the Assessment Tools tab, and select Assessment Materials to see the Language and Literacy Survey.

FIGURE 2.13 Levels of Oral Proficiency in English

Emergent/early receptive language. Very little or no understanding of oral English; may try to communicate in primary language or with body language and one- to two-word phrases

Beginning. Beginning proficiency; limited understanding of oral and English language; amount of receptive and expressive verb tense; phrasal talking

Early intermediate. Advanced beginning; limited proficiency, repertoire, and vocabulary; conversationally fluent phrasally and moderately expressive; limited academic knowledge means less verbal or written fluency

Intermediate. Intermediate proficiency; large receptive vocabulary; most verb tenses used correctly; basic vocabulary for conversation in place; most fundamental academic terms are known and used; academic and specialized vocabulary is limited and oral and written expression lack complex sentence structures

Advanced. High level of proficiency; academic, content knowledge, and syntax close to proficiency of monolingual English speakers

Comments

Source: Adapted from Zehler, A. M., Fleischman, H. L., Hopstock, P. J., Stephenson, T. G., Pendzick, M., & Sapru, S. (2003, September). *Descriptive Study of Services to LEP Students and LEP Students with Disabilities: Volume I: Research Report* (Contract No. EO-00-CO-0089). Office of English Language Acquisition, Language Enhancement, and Academic Achievement of Limited English Proficient Students (OELA). Retrieved from www.ncela.gwu.edu/resabout/research/descriptivestudyfiles.

Most language tests involve a combination of subtests that examine the speaking and listening domains: listening comprehension, vocabulary, sentence repetition, story retelling, and verbal analogies. Recordings are often played for the oral language measures. Several of these language assessments include reading and writing in subtests that include letter identification, word recognition, reading comprehension, writing through dictation for mechanics, spelling, usage, grammar, and handwriting.

Intermediate and Secondary Vocabulary Assessments

From high school onward, and often from sixth grade onward, nearly all of the vocabulary students learn comes from reading. The assessments presented in this section provide insights into how students' vocabularies will serve them in the intermediate and secondary grades.

Three assessments are presented: (1) a self-assessment students use to indicate and track what they know and need to learn about content vocabulary, (2) an academic vocabulary spelling assessment to understand what students know about procedural academic vocabulary, and (3) an assessment that examines students' knowledge of English prefixes and suffixes. The directions and forms to use are presented on the website.

CONTENT VOCABULARY SELF-ASSESSMENT.   Students are good at assessing their knowledge of vocabulary. The assessment presented on the website and illustrated in Figure 2.14 is a way for students to monitor their progress in learning content-related vocabulary (Templeton, Bear, Invernizzi, & Johnston, 2010). In this survey, students are provided with the key content vocabulary they will need to know in a subject they are studying, and with this survey, they become more responsible for learning the key terms in their content areas. Teachers often

PDToolkit

**for Words Their Way™
with English Learners**

Go to PDToolkit, choose your book, click the Assessment Tools tab, and select Assessment Materials to see the Content Vocabulary Self-Assessment.

FIGURE 2.14 Vocabulary Self-Assessment for Weather

Vocabulary	Knowledge Rating			
	Never Heard of It	**Heard It**	**Have Some Ideas**	**Know It Well**
meteorologist				× *weatherman meteorologist*
anemometer			× *measure, meter*	

select the vocabulary of bolded words from the text. As can be seen in Figure 2.14, students rate their knowledge of the vocabulary. Using different symbols, they track their knowledge of the vocabulary over time. This survey provides a good study tool as students summarize in their own words a definition of the vocabulary.

VOCABULARY BRAINSTORMING. Brainstorming is an individual and small-group activity that provides a sense of the content vocabulary students bring to their studies. The directions call for modeling by the teacher first:

1. *Introduce the vocabulary brainstorming activity.* Tell students, "This activity creates a page in your vocabulary notebook that you may share with classmates later in small groups, or with me when we review your vocabulary notebook."

2. *Share an example or model briefly how to brainstorm and write down ideas.*

3. *Choose a topic.* Choose a topic related to the content area that they know a lot about and are motivated to discuss.

4. *Take two minutes to write down as many words about the topic as possible.* "See how many special words you can think of that are related to the topic. Even if you do not know how to spell a particular word, go ahead and write it down as best as you can."

5. *Students work in groups.* Students divide into groups to discuss and combine the ideas they came up with individually. Develop groups in which the English learners can have plenty of support. There are several responsibilities that can be assigned among group members: scribe, timekeeper, discussion facilitator, and reporter. After 15 minutes of brainstorming, the reporters share the groups' ideas.

This activity will give you a sense of how easily the students work in groups and the role that the English learners play in groups. More detail for this activity can be found in *Vocabulary Their Way* (Templeton et al., 2010).

CONCEPT SORTS TO ASSESS SPECIALIZED ACADEMIC VOCABULARY. Sorting can provide a way to see what students know about their content areas and whether they can read the vocabulary that will be presented there. Write the words on a blank sorting template found on page 332 in the Appendix and on the website. Students are instructed to sort the words into particular categories or to take the words and sort them any way they would like. Afterward, students explain why they sorted the way they did. This can be conducted individually and then shared with a partner, or conducted first with partners and then shared in small groups. These sorts can be recorded in students' vocabulary notebooks and they can add additional terms as the unit progresses.

PDToolkit
for Words Their Way™
with English Learners

Go to PDToolkit, choose your book, click the Additional Resources tab, and select Template for Word Sorts in the Templates section.

Fifth grade teacher Mr. Ross conducted such a sort with content area words from a unit on the pre–Revolutionary War era. Students were instructed to sort the words into three columns: words that related to the British, those that related to Americans, and those that did not fit either category. Working as partners, students read the words aloud and discussed the categories. This activity offered excellent support in pronunciation for the English learners and provided Mr. Ross with a sense of what students knew about the topic. At the end of the unit he assessed students' growth by asking them to conduct the sort again. See *Vocabulary Their Way* for more details on this activity (Templeton et al., 2010).

INTERMEDIATE-LEVEL ACADEMIC VOCABULARY SPELLING INVENTORY. There is a vocabulary that is special to textbooks and other academic materials. No matter whether it is science or history, to complete their schools assignments, students need to know the meanings of many rather abstract words that are used repeatedly in students' textbooks—words like *examine, analyze, conduct, resources, appropriate, aspects,* and *required*. In this spelling inventory, students spell 20 academic vocabulary words, rate their knowledge of the words (Do you know the meaning of the word? Yes, No, Maybe), and then list related words (e.g., for *significance,* a student might include *signify, significant,* and *significantly*). The instrument includes the words *source, definition, conception,* and *majority*. A significant relationship between students' spellings of these words and their scores on standardized vocabulary and reading achievement tests has been found; there is also internal consistency for this instrument (Townsend, Bear, & Templeton, 2009).

This inventory can also be used to determine a stage of spelling for students in the later within word pattern stage and beyond. In the power score table found on the website, a spelling stage is determined by the number of words the students spell correctly. The results of this inventory provide some insight as to how students will understand their textbooks as well as the directions to the tests they take.

ASSESSING STUDENTS' KNOWLEDGE OF PREFIXES AND SUFFIXES. For intermediate English speakers and students in the upper levels of spelling, it is useful to examine what they know about English prefixes and suffixes. In this timed assessment, students produce as many words as they can think of that contain the prefix or suffix that is presented and also write the meanings of the affixes. For example, given the suffix *-al* and the word *magical* students are asked to produce words that have this same suffix. Two lists of 10 suffixes and prefixes with examples are presented. The prefixes and suffixes in Part I are more frequent than those in Part II. This assessment gives a clear sense of the depth and breadth of students' knowledge of inflectional morphology. Scoring and interpretation of this assessment are provided with the directions on the website.

MATCHING GREEK AND LATIN ROOTS WITH THEIR MEANINGS. This assessment is designed for students in the syllables and affixes or derivational relational stages of spelling; the directions and answer key are found on the website. It is drawn from the supplement *Words Their Way™: Word Sorts for Derivational Relations Spellers* (Templeton, Johnston, Bear, & Invernizzi, 2009).

In this assessment, students match word roots with their meanings. Afterward, students spell and define the roots. Students who have some sense of a few of these roots and who have mastered the inflectional morphology described in Chapter 7 are ready to examine the roots. Various activities to study Greek and Latin roots are presented in Chapter 8.

Talking with Families

Getting to know students' families is the best way to understand their literacy background. At whole-class meetings with parents, teachers can provide an overview of development and families can view books and word study materials arranged by developmental levels. Students can take their families on a room tour and follow a checklist of areas to visit. This meeting can often lay a foundation for individual teacher–family meetings.

PDToolkit

for Words Their Way™ with English Learners

Go to PDToolkit, choose your book, click the Assessment Tools tab, and select Assessment Materials to see the Intermediate-Level Academic Vocabulary Spelling Inventory.

PDToolkit

for Words Their Way™ with English Learners

Go to PDToolkit, choose your book, click the Assessment Tools tab, and select Assessment Materials to see Assessing Students' Knowledge of Prefixes and Suffixes.

PDToolkit

for Words Their Way™ with English Learners

Go to PDToolkit, choose your book, click the Assessment Tools tab, and select Assessment Materials to see Matching Greek and Latin Roots with Their Meanings.

English language development teachers may help to schedule individual meetings with families of entering children to find out about the child's language and literacy learning, involving translation services as needed. If possible, the person who will translate contacts the parents prior to the meeting to let them know that she or he will be there, that they may bring any information about the child's learning and development, and to ask if the parents have any questions. In the meeting, parents are asked to discuss their child's educational experiences and share any related reports or materials they may have. This is a good time to ask parents a few questions about language and literacy at home. Some guide questions can be found in the Language and Literacy Survey found on the website.

In addition to explaining the curriculum and school materials, students' instructional levels are discussed during parent–teacher meetings. Using the developmental chart from Chapter 1, children are identified along the learning continuum. Reading and word study materials used in whole-class and small-group activities at each developmental level are on display at separate tables around the room. The students' writing samples and current reading materials are highlighted when the teacher meets with the parents, and other work is exhibited so that parents see what their children are learning. Often, the children are in attendance, and while the parents are waiting to meet with the teacher, or after the meeting, the children walk their parents around the room to show them the various materials. The day before parent–teacher conferences, teachers can show students how to take their parents on a tour and provide a checklist of areas and materials that they should point out on their tours.

An important step is to ask parents what their goals are for their children's learning. Teachers should take careful notes and repeat back what they hear the parents say. At the end of the meeting, teachers have information about students' experiences and interests. Teachers can introduce and give parents samples of their children's writing, a book to read, and a word study game to play at home. They can also explain that when children come home with materials they have usually done the activity at school and are now practicing it. Show parents how to be involved in listening, talking about favorite pictures, or playing or timing the word study game.

Many schools are conducting evening programs for family literacy and learning. During these sessions, parents have an opportunity to study English language and literacy materials and they are taught to read to their children, often with texts that are written in the family's primary language (Roberts, 2009). We have observed that adults learning English follow the same developmental trends as younger students (Bear, Truex, & Barone, 1989). Word study has become a part of instruction in many literacy programs for adult English learners, and parents learning English also enjoy the word study activities presented in the instructional chapters that follow.

PDToolkit

for Words Their Way™ with English Learners

Go to PDToolkit, choose your book, click the Assessment Tools tab, and select Assessment Materials to see the Language and Literacy Survey.

3

Organizing for Word Study in Multilingual Classrooms: Principles and Practices

Rachel Benjamin teaches a second grade class that is alive with students from a variety of language backgrounds. Her students receive instruction in English, and she uses **sheltered instructional approaches** to support their learning. Ms. B has found that a traditional spelling program simply involving memorization does not seem to help her English learners understand the patterns and organization of the English writing system. Her students memorize individual words but do not generalize what they learn to their reading and writing. Their reading of early second grade materials is for the most part accurate, but they do not read with adequate comprehension. Their oral reading generally meets the district standard for fluency but is not particularly expressive, even in easy reading materials.

▶ **Sheltered Instructional Approaches**
Ways to present lessons so they are more easily understood by students learning English, such as using pictures and objects, clarifying language, and frequently checking for understanding.

After learning about word study and implementing the Elementary Spelling Inventory (see Chapter 2), Ms. B gained insights into her students' understanding of how words work in English. She began to see that the strategies her students use in their writing reflect their developmental levels, and that students from language backgrounds other than English also use what they know from their home languages to represent words they are learning.

Ms. B discovered that Marco, for example, was in the mid to late letter name–alphabetic stage of development based on the spelling inventory. He spelled *ship* as SHEP, *when* as WEN, and *lump* as LUBP. When it came to words with long vowel patterns, Marco spelled *train* as TRANE, *place* as PLEAS, and *float* as FLEUTE. Marco used but confused some short vowels as well as long vowel patterns that include silent letters. Some of his errors (e.g., the use of *e* to represent the long *a* sound) are typical of Spanish speakers using what they know from the Spanish language to represent the sounds they hear in English words.

As a teacher who has worked with English learners, Ms. B was pleased to find out that word study involves a set of active and collaborative learning opportunities for students. She knows that such activities support students as they learn challenging material in a new language. Based on the developmental spelling assessment, Ms. B assigned Marco to a word study group with four other students at a similar level.

In the teacher-guided portion of one recent lesson, Ms. B introduced a sort that compared *ump* and *amp* word families. She began with a small-group discussion, in which she modeled the sort and took time to talk about some of the vocabulary that was new to her students—in this case the words *champ, clamp, pump,* and *plump.* She asked if anyone knew the meanings for these words, and after the discussion, supplied her own definitions and used the words in sentences. Students then divided into pairs to sort their word cards together. They were encouraged to share what they knew about the words and to question and converse as they sorted. They were also asked to use some of the words in sentences to demonstrate their understanding of word meanings. Their final sort looked similar to the one shown in Figure 3.1.

FIGURE 3.1 Example Word Sort for Marco

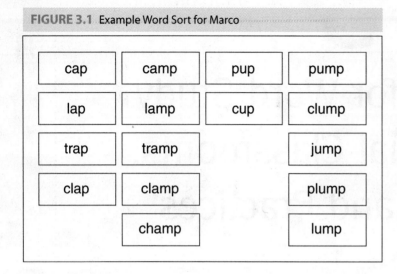

cap	camp	pup	pump
lap	lamp	cup	clump
trap	tramp		jump
clap	clamp		plump
	champ		lump

Just like Ms. B, once you have assessed the developmental levels of your students as described in Chapter 2, you are ready to gather materials, plan instruction, and organize your classroom for developmental word study. In this chapter we describe the important role of word study and how various types of sorts help your students actively and systematically learn about the structures and meanings of words in English. We also present many big ideas for how and why to tailor your lessons to support students who are not yet proficient in English, and recommend ways to adjust your instruction when you see that a lesson is too hard or too easy. The chapter closes with ten guiding principles of word study instruction and a list of other Words Their Way resources to assist you. The website provides you with video examples of word study activities such as concept sorts, word sorts, classroom scheduling, and room arrangements.

The Role of Word Study and Sorting

Word study is one of the essential activities in a balanced literacy program of Read To, Read With, Write With, Word Study, and Talk With (RRWWT) activities. Word study provides an opportunity to examine individual words at each student's level of development so that every learner can understand patterns and correspondences to apply in reading and writing. The act of sorting, or categorizing, words into groups with common attributes is at the heart of word study practice; for this reason the current chapter describes sorting in depth, outlining how to manage your classroom so that students have opportunities to do word sorting at their developmental levels.

Sorting is a powerful learning activity for all students, and especially for students learning a new language. Sorting tasks ask students to categorize items (words, pictures representing spoken words, or concepts) by how they are the same or different. As students sort, they call on higher-level thinking behaviors such as comparing, contrasting, identifying commonalities, and distinguishing core features of the items. Students are supported, when necessary, with pictures that help them learn new words and concepts. As students sort, the teacher receives immediate feedback about what they understand. Compared to workbook pages, word sorts offer students more opportunities for concentrated higher-level thinking, practice, and richer social interaction. In word sorting students have multiple tokens of the example features under study. They work with cards that are easily manipulated; activities are shared and discussed. Despite the fact that students are likely to be at different developmental levels in the same classroom, teachers can use similar sorting activities and routines across a range of word study levels to differentiate and meet all students' needs.

Types of Sorts

In the developmental chapters to follow, you will find specific sorts for different stages. Here we will describe some of the basic sorts used at all stages: sound sorts, pattern sorts, concept or meaning sorts, and then variations on these.

Sound Sorts

Sound sorts require students to compare commonalities and differences in what they hear in a word. For example, a simple sound sort may ask students to sort pictures by their beginning sounds. At a more advanced level, they can focus on the number and stress of syllables (for example, the reduced vowel sound in the middle of *composition* when a suffix is added to *compose*). Sound sorts provide an excellent way to build on the commonalities of sounds between a student's home language and English. Later, sound sorts focus on the specific sounds in English that may not be present in a student's home language, such as a sort for Spanish speakers of /sh/ and /ch/ words. Many examples of sound sorts that build on or highlight differences among various primary languages and English are presented throughout the next four chapters of this book. See the website for a look at a group of second-graders as they sort words that have the short *u* or long *u* sound in the middle of the word.

Pattern Sorts

Students at various developmental levels look to the visual representation of letter groups to understand patterns in the writing system. Pattern sorts are introduced with short and long vowels, and later include the ways syllables combine to form closed and open syllables (*hop/hopping, hope/hoping*). In these sorts, students begin with the sound and then explore the visual patterns in their sorts. English learners may find the visual sorting of words easier than hearing differences in the speech sounds. To ensure that students connect written patterns to the pronunciation of words, students are asked to say each word aloud as it is sorted. It is important to systematically introduce English learners to the common spelling patterns of English; students who speak and read highly alphabetic first languages may need extra support in transitioning to the deep and complex nature of English orthography. See the website for an example word sort that focuses on the patterns of *or, ore, oar,* and *w+or* with a group of fourth grade students.

Meaning/Concept Sorts

Meaning sorts may involve clustering words or pictures based on concepts, or sorting words that have a meaning–spelling relationship. For example, pictures can be sorted into weather-related items as in Figure 3.2 using any language. Concept sorts using pictures or objects are wonderful formats for English learners to gain vocabulary, especially when students are paired with English speakers who can supply English labels. See the website for a glimpse into a weather concept sort with young English learners. Spelling–meaning sorts allow students at the advanced levels from a variety of primary languages to look for common roots between their home language and English (see Chapter 8 for more examples).

Variations of Sorts

The following are among the many ways to conduct sound, pattern, and concept sorts.

- Teacher-directed closed sorts
- Student-centered open sorts
- Guess my category sorts
- Partner sorts
- Blind sorts
- Writing sorts
- Word hunts
- Picture hunts

FIGURE 3.2 Concept Sort for Hot and Cold Weather Items

for Words Their Way™ with English Learners

Go to PDToolkit, choose your book, click the Videos tab, and watch the videos titled "A Week of Sorting with Second Graders in the Early Within Word Pattern Stage" and "Activities with Fourth Graders in the Within Word Pattern Stage."

PDToolkit

for Words Their Way™ with English Learners

Go to PDToolkit, choose your book, click the Sorts & Games tab, and search for "Sort 9: Weather and Related Objects Picture Sort."

- Brainstorming
- Repeated individual sorts
- Speed sorts
- Draw and label/cut and paste sorts

What special considerations will be important as you plan variations of sorts for English learners? A few suggestions follow.

TEACHER-DIRECTED WORD SORTS. Teacher sorts are essential in introductory word study lessons for students with limited English skills. Teachers set up categories with key words, explicitly stating why each picture or word belongs in each category. English learners rely on the guidance and visual model that a demonstration provides. In seeing you sort, they learn more about the key words and their properties. It is critical that English learners know the names and pronunciations of the key words or pictures used in the sorts. This is the place for teachers to go over unfamiliar word meanings. As shown in Figure 3.3, after modeling, the teacher directs and guides students in their own sorting.

FIGURE 3.3 Teacher-Directed Closed Sort

STUDENT-CENTERED OPEN SORTS. In a student-centered or open-ended sort, students are given pictures or words and asked to create their own categories. Teachers can use these sorts to assess what students are learning about how words work or about students' conceptual understandings related to thematic vocabulary. English learners can show what they know. They control the pace of the demonstration, and they have props in the words or pictures as they explain why they sorted as they did. Even if English learners do not yet have the specific English vocabulary to clearly articulate their thinking, you must find ways for students to explain their sorts—perhaps through peer translators or by writing down the titles of their categories in their home language.

FIGURE 3.4 Guess My Category Sort

GUESS MY CATEGORY SORTS. The teacher can also demonstrate a sort without labeling the categories. Because pictures are a good bridge to conceptual understanding for English learners, it is important to start with picture sorts like Figure 3.4 and check with your students frequently to see that they are following the guessing game. Can they identify which category a new picture should go into? Can they express verbally, draw, or act out what makes each category unique? Checking for understanding with English learners will guide your pacing, also allowing you to know when Guess My Category word sorts may be appropriate.

PARTNER SORTS. Partner sorts are particularly important for students learning English because of the language support they can provide. One option is to pair students with a partner who provides the English label or who can explain the meanings of words. Another option is to pair students with the same home language so they can easily communicate their thinking to each other. Partners can work together to sort pictures or words for additional practice.

BLIND SORTS. After students have seen words sorted visually, an important step is to name the words without showing them and also indicate the appropriate category. Students can work in pairs to do this after they have sorted the words several times on their own. After setting up headers, one reads a word to the other who points to the correct category. The reader then lays the word down and lets the partner check the answer. Corrective feedback is immediate and a word in the wrong category can either be moved to the correct category or the reader can put it back into the pile to call again. Partners continue like this until all the words have been sorted and then they trade places.

WRITING SORTS. Students should record a sort by writing the words into categories after they have sorted as part of a standard weekly routine. In addition, a blind writing sort with a partner or parent for homework is valuable. After setting up the headers on paper, one partner calls out the words while the other writes them into categories. In class, save blind writing sorts for features that are well known to English learners, and use these writing sorts as opportunities for informal assessment in a low-pressure environment. Always show the word card immediately after writing so that students can self-correct.

WORD HUNTS AND PICTURE HUNTS. Variations in which students find the words are excellent ways for students to look through books, magazines, and environmental print for the features they are studying. It is important to be clear whether they are searching for a visual pattern or a sound. For example, students in a second grade classroom recently went on a word hunt for words with the long *e* sound after already sorting different *ee/ea/e-e* patterns. In addition to words like *tree*, *meat*, and *Pete*, José's list included *bread* and *dead*. José was searching for the visual pattern but did not have enough familiarity with the spoken versions of the words to differentiate the vowel sounds in these words. It is important for English learners like José to get feedback about the sounds of the vowels in these words and have opportunities to practice reading and saying them. *Bread* and *dead* then become good **oddballs** to discuss.

▶ **Oddballs**
Words with similar patterns that do not fit the targeted feature in a sort.

Assigning partners and asking students to say words aloud are ways to support English learners in word hunts. Children who are studying initial consonant sounds can look for pictures in magazines or alphabet books that begin with the targeted sounds. The printed materials that are available should have many words that are part of students' vocabularies.

BRAINSTORMING. Brainstorming involves thinking up as many examples as possible for a targeted feature. Teachers might ask students to think of words that begin with an initial sound (*p* for example) or with a prefix (*re-* for example) This may be one of the most difficult tasks for English learners to do because it requires a broad familiarity with oral and written words. Be willing to accept words in a student's first language that fit the feature. For example, *pan* (Spanish for bread) is a word that starts with *p*, while *repasar* is a Spanish word with a prefix having the same spelling and meaning as the English prefix. Create small groups with students at different levels of English proficiency, including, if possible, students who can translate for the most limited speakers. Write down brainstormed lists on charts such as Figure 3.5 that students can refer to in the future. Encourage students to copy brainstormed lists into a personal word study notebook for future reference.

REPEATED INDIVIDUAL SORTS AND SPEED SORTS. Provide many opportunities for students to repeat sorts until they can do them fluidly. This builds confidence and an expectation of mastery for student and teacher alike. Students in the within word pattern stage and beyond often find that timing the sorts and trying to improve their time is a challenge they enjoy. Students can work with partners; one sorts while the other uses a stopwatch or clock with a second hand to time the sort. Speed sorts can also be done in the whole class. Everyone gets out the sort they are working on and the teacher uses the classroom clock or a timer projected from a computer (find one at www.online-stopwatch .com). As students finish their sorts they look up to see the time and then record it. Soon after, or later in the week, they can repeat the sort to try to improve, competing always against themselves. These activities

FIGURE 3.5 Brainstorming a List of Words

Words for the at family

cat	pat
mat	Pat
rat	flat
sat	hat

FIGURE 3.6 Cut and Paste Sort with Labels

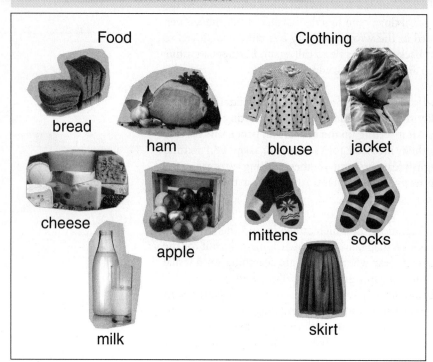

Food

bread

ham

cheese

apple

milk

Clothing

blouse

jacket

mittens

socks

skirt

help students gain fluency and automaticity in their word work. It is *as* critical for English learners as for monolingual students to be expected to achieve at this level of individual performance.

DRAW AND LABEL/CUT AND PASTE ACTIVITIES. Pictures are great ways to help English learners develop vocabulary as they learn a spelling or phonics concept. Students might be asked to draw pictures that start with a particular sound and then label them as best they can. Or they might paste down the pictures they have sorted several times and label them. When students are working with words they might be asked to illustrate words from their sort to demonstrate their meanings. Figure 3.6 shows how a student has looked for additional pictures of food and clothing after doing a concept sort. Pictures help anchor new vocabulary words, and students can even create their own picture dictionaries for reference and review over time.

Supporting Vocabulary Development during Sorting

At the early stages of language learning, picture sorts are most appropriate for English learners. Concept sorts with pictures or objects are the least demanding in terms of English language skills and can be good vocabulary learning activities. Picture sorts for sounds require students to know the names of enough of the pictures to demonstrate the sound relationship being sorted. Take care to support students' vocabulary knowledge by using common pictures and by teaching vocabulary within the lesson. When moving on to word sorts, ensure that students are making the oral–written language connection by saying words out loud. This should happen throughout the sort and will be reinforced when students "read" their sort out loud to a teacher after they have finished. When they do not know the meaning of a word, students refer to picture dictionaries or ask for help. Students will find it helpful to know that it is expected and valued for them to ask about words they do not understand or are having trouble pronouncing.

Concept sorts provide a visual, meaning-based support to students and offer a bridge to vocabulary learning. A student involved in a concept sort with pictures, such as sorting different kinds of animals, will be successful without knowing the names of words in English. Recently in Mrs. Johnson's first grade classroom, English learner Awa sorted her animal picture cards into groups. She had a group of sea animals, a group of furry animals, and a group of birds. She put animals that did not fit into these groups into a "leftover" category. Awa was able to explain the categories to her teacher using her limited English; however, she could not name all of the animal pictures. Mrs. Johnson encouraged her to say the names of the animals she knew, if not in English, then using her home language. Before completing the conversation, Mrs. Johnson practiced saying the names of three animals that Awa didn't know from her picture cards—shark, bear, and rabbit. She did not want to overload her with too many words at once, but wanted to use the teachable moment to reinforce Awa's developing vocabulary with some key words. This example shows how concept sorts with pictures can provide a useful bridge to help English learners become familiar with sorting procedures, use thinking skills, and learn new words in English in the process. For a video sample, see the picture concept sort used by Ms. Polanski with young English learners on the website.

for Words Their Way™ with English Learners

Go to PDToolkit, choose your book, click the Videos tab, and watch the video titled "Vocabulary Development and Concept Sorting with Kindergarteners in the Emergent Stage."

Picture sorts provide a bridge for students to learn new vocabulary.

Sound sorts using pictures provide similar visual support for English learners. Because a student needs to know the name of the picture in order to sort it correctly, however, the task is more language driven. The names of the pictures should always be discussed before the sound sort begins. For example, a kindergarten teacher introduced a picture sort to classify beginning sounds *b*, *m*, *r*, and *s*. The teacher began by holding up each picture and naming it, then asking the students to name it. The sort was modeled and the names of the pictures were again emphasized. After sorting, all the words in each category were named again as the children joined in. The teacher knew that English learners might need more support. When Alfredo sorted on his own and got to a picture of a seal, he didn't know where it went, because he didn't know its name. His options were to set the picture card aside for the time being, ask a schoolmate or the teacher what the name is, or sort it based on his home language. The Spanish name for seal, *foca*, does not help Alfredo sort the picture into the given letter–sound categories, so in this case he sets the picture aside. If too many pictures are unknown to Alfredo, he will not get the practice he needs sorting sounds, and the task may become frustrating for him. In that case, it would be more effective for him to wait on the sort until more time has been spent on a structured vocabulary lesson.

Sound–picture sorts can also be conducted in the student's home language as a bridge to English literacy. Try adding pictures that have the same beginning sounds as in a student's home language, allowing students to sort these pictures in the given categories. For example, if Alfredo had pictures of a *sandía* (watermelon), *mesa* (table), or *ballena* (whale), he could add those to the beginning sound picture sort he was doing in English for *b*, *m*, *r*, and *s* without the same vocabulary challenge. As Alfredo's vocabulary grows in English, he will rely less and less on the labels for words in Spanish to complete his sorts.

Use the list of picture words in other languages found in the Appendix (page 309) to create sound sorts that you would like the student to eventually do in English. Start simply with several words in a student's home language (for example, in Spanish, *s*: sol, seis, suéter, silla; *m*: mano, muñeca, mapa, mitón). After modeling the sort, introduce some English words that would fit in, such as *soap*, *saw*, and *moon*. Certain Spanish words can even be translated as cognates, related in spelling and sound across languages, such as *suéter/sweater*, *seis/six*, *mapa/map*, and *mitón/mitten*. This may help students remember the English words they are learning.

Word sorts reinforce visual spelling patterns but do not necessarily teach vocabulary on their own. Go over all the words before sorting, pronouncing them and talking about what they mean. It is important that English learners say the words aloud as they sort; this ensures that students connect spelling patterns to what they hear in spoken words. In addition you might supply pictures along with words, starting with common words students might already know. In the Appendix are many pictures that can be used for not only beginning sounds but vowel sounds as well. Students might sort the pictures first as they do in the website example, where long and short *u* are contrasted and then words are matched to the pictures. Another suggestion is to have the students draw simple illustrations to the side of a word or on the back of a word card as a reminder. See an example in Figure 3.7.

Three steps to consider for instructing English learners when sorting on their own:
1. Set unknown pictures and words aside, and return to them with assistance.
2. Ask a classmate.
3. Use words from the student's home language to sort.

for Words Their Way™ with English Learners

Go to PDToolkit, choose your book, click the Videos tab, and watch the video titled "A Week of Sorting with Second Graders in the Early Within Word Pattern Stage."

FIGURE 3.7 Students Illustrate Words to Develop Vocabulary

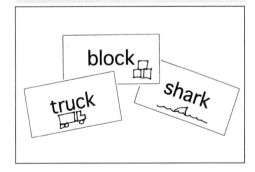

Supporting Vocabulary Learning during Sorting

1. Start with picture sorts for concepts and sounds.
2. Select pictures of common everyday objects or actions for simple sorts in English or use pictures to sort in primary languages by sounds.
3. When doing word sorts provide pictures that match. Sort the pictures first and then match words.
4. Reduce the number of words in sorts for English learners.

5. Name pictures and words before, during, and after sorting. Introduce the words, say them aloud as they are sorted, and name them as the sort is checked. Repeat this as needed.
6. Have students illustrate words with simple drawings to remind them of meanings.
7. Pair English learners with English-speaking partners in activities.
8. Encourage English learners to always ask questions about words whose meanings or pronunciations they do not know.
9. Check for understanding of sorting words as you meet with students.

Always check for understanding of the meanings of words being used in sorts. Choose a few important words that students do not know to define and use in context during the lesson.

To be effective, word sorts require students to know how to read, say, and attach meaning to words being sorted. When students are learning vocabulary at the same time as they are learning spelling patterns in sorts, it is crucial to provide them with built-in vocabulary instruction for the words they are working with, as well as access to resource people who will respond to their pronunciation and meaning questions. This allows word study to become a process of integrated learning for spelling, phonics, and vocabulary.

Word Study Instruction in Multilingual Classroom Settings

All students in your classroom will profit from participating in word study. Whether you teach in a classroom in which instruction is conducted in English or another type of program, you will want to arrange a management system for your literacy instruction that allows you to meet with small groups of students for word study on a regular basis. Consider students' developmental levels in forming these groups, but also take into account whether or not students are English learners who need additional language support. At certain times it will be important to have heterogeneous language groups so that you have a range of oral proficiency in your small groups; at other times you will want to group students who need the most help in oral English skills together to give them focused support.

Students benefit from learning the procedures you expect them to use in word study activities. These include how students get access to materials; when they work in a teacher-guided group and when they work independently; how they collaborate with peers; and common procedures for sorts, games, and other literacy activities. For a glimpse into a third grade multilingual classroom, view Ms. Nguyen's class on the website. You will see how the room is organized to clearly communicate procedures and expectations to the students. The processes used in word study can be described and practiced until the routines are well established. In the next section, a variety of support strategies are outlined that apply to many multilingual classroom situations.

for Words Their Way™ with English Learners

Go to PDToolkit, choose your book, click the Videos tab, and watch the video titled "A Look into a Third-Grade Classroom Literacy Environment."

Strategies to Support English Learners

Many challenges face students learning to read and write in a new language. Language learners need effective teachers and well-thought-out instruction in literacy (Helman, 2009). Research on diverse learners has found that a core set of teaching practices helps ensure successful learning for all students, including language-minority students (Center for Research on Education, Diversity & Excellence, 2004; Echevarría, Vogt, & Short, 2008). Other studies describe the benefits of bilingual instruction and the use of specific instructional strategies for English learners (e.g., August & Shanahan, 2006; Bialystok, Luk, & Kwan, 2005; Cummins, Chow, & Schecter, 2006; deJong & Harper, 2005; Genesee, Lindholm-Leary, Saunders, & Christian, 2005; Gersten & Jiménez, 1998; Slavin & Cheung, 2005).

When the research is taken as a whole, findings can be organized around several general principles about the most effective practices for English language learners:

- Instruction that is explicit and systematic
- Formats that allow students to interact with others in their learning community
- Guidance to help students make connections to what they already know
- Arrangements in which students actively construct knowledge

Figure 3.8 provides a graphic organizer outlining these four overarching themes, as well as examples of how these come to life in particular instructional practices. Throughout the discussion of these support strategies you will also find specific examples of how these practices relate to word study instruction.

EXPLICIT AND SYSTEMATIC INSTRUCTION. Organization and clarity make it easier for English learners to understand the material and teachers' expectations for reading and writing tasks. Hearing something explained once orally will not be sufficient for learners of a new language to "get it." Think back to a time when you may have been immersed in a language that you did not understand well, perhaps on a trip or in a language class. What did you do to help yourself get a handle on the information coming your way? Did you look for picture clues? Ask someone to tell you again slowly? Look for a map or other graphic to orient you? English learners in your classrooms grasp for the same kinds of support. Table 3.1 summarizes a variety of ways that teachers can provide clear and explicit instruction.

- *Modeling* involves performing a sample activity while students watch. Whatever you are making or doing in class can be physically demonstrated to provide multisensory input for students.

FIGURE 3.8 Strategies to Support English Learners

Explicit and Systematic Instruction

- Modeling
- Visuals and contextualization
- Guided practice
- Metacognition/think-alouds
- Instructional-level teaching
- Focus on language and vocabulary
- Simple to complex
- Clustering

Engaging in a Learning Community

- Low-anxiety environment
- Student-to-student interactions
- High expectations
- Student-to-teacher connections

Strategies to Support English Learners

Highlighting Connections

- Whole to part to whole
- Oral and written language
- Schema building
- Graphic organizers
- Personal experiences
- Background knowledge

Active Construction of Knowledge

- Hands-on activities
- Purposeful activities
- Time to talk
- Modified questioning strategies
- Multiple intelligences
- Music and rhythm
- Total physical response

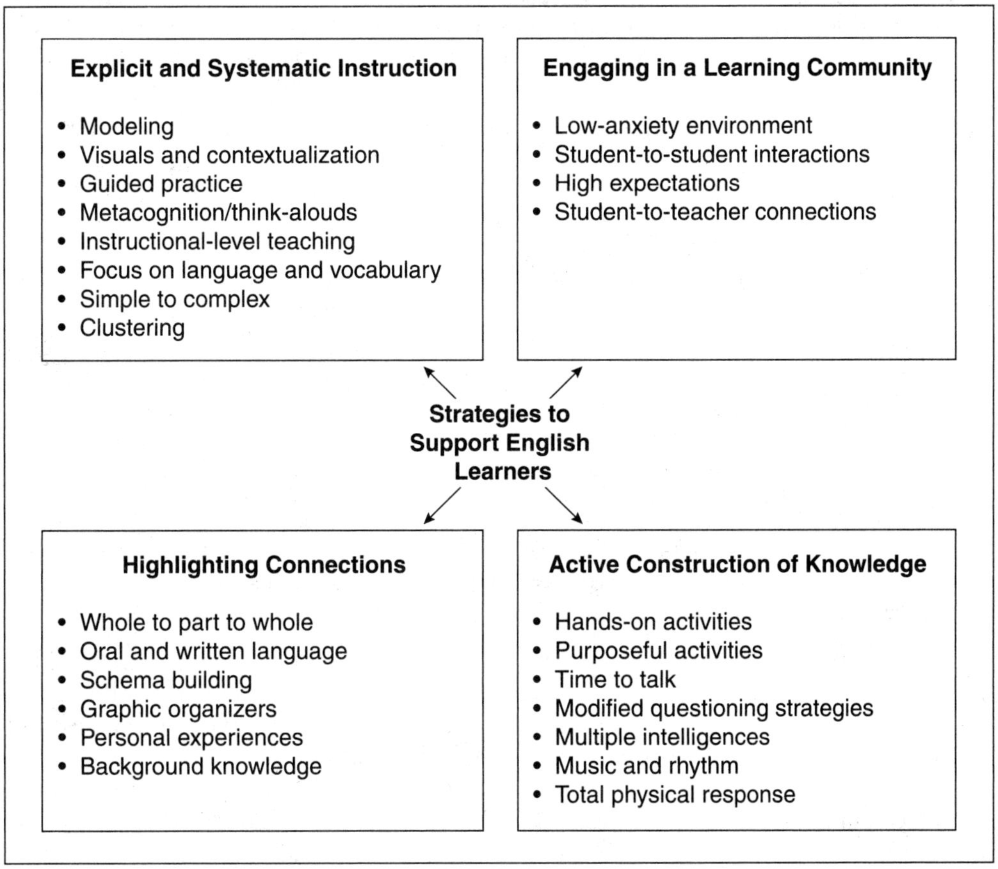

TABLE 3.1   **Explicit and Systematic Instruction in Word Study**

STRATEGY	EXAMPLE WORD STUDY APPLICATIONS
Modeling	Teachers model writing in a way similar to how students would do it so that students feel comfortable writing in the best way they know how. New sorts may be modeled to highlight a pattern that will be prominent in upcoming studies.
Visuals and contextualization	Real objects are used often in a concept sort. A common stimulus or experience is used as the basis for a group experience story.
Guided practice	Many word study sorts and lessons, especially those that involve a new concept or pattern, involve teacher guidance and informal assessment. Students are asked to explain their thinking for decisions made in the sorting process and this provides an opportunity for teachers to talk through misconceptions with them.
Metacognition	"Think out loud" with students about writing conventions and spelling as chart-sized messages are created in a group setting.
Instructional-level teaching	A developmental spelling inventory is used to assess students' word knowledge and to place them in word study activities at the appropriate developmental level.
Focus on language and vocabulary	Vocabulary development is explicitly integrated into word study activities for English learners: Words are reviewed and discussed before sorting. In addition, students are encouraged to identify and set aside unknown words in the sorts they are doing.
Simple to complex	Developmental word study builds from simple to complex relationships in the writing system. Sorts are simplified early on to be comprehensible to students.
Clustering	Word study activities involve consistent procedures and regular activities that can be clustered and taught to students for their ongoing use—for example, demonstrate, sort and check, reflect, and extend. Students become familiar with the regular routines and do not see individual word study activities as isolated experiences.

- *Visuals and contextualization* help to clarify instruction with real-life objects, "being there" experiences, expressive body language, role playing, puppets, visual depictions, and so on. Contextualizing lessons gives students a better chance to connect an activity to "real life."

- *Guided practice* allows the teacher to lead students in applying a skill or concept that has already been introduced. The teacher oversees, gives feedback, and reinforces the students in their application of the new skill.

- *Metacognition* occurs when people become conscious of and articulate in-the-head processes they are using during a literacy event. It can be seen as "thinking out loud."

- *Instructional-level teaching* matches classroom tasks and materials to the background knowledge and developmental levels of individual students. Instruction should not be above students' heads nor too easy but rather "just right"—challenging but doable.

- *Focus on language and vocabulary* sharpens a teacher's emphasis on making instructional language more comprehensible to English learners, who are often overwhelmed by the fast and complex stream of words coming their way. Teachers can help alleviate this overload with several simple but important practices: Monitor the speed of their talk, clearly articulate words, face the listener, emphasize key words, and avoid idioms such as "chewed her out," which can be very confusing to English learners. Teachers can also identify and teach key words that students may not understand to help them meet the lesson objectives.

- *Simple to complex support* breaks down tasks into sequential steps or uses scaled-down examples first. The goal is to help students move from an easy format to progressively more complex versions.

- *Clustering* provides a strategy for putting together pieces of information that go together. It may also involve chunking activities into sections so that students can work through them piece by piece.

ENGAGING IN A LEARNING COMMUNITY. It is not enough for students to receive clear and understandable instruction. Students also need to use what they are learning with others, and feel confident that they are valued members of their learning community. If students get the feeling they are not expected to learn or that the new knowledge is not useful to share with others, they are less likely to be successful. The following support strategies (Table 3.2) build on the foundation that students are social beings who strive to have successful personal interactions:

- *Low-anxiety environments* enable interactions and learning activities that are not stressful but rather allow students to make mistakes or discuss concepts they are not sure about. This leads to an atmosphere where deeper thinking flourishes and students do not need to have the "right answer" in order to speak up.

- *Student-to-student interactions* help build a positive learning community as students use oral and written language with peers in partnerships, cooperative learning teams, and other small-group activities.

- *Holding high expectations for students* means that teachers believe in their students' learning potential. It is communicated by what teachers say and do. Teachers who say, "You don't have . . . ," "You don't get . . . ," or "You can't . . ." may communicate a lack of faith in students' abilities and possibilities. On the other hand, teachers who view students on a developmental continuum assess students to find out their current knowledge base and then plan appropriate next steps for instruction.

- *Student-to-teacher connections* form bonds in the learning community. Teachers who build strong personal connections with students, and work persistently with them, help ensure their success.

TABLE 3.2 **Engaging in Word Study in a Learning Community**

STRATEGY	EXAMPLE WORD STUDY APPLICATIONS
Low-anxiety environment	Games, songs, and chants are integrated into word study activities. Students are encouraged to share ideas and say when they do not know a word.
Student-to-student interactions	Word study provides numerous opportunities for student interactions such as when sorting with a partner, playing games in a small group, going on a word hunt together, and brainstorming word derivations with others.
High expectations	Effective word study teachers provide rigorous instruction and hold high expectations for student accomplishment at their developmental levels. All students, including English learners, are expected to become accurate, fluent, and automatic in their sorting.
Student-to-teacher connections	Opportunities for student-to-teacher interactions in word study include individualized writing conferences, using student dictations for rereading, and structuring extra time for dialogue to communicate students' understanding of spelling patterns.

HIGHLIGHTING CONNECTIONS. When students see how new knowledge fits into their current understanding of the world, learning takes root most effectively. English learners bring their home language and previous experiences with literacy activities, as well as their other personal, academic, and cultural experiences, with them to the classroom. Table 3.3 outlines ways of connecting instruction with students' knowledge base to show students the "big picture" of how academic information interrelates.

- *Whole to part to whole* involves instruction that gives students the big picture first, such as using a whole piece of text (book, poem, song, and so on). Next, a component or skill is pulled out for a minilesson or practice. Afterward, the skill is applied in context again.

- *Oral and written language connections* encourage students to highlight relationships. Use any occasion you can to help students see the correspondence between what they say or hear and how it is written in English. The alphabetic nature of written language will become more apparent to students the more they engage with it.

- *Schema building* helps students see where new information fits into their "mental file cabinet." Teachers encourage schemata when they point out relationships between things instead of studying isolated bits that do not seem connected.

- *Graphic organizers* provide visual tools that help organize our thinking with symbols or designs. They support students in seeing conceptual relations, and their use by students in the classroom also lets teachers know whether they understand the big picture.

- *Connections to personal experience* relate concepts, ideas, or skills to events in students' lives or in the classroom community. This emotional link aids learning.

- *Connecting to background knowledge* assists students in finding something they know that relates to the new information being learned. This may involve building on academic

---

TABLE 3.3 **Highlighting Connections in Word Study**

STRATEGY	EXAMPLE WORD STUDY APPLICATIONS
Whole to part to whole	Start by reading a whole piece of connected text that contains examples of a spelling feature. Next pull out the words that fit the focus for word study. Finally, look for the feature in other contexts through word hunts.
Oral and written language	Connect oral and written language in word study activities through blind sorts, story dictations, and vocabulary notebooks.
Schema building	Word study helps students build schemata by seeing how word families, patterns, and morphemes fall into categories.
Graphic organizers	Organizing like words in columns in word study notebooks and sorts, classifying words into Venn diagrams, and analyzing words by semantic features are some examples of how graphic organizers are used in word study.
Personal experiences	Investigate words of personal interest and meaning, use the names of children in class for letter and sound learning, and create personal readers of dictated stories to help students build on their personal experience in word study activities.
Background knowledge	Word study builds on background knowledge when words and pictures for sorts are familiar to students and are connected to vocabulary in their home language. Look for cognates between students' home languages and English, and compare word roots and affixes to those in students' home languages.

knowledge in a student's home language or making a connection to information that has been previously learned.

ACTIVE CONSTRUCTION OF KNOWLEDGE. English learners who are engaged in and contributing to the learning process will remember more, be able to apply their learning, and show teachers if and where confusions exist. The following support strategies, summarized in Table 3.4, help teachers provide active learning opportunities for their students:

- *Hands-on activities* involve manipulating learning materials, creating objects, going on field trips, and doing experiments or simulations. Hands-on activities provide nonverbal support for students to learn and demonstrate their growing understanding.

- *Purposeful activities* accomplish tasks or solve problems in students' immediate lives.

- *Time for students to talk* allows participation that goes beyond simply listening to information or reading about it. It helps students actively engage with a topic and share their understandings with others, linking the content to individual and group personal experiences.

- *Modified questioning strategies* use a range of questions in the classroom to allow all students, even those with very limited English language skills, to respond. Questions can be adapted so that student responses involve pointing or gesture; yes or no indicators; one-to two-word answers; simple sentences; or open-ended, hypothetical replies.

- *Involving multiple intelligences* means helping students learn and practice concepts through a variety of activities such as writing, sharing, singing, listening, counting, graphing, moving, doing, speaking, drawing, constructing, and so on.

TABLE 3.4   **Active Construction of Knowledge in Word Study**

STRATEGY	EXAMPLE WORD STUDY APPLICATIONS
Hands-on activities	Sorts, games of all types, word hunts, and language experience activities make word study full of hands-on activities.
Purposeful activities	Write letters, cards, and lists for families, friends, and the community. Connect word study to lots of reading and writing practice.
Time to talk	Sorts and games may be played with partners and groups. Students discuss words and reflect on decisions they made while sorting.
Modified questioning strategies	Begin with concept sorts that do not require the names of specific words. Move to simple sorts that compare "words that do" with "words that don't." Allow students to explain their word study decisions in their home language.
Multiple intelligences	Word study activities encourage students to learn and practice concepts through writing, sharing, singing, listening, counting, graphing, moving, doing, speaking, drawing, and displaying.
Using music and rhythm	Songs, chants, rhymes, and rhythms are integrated throughout word study to help students understand and remember patterns.
Total physical response	Word study may be expanded to involve physical actions such as people sorting, acting out spelling patterns with movements, or demonstrating word relationships through physical lineups.

- *Music and rhythm* helps students remember a skill or concept by putting a tune or rhythmic pattern to it. Students actively participate by chanting, singing, clapping, or keeping the beat.

- *Total physical response* augments student learning by moving, touching, pointing, and role playing. It allows the body to reinforce new learning.

Organization of Word Study Instruction

How does word study work in a multilingual classroom? Which materials and resources are needed? What might daily and weekly schedules look like? This section addresses how to adjust instruction for English learners.

Preparing Your Word Sorts

In classrooms with students of diverse language backgrounds and from different literacy experiences, the range of developmental levels may be quite wide. For instance, fourth grade teachers may have readers from emergent to advanced levels. In addition, teachers often have students who speak little to no English along with others those who are extremely knowledgeable speakers, as well as some who fit in between. Each of these groups will require a modification of instructional materials. What can you do to be prepared for these multiple needs? Here are some tips:

1. Use word study materials that are already available. This book and accompanying website have many reproducible sorts, games, and activities for you to copy and put right to use, and you can find valuable reproducible resources in other Words Their Way products listed at the end of this chapter. In addition, your school's adopted reading or spelling program may include sorts that fit into this developmental model.

2. Gather nonconsumable materials for concept sorts that can be used for multiple purposes. Many educational publishers have picture dictionaries, picture card sets, and small collections of manipulatives suitable for concept sorts. These materials are very versatile and quite helpful for extending English learners' vocabularies. Online searches such as Google Images are a wonderful source for pictures you can add to sorts or download for other purposes. Students can also go on "hunts" in magazines and newspapers to find pictures for sorts. Use these language-building resources over and over again for many sorts and games in your classroom. Also see the list of multilingual and language development materials in the reference section (p. 343) of this book.

3. Enlist parents, aides, older students, and other volunteers to put together the games and sorts from this book and website. Games and sorts can be colored, cut out, glued onto file folders, and laminated for long-term use.

4. Have older students make their own sorts as part of word study. If students are mature enough to quickly write the sorting words, they can create the cards just prior to sorting. This activity may even come to take the place of more traditional (and isolated) handwriting lessons.

5. Integrate the word study notebook as an ongoing reference book for students, possibly including a **sound board** for the vowels and consonants in English or with space for notes about how the letters compare to the sounds in the students' home languages. Word study notebooks can contain personal dictionaries of words students are learning in English, with translations of key vocabulary words. They are also a place for students to record written versions of sorts they have completed and add words they have found

▶ **Sound Board**

A page with pictures and letters illustrating the sounds in English.

on word hunts. A well-developed word study notebook is a valuable resource for English learners to come back to over and over as they are cementing their familiarity with English words.

6. Maintain consistent procedures for where and how word study materials are stored, and teach students to oversee their care. Figure 3.9 shows sorts organized in baskets. File folder games are easily stored in a plastic tub that can be labeled or color coded so that students return materials to their proper place. A rotating leadership job in the class might be to straighten up word study materials at the end of the day or week. The more that students can take over these responsibilities, the easier the word study system will be to manage.

FIGURE 3.9 Sorts Organized in Baskets for the Week's Word Study

Courtesy Amy Frederick.

7. Begin collecting materials from the primary languages of students in your class. Books, flash cards, newspapers, and other print-related materials can be found in a variety of languages—see the list of multilingual and language development materials in the reference section (p. 343) for some examples of where to find them. Having these materials available allows teachers and students to compare and contrast languages. If possible, create sorts for other languages using the picture cards in this book (pp. 262–297). Store these sorts in color-coded tubs to identify different languages so that students gain experience with word study activities in a familiar language.

The Big Picture: Scheduling Word Study

Your schedule for word study activities will depend on many factors, including your grade level, the overarching structure of the school day, and how supplemental services for students are delivered. Most teachers, however, are able to set aside a literacy block of at least 90 minutes in the elementary grades to focus on literacy-related activities. Your daily morning schedule might look something like this:

- Welcome/school business: 5–10 minutes
- Transitional independent activity: 10 minutes
- Preview of literacy block activities: 5–10 minutes
- Literacy block (teacher-guided and independent small-group activities): 90 minutes.

Set aside time for listening to and reading a variety of literature and expository texts throughout the day according to your specific schedule.

Word study activities fit well into the literacy block either as a portion of the time or integrated into your group rotations. Some teachers divide their class into three or four developmental groups and find time to work with each small group every day. Other teachers construct a rotation in which they see each small group every other day, and an assistant or specialist teacher works with the group on alternating days. Having a predictable routine helps ensure that the 10 to 15 minutes of word study each student does every day will achieve productive results. In the basic progression of a word study lesson over the course of a week, you and your students will move from a teacher-directed group sort to independent

FIGURE 3.10 Teacher Checklist of Word Study Activities

Group _____

Sort title	Read rhyme	Introduce sort	Practice sort	Play game	Sort with partner	Paste sort	Apply skill (write)	Assess	Observation notes
at, ad, an	10–16	10–16	10–17	10–18	10–19	10–19	10–20	10–20	*Replay game—hard!*

Courtesy Linda Woessner.

**PDToolkit
for Words Their Way™
with English Learners**

Go to PDToolkit, choose your book, click the Videos tab, and watch the video titled "Activities with Fourth Graders in the Within Word Pattern Stage."

follow-up activities and assessment, usually spending a week with each sort before moving on to a new one using the following general pattern:

- Demonstrate the sort
- Sort and check
- Reflect
- Extend

Linda Woessner, whose teaching is featured on the website, keeps track of where she is by using a teacher checklist similar to Figure 3.10. Claire Roberts, who is also featured on the website, describes the weekly routine that her students follow in their 15 minutes of daily word study: Monday—demonstration and guided sort, Tuesday—buddy sorts/speed sorts, Wednesday and Thursday—word hunts and games, Friday—assessment. Students learn the routine and with just a brief reminder move to the word study activity for the day. A common weekly word study schedule is outlined in Table 3.5.

Word Study Lesson Plan Format

Four steps comprise the word study lesson plan format: demonstrate, sort and check, reflect, and extend:

DEMONSTRATE. The teacher demonstrates the sort to the students and enlists their participation (Figure 3.3). Name the pictures and go over the words to be sure students know the pronunciations and meanings of the words. Ask students what they notice about the words and get their ideas about what the categories will be. Introduce the key picture or word for each category and place it as the header for each column. Model several words and think aloud about what you do: say the word, compare it to the first key picture or word, and then explain why it fits the category. Sort at least one word for each column before enlisting students' help.

SORT AND CHECK. Complete the sort with the students' help, saying each word and deciding where it belongs. After the sort, read through each column of the sort to check for accuracy and to make changes. Check for the meanings of words as needed.

REFLECT. To reflect, students form generalizations about the feature of study and reach some conclusions about the sounds, patterns, or other features of the words. Teachers might ask, "Why did we sort the pictures [words] this way?" Avoid telling students what they should learn and instead use open-ended questions such as "How are the words alike in this column?"

or "What can we learn from this sort?" Talk about oddballs and why they do not fit the categories. Check for word meanings again as needed. At this point the teacher may repeat the group sort or students may get their own set of pictures or words to sort under the teacher's supervision or at their desks. As students sort they should repeat the sort, check, and reflect steps described here.

EXTEND. Introduce students to basic routines, such as how to cut apart their words or pictures and store them in a baggie or envelope. To help keep their sorts separated, students scribble with crayons (students should use a different color from others in their group or at their table) on the backside of the sorting page before cutting. Students then try out the sort on their own as time allows. Finally, the sort is bagged, ready for the next day. Some teachers have multiple copies of sorts ready for students when they gather in small groups. After sorting, instruct students to set aside the headers and then shuffle or mix up the word cards so that next time the words are not already sorted.

For repeated practice, students sort again at their seats or in centers over several days. They also record the sort in their word study notebooks; work with partners in a blind sort, blind writing sort, or timed sort; and hunt for related words to record on charts—all variations of sorts described earlier in this chapter. In addition they might play word study games from the activity section for each stage. Many of these extensions can be completed independently in the classroom in centers, for seatwork, and at home.

ASSESS. When students have completed their study of the week's sort, use informal assessments to gauge their learning. Examples include dictating some of the words for students to write on whiteboards, conducting a developmentally appropriate spelling test, or observing the fluency and accuracy of the student's sorting.

If you have a mixed group with some students who need vocabulary support and others who do not, arrange 5 to 10 minutes for a small-group preview of the vocabulary involved in the week's sorts on Monday. This could happen during transitional independent activity time. Teachers will also need to provide ongoing support for English learners by checking in as frequently as possible throughout the week to offer help or by using peers or other helpers to explain words in question. The next section outlines some of the ways in which peers, volunteers, and school staff can be a part of the weekly word study schedule.

Structuring Interactions

In previous discussions in this book, we have noted the importance of socially mediated learning for English learners. Many aspects of learning a new language involve using language with others and being able to practice and ask questions. Quiet seatwork is not often an effective

TABLE 3.5   **Weekly Schedule for Word Study**

MONDAY	TUESDAY	WEDNESDAY	THURSDAY	FRIDAY
Introduce sorts in small groups	Students re-sort and record the sort in word study notebooks	Buddy sorts, blind sort, writing sort, speed sorts	Buddy sorts and/or word hunts	Assessment Games

technique for English learners' optimal growth! So how do teachers structure productive word study interactions in the classroom? First let's consider possibilities for student-to-teacher (or tutor) interactions before looking at peer interactions within the classroom.

STUDENT-TO-TEACHER (OR TUTOR) INTERACTIONS. Many elementary school teachers set up their language arts schedule around a concentrated block of instructional time of at least 90 minutes. In that typical arrangement, it is possible to structure three rotations of 30 minutes each. Once procedures for these rotations are well established, a teacher can meet with each group for 30 minutes every day, and in this way have a chance to interact with all students in the class. These groups are developmental, and although the teacher's main objective during this small-group time is to focus on instructional-level reading with students, there should also be time for word study.

A variety of word study activities take place during the three literacy-block rotations, and the amount of word study that is included in the teacher-guided versus follow-up or center rotations may vary throughout the week. For instance, on Monday, when the new sort of the week is introduced, a teacher may spend 15 minutes of the 30-minute small-group time on a teacher-guided word sort. On Tuesday, when the word study sort is practiced, most of the time spent on word study will not be in the teacher-guided small group but rather in the follow-up period for independent activities. On Friday, the weekly assessment can take place during the teacher-guided group, but games will likely occur during the center rotation.

After spending time with a teacher, a group moves on to an independent seat activity. On some days this may mean writing out words for a sort, doing a word sort with a partner, reading or writing independently, and so on. During center times, students participate in learning activities that have been previewed ahead of time in the whole group, or they work on continuing projects. Examples of center activities are word study games, reading projects, listening to prerecorded stories, writing or creating books, and so on. Center activities will vary depending on the age and independence level of your students; it is helpful to set up consistent centers that students can come to do automatically.

Although a literacy-block rotation schedule will ensure daily contact between the teacher and each student, it also requires a lot of energy from a teacher who is managing it alone. Here are some thoughts on how to involve others to support your students during the literacy block:

1. Coordinate your literacy time with the support teachers at your school, and encourage these teachers to follow a "push-in" model of support services. Support staff can also meet with English learners during center and seatwork activities to provide more directed language instruction.

2. Recruit volunteers from the parents in your class, your school's parent organization, or local community organizations. They can support students' independent work or do one-on-one tutoring. These adults can run a center and make the learning time even more productive. Adults with limited background in teaching will appreciate the consistency of becoming an expert at a specific center and running it each week.

3. Build a relationship with local colleges and universities that could send practicum students to your classroom.

4. Find a classroom of older students that can send cross-age tutors to your classroom on a regular basis during your literacy-block time. These could be upper-grade elementary, middle school, or high school students. Depending on the age level of your volunteers, they can run center projects, support students in their independent work, or do one-on-one literacy tutoring.

PEER INTERACTIONS. There are many ways to encourage students to share with and learn from each other during literacy time and other periods of the school day. This cooperation begins with an atmosphere of respect and helpfulness that is established and modeled by the teacher and other adults. The time a teacher spends in reinforcing positive interpersonal relations in the classroom will be repaid many times over by the productive learning atmosphere that is created. Consider the following collaborative structures for your students.

Flexible Grouping. You will be working with small groups of students at similar developmental levels throughout the literacy-block time, so plan ways for flexible grouping when students are not at the teacher-guided group. As often as possible, make working groups heterogeneous by ability and language proficiency level so that students get to know each other and practice their English skills. Numerous opportunities for heterogeneous groupings are available in science, social studies, and thematic investigations; art, music, and other creative arts; physical education and life skills; and in language arts, in writer's workshops, in literature response groups, and during comprehension strategy instruction.

FIGURE 3.11 Volunteers Serve as Literacy Tutors in Class

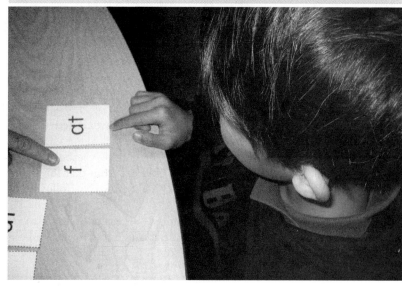

Courtesy Amy Frederick.

Proximal Partners. Create partnerships so that students have a "buddy" to practice with. These proximal partners can read to each other and work on interdisciplinary projects together. It is especially helpful for English learners if their buddy can provide a role model as a proficient English speaker. If you do not have enough language models to go around in your partnerships, it is often helpful to pair a more outgoing but less proficient English speaker with a shyer, more proficient student. They will both learn from this balance of skills. Set procedures for how you expect partners to work. Demonstrate how they can be supportive without doing things *for* their partner, how they can ask questions instead of telling answers, and how they can state things positively and not negatively when working together.

Making Sorts Harder or Easier

As you work on sorts with your students, it is important to constantly assess whether the sort you are presenting is too difficult, just right, or not challenging enough. Because English learners have fewer words in their repertoire to call on, making sorts easier or more difficult may relate to the number, frequency, or academic intensity of the vocabulary words included. Here are some tips for making sorts easier or harder for students:

To Make a Sort Easier	To Make a Sort Harder
Decrease the number of words	Increase the number of words
Limit the sort to common, familiar words	Include unfamiliar words
Choose obvious contrasts such as long *a* and short *a*.	Ask students to differentiate subtle contrasts such as short *a* and short *e*
Sort by two categories—items that "do" and items that "don't"	Increase the number of contrasts in the sort or add an "oddball" category
Take away any time pressure	Ask students to do the sort as quickly as they can

Teaching Vocabulary

As has been noted throughout this chapter, vocabulary support and instruction are crucial challenges in the multilingual classroom. Without knowing the meanings of words, word study and other literacy tasks become abstract, confusing, and frustrating. Students who are working at a frustration level in language may develop some ill-founded understandings. Yet there are so many words to learn; how can enough vocabulary be taught to make word study meaningful? In each of the instructional chapters of this book, vocabulary instruction is integrated into the word study activities. Vocabulary instruction may look different at each developmental level, as well as for students of varying language proficiencies within a developmental level. For example, vocabulary instruction for an emergent reader who is 5 years old may look quite different from that for an emergent reader who is 15 years old and recently arrived in the United States. The following important ideas extend throughout the stages:

- It takes multiple experiences with a word to learn it. An English-learning classroom needs to be print rich and full of formal and informal activities to practice language throughout the day.

- Some preteaching of vocabulary will be necessary in word study lessons for English learners, and more will be needed for students with very limited proficiency. It is not efficient to wait for students' oral language to develop naturally before beginning literacy instruction—they will lose too much ground in the curriculum.

- It is important to focus on useful words as opposed to those that students will rarely encounter or use. When an uncommon word is encountered in a text or word study lesson, it will probably be better to set it aside and focus instructional time on high-frequency, conceptually important words that students are likely to need on a regular basis.

- English learners need practice in saying words orally, seeing them in written forms, and using them in the contexts of conversations and writing.

- In word study, if a word is not known, students should learn to put the word to the side for the time being. This is an informal assessment that will help teachers plan the vocabulary-learning agenda. It also communicates to the student that meaning is an integral part of the word study process.

Integrating Word Study into the Language Arts Curriculum

Word study is an integral part of the essential literacy activities that are a part of each day in the classroom—Read To, Read With, Write With, Word Study, and Talk With (RRWWT) activities. The literacy-block rotation schedule discussed in the preceding section includes word study activities as an integrated part of the language arts curriculum in both the teacher-guided and independent group activities. Word study and spelling activities should not be seen as isolated skills to be practiced independently; rather, they are in synchrony with reading and help inform a teacher's understanding of each student's literacy development. It is critical for English learners that the Talk With component of the essential literacy activities be consciously implemented in a word study program. Learning will gel and confusions will come to light when students have time to talk with teachers and peers.

How will teachers decide which skills to focus on in word study? The assessment process described in Chapter 2 will guide you as you begin, but once your developmental groups have been established, you need to use regular informal assessments, such as reviewing students' writing samples and watching how students do in sorting tasks to monitor their progress. Some teachers conduct weekly spelling assessments of the words students have sorted that week. Students who are appropriately placed and participate in a variety of word sorting routines across the week should score high when tested on the words. It is very natural for the developmental groups you work with at the teacher table to need periodic readjustment, because students will vary in the pace of their learning. Once you know the word study features you will focus on in each group, remember to teach and reinforce unknown vocabulary for English learners. For example, a group that is examining long *a* patterns will need to know the meanings of *tale* and *tail*, *mane* and *main*, *made* and *maid*, and so on. Without the background vocabulary, this exercise will be confusing and esoteric to students.

What standards of accuracy should students be held accountable for in their writing, and what expectations should teachers have for how much editing to do with English-learning students? As with all students, English learners will need to be held accountable for those skills they have mastered at their developmental levels. For instance, students who are comfortable with putting beginning and ending sounds in the words they are writing should be expected to do that in their daily work. It would be inappropriate to hold these same students to accuracy in representing the vowel sounds. English learners may have specific difficulties with English letter and sound representations that contrast with their home language. For example, a Spanish-speaking student, on occasion, may use *r* to represent the sound of *d* in English. When students know a good number of sound–symbol correspondences, it is important to fine-tune and begin to hold expectations for accuracy even in areas of interlanguage confusions. Focused supplemental instruction for students from specific language groups may be necessary to support this expectation.

At any developmental level, work that is to be published or presented in a public way should proceed through an editing process. The amount of time students invest in this process will depend on their skills and maturity level. Ask students to review and self-correct those items that they are generally able to manage at an independent level. Items that students are "using but confusing," or items at the students' **zone of proximal development** (ZPD) can be edited with teacher direction during a small-group lesson or writing conference. Writing errors that are beyond a student's developmental level can be corrected as needed by a teacher but should not yet be the focus of lesson instruction.

▶ **Zone of Proximal Development**

Students' instructional level: what they can do with some assistance.

Involving English-Learning Parents in Word Study

Most parents are interested in doing whatever they can to support their children's literacy learning in English. To encourage parents who do not speak English well or who do not have literacy skills in English to participate in the classroom or to help with homework, teachers can scaffold their participation. Often it is necessary to send notes home in the students' home languages. It is also helpful to train students in class to show them what they can be practicing with their family at home.

Do not ask parents to teach new content to students. That can be confusing for all involved. Homework assignments should be practice, not instruction. Some do's for family involvement might include the following:

- *Do* encourage students to talk with families about what they are learning in school. They do not need to use English—more than likely, using English will severely limit the conversation—so they should be encouraged to use their home language.
- *Do* send envelopes containing duplicate sorts home with students to practice on with their families. Have students read their word study words to family members, demonstrate their sorts, and explain the categories. Sorting at home can become a learning experience for the whole family!
- *Do* have students share the meanings of words in English, and ask their families to teach them how to say these words in their home language. For English learners, learning the translation of a word makes it easier to remember the meaning of a word.

Ten Principles of Word Study Instruction with English Learners

Words Their Way™ (Bear, Invernizzi, Templeton, & Johnston, 2008) outlines ten guiding principles for word study instruction (see Figure 3.12). In the following paragraphs, we have expanded on these principles to highlight issues of particular importance to English learners.

1. *Look for what students use but confuse.* As noted in the assessment procedures in Chapter 2, students' spellings give us information about their developmental understanding of the English writing system. For English learners, writing and spelling samples may also show how they are applying principles from the sound system, grammar, vocabulary, or orthography of their native language to their learning in English. For example, a Somali student who spells the long *i* in English by writing two *i*'s may be applying his or her knowledge of how this sound is written in Somali.

2. *A step backward is a step forward.* Often students learning English are pushed too quickly in the curriculum without a firm understanding of the word study concept they are working with. At times, some students seem to suddenly forget the letter–sound correspondences of the short vowels as they move into studying the long vowels in English. Older students may attempt to memorize individual words without perceiving the principle or pattern these words represent. In these cases, it is important to take a step back to assess what the student truly has internalized about the English writing system. This understanding will be the solid ground on which to build more complex concepts. The lack of a firm foundation will lead to confusion and indecision at the higher levels of word study and reading.

3. *Use words students can read and understand.* It is important for word study to help students connect oral language to written language and match written words to the concepts they represent. In this way, word study reinforces the language learning process. Because too many unknown words will turn the word study activity into an esoteric visual game, introduce words and their meanings before sorting and have students say words aloud as they sort. Encourage them to ask partners if they do not know word meanings. Perhaps a few of these words can be incorporated into a vocabulary lesson. English learners should be encouraged to set aside words they do not understand or cannot read.

   Do not overstress pronunciation. If students consistently pronounce a sound in a nonstandard way, for example, mispronouncing the *i* in saying *sit* as "seat," informal practice and refinement over time will be more effective than attempting to require students to hear a sound difference that does not exist in their dialect or language. Students will come to differentiate these sounds better as they encounter and discuss these features in words they hear and see in print and make the connection between oral sounds and writing. Wide reading will present numerous examples of words to students, and as they compare slight differences in spelling patterns across words, it will spark insight into the spelling/pronunciation contrasts.

4. *Compare words "that do" with words "that don't."* As stressed earlier in this chapter, it is important for English learners to receive clear instruction and have many opportunities to test out their new learning. Comparing words "that do" with words "that don't" provides a simple contrast that supports students in seeing the "big idea" of an orthographic concept. When a teacher is not sure if students understand a certain word study pattern or the way words are contrasted in the two

---

FIGURE 3.12 Principles of Word Study

1. Look for what students use but confuse.
2. A step backward is a step forward.
3. Use words students can read.
4. Compare words "that do" with words "that don't."
5. Sort by sound and sight.
6. Begin with obvious contrasts.
7. Don't hide exceptions.
8. Avoid rules.
9. Work for automaticity.
10. Return to meaningful texts.

or three columns of a sort, it is a good idea to return to this most basic contrast and build on it.

5. *Sort by sound and sight.*   Connecting written words to their spoken counterparts is critical for students learning a new language. For this reason, plenty of occasions to use sound sorts with pictures and words as in Figure 3.13 should be provided. Even as English learners progress to word sorts based on spelling patterns, help them to say the words and reflect on pronunciation issues. Remember, English learners do not have to say words exactly as the teacher does. Their version of the pronunciation will attach to the spelling patterns, and that is a good start.

6. *Begin with obvious contrasts.*   In the spirit of moving from simple to complex, it is always good to introduce a new concept by comparing it to something that is very different. This is one reason kindergarten teachers may introduce three letters like *m*, *s*, and *l* at the beginning of alphabet study. These letters look very different in print, and the sounds they represent are very distinctive. This makes common sense.

   Complications arise for teachers who work with students learning English as a new language. What if a student's home language does not have the same distinctions that English does? What if *l* and *r* sound the same in that language? What if there is no distinction between *sh* and *ch*? For this reason, it is important for teachers to know something about the phonology of their students' home languages. The obvious contrasts that are selected for classroom study should be distinctive in all student home languages. As such, they will be a good place for everyone to start. After students have gained a beginning base in English sounds or patterns, focus on contrasts in English that may be confusing for English learners because of the sounds, grammar, or orthography of their home language. For example, begin short vowel contrasts with short *a* and short *o*; save harder contrasts such as short *e* and short *i* for much later along. You will find contrast-type sorts throughout this book for English learners from different primary languages. For example, Sort 81 on the website is a *th/t* sound sort that will be especially helpful for Spanish speakers who have difficulty with this contrast. Not all sorts will be appropriate for students from all language backgrounds, and these "fine-tuning" sorts should always come after the obvious contrasts have been established.

7. *Don't hide exceptions.*   English has a deep orthography, and many of its patterns require looking below the surface. Sometimes the reason for a spelling pattern may need to be unearthed through a book on etymology. You do not need to pretend that English is a simple and straightforward system, but as a teacher you do need to communicate a confidence to students that you will guide them to understand it in a systematic way. When you discover words that do not follow the pattern you are studying, feel free to talk about them, and note their uniqueness. Think out loud with students about the consistencies in the language and also the occasions in which it challenges us. Encourage students to develop a thoughtful and inquisitive attitude about words and spelling, and see where it leads you.

8. *Avoid rules.*   Novices tend to want a "how to" formula, and those learning a new language are no exception. Unfortunately, sharing spelling "rules" may lead to a mechanistic attitude in students, making it more difficult for English learners to gain the flexibility required to adapt to the ever-more-complex layers of the orthography. "Just teach me the rule" is what students want, but what happens when the rule does not apply in all situations? They may lose faith that the system works. Often, the rules they memorize are beyond what they can use in their own writing.

FIGURE 3.13 A Sound Sort with Pictures and Words

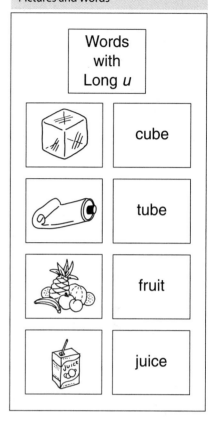

Words with Long *u*

cube

tube

fruit

juice

for Words Their Way™ with English Learners

Go to PDToolkit, choose your book, click the Sorts & Games tab, and search for "Sort 81: /th/ /t/ Focused Picture Sorts to Contrast Beginning Consonant Digraphs & Blends."

A more helpful teaching approach is to build on students' current developmental understandings and help them see patterns in the written language. A word study notebook in which students have recorded related words can support English learners' exposure to common spelling patterns. These lists can be reviewed, reread, and referred to over time. In this way, students are encouraged to actively notice relationships among words and question words that do not follow the pattern.

9. *Work for automaticity.* English learners need a firm foundation on which to build their English literacy learning. Accuracy and speed are the two important signs that students have mastered a sort. Teachers must expect the same high level of mastery for all students, including English learners. It is no favor to expect less than mastery, despite the many challenges to learning to read while learning to speak English. If English learners are pushed into harder and harder material without attaining automaticity, in the long run the foundation for their literacy learning may crumble under the weight of more complex material.

10. *Return to meaningful texts.* This principle is essential for English learners as they struggle to make meaning from literacy activities in the classroom, despite their limited oral language. What vocabulary words and language patterns do students understand? Are they experiencing these in their reading materials? How can teachers connect students with texts that are purposeful and understandable? If necessary, students may need to write the material themselves and use their personal narratives as meaningful texts, as in Figure 3.14. When commercial texts are at a level that is difficult for English learners, whether because of their unfamiliar content, vocabulary, or language structures, teachers can support comprehensibility with visuals and hands-on experiences and also by giving students time to reflect on and discuss the material in groups. This contextualization will give students the experience of reading as a meaning-making activity.

Throughout this chapter we have described the power of word study as part of an effective literacy instruction program for English learners. Word study is based on the assessment of students' orthographic understanding of English words and invites teachers to meet students at their developmental level and build on it in a systematic and explicit way. Word study helps English learners interact with others in their learning community as they investigate words in partnerships and groups through sorts, games, and other learning activities. In word study, English learners make connections between oral and written versions of English and between their home languages and English. In addition, at all levels word study is an active process of pattern identification that involves many hands-on materials and procedures.

Word study activities for English learners build on the same child-centered principles as for those students from monolingual English backgrounds. Organization of word study instruction, and the corresponding scheduling, structuring of interactions, and integration of content into the language arts curriculum, however, are even more complex for teachers working with multilingual classrooms. In the next four chapters we offer materials and activities to take these foundational support strategies for working with English learners and put them into practice in a word study program for all students in your classroom.

FIGURE 3.14 A Student's Personal Narrative

Mexico

People celebrate the Day of the Dead. People speak Spanish. Their skin is light brown. They use different money called pesos. There are many great artists.

Words Their Way Word Study Resources

WORDS THEIR WAY™ WITH ENGLISH LEARNERS WORD STUDY RESOURCES

PDToolkit for *Words Their Way*™ *with English Learners*	The website that accompanies this text prepares you for word study by examining successful classroom instruction with English learners across grade and developmental levels. You'll hear teachers explain the process, watch students learn skills, and see how a successful word study approach is established and managed. An example classroom is featured to demonstrate how the classroom physical environment and instructional routines support learning for English learners. The website also includes all of the assessment and instructional reproducibles mentioned throughout the text.
Words Their Way™: *Emergent Sorts for Spanish-Speaking English Learners*, by L. Helman, D. R. Bear, M. Invernizzi, S. Templeton, and F. Johnston	This text provides strategic assistance for teachers working with native Spanish speakers who are learning English. The text provides instructional activities for the emergent speller, whether young or not so young. The text is careful to include sorts more appropriate for older learners. Teachers of English learners from other language backgrounds or native-English-speaking students with limited vocabularies may find the extensive body of picture sorts and language development ideas in this text useful for their students as well.
Words Their Way™: *Letter Name–Alphabetic Sorts for Spanish-Speaking English Learners*, by L. Helman, D. R. Bear, M. Invernizzi, S. Templeton, and F. Johnston	This text provides strategic assistance for teachers working with native Spanish speakers who are learning English. It begins with a series of picture concept sorts that teach students how to sort, providing guidance to help teachers make sorting meaningful. The text develops a routine for introducing vocabulary in English, helping students learn the vocabulary before they sort. The text addresses the needs of the letter name–alphabetic speller, whether young or not so young. Teachers of English learners from other language backgrounds or native-English-speaking students with limited vocabularies may find the wealth of picture sorts and language development ideas in this text useful for their students as well.
Words Their Way™: *Word Study in Action with English Learners*, by L. Helman, D. R. Bear, S. Templeton, M. Invernizzi, and F. Johnston	This K–5 program has materials for teachers to use with their students, including teacher resource books, student notebooks, big books of rhymes, and a supplementary leveled book series. Available from www.pearsonschool.com (key words: Words Their Way with English Learners).

WORDS THEIR WAY™ WORD STUDY RESOURCES

Words Their Way™: *Word Study for Phonics, Vocabulary, and Spelling Instruction* (Fifth Edition), by D. R. Bear, M. Invernizzi, S. Templeton, and F. Johnston	The developmentally driven *Words Their Way*™ instructional approach is a phenomenon in word study, providing a practical way to study words with students. The keys to this successful, research-based approach are to understand your students' literacy progress, organize for instruction, and implement word study. The fifth edition of *Words Their Way*™ features an innovative redesign and introduces technology integration aligning text to all-new classroom video, an interactive classroom assessment application, prepared and create-your-own word sorts, games, and more. It gives you all the tools you need to carry out word study instruction that will motivate and engage your students, and will help them to succeed in literacy learning. Sequenced developmentally, *Words Their Way*™ complements the use of any existing phonics, spelling, and vocabulary curricula.
Words Their Way™ Online Workshop	Meant to complement *Words Their Way*™: *Word Study for Phonics, Vocabulary, and Spelling Instruction* (4th ed.), this online workshop helps develop literacy skills like never before. Author Michelle Picard and the design team of Kristin Gehsmann and David Picard join Donald Bear, Marcia Invernizzi, Shane Templeton, and Francine Johnston—authors of the popular word study method, *Words Their Way*™—to present educators with a self-paced, interactive, professional development workshop designed to help primary, elementary, and middle grades teachers, as well as reading specialists, literacy coaches, facilitators, and staff development trainers master the methodology of the *Words Their Way*™ word study approach for their students.
Words Their Way™ *with Struggling Readers: Word Study for Reading, Vocabulary, and Spelling Instruction, Grades 4–12*, by K. Flanigan, L. Hayes, S. Templeton, D. R. Bear, M. Invernizzi, and F. Johnston	Intended for the classroom teacher, this handy book provides specific guidance, strategies, and tools for helping struggling students, grades 4 and up, catch up with their peers in literacy. The thrust is intervention—specifically, utilizing word study with its hands-on, assessable approach to aid students struggling with the vocabulary, fluency, and comprehension load of middle and secondary classrooms. This text will help you determine student needs, provide you with the strategies to guide each student toward success in content area comprehension, and even outline ideas for fitting these strategies into your crowded schedule. You'll have the tools you need to help your students acquire the literacy skills they need to meet the ever-increasing demands of school life.
Vocabulary Their Way™: *Word Study with Middle and Secondary Students*, by S. Templeton, D. R. Bear, M. Invernizzi, and F. Johnston	By relying on students' natural inclination to look for patterns, *Vocabulary Their Way* gives intermediate, middle, and secondary teachers the foundational information and strategies they need to help students develop vocabulary knowledge.

WORDS THEIR WAY COMPANION VOLUMES

Each of the following stage-specific companion volumes provides a complete curriculum of reproducible sorts and detailed directions for the teacher. You'll find extensive background notes about the features of study and step-by-step directions on how to guide the sorting lesson. Organizational tips and follow-up activities extend lessons through weekly routines.

Words Their Way™: Word Sorts for Letter Name– Alphabetic Spellers (Second Edition), by F. Johnston, D. R. Bear, M. Invernizzi, and S. Templeton	Primarily for students in kindergarten through grade 3, blackline masters include picture sorts for beginning consonants, digraphs and blends, word families with pictures and words, and word sorts for short vowels.
Words Their Way™: Word Sorts for Within Word Pattern Spellers (Second Edition), by M. Invernizzi, F. Johnston, D. R. Bear, and S. Templeton	Teachers of grades 1 through 4 will find reproducible sorts that cover the many vowel patterns.
Words Their Way™: Word Sorts for Syllables and Affixes Spellers (Second Edition), by F. Johnston, M. Invernizzi, D. R. Bear, and S. Templeton	This text includes sorts for syllables and affixes spellers in grades 3 to 8.
Words Their Way™: Word Sorts for Derivational Relations Spellers (Second Edition), by S. Templeton, F. Johnston, D. R. Bear, and M. Invernizzi	Teachers in grades 5 to 12 will find upper-level word sorts that help students build their vocabulary as well as spelling skills.

4

Word Study
with English Learners
in the Emergent Stage

The emergent stage of literacy development is characterized by a budding awareness of how print works and how oral language connects to written language. The emergent learner knows that speech can be written down and that words on a page can be read, but does not yet understand the code through which this happens. The emergent stage is a time of great discovery and excitement in literacy learning!

English learners at the emergent stage do more than connect print to language; they do it in a new language. Unlike students who have been learning the vocabulary, syntax, and sounds of English from birth, English learners enter the realm of the written code in this new language with limited oral resources. These students critically need a language-rich classroom that provides multiple daily opportunities to talk, chant, sing, listen to comprehensible language, and connect English to what they know in their first language. Before we share more details about the emergent stage and the components of a rich early literacy program, let's take a peek into one language-rich classroom for English learners.

Ms. Rosa's kindergarten classroom is cheerful and active. She has a library with many picture books and nonfiction reference materials. Her science center has a display of different kinds of rocks and hands-on materials such as rock pieces, magnifying glasses, magnets, bowls, and spoons for students to use in their manipulations.

An easily accessible writing center contains paper products of all sorts and pens, pencils, markers, and crayons. Ms. Rosa has arranged the room with a floor space where the group can gather to meet, listen to stories, present work, sing, move, and share. She also has four large tables where students work on literacy and other projects. Her room is decorated with student writing and student-created artifacts, interesting posters relating to the current theme, and sign-up lists where students will put their name cards. She has labeled some of the major areas in the class such as "library" and "writing center" as well as objects like "scissors."

The students in Ms. Rosa's class come from a variety of linguistic backgrounds including Spanish, Hmong, Somali, and Vietnamese. Most are learning English as a new language. At the moment, Ms. Rosa is guiding her students in a writing project. Each student has a picture of someone or something connected to the school—the custodian, the principal, special teachers, the play structure, the cafeteria, and so on. Students are writing about their pictures and will share them as a group in a few minutes. Some students are drawing the words to tell their stories; others have used squiggly lines; and still others, random strings of

Courtesy Linda Woessner

letters. One student is sounding out her words and putting the letters she believes fit the sounds she hears. Her paper says *K D S* ("clean the school"). Ms. Rosa moves from student to student, modeling language and asking questions: "Yes, that is Mr. Yang, the assistant principal. What did you say about Mr. Yang? Do you know what he does?"

Following the writing activity, Ms. Rosa calls the students to the rug area, where they share their pictures and stories with each other. When students are unable to find the words to communicate in English, Ms. Rosa asks simple questions or encourages them to speak in their first language. Sometimes peers will help with a translation. With each sharing, Ms. Rosa clearly states the name of the person or object in each picture and has students try to say it along with her. On another day, she will use these pictures to play a guessing game. She will come back to these photos over and over throughout the year to reinforce meaningful vocabulary. This is also the way she helps students learn the names of schoolmates and helpers in their classroom community.

Ms. Rosa understands that students beginning to learn about reading and writing in English need many opportunities to hear language, connect language to their experiences, practice language in supportive environments, and see the relationship between oral language and print. She has structured her learning environment to provide maximum literacy support and practice for her students.

From Speech to Print with English Learners

All students bring many oral language resources with them to school. Most students know how to communicate their basic needs to the people who take care of them. They have vocabulary words for many of the people and objects in their lives, can distinguish and articulate the sounds that are used in their home language, and understand the patterns of the rhymes and stories that are told in their families. These strengths provide a foundation for connecting speech to print in the early literacy classroom. But how is the experience of learning about print in English different for those students who come to reading and writing without an oral language foundation in English?

English learners entering U.S. schools for the first time are likely to have less depth in their knowledge of English vocabulary and syntax than do their peers from English-speaking households (August & Shanahan, 2006). This limited experience with English words can influence other literacy skills for students. For example, they may perceive the sounds of English as though filtered through the framework of their home language. Consonant and vowel sounds may be "heard" as resembling sounds in the students' home languages. For example, students from some Asian languages may hear /l/ and /r/ sounds as being the same. Phonological awareness skills from identifying **alliteration** to **phonemic segmentation** are supported by students' knowledge of a large number of spoken words. For instance, students who know many words that start with /s/—*sun, sandwich, soap, school, store*—will find it easier to recognize and distinguish the /s/ sound in early literacy activities (Metsala & Walley, 1998). Students who do not have a significant oral language base in English will need to have many opportunities to experience the rhythms and rhymes of language through poems, songs, and movement activities. These activities should introduce English sounds and rhythms and build on the home language experiences that students bring to the classroom.

▶ **Alliteration**
The occurrence of two or more words in a phrase or line that begin with the same sound, such as in *nine noisy neighbors*.

▶ **Phonemic Segmentation**
The process of dividing a spoken word into the smallest units of sound within that word. The word *sun* can be divided or segmented into three phonemes: /s/ /uh/ /n/.

What is key to literacy development for English learners in the emergent stage is that they use language with teachers and peers and see oral language they understand captured in print (Helman, 2009). English learners need structured opportunities to learn many new words to add to their repertoires so that these words can become the material of their literacy learning. Informal experiences using oral English, such as those that occur naturally in a mainstream primary grade classroom, will simply not be enough to support the extensive language development needed for English learners' literacy development (Saunders, Foorman, & Carlson, 2006). Literacy teaching for English learners demands the dual task of teaching vocabulary and language patterns, along with any specific reading or writing skill (Dutro & Helman, 2009). Every day in the classroom and in each literacy lesson taught, vocabulary learning and language practice must be a key focus.

As we discussed in Chapter 1, students bring specific language and literacy resources with them to the classroom. Emergent English learners may represent a variety of backgrounds. They may be students at the same age and grade level as their monolingual English peers, with past school experiences in English instructional programs but having not yet developed full fluency. They may be students who are new to the country and bring an equivalent grade level of reading and writing proficiency in a home language but limited literacy experiences in English. Although these newcomers are emergent in English reading and writing skills, they are more literate in their home language and are likely to move quickly beyond the emergent stage as they transfer reading and writing skills from their first language into English. Or emergent-level students may come to their grade-level classroom with limited literacy experiences in their home language and limited literacy experiences in English. Throughout this chapter we describe activities for the range of emergent English learners, including older learners.

Characteristics of the Emergent Stage of Reading and Spelling

Emergent readers "try out" reading and writing behaviors as their awareness of print and knowledge of writing conventions grow. At the early emergent level, students "pretend read" a story, mimicking the tone and content of what has been modeled to them in book-sharing experiences. Later, students reread texts that they have memorized—often without missing a word! Eventually, emergent readers notice the speech–print connection in the texts they are reading and they begin to fingerpoint as they reread memorized texts. This one-to-one correspondence, or *concept of word*, is highly connected to students' developing phonemic awareness skills and facilitates both their learning of sight words and letter–sound correspondences (Morris, Bloodgood, Lomax, & Perney, 2003).

English learners moving through the emergent stage profit from formal as well as informal opportunities to experience books and conversation. Remember, English learners have not had the same number of years of being immersed in book sharing and conversations in English as monolingual English speakers. It will be difficult for English learners to invent their own stories based on the pictures in a book when their verbal planning is limited by their English vocabularies and knowledge of syntax. Allow students to "read" books using their home language. Teach students key vocabulary words as you introduce a new book; encourage them to tell stories using this vocabulary. For instance, Ms. Mason recently introduced her class to the book *Mary Wore Her Red Dress and Henry Wore His Green Sneakers* (Peek, 2006). She knew that after several readings, this book would become a favorite for students to reread to themselves and others. To support her English learners' ability to do this, she spent some time with them introducing key vocabulary words: *dress, red, green, yellow, blue, brown, purple, orange*, and *pink*. In future lessons, she will practice some of the clothing words such as *sneakers*, *sweater*, *jeans*, *pants*, *shirt*, and *hat*. These important words will give her students immediate help in retelling the new book.

Emergent writers begin with random marks or scribbles, progress to representational drawing, and later move to linear and letter-like forms. Eventually, students begin to write with the letters of the English alphabet, and by the end of the emergent stage they incorporate letters that correspond to the salient sounds of words they are trying to spell (Ferreiro & Teberosky, 1982; Read, 1971). An early emergent writer may write a shopping list to "buy milk and eggs" as some scribble marks on a page. Later in development, perhaps the same list will appear as three curly-cue lines. With more experience, the attempts take on letter-like shapes. When emergent writers begin to use real letters, their spellings are often random strings such as *AX, LTV, AAM* for the shopping list just mentioned. A major accomplishment takes place when students begin to perceive that the sounds in the words they are attempting to spell are related to the letters they choose to represent them. The late emergent speller may represent our previous shopping list as *B MK N Z* ("buy milk and eggs")—representing the most obvious sounds heard.

English learners will exhibit the same kinds of emergent writing but are likely to bring their background experiences with print to the developmental writing process (Helman, 2005). Students who come to school with limited exposure to print, no matter what age they are, may demonstrate writing that is less letter-like. Students whose home language script is very different in form from English (Arabic, Chinese, and others) will need time and experience to start writing "like English." Depending on their home languages, immigrant students may also need added support to learn the left-to-right directionality of writing in English.

When students come to English schooling with some literacy skills in their home language, they may temporarily look like emergent learners, but they will quickly move into the beginning reader/letter name–alphabetic spelling stage. These students already have many of the skills that emergent learners are only developing—a knowledge of the connection between letters and the sounds they represent (the alphabetic principle), conventions of print such as directionality and spacing between words, and awareness of sounds in words (phonemic awareness). Their stay in the emergent level is only a temporary stopover to learn the shapes and names of English letters. This group will quickly be on its way to identifying and comparing the sound systems of the two languages in the beginning reader/letter name–alphabetic spelling stage described in the next chapter.

Components of Early Literacy Learning

Many building blocks of literacy learning are addressed in the emergent stage. These include expanding language and vocabulary skills, developing phonological awareness, and learning the alphabet. These skills are enhanced as students learn to track print and develop a beginning sight word vocabulary. Students at the emergent stage also refine their abilities to sort and categorize conceptually, and they attach language to their conceptual understandings. Effective instruction for emergent learners consists of a literacy "diet" that aims at developing six components of the learning-to-read process (Invernizzi, 2002):

1. Oral language, concepts, and vocabulary
2. Phonological awareness (PA)
3. Alphabet knowledge
4. Letter-sound knowledge
5. Concepts about print (CAP), such as identifying words, letters, and directionality
6. Concept of word in text (COW), matching spoken words to printed words while reading

Teachers of emergent students look to provide many activities that develop vocabulary and concepts, engaging students in the rhythms of oral language while connecting sounds to written texts and helping them learn the letters of the alphabet.

In previous chapters we have outlined essential literacy activities for the classroom: Read To, Read With, Write With, Word Study, and Talk With—or RRWWT. These activities are formats for delivering a productive literacy diet for emergent learners, taking place throughout the day, as described in Ms. Rosa's kindergarten, during whole-group, small-group, and individual lessons with students. Formats vary from listening to interesting stories, to rereading familiar rhymes in a **Personal Reader** notebook, to constructing a **group experience story** that is reread and discussed over and over again. The essential literacy activities take place when students sort objects, pictures, letters, and words into categories and reflect aloud on their learning. The essential literacy activities can become a routine part of your classroom's literacy block; they can also be a part of integrated classroom themes that facilitate students' content area and vocabulary learning (Helman, Bear, Invernizzi, Templeton, & Johnston, 2009a). In the next section we offer some suggestions for implementing RRWWT with emergent learners to ensure a comprehensive early literacy diet that will support their growing development as readers.

Read To

Reading aloud to students is a critical component in the emergent literacy classroom and of special importance to English learners. While reading to students, teachers introduce and reinforce new vocabulary and oral language structures, share interesting and motivating texts that are beyond a student's reading level, model fluent reading, and engage in discussions of content that encourage higher-order thinking (Cunningham & Stanovich, 1991). To make the most of the listening experience, English learners will need material that is engaging but not too difficult for them to understand.

Read to your students at the start of the day, at the end of the day, and during other transitional times throughout the school day. Read to your students whenever you can find a moment. Have a book of simple poems always at hand, and read one when you have 30 seconds to spare. Find a range of narrative and nonfiction texts to share aloud. Read notes, lists, and school announcements. Pay attention to the complexity of the message. Do your English learners understand the text? How do you know? Look for body cues such as eye contact and attentiveness. Do students respond to the humor? Can they make predictions about what is coming next? Check for understanding of key vocabulary words and important events in the material by engaging in discussion and review. Or have students "show you they know" with a drawing or demonstration. If you find that the material is above students' heads, search out texts that deal with the same ideas using simpler language and more visual support. Patterned texts such as *I Went Walking* (Williams, 1992) offer repetitive language and simple sentence structures that listeners can understand and echo along with the teacher during readalouds.

In the pre-K or kindergarten classroom, your read-aloud sessions will be short in duration (5 to 15 minutes) and will often involve student participation such as helping to make sound effect noises or role-playing the story. Preview literature so that you can scaffold unknown vocabulary or complex language structures with students. Books with expressive illustrations or photos and easy-to-understand text will be critical. Consider taking a "book walk"—talking through the storyline as you look at the photographs or illustrations—with English learners, or having them preview the material with someone who speaks their home language before they listen to a story in English with the whole class. Using characterization in creative dramatics can provide opportunities to move to your descriptions; for example, *walking with a cane, stirring soup with a large spoon,* and *walking slowly like a proud lion* are all characterizations that young children of all language levels can enjoy. Take for example the story of *Froggy Gets Dressed* (London, 1992). The story shows Froggy getting dressed, one article of clothing at a time, and includes numerous opportunities for participation and clarifying vocabulary. The initial "book walk" will help students understand the context for the story, while acting

▶ **Personal Reader**

An individual collection of familiar poems, dictated stories, or other pieces of text that students have memorized and can read with good accuracy. These reading materials are copied or typed and placed in a booklet for students to read again and again.

▶ **Group Experience Story**

A chart story created after students have shared an interesting experience together, such as a field trip, hands-on activity, or exciting read-aloud story. The teacher guides a small group of children, each in turn, to dictate a comment about the experience; their words are transcribed onto a piece of chart paper, and the story is reread for reading practice.

out getting dressed to go play in the snow will be a way for students to hear and work with vocabulary such as *boots, hat, scarf,* and *mittens.*

In the primary grades, the best read-aloud materials will be picture book stories and expository texts that have interesting themes and information expressed in uncomplicated language. Books with not more than three sentences of text per illustration are ideal. Read-aloud materials aimed at the whole class may be too difficult for English learners to understand without additional support. Plan to introduce your read-aloud text to English learners in a small-group lesson so that students will have the background and vocabulary needed to contextualize the material when it is read aloud. Look for bilingual editions of books, books on tape in other languages, and support personnel to read stories in the home language first. Students will understand much more of the text in English when they have already heard it in their home language.

Older emergent learners in the upper grades will find most of the content of read-aloud materials presented in class to be over their heads. Provide opportunities for students with limited English proficiency to discuss the material with bilingual students or aides who can translate for them before and after a read-aloud session. Provide English learners with simpler texts that focus on the same content. Use additional visuals for reference. Help students focus on three to five key vocabulary words in each read-aloud session by showing pictures, talking about their meanings, or using them in sentences. Or let students listen to simpler books on tape while you are reading aloud a harder text. Do not expect English learners to sit for extended periods of time listening to material in English that is beyond their listening comprehension levels.

Provide older emergent learners with simpler texts, visual and other vocabulary support, and opportunities to interact with bilingual peers.

Read With

Spending time with the teacher in Read With activities is a key part of the literacy block time in an elementary classroom. Emergent readers need time to practice their blossoming skills with the support of a more experienced guide. This practice will reinforce one-to-one matching of oral language to print (COW), support directionality and other important concepts about print, and teach beginning sight words. Read With activities are most effective when a teacher can work with a group of students who are at similar developmental levels so that activities are appropriate to their instructional level. Teachers are encouraged to implement a center system so they can work with small groups of students having similar needs over the course of the literacy block time, while other students participate in more independent activities.

Reading with students takes place through a number of ongoing literacy experiences in the early education classroom. Pre-K and kindergarten teachers help students read along with big books and chart stories as they model tracking, or following along with the printed words (COW). By using enlarged text and having multiple opportunities to reread these stories, students will memorize the text and point to words as they follow along. Little leveled books with predictable text help students "try out" reading in highly supportive situations. Look for predictable texts with common language patterns and sentence frames such as "I can see a _____" or "There's a _____ at the zoo," and so forth. In this way, students not only get to practice the agency of reading, but they also learn vocabulary that is supported by illustrations and practice natural language patterns (Johnston, Invernizzi, Juel, & Lewis-Wagner, 2009).

Create a book box of familiar reading materials for each of your students. These book boxes should house little books that students have memorized and can read on their own. Include a Personal Reader in each student's book box. As previously noted, the Personal Reader is a notebook or folder that contains copies of familiar poems, stories, and **dictated accounts** that students have memorized. Each time students reread a page of the Personal Reader, they can put a tally mark on it to document their efforts (see Figure 4.1). Word banks can be created as students select familiar words to write on cards and add to a baggie of known words.

▶ **Dictated Accounts**
Retellings, personal sharings, or other oral language samples you have written down from students.

FIGURE 4.1 Personal Reader

Write With

Write With activities engage emergent students in sharing how spoken words get translated into print. Typical examples include taking **language experience** dictations from individual students, creating group experience stories, and working with a Morning Message or shared writing (Nelson & Linek, 1998). These formats are explained in depth in the emergent activities section that follows. As teachers model how to put words and sentences onto paper, they describe what they are doing, giving students insight into the encoding process. Teachers should focus on skills that are at the developmental level of their emergent learners, such as left-to-right sweep, spacing between words, and choosing the beginning letters of words, important concepts about print.

    Providing time for emergent learners to practice their own developmental spelling as we saw in Ms. Rosa's kindergarten is also an excellent Write With activity, as well as a wonderful informal assessment of their phonemic awareness abilities. Developmental spelling challenges students to produce their best approximation of what English writing looks like and exercises their phonemic awareness and letter-sound knowledge as they separate sounds to match to letters. It also provides an informal assessment of students' letter knowledge and phonemic awareness abilities. Look to see if students are writing with letters or other symbols. Notice if they are selecting words from the environment, their personal lives, or using any letter–sound associations. Students may do their own unassisted writing through journal activities or in free-writing assignments that include drawing a picture and writing about it. Have students reread their writing to you, and when you want to remember their messages, write down their dictated words below their personal efforts. Your writing will serve as a model for students' later approximations.

    Scaffold your students' writing to a greater or lesser degree. As in the examples mentioned, dictated stories involve a high degree of teacher support. The student is required to tell the story, but the teacher or a tutor records it. Journal writing involves a high level of student responsibility and less teacher support. Always consider the task and the student as you implement Write With activities. There are times when your English learners will need a highly structured lesson, such as a piece of writing built on frame sentences, in order to learn a language pattern or to reduce the complexity of a task. For instance, instead of asking students who are just learning English to come up with their own stories from scratch, you can provide

▶ **Language Experience**
After experiencing a real-world activity, student language is elicited and recorded in print.

FIGURE 4.2 Creating an Interactive Message on Chart Paper

We will see the
school play today.

them a framework in which to include their ideas (Koch, 1999): "I like _____. I like _____. I like _____. But I don't like _____." ("I like to run. I like to jump. I like to eat. But I don't like to go to bed.")

At other times, a more interactive approach is called for. Teachers often find that co-constructing a message with a student on paper or group of students on a chart is a useful way to support students' beginning writing skills. To create an interactive message on chart paper, work with students to generate a meaningful one-sentence message (see Figure 4.2). Discuss how many words are in the sentence and "think out loud" about the spelling and punctuation involved. Share the pen with students who feel they can write a certain letter or word on the chart paper. When your message is written, review the text for specific letters and other concepts of print. Have students highlight or circle the letters or words you are discussing.

Write With activities are most effective when they take place within a teacher-directed small-group reading lesson. When done in the context of small groups, minilessons can be directed at the needs and developmental levels of the individuals involved. Certain Write With activities such as journaling may also be appropriate for independent centers or seatwork stations. Even when writing is used as an independent activity, students will profit from "reading" their story to a teacher at the end of the work time.

Emergent students at the kindergarten and pre-K level may have an attention span of only five minutes for Write With activities each day. Short lessons integrated regularly into small-group work will have a powerful impact in the long run. Emergent students in the primary grades will have longer attention spans and can draw and write on their own for 15 to 20 minutes. You may find that with increased fine motor skills, these students copy more words from books and environmental print in the classroom. Older emergent learners are likely to know the mechanics of handwriting and may copy or memorize a small set of essential words. Asking older emergent learners to use developmental spelling, and not just copy words from books, will help you understand what they have internalized about the English orthographic system.

Word Study

The focus of word study at the emergent level is to support students' learning of sounds, letters, and words in English. At the sound level, word study activities involve phonological awareness experiences such as working with rhymes in songs, books, and games; alliteration activities that encourage students to hear beginning sounds; and the blending and segmenting of sounds in words. Through these kinds of activities, students develop the phonemic awareness skills that will allow them to hear individual sounds in words and eventually attach related letters to represent those sounds.

Many word study activities at the emergent level are designed to teach the alphabet and letter sounds, often through the use of books, songs, games, and sorting and matching tasks. Because English learners have not grown up experiencing the English alphabet song and may have only limited exposure to print in English, they will require additional and more extensive opportunities to experience English letters in a variety of ways. The activity section that follows presents numerous ideas for teaching letters to students who have limited experiences in English.

Vocabulary and concept development are also crucial aspects of the word study component of the essential literacy activities. Concept sorts with pictures and objects extend English learners' higher-order thinking skills as they reinforce word learning. These sorts also help

FIGURE 4.3 Previewing Vocabulary with English Learners before Sorting

Materials: Picture cards for sorts

Procedure:

1. Select up to ten pictures from the sort for the vocabulary study.
2. Preview these pictures with students. Name the picture and have students repeat the name.
3. Talk about the pictures. Have students generate examples. Teacher paraphrases and provides a simple definition. For example, in a transportation-related sort, Edgar may say, "I see a *jeep* on TV." Paraphrase the student response, for example, "Edgar saw a *jeep* on TV." Provide a simple definition of the word, for example, "A *jeep* is like a square car that can go off the road."
4. If students do not have enough English words to say something about a picture, the teacher should move into a more directive role. For example, "This is a tractor. A tractor helps a farmer plant." Body language and translating the definition into a student's home language is recommended to support this new language learning.
5. When all of the cards have been discussed, chant each word as a group one last time.

students practice the sorting procedure; students who are not yet reading and those who are just learning the English vocabulary for the pictures will still be able to profit from sorting by concepts (see Figure 4.3).

Word study activities are an integral part of teacher-guided small-group lessons during your literacy block time. If you have 15 to 20 minutes to work with each small group, plan to spend 6 to 8 minutes on the word study component. On a typical day you may use this 6 to 8 minutes to introduce a new concept sort or letter matching game or listening to a story for words that sound alike at the beginning. Your word study activities can also be integrated into other components of the lesson such as your Write With activities. For instance, you can have students write a page for a personal alphabet book featuring a letter you worked with in word study or write a traveling story on a day you did a transportation concept sort.

The content of your concept sorts and vocabulary development may look different for various age groups of emergent learners. Young students will likely be working with simple concepts and vocabulary involving items such as living things, colors and shapes, or toys. Primary-age students are ready for more complex topics such as items around town, weather and related objects, or occupations. Older emergent learners should be exposed to concept sorts appropriate to their grade level, such as technology, biology, and geography (Helman et al., 2009a). Older emergent learners will need pictures and other visual support materials that do not look like they came from a preschool classroom. **Photograph libraries** and picture dictionaries for older learners provide useful references for the English learning classroom. See the list of language development resources at the end of this book (p. 343) for sources of these materials.

Talk With

A crucial component of an effective literacy program is having time for students to put their language learning into practice through Talk With activities, and this is even more crucial for English learners (Center for Research on Education, Diversity & Excellence, 2004; Echevarría, Vogt, & Short, 2008). Remember, it is hard to connect literacy to language in the classroom if there is no talking going on! Integrate conversation and dialogue many times throughout your school day. Structure regular routines at the beginning and end of the day and during small-group lessons. You do not need to have a separate time of the day for Talk With. For examples, structure community circle discussions on a regular basis. If procedures are well known and

▶ **Photograph Library**

A collection of photograph cards illustrating common words and everyday activities, usually organized by topics such as household items, colors, actions, tools, food, and so forth. These photograph collections are available from commercial publishers and provide a useful tool for teachers to clarify their instruction and develop new vocabulary with students.

FIGURE 4.4 Ten Ways to Get Students Talking

1. Partner sharing or turn and talk
2. Read or chant along with teacher
3. Echo reading
4. Small-group discussions
5. Games
6. Individual conference with the teacher
7. Reflect out loud on reading or sorting activity
8. Go around the circle so all share a thought
9. Singing songs or reciting poems
10. Frequent checking of students for understanding

input can be framed with a starter sentence, English learners are likely to feel comfortable about contributing. For example, Ms. Sanders's kindergarten students have learned that every day in their class they will go around the circle and contribute one idea to a class discussion. At first, many of the English learners were shy about speaking up, so they "passed" on their turn. With a predictable routine and a simple starter sentence such as "This weekend, I will . . ." or "My favorite animal is . . . ," the students have begun to contribute regularly.

Build in partner sharing as you present literature and nonfiction texts in class. Encourage students to read their writing in an Author's Chair format, and let peers give feedback. Ask open-ended questions and leave wait time for students to think and respond. Call on all students over the course of the day. Find ways to limit teacher talk, and open the floor to more student voices. For example, instead of always asking students to respond to the teacher (when only one child can talk at a time), ask the students to turn and talk to the person beside them to answer a question, offer a personal response, or ask a question. This increases the amount of talk time dramatically and gives less-verbal children a chance to talk in a low-risk setting. English language learners can be paired with peers who speak their home language or with monolingual English speakers. Also provide opportunities for students to sing, chant, and tell stories. Set the context of your classroom to be accepting of *all* students' voices and to show respect even when students do not know the "right" answer or the right word. Figure 4.4 shows ten ways to get students talking.

Older emergent learners in particular need opportunities to dialogue with fellow students about the content of what they are learning. Let talk be a bridge to the content they cannot yet read on their own. Encourage bilingual peers to translate what is being learned for students with less proficiency in English.

The rest of this chapter outlines numerous specific teaching activities for structuring a language-rich literacy diet for your students. These activities can be used for informal assessment of language development and will help students to hear rhymes, syllables, and sounds in words; develop new vocabulary; share stories; see their words written down in English; and build their letter and print knowledge in English.

ACTIVITIES
FOR ENGLISH LEARNERS IN THE EMERGENT STAGE

Activities are provided for this stage that complement the fundamental activities presented as RRWWT. The activities are numbered and organized under basic headings: Concept Books and Sorts, Talk With and Read With Activities, and Alphabet and Letter-Sound Knowledge.

Concept Books and Sorts

4.1 Concept Book Walks

MATERIALS. Gather a collection of simple concept books to share with a small group of English learners. The best books to choose have photographs or clear pictures so that vocabu-

lary is easily understood. Often these concept books will be in the toddler or "board book" sections of bookstores, but it is important to choose books that are not too babyish. Some examples of engaging concept books include the following:

Panda Big and Panda Small (Cobrera, 2000)
Horn to Toes and in Between (Boynton, 2000)
The Eye Book (LeSieg, 1999)
Bears on Wheels (Berenstain & Berenstain, 1983)
Going Places (Parr, 2002)
From Head to Toe (Carle, 1997)
Actual Size (Jenkins, 2004)
Move! (Jenkins & Page, 2006)

PROCEDURES. In your small-group lesson, share the book in an interactive way. Make the words come alive with dramatic effects or body language. Encourage students to act out or share experiences about the words or concepts being introduced. For example, while reading *Move!*, invite students to move along with the actions of animals in the story. Read the story, point out the names and pictures of individual animals, invite students to talk about the pictures, have students touch the part of their own body represented on the page, and encourage students to chant the lines as they act them out. Make the most of these simple concept books. Keep them easily accessible around the classroom so that students can come back to review them whenever they have a chance. Follow-up with concept sorts described in Activity 4.4.

4.2 Bilingual Concept Books

MATERIALS. Concept books that are written in two languages can teach you about your students' home languages while your students are learning English. Bilingual concept books also support students in making connections between their primary language and English, and this will help cement important vocabulary and conceptual learning. Some good examples of bilingual concept books to use in this lesson include the following:

My Opposites/Mis opuestos (and others in the series) (Emberley, 2000)
My City/Mi ciudad (and others in the series) (Emberley, 2005)
My Family and I/Mi familia y yo (and others in the English/Spanish
    Foundations Series) (Rosa-Mendoza, 2001)
Food/La comida (and others in the Bilingual First Books series) (Beaton, 2003)
Where's the Kitten?/Kote Ti Chat La Ye? (English/Haitian Creole bilingual
    edition) (and others in the Photoflap Board Books series) (Christian, 2005)
America: A Book of Opposites/Un libro de contrarios (Nikola-Lisa, 2001)
Brian Wildsmith's Farm Animals (Available in seven languages including Tagalog,
    Korean, Vietnamese, Spanish, and Chinese) (Wildsmith, 2001)

Additional examples of bilingual books can be obtained from the publishers and bookstores included in the list of multilingual and language development materials in the reference section of this book (p. 343).

PROCEDURES. Share the bilingual concept books with your students, and encourage them to say the words in their home language if they know them. Have them chant and act out the words in English. Ask students if the translation in the book is one that they would use in their home or if they have a different way to say it. Keep a small reference section of bilingual concept books for students to use when they are struggling with a word. Use the bilingual books to compare letters and sounds across languages. Encourage monolingual English-speaking students to learn words in other languages by referring to the bilingual concept books, too!

VARIATIONS. Have your students make bilingual concept books that expand on the words in the commercial books, and add them to the classroom collection or donate them to a partner class.

4.3 Using Illustrated Word Books

MATERIALS. Another important source of vocabulary activities for English learners is illustrated books of words or simple picture dictionaries. These texts can be used as student reference materials or as the source material and content for word-learning games. Some examples of these books include the following:

DK Children's Illustrated Dictionary (McIlwain, 2009)
The American Heritage Picture Dictionary (American Heritage, 2009)
My Big Word Book: Over 1000 Essential First Words and Pictures (and others in the Smart Kids series) (Priddy, 2002b)
My Big Animal Book (and others in the Big Ideas for Little People series) (Priddy, 2002a)
My First Dictionary (Root, 1993)
Richard Scarry's Best Word Book Ever (Scarry, 1999)

And for older emergent students:

Oxford Picture Dictionary (Adelson-Goldstein & Shapiro, 2008)
Side by Side (Molinsky & Bliss, 2000)
Word by Word (Molinsky, 2005)

PROCEDURES. Introduce these resource books by pointing out the word–picture match and any thematic or alphabetical organization to the text. Encourage students to use the books to look up and copy words. Students can use picture dictionaries to help them create their own desktop word walls or personal picture dictionaries. Use the photos or drawings in the books to create concept sorts.

VARIATIONS. Play "I Spy" on individual pages of word books for students to guess what you are thinking of. For instance, on the "around town" page of a picture word book, tell students you are thinking of something that travels on the road. It has tires and carries people going to work. People ring the bell when they want it to stop. Provide clues until students can identify *bus*.

4.4 Concept Sorts with Pictures

PDToolkit

for Words Their Way™ with English Learners

Go to PDToolkit, choose your book, click the Sorts & Games tab, and select Picture (Concept) Sort from the Type filter.

MATERIALS. Table 4.1 lists the picture sorts that are included on the website that accompanies this book. The final column offers suggestions for ways these cards can be sorted. Make copies of these sorts, cut them apart, and place them in envelopes or small plastic bags. To help keep multiple sets organized, consider using various colors of paper, or scribbling on the back of each sheet with a colored marker so that it can easily be reorganized if students' cards get mixed up.

PROCEDURES. Demonstrate with students how to sort pictures into categories. For example, a concept sort related to transportation such as Sort 8 features pictures of cars, vans, motorcycles, buses, skateboards, boats, planes, and so forth. In an initial closed sort, the teacher guides students to sort the pictures by water, air, and land travel, as in Figure 4.5. Create labels for these categories and ask students to help listen for sounds and think of letters to record the words on cards that will become headers for the sort. Later, students may be encouraged to sort the items by whether or not they have personally experienced this form of transportation. At other times the students may do an open sort, in which they create the categories. One student sorted by whether the vehicle held one person or a whole family. Another student sorted by how many wheels the item had. A list of possible ways to sort the picture cards is listed in column 3 of Table 4.1. You and your students are invited to think of all kinds of variations of these sorts, too.

FIGURE 4.5 Transportation Concept Sort

TABLE 4.1   **Overview of Concept Sorts in This Book**

SORT	CARDS PROVIDED (SEE WEBSITE)	IDEAS
Sort 1: Furniture and Household Items Picture Sort	Broom, kitchen table, dining room chair, armchair, couch, lamp, door, kitchen, rug, tub, towel, vacuum, window, bed, closet, refrigerator, television, stove	In your house/not, plugged in/not, heavy/light
Sort 2: Living Things Picture Sort	Cat, dog, fish, bird, cow, duck, man, woman, boy, girl, plant, spider, whale, fruit tree, snail, fox, vine, pine tree	Animals/plants, legs/no legs, live in a house/live outdoors
Sort 3: Occupations Picture Sort	Doctor, police officer, firefighter, teacher, sales clerk, postal worker, artist, construction worker, custodian, librarian, farmer, cook, astronaut, gardener, veterinarian, truck driver, actor, bus driver	Someone you know/not, work outdoors/work indoors
Sort 4: Personal Care Picture Sort	Comb, toothbrush, toothpaste, towel, tissue, hairbrush, soap, sink, person sleeping, hair dryer, razor, vitamins, shampoo, floss, fingernail clippers, Band-Aid, scarf, glasses	In bathroom/not, cleans you/helps you in other ways
Sort 5: School and Office Items Picture Sort	Key, chair, desk, pencil, stapler, lined paper, clock, scissors, envelope, glue, tape, book, map, waste basket, markers, computer, crayons, ruler	School/office, big/small, use to draw/no
Sort 6: Technology and Numbers Picture Sort	Computer, thermometer, watch, plug, camera, telephone, date (March 12, 2010), add (2 + 1 = 3), subtract (7 – 6 = 1), dice, ruler, measuring tape, price tag, checkbook, calendar, digital alarm clock	Has numbers/no, plugs in/no, used at school/no
Sort 7: Toys Picture Sort	Block, drum, board game, kite, toy car, doll, ball, teddy bear, scooter, train set, Legos, sand bucket and shovel, paint set, model plane, comic book, baby book, puzzle, toy house	Outside/inside, by yourself/with others, noisy/quiet
Sort 8: Transportation Picture Sort	Car, van, motorcycle, train, bike, skateboard, boat, airplane, ship, truck, jet, sailboat, taxi, jeep, helicopter, school bus, horse with rider, unicycle	Water/air/land, one person/lots of people, you have done it/no
Sort 9: Weather and Related Items Picture Sort	Sun, rain, snow, wind, sunglasses, scarf, mittens, umbrella, galoshes, sunscreen, bathing suit, sandals, fall tree, rake, thermometer, snowman, night, raincoat	Seasons, nature/man-made, for cold/hot weather

VARIATIONS. Explicit vocabulary instruction fits very well with concept sort activities. Share the names of picture cards being used in sorts. Have students echo these names for you. Let them "quiz" others to see if they remember the names of each picture. Have students sort the picture cards into a group for which they do remember the English name and a group for which they don't. Encourage them to see if they can make the "don't know" group smaller each time. Have students use their home language to describe the pictures, while you help them to learn the English labels. Have students write the sounds in the words "as best they can" to get practice hearing and representing the sounds in words.

OTHER CONSIDERATIONS. In addition to using the resources in this book, you can also find pictures for concept sorts in old magazines, calendars, or commercially produced picture or photo libraries or by searching for images through a search engine online. Creating a picture collection is a task in which students, family members, and community volunteers can often help. This is also one way that your collection of pictures can begin to represent the variety and focus of your school community and the themes that you teach in class.

Games Using Concept Picture Sorts

The picture cards you use in concept sorts can be transformed into vocabulary-building games without much difficulty. Here are some sample ideas that can be used as follow-ups to sorting.

FIGURE 4.6 Students Can Play Matching Games with Concept Picture Cards

PDToolkit

for Words Their Way™ with English Learners

Go to PDToolkit, choose your book, click the Sorts & Games tab, and search for "Sort 5: School and Office Items Picture Sort" and "Sort 1: Furniture and Household Items Picture Sort."

PDToolkit

for Words Their Way™ with English Learners

Go to PDToolkit, choose your book, click the Sorts & Games tab, and search for "Sort 3: Occupations Picture Sort" and "Sort 7: Toys Picture Sort."

4.5 Memory or Concentration Games

MATERIALS. Make two copies of one of the concept picture sorts provided on the website, such as the School and Office Items pictures. Cut the pictures apart.

PROCEDURES. Shuffle the cards and lay them face down on the table or floor. Students turn two pictures over to try to make matches such as two pencils, two desks, or two staplers (see Figure 4.6). If students cannot remember the name of items when they make a match, they may not keep it as a pair. However, someone (a teacher, assistant, volunteer, or peer) should be ready to supply the English word.

4.6 Musical Cards

MATERIALS. Make a copy of one of the concept picture sorts provided on the website, such as the Furniture and Household Items cards. Cut the pictures apart.

PROCEDURES. Spread individual picture cards around a rug area or on desktops in your classroom. As you play a bit of music, have students move from picture to picture seeing how many names they can identify. When the music stops, each student must find one and only one card to pick up. The teacher may ask students to say the name of their picture to the whole group. For instance, students reply with "broom," "table," "vacuum," and so forth. If students can't remember the name of their item, they can ask a peer for help.

VARIATIONS. The teacher can also have students do physical sorts with the item they are holding. "If what you have belongs in the kitchen, come stand over here." Or "If you need to get plugged in to work, make a group over here." Students can also think of ways that the household items could be described and sorted. There are so many possibilities! Another variation of Musical Cards is for the teacher to ask questions about the items students are holding: "Who has something that helps us cook?" "Who has something that helps us clean?" "Who has something that makes sound?" Specific sentence patterns such as "I have a _____" can be practiced in this way. After each round, the music starts again and students find a new card to work with.

4.7 I Spy

MATERIALS. Make a copy of one of the concept picture sorts provided on the website, such as the Occupations cards. Cut the pictures apart.

PROCEDURES. In a small group of students, take four or five cards from the concept picture sort. For example, you might take the doctor, police officer, firefighter, teacher, and sales clerk cards from the Occupations sort. The teacher gives clues about a focus picture: "I'm thinking of someone who comes when there is a fire. This person rides in a big truck that has hoses for spraying water." Students guess which person the teacher is thinking of. As students' language proficiency increases, they can take turns being the "teacher" and being the leader of the I Spy game. Students may also be encouraged to add statements about the picture card once it has been identified. ("There was a firefighter on TV last night.")

4.8 Build a Story

MATERIALS. Make a copy of one of the concept picture sorts provided on the website, such as the Toys cards. Cut the pictures apart.

PROCEDURES. Use this set of concept picture cards to help students create oral or written stories. Give four to six pictures from the Toys set to each student in a small group (see Figure 4.7). Have students create their own stories about the pictures they have. "I went to the store with my mom and we saw some toys. I asked her to buy me a drum, but she said no. Then I saw a kite and a board game, but she still said no. Finally, when we were leaving the store she said I could have one thing because I was good. I got a bucket and shovel." Students can tell their stories to each other or try to make one long group story.

FIGURE 4.7 Concept Picture Cards Can Be Used to Learn and Practice Language

VARIATIONS. The teacher may choose to write a line from each student's story on chart paper for the group to reread.

4.9 Charades

MATERIALS. Make a copy of one of the concept picture sorts provided on the website, such as the Personal Care cards. Cut the pictures apart.

PROCEDURES. Review the set of pictures with a group of students. Have students take turns secretly picking a card and acting it out for others in the group to guess. Action words such as *sleeping, combing,* and *washing* will be especially good for this game, but nouns such as *toothpaste, fingernail clippers,* and *hair dryer* will also be fun to try!

4.10 Concept Board Games

The picture cards for concept sorts can also be incorporated into board games that students play independently with their peers.

MATERIALS. Make a copy of the Weather and Related Objects sort cards included on the website. Use one of the blank board game models from the website to create your own weather board game by drawing or pasting some weather-related pictures on the game board.

PROCEDURES. To play, the student rolls a die and then turns over a picture card—let's say *umbrella.* If the student can say the name of the picture, she can move the number of spaces on the die. If not, she must stay where she is. To make this game more challenging for advanced speakers, students may be asked to put the word in a sentence before moving ahead. ("I have a red umbrella.") Or they can be asked to share as many describing words about the item as the number on the die. ("It is big. It is shiny. It folds up." Move three spaces.)

4.11 Bingo

MATERIALS. Make multiple copies of one of the concept picture sorts provided on the website, such as the Living Things cards (see Figure 4.8). Cut the pictures apart. Teachers can use the cut-apart picture cards to create Bingo cards for students to play with. For example, the cards from the Living Things set can be mixed up so that every student's Bingo card has nine pictures from the collection, laid out in a grid format. No two Bingo boards should have exactly the same pictures in the same order.

PROCEDURES. A teacher or student leader can call out the picture names as they are picked, and students use tokens to cover the items on their board. When a "Bingo" or "Blackout" is achieved, that student wins. Encourage students to repeat the names of all of the pictures on their boards when the game is over.

PDToolkit
for Words Their Way™
with English Learners

Go to PDToolkit, choose your book, click the Sorts & Games tab, and search for "Sort 4: Personal Care Picture Sort."

PDToolkit
for Words Their Way™
with English Learners

Go to PDToolkit, choose your book, click the Sorts & Games tab, and search for "Sort 9: Weather and Related Objects Picture Sort" and "Sort 2: Living Things Picture Sort." Blank board game models can be found in the Templates section of the Additional Resources tab.

FIGURE 4.8 An Example of a Bingo Card

ACTIVITIES   EMERGENT STAGE

4.12 Concept Picture Sorts for Older Emergent Students

MATERIALS. Make a copy of one or more of the concept picture sorts provided on the website. Cut the pictures apart. Cut blank cards for students to write the name of each item on its own card.

PROCEDURES. Have older emergent students write the names of objects onto word cards, such as the Technology and Numbers cards, and then match the pictures with the labels (see Figure 4.9). These labels may be done bilingually if students are literate in their home language.

VARIATIONS. Older emergent learners may also appreciate having copies of the concept picture pages to keep in a word study notebook for reference. They can write the label for each picture on the page. Students can also use these reference pages to support themselves when completing simple writing projects.

FIGURE 4.9 Students Can Create Labels and Match Them to Pictures

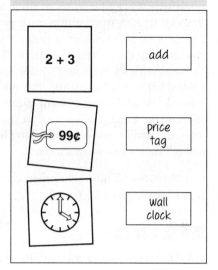

Talk With and Read With Activities

4.13 Rhythm, Rhyme, and Phonological Awareness—"Rain, Rain, Go Away"

MATERIALS. Start with a simple rhyme or poem that uses natural language patterns. Many excellent rhymes and chants are available in books of poetry, children's songbooks, and collections of jump-rope jingles (e.g., Merriam, 1994; Prelutsky, 1986, 1983). Look for a rhyme that is fairly simple and presented in a relatively natural oral language pattern (e.g., "Rain, rain, go away, come again another day"). Rhythm and rhyme help students memorize the verses. Simple, straightforward phrases may also be transformed into fun and useful sentences in students' lives (e.g., "Bus, bus, come this way, don't forget me here today!").

Although classic nursery rhymes share the cultural heritage and help students appreciate the rhythm of English rhymes, carefully select the rhymes you use with beginning learners of English to make sure they follow simple syntactic structures and contain meaningful and useful vocabulary. For example, "Hey Diddle Diddle" may be rhythmic, but it also contains many words and phrases that may be nonsensical to students (e.g., *fiddle, such sport, jumped over the moon*). Memorizing rhymes will be especially difficult for English learners when there are too many unknown words and the students do not have many clues as to the meaning of the text. In addition, early on it is important to spend teaching time on language that will serve students in their daily speech. There are numerous examples of simple rhymes to use with emergent learners that are playful and rhythmic while teaching useful vocabulary and modeling important language structures. For additional rhymes and activities see *Words Their Way™: Emergent Sorts for Spanish-Speaking English Learners* (Helman et al., 2009a).

PROCEDURES. Read the poem to your students several times, and encourage them to join in. Use expressive language, body motions, and rhythmic clapping so that students can participate more fully. Write the poem on a piece of chart paper (see Figure 4.10) or sentence strips in a pocket chart and point to the words as you reread the poem. Add pictures to aid understanding. In later readings, cut apart the chart or sentence strips and help students put the poem back together in the correct order. Make a notebook-sized copy of the poems you have learned for students to put in their Personal Readers (folders of familiar materials for students to reread). Students will "try out" reading as they come back to these rhymes over and over, and their tracking/concept of word, sight word reading, and phonological awareness skills will get much-needed reinforcement.

VARIATIONS. Letter and counting songs like "Five Little Ducks Went Out One Day" help students internalize the alphabet, numbers, and the days of the week in English.

4.14 Rhymes in Other Languages

A concept of rhyme will set a foundation for students' later development of more discrete phonological awareness skills. To scaffold this process, consider bringing rhymes from other languages into your classroom program.

MATERIALS. Find rhymes from other languages by researching your local public library or the resources and vendors in the multilingual and language development materials list in the reference section of this book. Parents and neighborhood community members are especially good resources for sharing the oral language traditions of your students. Many immigrant languages are primarily based on oral traditions, and sharing children's rhymes is a powerful way to bring parents into the classroom learning community!

A fun online resource for poems from around the world is Mama Lisa's World: Kid Songs from Around the World (www.mamalisa.com/world/atoz.html).

The following example demonstrates a rhyme about frogs and toads in Spanish that all students will enjoy learning:

FIGURE 4.10 A Simple Rhyme on Chart Paper

Rain, rain, go away!

Los Sapitos

La ranita soy yo
Glo, glo, glo.
El sapito eres tú
Glu, glu, glu.
Cantemos así
Gli, gli, gli.
Que la lluvia se fue
Gle, gle, gle.
Y la ronda se va
Gla, gla, gla.
    TRADITIONAL

To summarize in English, silly syllables are put into a rhyme about the song of a little frog and toad.

PROCEDURES. Follow the same procedures listed in Activity 4.13 to help your students memorize this poem. Encourage native speakers to help others get the rhythm and pronunciation right. Act out the poem or clap to its beat. Have students point to the words as they reread it over numerous occasions.

Ask your students if they have ever heard the rhyme you have selected. Encourage them to help you pronounce it correctly, and ask them to tell you what the words mean. After helping your students memorize the rhyme, show them how to fingerpoint to the text you have written on paper.

4.15A Rhymes to Assess Concept of Word in English

Here we give sample rhymes in both English and Spanish that illustrate an opportunity to informally assess concept of word.

MATERIALS. Select one of the following rhymes and copy it onto a piece of chart paper or sentence strips for the pocket chart.

Mix a pancake,
Stir a pancake,
Pop it in the pan.
Fry the pancake,
Toss the pancake,
Catch it if you can.
 CHRISTINA G. ROSETTI

Rain on the green grass,
Rain on the tree,
Rain on the rooftop,
But not on me!

PROCEDURES

1. Teach your students one of the rhymes orally before doing this activity with the printed version. Practice the rhyme many times, using any support cues you can think of, such as body movements, voice intonation, or pictures reflecting the text.

2. When your students have memorized the rhyme, introduce the written version on a chart or printed page. Model how you point to the words as you read and then have the children read along with you.

3. Call on individual students to read the rhyme to you and point to each word along the way (Figure 4.11). Notice the student's fingerpointing accuracy: Does he correctly match the word he is saying to the word he is pointing to? Do multiple-syllable words such as *pancake* or *rooftop* throw him off? What happens when he gets to the end of a printed sentence but hasn't yet finished saying the line? These observations will let you know whether or not your student has developed a concept of word.

FIGURE 4.11 Trying to Match Voice to Print

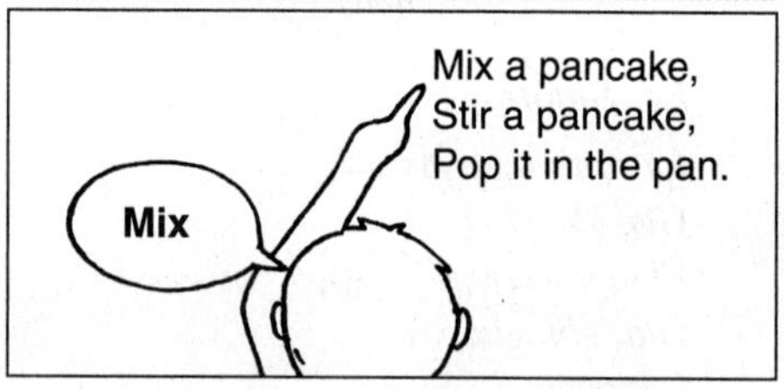

Mix a pancake,
Stir a pancake,
Pop it in the pan.

Mix

4. In subsequent Read With sessions, take turns echo reading line by line. Have the student echo read and fingerpoint to each word in a line after you model.

5. Make a copy of the rhyme for each student so they can all fingerpoint during choral and echo reading. This copy can be added to their Personal Readers.

4.15B Rhymes to Assess Concept of Word in Spanish

MATERIALS. The Spanish language has far fewer one-syllable words than does English, so students attempting to fingerpoint words in a rhyme are immediately thrust into the multiple-syllable word challenge. Here are two relatively simple rhymes that you can use to teach and informally assess your Spanish-speaking students' concept of word in Spanish. Select one of the following rhymes and copy it onto a piece of chart paper or sentence strips for the pocket chart. The first rhyme is about the sun and its lovely color and heat. The second rhyme is about a snail that crawls from branch to branch carrying a flower.

El Sol	*El Caracol*
El sol que yo pinto	*Aquel caracol,*
de lindo color	*que va por el sol,*
nos brinda su luz,	*en cada ramita,*
también su calor.	*lleva una flor.*
TRADITIONAL	TRADITIONAL

PROCEDURES. As you would in English, help your students to memorize the rhyme by repeated practice and by adding physical and visual clues. When students know the rhyme by heart, ask them to fingerpoint the words as they read from a chart or paper version. Notice if your students are able to correctly touch the words they are reading. When and how do they get off track? Do they attempt to recover their rhythm by starting the line again or noticing beginning letters? The answers to these questions will give you many insights into your students' developing concept of word. Now go back and show your students how to fingerpoint read as outlined earlier in this activity.

4.16 Sharing Stories

One way to learn more about students' oral language proficiencies in English (and their home languages) is to elicit personal narratives about exciting real-life events. In this way, teachers have an opportunity to see students using language in a group setting with peers, where maximum fluency is likely to be found.

MATERIALS. Come prepared to share an interesting real-life story with your students, one that you hope will spark stories of their own. If your story is thematic, bring support materials such as concept sort cards from the website or simple word books such as those in the children's literature list in the reference section of this book.

PROCEDURES. In the Language and Literacy Survey on the website we outline how to use Tell a Story to Get a Story (McCabe & Bliss, 2003) as an informal oral language assessment. This technique may be used on a regular basis informally in your small-group lessons as well. Sharing stories is a good way to open a lesson, find out about students' background experiences, and "prime the pump" for the upcoming activities. Share your story with enthusiasm. Try to make it as dramatic as possible. When you are finished, ask an open-ended question to get students to tell their own stories. As they share, ask follow-up questions as necessary. Bring out your picture resources to help in case students have difficulty with specific vocabulary words. Figure 4.12, Mr. Chang's Lesson, illustrates how one teacher implemented this lesson.

VARIATIONS. If time permits, build on Sharing Stories by having students do a language experience or group experience story (see Activity 4.17). This provides an opportunity to connect oral language to written words, and the stories will be available in future lessons to examine conventions of print and letter–sound correspondences. It will also provide comprehensible text for students to use in repeated readings of familiar materials.

4.17 Language Experience Dictations

Use students' background experiences and knowledge of English to create texts that you know they will understand. The Language Experience Approach (Stauffer, 1980) shows students the connection between oral language and print, validates students' experiences, and helps teachers understand their students' oral language development.

for Words Their Way™ with English Learners

Go to PDToolkit, choose your book, click the Sorts & Games tab, and select Picture (Concept) Sort from the Type filter.

for Words Their Way™ with English Learners

Go to PDToolkit, choose your book, click the Assessment Tools tab, and select Assessment Materials to see the Language and Literacy Survey.

ACTIVITIES EMERGENT STAGE

FIGURE 4.12 Mr. Chang's Lesson

Mr. Chang is a kindergarten teacher who combines a sharing stories activity with a concept sort and a brief phonemic awareness lesson. Mr. Chang is working with a group of six English learners in his kindergarten class. Today he will focus on building the vocabulary of animal names, and he will do some phonemic awareness tasks to discriminate the beginning sounds in words. He knows that students need some meaningful words to work with in order to participate in phonemic awareness activities. He has decided to use Tell a Story to Get a Story as a way to get students talking. Mr. Chang begins, "I saw something very exciting this morning before I came to school—something I had never seen before. I looked out of my window at home, and in a little grassy area I saw a wild rabbit. It was sitting still, and every once in a while it would hop down the way. It did not see me, so it wasn't scared. I have never seen a rabbit by my house before. I didn't even know that rabbits live there! I wonder where it sleeps. Have you ever seen an animal that you can tell us about?"

Mr. Chang calls on students to share their experiences and asks clarifying or open-ended questions as needed to support their narratives. If students cannot name the animal they have seen, he pulls out the animal sort picture cards to see if they can point to the animal they are discussing. He also has simple picture dictionaries or a photo library set at hand to help them point out their animals as needed.

Once students have had an opportunity to share their stories, Mr. Chang moves to a picture sort of animal cards. He starts by sorting the cards into "Animals we told stories about" and "Animals we didn't." Next he moves into a sort of wild animals and animals that live with people. In each round of sorts, students work with the teacher to remember and repeat the animal names and sort them into categories. Finally, Mr. Chang uses this new vocabulary to discuss beginning sounds. He works with students to find animal names that sound alike at the beginning such as *cat–cow, fox–fish, dog–duck,* and *bee–bug.* After all the correct matches have been made, the teacher picks three pairs and mixes them up. He hands individual cards to students and asks them to find the person whose animal starts with the same sound. Students must say the name of each animal out loud to find this sound match.

MATERIALS. It is usually helpful to have a warm-up conversation or a hands-on experience to lead into the language experience dictation. For instance, the Sharing Stories activity (Activity 4.16) prepares students for drawing and dictating a story about an animal they have seen. A field trip or an in-class activity such as making playdough, constructing a house with blocks, or observing a pet hamster are also examples of experiences that can lead to a dictation. Thus, materials will vary depending on the activity you choose. Have drawing and writing materials available for the students to illustrate their experience.

PROCEDURES

1. Provide an interesting activity such as making pancakes as you model the use of vocabulary such as *batter, sugar,* or *spoon.* Provide time for oral language.
2. Encourage the students to talk about what they see and do for the "language experience." Then invite individual students to offer sentences that you write down on paper. Say each word as you write it and point out concepts of print such as capital letters and punctuation. Reread the entire sentence, pointing to each word, before eliciting a new comment.

Help each student to shape a sequential coherent account that is not too long. Repeat the sentences, pointing to the words, and have the student read along with you. Finally, ask the student to reread the dictation to you while pointing to each word. Make a copy of the dictation for the child to reread and illustrate. Keep the dictation in the student's Personal Reader folder to reread on an ongoing basis and for harvesting words for word banks. This can be used as another informal assessment of the child's concept of word.

CONSIDERATIONS. Language experience dictations are designed to bridge the natural language of students to the printed word. Students who are learning English as a new language or who speak dialectical variations of academic English may use nonstandard forms in their oral speech. For example, one student recently dictated the phrase "He goed to the store to get a cake." A teacher may be torn about whether to write this language verbatim for the student or whether to correct the sentence to "He went to the store to get a cake." On the one hand, the student will probably reread the text as spoken, and when she gets to the verb, she will say "goed." If the word has been written as "went," she will misread the text. On the other hand, many teachers feel uncomfortable having students reread text that may reinforce incorrect patterns. You will need to make a decision in context about which approach is most appropriate for the situation. If the primary goal is to show the oral language to written language connection, and this story is not aimed at a wider audience, write exactly what the child has said. If you can rephrase the sentence for the child and she repeats it correctly (e.g., "He *went* to the store"), and if the story will be shared with others, use the occasion as a teachable moment to correct and practice the standard language form.

4.18 Group Experience Stories

Group experience dictations provide a way for students to see their spoken words take form in much the same way that individual language experience activities do, this time in a small-group context.

MATERIALS. Provide a memorable activity for students—a field trip, a hands-on science or art experience, a construction project—anything that involves the senses and sparks interest. Activities that connect to your classroom unit of study are particularly valuable. Materials will vary depending on the specific activity. You will also need chart paper and colored markers to write students' sentences.

PROCEDURES. Pull aside a group small enough so that you can see each person's eyes as you reread the text. Usually groups of four to eight students work well, and this ensures that everyone in the group has a chance to create a sentence. Elicit a comment about the experience from each student in turn, and write these statements on a large chart (see Figure 4.13). For example: "Mohamed

FIGURE 4.13 A Group Experience Story on Chart Paper

Mohamed said, "My airplane went in the tree."

said, 'My airplane went in the tree.' Marika said, 'I made a paper airplane that went up and down.'" Some teachers find it helpful to change the color of the text to differentiate each student's comment. When all of the students' sentences have been written, reread the chart as you fingerpoint to each word. Discuss and clarify specific words and conventions of print. Students will love reconnecting to the meaningful text of the shared group experience and will eagerly point out what each of their peers said.

VARIATIONS. Students can also be invited to dictate sentences that fit a predetermined pattern selected by the teacher that introduces targeted vocabulary or reinforces language from a familiar book. If the focus is on color words and clothing (after reading *Mary Wore Her Red Dress*) the account might read like this: "María said, 'I wore my yellow shirt.' Kia said, 'I wore my pink shorts.' Bao said, 'I wore my blue sneakers.'" Or, an account about pets might read "Ramón has a dog for a pet. Leeza has a cat for a pet."

Alphabet and Letter-Sound Knowledge

4.19 My Name, Your Name

Students' names are a great source of meaningful print for learning words and letters!

MATERIALS. You will need pieces of cardstock approximately 3 × 7 inches. Write the name of each student in your class clearly on its own piece.

PROCEDURES. At transitional times in the school day, use these cards as flash cards to help students begin to memorize each other's names. Use the name cards to select class helpers or a "student of the day." Play games with the name cards: Have students pick a name at random and deliver it to the correct person, use physical actions such as "hop" to Yasmin's name or "skip" to Miguel's name, or use the name cards for students to "sign into class" in the morning or express their opinion on a topic of the day.

As students become more familiar with each other's names, use the cards to do group sorts. Lead the group to sort by how many letters each name has or by whether it contains a certain letter, such as *o*. Eventually, have students sort the names by beginning letters. Work with names in each letter group to see if they sound the same at the beginning. Compare these groups to alphabet books that feature names such as *A My Name Is Alice* (Bayer, 1992), *Matthew A.B.C.* (Catalanotto, 2005), or *What's Your Name? From Ariel to Zoe* (Sanders, 1995).

VARIATIONS. The name cards may also be used to stimulate oral language in a variety of ways. In a small group, choose a student's name card and encourage other students in the group to make sentences about the featured person. "Miguel has a green shirt." "Miguel runs fast." "Miguel rides the bus." The teacher may choose to write some of the sentences down on chart paper for a group experience story. Another way to elicit discussion is for students to pick two name cards and discuss how the spellings are the same or different. "Yasmin and Miguel's names both have the letter *i*." "They both have *m*s, but Miguel's *M* is big." "They both have six letters." "There are many letters that are in one of the names, but not the other, like *y*, *a*, *s*, *n*, *g*, and *u*."

4.20 A Community Alphabet

The names of students in your class, as well as familiar people, places, and objects in the school and neighborhood, can be used to create a relevant and meaningful way for students to connect letters to the real world—a community alphabet.

MATERIALS. Using photographs or drawings, illustrate each letter of the alphabet on a bulletin board area or pocket chart stand. Each of the uppercase and lowercase letters can feature someone or something from your school community. To help everyone feel a part of the community, all students' names should be included in the alphabet, even if it means you have five illustrations for *A*! If you are lacking someone for a particular letter, consider giving a classroom pet a name that starts with the unused letter (Zorba the guinea pig? Quentin the goldfish?). Find a book of baby names (or find lists on websites) and read through them with your students. They will hear the sound repeated many times and you can write down choices on the chalkboard for voting purposes.

PROCEDURES. Use the community alphabet to practice singing the ABC song or to play guessing games. If it is possible to duplicate the alphabet at an 8 ½-×-11-inch size, make copies for students to keep and refer to at their tables.

4.21 Personal Alphabet Books

MATERIALS. Provide each student with a folder having enough pages for each letter of the alphabet. Old magazines can be cut up to provide pictures, or use pictures from concept sorts, photographs, and drawing materials to illustrate the personal alphabet book.

FIGURE 4.14 Alphabet Scrapbook

PROCEDURES. Create an alphabet scrapbook of pictures and important words to go with each letter of the alphabet (see Figure 4.14). English learners will find this an especially helpful reference as they learn the letters and build their vocabularies in English. Encourage students to write the names of family members, friends, and school personnel in their personal alphabet books. They can illustrate the words with pictures and drawings. Important words that students use in their free writing (*like, I, have,* color words, etc.) should also be included, whenever possible, with a key picture. If students are literate in another language, they may want to write a translation of these words in their alphabet book. Students are encouraged to refer to these books throughout the day as needed.

4.22 Playing with Letters

MATERIALS. Manipulatives, such as plastic or wooden letter tiles, magnetic letters, sandpaper letters, and alphabet puzzles.

PROCEDURES. Help students to become familiar with the letters in the English alphabet as they examine, sort, and manipulate letters in a variety of hands-on games and activities. Manipulatives, such as plastic or wooden letter tiles, magnetic letters, sandpaper letters, and alphabet puzzles, can be used by students to match, sort, trace with their fingers, and spell simple words. Each time students handle the letters, their shapes become more familiar. The manipulative activities provide contexts for students and teachers to discuss and describe letter names and sounds, what is "right side up," and a burgeoning sight-word vocabulary. ("Is that a real word?" "Look, it's my mommy's name." "Teacher, I made a word from our word wall.")

Alphabet puzzles are a good example of what can be done with letter manipulatives. The simplest puzzles require students to match a letter to its own shape. Often, the puzzle piece itself is shaped like the letter. The puzzle may be practiced over and over, and students are encouraged to say the letter names or sing the alphabet song as they work to put it together. Students can work with a partner to complete the task, thereby encouraging literacy-related conversation (and partners can supply the names of unknown letters). Give students individual puzzle pieces and ask them to find other examples of that letter around the classroom. More complex alphabet puzzles may require students to match an uppercase letter to its lowercase counterpart, or a letter shape to a word that starts with that letter. The repeated practice of identifying each letter and matching it to its picture or letter pair provides English learners with much needed visual support and reinforcement.

4.23 Letter Hunts

MATERIALS. A print-rich classroom or area with charts, labels, signs, and so on for students to look for letters and words; books and magazines with print big enough for students to work with; notetaking paper, writing materials, and highlighter pens.

PROCEDURES. To help students recognize letters and see that they are everywhere, send students on a letter hunt. Have them search for examples of the first letter in their names or a letter featured in your shared reading or writing activity. They can look on classroom walls, on labels and packages, and in big books or chart stories. Have students write the letter on a small piece of paper each time they find one, or they can write words they find that contain that letter. Students can also use highlighter markers to spotlight the focus letter in printed materials such as old workbooks or outdated magazines with big print.

4.24 Sharing Alphabet Books

MATERIALS. There is an incredible range of excellent alphabet books on the market that can support your language and literacy teaching for emergent English learners of all ages. ABC books from the simplest wordless books to those using complex content area vocabulary can be used. Let the artistry of master wordsmiths and illustrators support your English learners' attempts to recognize the English alphabet, build their vocabularies, and engage in meaningful conversations. Please see the reference list of suggested literature featured at the end of this book for additional titles. Alphabet books are coded "ABC" at the end of selected references. Books for specific activities are listed in procedures.

PROCEDURES. Wordless alphabet books and other concept books show rather than tell, providing a platform for student participation in storytelling activities. For example, *Alphabet City* (Johnson, 1995) features realistic paintings of objects in New York City that resemble letter shapes. *A* is the side view of a sawhorse, *B* a set of fire escape stairs, and so on. While the book is simple, it is not "babyish." Both young and older emergent learners profit from discussing where in the picture the letter is represented, which object is depicted, what the object does, and the words that could be used to describe the pictures. Use this and other wordless books to elicit content-based conversation from your students.

Some alphabet books focus on the sounds that letters make in funny ways. Two examples include *Achoo! Bang! Crash! The Noisy Alphabet* (MacDonald, 2003) and *Talk to Me about the Alphabet* (Raschka, 2003). MacDonald's book provides sounds in nature as well as the sounds of words to narrate a humorous picture for each letter of the alphabet. For instance, the *K* page shows a knight who has been ejected from his horse while walking over a dragon. The text depicts klanking and klopping sounds (MacDonald, 2003). Second-language learners may think that the English language sounds like a bunch of noise, and this book is one way to have fun with that idea. *Talk to Me about the Alphabet* works its way through each letter, incorporating words and sounds the letter represents. Even if students do not understand the meaning of every word, the repetition of sounds provides a connection to learning the written code of English.

Read these alphabet sound books to your students aloud in an energetic and theatrical way. Exaggerate the sounds that are illustrated in the texts. On repeated readings have students echo read the "noisy" lines. Let your students become the chorus of sounds as each page is read. Have students pick their favorite pages and lead the group in chanting the rhythmic and onomatopoetic lines with words such as *crunch, clank,* and *crash* (MacDonald, 2003).

Many simple alphabet books serve as learning tools that can help build your students' basic vocabulary in English. For example, *Charley Harper ABCs* (Harper, 2008) features elegant artistic representations of animals. *Alphathoughts* by poet Lee Bennett Hopkins (2003) simply but eloquently describes a series of common and useful words. The beautiful illustrations help English learners connect the word and poem to an easy-to-understand visual. Read this book over and over, each time clarifying or informally checking that students understand the use of words and their meaning. Ask students to share what they know about individual words or topics.

Other simple definition-type alphabet books focus on specific content areas such as a kind of animal, a job, or a place. *Alphabeep: A Zipping, Zooming ABC* (Pearson, 2006) involves vehicles and road signs that might be seen as you drive. Use a book like this when you want to develop vocabulary related to a unit on transportation or the city. Build on the book by learning the names of various kinds of vehicles; cut out pictures of traffic signs and vehicles from magazines; sort these pictures in multiple ways such as by their appearance or function; or have students create their own transportation books. Using content area alphabet books in thematic units integrates letter–sound awareness within meaningful vocabulary development and conceptual learning.

Alphabet books provide opportunities to create a supportive climate for multicultural and multilingual experiences in the classroom. ABC books such as *Ashley Bryan's ABC of African American Poetry* (Bryan, 1997), *Gathering the Sun: An Alphabet in Spanish and English* (Ada, 2001), and *Handsigns* (Fain, 1995) add to students' understanding of the English alphabet while broadening their knowledge of specific cultures and languages. Guide students to dialogue in class about the many ways in which people express themselves; this often helps them feel more comfortable about sharing their own experiences. As students share their personal background experiences, consider ways to bridge your classroom curriculum to their languages and cultures. Look for the "ABC" code in the children's literature references at the end of this book for additional examples.

VARIATIONS. Older emergent English learners will appreciate alphabet books that use humor or more grown-up themes to elucidate the letters. In *Z Goes Home* the letter *Z* maneuvers through an ABC of obstacles to reach home at the end of the day (Agee, 2003). Using a very simple text line—each letter is represented by only one word—the illustrations and continuity of the story are appealing to students of many ages. It is a fun book for mature students just beginning to develop letter knowledge and vocabulary in English. Another humorous book for students with more advanced English vocabularies is *What Pete Ate from A–Z (Really!)* (Kalman, 2003). The text describes a mischievous dog that eats his way through people's personal items. The bold and silly illustrations are especially engaging to upper-grade students and lend themselves to extension activities and discussions. Imagine having students create their own alphabet books of "What Pete ate" as they expand their English vocabularies.

4.25 Sorting Alphabet Books

As your classroom collection and group experiences with alphabet books grow, consider using the books you have shared to conduct open or closed sorts.

MATERIALS. Gather a stack of eight to ten alphabet books you have previously shared with your group.

PROCEDURES. Spend a few minutes reminiscing about the story line, content, or artwork in the books. For open sorts, invite students to think about all of the books, and share ways that the books might be grouped by commonalities. For instance, students might suggest grouping books by the kind of illustrations they use (photographs, collage, drawings, etc.); students may notice letters being displayed in certain styles of fonts; or they may want to classify books by how they were used in your classroom ("We read these ones when we studied about animals"). For closed sorts use a key picture card to represent your category. Invite students to review and discuss which books belong in each group. On one sort, your categories might relate to each book's theme or topic, such as ABC books about animals, school, the community, or a specific habitat.

Another sort might involve sorting books by how much text is presented for each letter: Is the book wordless; does it have single-word descriptions, short phrases, simple sentences,

or more complex texts? In still another sort, students might sort the alphabet books by level of sophistication: What age-group audience would most appreciate each book, and why do they think that? Make up categories that fit your classroom studies and students' interests.

4.26 Hands on the Alphabet

MATERIALS. Begin a collection of magazine pictures or small objects to keep in small containers for each letter of the alphabet. For example, the *A* box may include pictures or mini-versions of an apple, an acorn, an alligator, an armchair, an astronaut, and so on. Many educational supply companies sell these sets ready made. It is also fun to have students contribute to the collection.

PROCEDURES. Work with one or two letters at a time. Use the objects or pictures to teach students the names of words. Mix up two letters' worth of items and see if students can correctly sort them into the appropriate container. Give one item each to students and ask them to form themselves into two lines depending on their letters. In order to do that, students will need to know the name of their item and remember to attach it to the appropriate letter. Always begin with two letters that have very different sounds.

VARIATIONS. You can use the pictures or objects to play guessing games. Give one item from a specific letter group to each student to keep hidden. Have the student give clues about what the object is until other students have identified it. You can also play a memory game by laying out all of the objects from a certain letter on a tray. Ask students to close their eyes while you remove one object. Students will need to use their memory and vocabulary skills to identify which object is missing.

4.27 Alphabet Strips

MATERIALS. Obtain enough alphabet strips (Figure 4.15) from educational materials stores for each student in your group to have his or her own piece. These can be purchased as rolls of stickers (which can be attached to cardstock) or as individual desktop alphabets with a key illustration for each letter. Photographs as illustrations are especially helpful for English learners who may find some caricatures or drawings difficult to decipher.

FIGURE 4.15 Portion of an Alphabet Strip

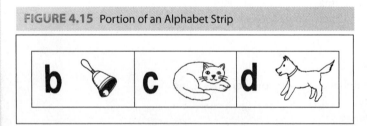

PROCEDURES. Desktop alphabet strips are a useful tool to aid in letter recognition and sorting. Use these alphabet strips to have students touch each letter as they say it or as they sing the alphabet song. Have students "quiz" a partner on the names of letters. Mix up an alphabet set of letter tiles for students to place under the correct letter on the strip. In small-group discussions, encourage students to identify letters and describe their shapes and sizes. Invite students to sing or chant their way through the alphabet to find the names of unknown letters.

VARIATIONS. Extend these tasks by giving students small word cards with the names of their fellow students on them, and guide them to put each name below the letter on the alphabet strip according to its first letter. As students learn new sight words, have them demonstrate how the first letter of the word they learned matches a letter on the alphabet strip and line it up below that letter.

4.28 Many Kinds of Alphabets

MATERIALS. Make copies of some of the sample alphabets from the Appendix of this book.

PROCEDURES. Emergent students of all ages will enjoy looking at and comparing the alphabets of many languages. Let students examine the various alphabets, and ask them to share their perceptions. What does the writing remind them of? How does it compare to English? Can students distinguish the English alphabet from the others? Try to make some letters from other languages by tracing through a thin layer of salt on a shallow tray.

VARIATIONS. Discuss key ideas about why people from a variety of cultures have created writing systems. You may want to share portions of books that highlight writing in a variety of languages, such as the *Day of Ahmed's Secret* (Parry, 1995). Invite in a classroom parent or community member who can share a different writing system with the students. Show examples of how students' names might be written in this other language. Let this be an opportunity to validate the diversity of written languages in the world, and help students make connections to background knowledge they bring from their primary languages.

4.29 Comparing Picture Books in Different Languages

MATERIALS. Begin to build a collection of picture books from many languages to share with your students. The most effective of these will be books that have simple text-to-picture matches and clear print. It is also helpful to have bilingual books in which the text is printed in both English and another language. A list of sources for bilingual books is included in the reference section of this book.

PROCEDURES. Introduce a bilingual book to your students by showing the cover of the book and pointing out how the text looks in both English and the other language. For example, *My First Book of Proverbs/Mi primer libro de dichos* (Gonzalez & Ruiz, 1995) puts the English print and Spanish print in separate banners across the page. Read the text in English, and then point to the words in Spanish. If you are not fluent in the language presented, do your best to sound out the words, and ask your students to help you say them. If the text uses a script you cannot read, point it out anyway, and ask students who speak the language to make a prediction about what the text might say. Encourage students to share vocabulary words that relate to the picture, which they could teach to the rest of the group. For instance, in *My First Book of Proverbs* one of the pages quotes a Mexican proverb, "Una abeja no hace una colmena" (*One bee doesn't make a hive*). Students who are learning English, but do not speak Spanish, can be guided to describe the picture and share words in their primary language that relate such as *bee*, *flowers*, and *tree*. Help students understand the moral behind the proverb, and ask how this might be expressed in their home languages.

VARIATIONS. If you have bilingual support staff, colleagues, parents, or community members who can share bilingual books with students, build in time for them to come in on a regular basis. Students who have heard a book in their primary language will be able to understand and appreciate the English version much better. If your guest does not speak English, the sharing of a bilingual book can be a team affair! Look for translations of popular children's books from your grade level to include in your classroom library. Students can compare the scripts, make oral language to print connections with their primary language, and pull these books out for bilingual visitors who may be able to read them to individuals informally.

4.30 Bilingual Picture Alphabet

MATERIALS. Make copies of the bilingual picture alphabet for the letters in Spanish and English from the Appendix of this book. The same illustration represents each letter in both languages.

PROCEDURES. Bilingual picture alphabets help English learners make connections among their home oral language, oral English, writing in their home language, and written English.

Tt
turtle   tortuga

Bilingual picture alphabets also provide a common vocabulary with which teachers can explain letter–sound correspondences in English by relating these to the language students already know.

Use the Spanish-English picture alphabet to teach vocabulary: "*B* is for *boat*, or *barco* in Spanish; *boat–barco*, they both start with *B*." Let the bilingual alphabet be a scaffold for helping students find letters as they are learning English key words: "Point to *tortuga*; *tortuga* starts with the letter *T*."

VARIATIONS. As you learn more about the background languages of your students, begin to collect resource materials to share in class and consider creating bilingual picture alphabets in numerous languages. Some of these resources may already be available from educational publishers or on the Internet (see the multilingual and language development materials list in the reference section of this book). These activities build an appreciation and interest in languages and literacies among monolingual English speakers. Have students share the names of illustrations in their home languages. Ask students or their parents if the English letters are used in the script of their home language. Use an affirming manner and open inquisitiveness to discuss commonalities and differences among languages in your multilingual community.

4.31 Learning My Letters Game

Use simple games to help students practice the names of letters.

MATERIALS. Copy the blank game board from the website. Choose four or five letters to focus on, and fill in one letter per space, in random order throughout the board. You will also need the same letters on plastic or wooden tiles and a cup to draw from.

FIGURE 4.16 A Sample Learning My Letters Game Board

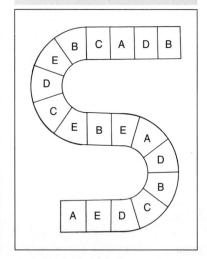

PROCEDURES
1. Put four or five letter tiles in a small cup—let's say you picked *A*, *B*, *C*, *D*, and *E*.
2. Students take turns picking one letter from the cup and moving to the next spot where that letter appears. Students must say the name of the letter before advancing.
3. The first person to reach the end wins (see Figure 4.16).

VARIATIONS. Many variations can be devised for the Learning My Letters game. As students become more proficient with recognizing the letters, letter tiles can focus on similar shaped letters such as *c*, *o*, *d*, *b*, and *p*. You can make the game more difficult by using uppercase versions for the letter tiles and lowercase for the game board letters. Or have students work with the vowels only. As students' language development progresses, you can ask students to think of a word that starts with the letter before they may advance to each new space. It is always helpful to have a copy of the alphabet or simple picture dictionaries handy when creating more complex variations of this game.

4.32 The Winning Letter Game

Here is a game to build letter recognition and encourage discussion about the alphabet.

MATERIALS. Choose six letters you want to reinforce with your students. You will need a blank die that you can write letters on for this game. If this is not available, put a small sticker on each side of a numbered die—one letter per side. Each student needs a game sheet printed from the website that contains a grid with six rows and six columns (Figure 4.17). Label each row with the name of one of the letters.

PDTooIkit

for Words Their Way™ with English Learners

Go to PDToolkit, choose your book, click the Additional Resources tab, and select S Game Board (left) and Grid Game Board in the Templates section.

PROCEDURES
1. Students take turns rolling the die and naming the letter that turns up on top.
2. Students write the letter in the grid in the appropriate row and the turn passes to the next student.
3. The first person to color in five boxes for the same letter has "The winning letter!"

4.33 The Piñata Game

MATERIALS. You will need two sets of letter tiles or one set of uppercase and one set of lowercase letters for students to match. The piñata can be a cup or other small container that holds letters.

PROCEDURES. This is a letter-matching game. It is a fast game, just like a race for candy in a real piñata. Students take turns tipping the piñata. When the letters fall to the ground, all students quickly find as many matches as they can, and pair them up in their work space. When all of the letters have been partnered, students share the letter names and see who has the most pairs. Then put the letter tiles back in the piñata and play again.

FIGURE 4.17 A Sample Winning Letter Game Sheet

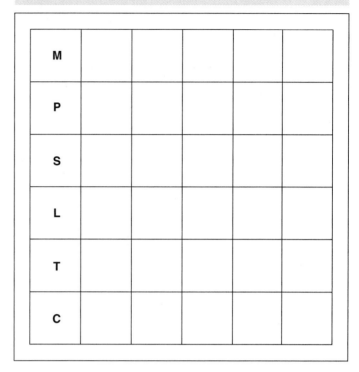

4.34 Sound Boards

MATERIALS. Make copies of the sound boards for beginning consonants in English or the bilingual alphabet from the Appendix in this book.

PROCEDURES. Sound boards visually help students connect sounds to a key picture. They are exceptionally helpful in giving students a consistent visual key for the sounds of English letters. Keep these sound boards handy for English learners. Students can have their own copies to paste on the inside covers of their Personal Readers or writing folders. Review the key word pictures so students can make an oral language connection to the letter and word.

VARIATIONS. Your Spanish-speaking students connect the letters to words in their home language by using the bilingual picture alphabet. Even if you do not speak Spanish and your students do not have the opportunity to learn to read and write in Spanish, the bilingual alphabet will facilitate an understanding of the alphabetic principle that smoothes the path to learning letters in English. Encourage your students to point to the consonants and say the name of the associated picture in each box. Chant the sounds along with the word, such as "B-b-b, barco."

Use the same phonemic awareness games and activities with the Spanish key words as you would with English words. Remember, learning to play with and distinguish individual sounds in words is a skill that transfers across languages!

4.35 Beginning Consonant Picture Sorts

By the end of the emergent stage students are ready to work with sound sorts to identify and discriminate some of the more obvious beginning sound contrasts. An in-depth discussion of these sorts is provided in Chapter 5, Activity 5.18, because these sorts are also an important aspect of word study for early letter name–alphabetic students.

for Words Their Way™ with English Learners

Go to PDToolkit, choose your book, click the Sorts & Games tab, and search for "Sort 13: /s/ /m/ Beginning Consonant Picture Sorts."

DEMONSTRATE. Prepare Sort 13 from the website. Copy and cut apart the pictures you will need for the sort. For example, you will begin with a sort contrasting /s/ and /m/. Before doing the teacher-guided sort, hold up each picture card and ask students to give its name. Consider teaching the names of up to five unknown items. Additional unknown items can be set to the side for another time. Proceed through the sort by holding up each picture and sharing your thinking in the following way: "Here is a picture of a sink. Does *sink* sound like *sun* at the beginning or like *monkey*? Right! I'll put *sink* under the card with *S* and the sun on it. Now, you help me sort the rest of these pictures." Continue with the children's help to sort all of the pictures. Model how to isolate, identify, and then categorize the beginning sound in each word.

SORT AND CHECK. Give each student (or pair of students) a set of the pictures to sort. Now have the students repeat the sort under your supervision using the same key pictures as headers. You may want to have students work with partners to mix up the pictures and take turns drawing a card, saying the picture's name out loud and sorting it in the correct column. After sorting, remind students to check their sorts by naming the words in each column to be sure the beginning sounds are the same.

REFLECT. Ask students to reflect about how the words in each column are alike. Have them share their comments with others in the group or think of other words that start with the same sounds. These are excellent ways for students to use English vocabulary in real conversations.

5

Word Study with English Learners in the Letter Name–Alphabetic Stage

First grade teacher Ms. Atchison has just completed a teacher-guided Read With and a Word Study activity with her third group of the morning, and she is ready for a whole-class meeting to introduce the theme for the week: animals and what they eat. In the class meeting, she models a concept sort in which students match pictures of animals and the foods they eat: rabbit–lettuce, squirrel–nuts, child–sandwich, cow–grass, bird–worm, deer–plants, dog–dog biscuit. Next Ms. Atchison demonstrates how she could conduct a sort. She puts a card that says *Animals* and another that says *Food* at the top of two columns and then helps students sort the pictures that go in each column. This sort just takes a moment and Ms. Atchison explains that students will complete a similar sort after their meeting.

Ms. Atchison asks students what pets they have at home and what their pets eat. Students share for a moment or two and then she asks them to form small groups of two or three students from within their cluster, or pod, of desks to sort their pictures. She also asks them to think about what dogs, cats, gerbils, fish, and other pets eat. "When you are done sorting, each person will draw about pets and what they eat. I'll come and visit you in your pods as you sort and write."

Students work in small groups to match the animals to their foods and paste them onto pages. As they work, Ms. Atchison moves among the groups to encourage their conversation, giving additional support to a few English learners in the pod. As she talks to students in each small group, she asks them to tell her in a sentence about their animals and what they eat. Ms. Atchison records the following individual one-sentence dictations into her laptop:

> Hector said, "Rio eats the cat food and the dog food."
> Brian said, "Lucky gobbles dog food like a pig!"
> Luis said, "¡Mi gato come pepinos!" (*My cat eats cucumbers.*)
> Elivia said, "My cousin has a cat."
> Teresa said, "My cat eats people food."

Everyone in the group agrees that they have drawn some funny pictures, and Ms. Atchison then asks whether students are ready to write on their own. She tells them that she will print copies of their sentences for them as soon as she gets back to her desk. They may use these sentences to make an illustrated book for the class or put them in their Personal Readers to read again on other days.

In these mixed-ability groupings, students are at different levels of literacy development, and the spelling development of students in the pod of desks spans the entire range of the letter name–alphabetic stage. This range is evident in Luis and Teresa's spelling samples as seen in Figure 5.1. Although Luis is just learning English, there is nothing in his spelling of these five

FIGURE 5.1 Early Letter Name–Alphabetic Spelling by Luis (left) and Middle to Late Letter Name–Alphabetic Spelling by Teresa (right)

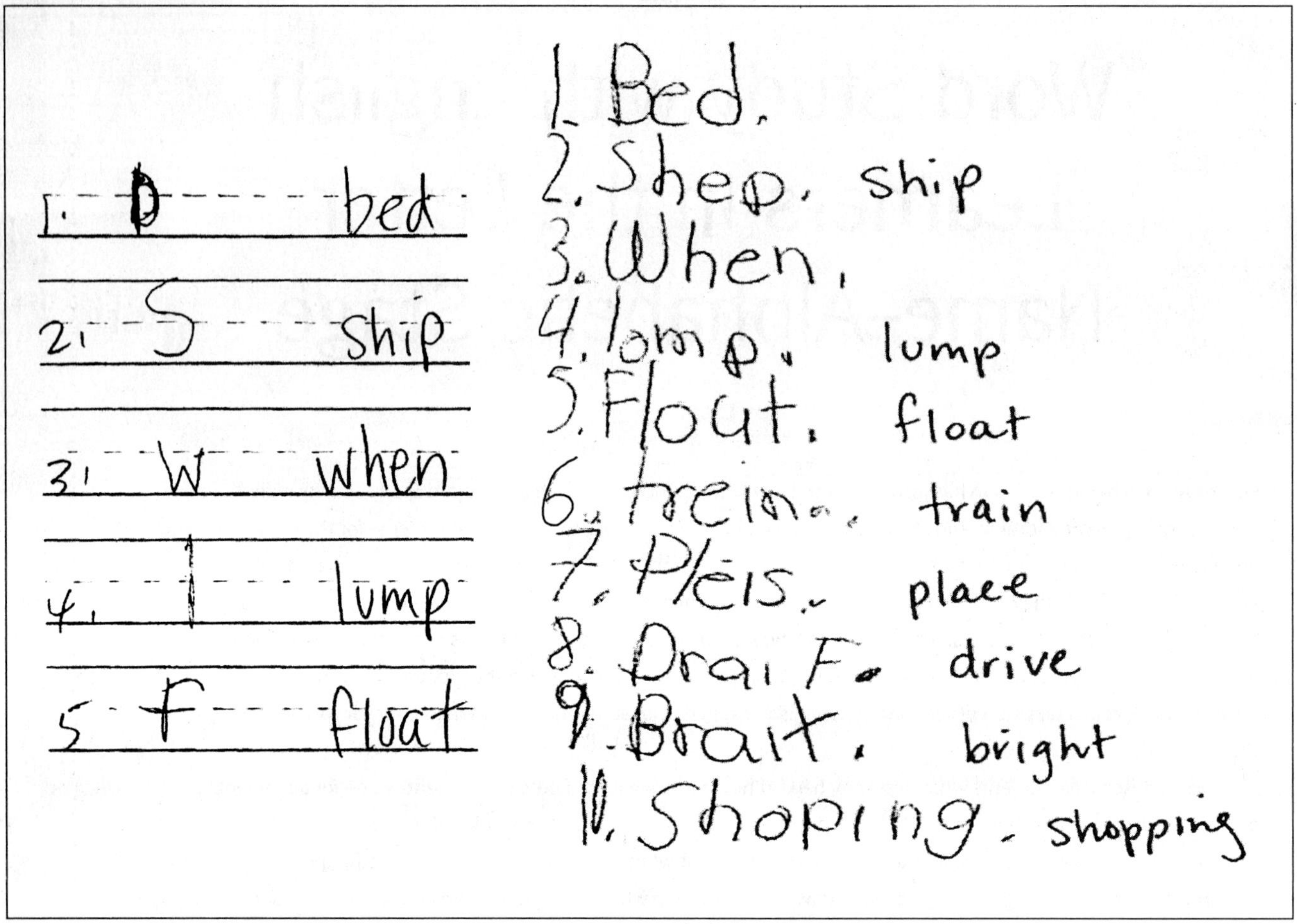

words that shows the influence of Spanish on his spelling. He spells the beginning sounds of the five words and we would say he is an early letter name–alphabetic speller.

Teresa's spelling indicates that she is in the late letter name–alphabetic stage. She has an excellent grasp of consonant blends and digraphs, and she is spelling some short vowels correctly. Her substitutions of *e* in spelling *ship* as SHEP and of *o* in spelling *lump* as LOMP are typical of many letter name spellers. The influence of her native language, Spanish, can be seen in the way that Teresa includes two vowels for the long *a* sounds in *train* and *place*. When sounded out slowly, the long *a* can be perceived as two vowels, which she represents with Spanish letter–sound correspondences: *e* for the first long *a* sound and *i* for the long *e* sound spelled with an *i* in Spanish. The same extended sounding out and matching with Spanish letter–sound correspondences is also seen in her spelling of the long *i* words with *ai*.

Given the wide differences in development in her class, Ms. Atchison prepares word study activities for three distinct groups. Although Luis and Teresa are in different spelling stages, they often work together in one cluster to explore themes through talking, reading, drawing, and sorting. Students like Teresa choral read with Luis to offer support when he rereads familiar passages in his Personal Reader.

The first part of this chapter presents the background, instructional scope and sequence, and routines for this stage. These basic routines are fundamental to many of the word study activities that follow. Activities for this stage are included following the introductory material and are arranged in developmental order. The concept sorts are designed to teach vocabulary commonly found in curriculum themes and units in primary classrooms. After the concept sorts, students sort by how words sound and look alike to make sound–symbol correspondences. Through these activities students acquire an understanding of consonants, digraphs and blends, word families, and the consonant-vowel-consonant (CVC) pattern, the predominant short vowel pattern. Student and teaching materials for sorts and games are included on the website.

Word study instruction during this stage explores the letter–sound correspondences of consonants and vowels.

for Words Their Way™ with English Learners

Go to PDToolkit, choose your book, and click the Sorts & Games tab.

Literacy Instruction for English Learners in the Letter Name–Alphabetic Stage

A number of important ideas apply to letter name–alphabetic stage English learners who are learning about the letter–sound correspondences of English spelling.

Students May Know Different Sounds Than Those Found in English

Many students learn the sounds of English at the same time they learn how the sounds are spelled. Word study can highlight English sounds and vocabulary. For instance, Spanish speakers may have difficulty saying and sometimes spelling the beginning sounds of the following words because the beginning consonant sounds do not exist in Spanish: *den, jam, rail, van, zipper, shut, thin,* and *trade* (Helman, 2004; Swan & Smith, 2001).

Word study is another way students can learn about oral English.

Consider the Role of Correct Pronunciation

Do not expect students to pronounce words correctly because many sounds of English will be new to students and accurate pronunciation takes time. In lessons, do expect students to make contrasts and distinctions among sounds. Think of how sounds are made in the mouth. Begin with larger contrasts such as /m/ and /s/ and then sort for finer gradations that focus on the specific confusions that students experience between sounds in their first language and in English such as /d/ and /t/. For example, although students may not pronounce the /v/ sound completely correctly, we do expect them to eventually hear that /v/ is distinctive from other sounds such as /b/ or /f/.

Students Use Their Primary Language Literacy

Students use what they know about phonics in their primary languages to spell, but the letter–sound relationships in their first languages are not always the same as they are in English. For example, students who speak Spanish may turn to the /ch/ sound to pronounce the /sh/ sound in English because there is no /sh/ sound in Spanish. Students who speak Chinese often have difficulty pronouncing the /th/ sound. You will find word study activities in this chapter that compare the difficult contrasts of /ch/ and /sh/ or /th/ and /t/. Select one of these activities when your students' writing shows you they are ready to examine these tricky sounds.

Students' Primary Languages Support Their Literacy Development

Vocabulary from students' first language assists them in making the transition to learning solely with English texts. For example, when asked to draw pictures of words that begin with the /t/ sound, students may be invited to include words from their primary language that begin with this sound.

Students may include words from their primary language when they brainstorm words related to the content studies. For example, encourage students to use or add concepts from their first language such as *pan* or *mkate* (*bread* in Spanish and Swahili, respectively) to a food theme sort.

Vocabulary Is a Partner in All Sorts

Even when there is an emphasis on phonics instruction, vocabulary instruction continues to play a key role in each word study lesson. Use pictures like those in the Appendix and website of this book to assist in vocabulary instruction. The activities for this stage begin with concept picture sorts that are suitable for learners of all ages. Concept sorts show students the importance of making meaning and encourage discussion, thinking, and development of big ideas. Vocabulary learning supports all three of these actions. In word study routines like those presented in Chapter 3, students are repeatedly exposed to important vocabulary words. Choose words that have high utility and can be used easily in conversation.

In word study lessons, many older English learners will want to keep a short list of words they see or hear and want to learn. Often, the key content vocabulary is what students bring to the discussion, as well as some of the general academic and descriptive language in their assignments (e.g., *weather forecast*, *reverse*, *subtract*). Students in this stage who are in the intermediate elementary grades may not be able to read many of the words in their content texts and will need extra support, such as through **vocabulary word walls.** Provide opportunities for students to identify key vocabulary in their texts that they do not understand. Then show them examples of what the words mean and engage in dialogue to see whether students can use the words in context. Students' school success in the upper elementary grades is rooted in their knowledge of content vocabulary and academic language. Through word study, teachers help students grow vocabulary and provide some of the student motivation to engage in academic inquiry.

Pictures Are a Part of Many Sorts during This Stage

During the letter name stage, the sorts teachers use are a blend of pictures and words, starting with mostly pictures at the early part of the stage, as in Figure 5.2. By the time students have mastered beginning consonant sounds, they have learned enough sight words to use mostly words in sorting, but pictures are often included for vocabulary instruction or to double check sound discrimination.

Sort with Known Words and Pictures

To create word sorts, teachers must have a good sense of the words students can read. The few words students do not know are set aside and reviewed at the end of the sort once categories are established. If they remain unknown after several days of review and sorting, they can be discarded. After supported practice reading the words in a sort, if there are more than four words that students cannot read, choose a slightly easier sort. Remember to check that students know the meanings of words, even if they can read them.

Letter Name–Alphabetic Spellers Are Beginning Readers

Beginning readers read slowly and read out loud. Beginning readers who understand many letter–sound correspondences and have learned a group of sight words will have a concept of word. They will be able to read appropriate leveled texts with good accuracy and at a natural pace, especially with repeated practice. Parents and teachers may say, "Students read the words but do not comprehend

Word study instruction for English learners varies with the depth of each student's vocabulary knowledge.

▶ **Vocabulary Word Wall**
A posted collection of words with photos or illustrations that relate to a particular topic or theme being studied in the class.

Word study can be a vehicle for oral language learning.

FIGURE 5.2 Sorts Include Pictures

what they read." This ability to read and not comprehend is related to their developing language and vocabulary skills that continue to grow through both oral and written language use. Because some students read with accuracy and fluency, they may surprise us in what they do not understand. Vocabulary knowledge is a factor in their understanding. Take time to focus on comprehension activities even when students seem proficient in their decoding.

Students' decoding skills may be progressing, but they may not understand what they read.

Understanding Is the Key to Successful Reading

By concentrating on what students do understand, we help their motivation to have integrity while they read; by integrity, we mean that students are able to keep a *vigil to understand* what they read (cf. Deese, 1969). It is the skill of thinking while reading that we want to promote in all essential literacy activities, whether in a Read To or Word Study activity. Students must learn to ask about the words they do not know, seeking clarification from their classmates and teachers when needed.

Teach students to keep a vigil for understanding in reading and word study.

Concept Sorts Encourage Discussions

How do teachers know if students understand the meanings of the words they read and sort? One way to assess understanding of the words is to have students talk about why they sorted the way they did. To encourage verbal interaction, ask students to sort words conceptually. Then have students play guessing games or ask each other questions about the words. For example, a student may say, "Find two words in this sort that are colors" (black/red) or "Find two words for things that you would find in your house" (lamp, bed). In open concept sorts, students develop their own categories and talk about the categories that underlie the words.

Help English learners to notice when they are able to say a word but do not know what it means.

. . . .

Characteristics of Orthographic Development for English Learners in the Letter Name–Alphabetic Stage

The Letter Name Strategy, Reliance on Articulation, and the Alphabetic Principle

In reading and spelling, students in this stage approach words with three common strategies:

1. They use the names of the letters as clues to spelling.
2. They select letter–sound matches for spelling based on how sounds are articulated in the mouth.
3. They master the principle that the letters of the alphabet represent individual sounds.

In these three ways students match unfamiliar sounds and letter sounds in English with the sounds of their first language. Students who bring literacy from a home language also make informal associations across the writing systems of both languages. Students use information about *where* sounds are made (their point of articulation) and *how* they are made as air is forced through the mouth and nose (their manner of articulation). Table 5.1 outlines some useful vocabulary that will help you better understand the role of sounds, how they are made, and what makes them similar or distinct as we navigate this linguistic terrain.

Descriptions of where and how sounds are made in the mouth are presented in Table 5.2. This table helps explain why students may experience difficulty discriminating among specific sounds in English. Minimal pairs are sounds that differ in only one minor way. For example, in saying the words *fat* and *vat*, one can feel the similarities and slight difference in the beginning consonants as the two words are said. As can be seen in Table 5.2, /f/ and /v/ are articulated the same way: They are both made with the air coming between the top teeth and bottom lip (see

TABLE 5.1 Helpful Linguistic Vocabulary

TERM	WHAT IT IS	EXAMPLES
Consonant	Speech sounds (and the letters that represent them) that are produced by constricting or closing the flow of air through the upper vocal tract.	/s/, /t/, /f/, /m/
Vowel	Speech sounds (and the letters that represent them) that pass through a relatively open, unobstructed airway in a continuous stream.	a, e, i, o, and u
Minimal pair	Two words that differ in only one articulatory way, such as having a sound that is voiced or voiceless.	pie/by, half/have, chin/shin
Voiced sound	A sound in which the vocal chords vibrate.	that, zoo, big
Voiceless sound	A sound in which the vocal chords do not vibrate.	thin, soon, pig
Open syllable	A syllable that ends with a vowel.	pilot, reason.
Closed syllable	A syllable that ends with a consonant sound.	battle, racket.
Plosive sound	Sound made by closing the air flow and creating a puff of air (/b/, /p/, /t/, /d/, /k/, /g/).	bat, tell, don't, keep
Glottal sound	A sound made using the vocal cords or the area around them—the glottis.	
Short vowel	A set of sounds the five vowels can represent, typically in closed syllables such as am, em, im, om, um.	cat, bed, him, not, run
Long vowel	A set of sounds the five vowels can represent often described as "saying their names."	play, he, ice, loan, rule

Nilsen & Nilsen, 2002, for additional information). The biggest difference is *how* the sounds are made: /f/ is voiceless and /v/ is voiced. *Feel* how the vocal cords are engaged when saying /v/ and not in saying the /f/ sound. *The way sounds are made is as important as the actual sounds the students hear.* This is why students say the words as they sort. Many of the substitutions in the spelling of English learners are phonetic, letter–sound substitutions according to minimal pairs. This is why it is common for students to substitute *f* for *v* as in FAFRIT for *favorite*.

Why would a student spell *boat* as POT and not BOT? How can the substitution of *p* for *b* be understood? Refer to Table 5.2, and draw a line from the /b/ to the /p/. Both sounds are made with a puff of air leaving the two lips, but /b/ vibrates the vocal chords and /p/ does not. They are similar, however, and this may be experienced by saying *pumper–bumper* several times. Feel the slight difference in the shape of the lips as you say the words. If an English learner's home language does not differentiate between the /p/ and /b/ sounds, such as for Hmong speakers, students are likely to interchange these letters in their spelling attempts such as writing ROP for *rob*.

Instruction for English learners at this stage begins with easy contrasts and gradually works toward these more difficult comparisons between minimal pairs. What are the sounds that English learners find difficult? This will depend on the languages students speak. For this book we compared 15 languages to English and developed a series of sorts for English learners based on the contrasts that linguists have described.

Consonants and the English Learner

The number and types of consonants vary from language to language. The consonants and vowels of English are arranged into open or closed syllables. More common are closed syllables, which end in a consonant sound. Spanish, in comparison, is composed mostly of open

The voiced/voiceless distinction explains many of the logical substitutions spellers make.

TABLE 5.2   **Where and How Sounds Are Made and Feel in the Mouth: Manner and Point of Articulation for Consonants**

WHERE POINT OF ARTICULATION →

HOW MANNER OF ARTICULATION/ FLOW OF AIR	Bilabial—two lips	Labiodental—top teeth/ bottom lip	Interdental—tongue tip/top teeth	Alveolar—tongue tip/ tooth ridge	Retroflex or alveolar flap or tap—tongue tip/hard palate	Palatal—tongue mid/ hard palate	Velar—tongue back/ soft palate	Glottal—not localized
STOPS/PLOSIVES a closing of air flow and a puff of air	p pen / **b ball**			t tail / **d donkey**			k kite / **g gate**	
CONTINUANTS/FRICATIVES continuing air forced between two places in the mouth	hw which / **w water**	f file / **v view**	ө thank / **ð then**	s sun / **z,y,l zipper yellow lake**	r butter	š ship / **ž measure**		h hen
NASAL CONTINUANTS air forced through nasal passage	**m mat**			**n night**			**ŋ sing**	
AFFRICATES stop + air flow made with some friction between two places in the mouth						č chip / **j Jim**		

Key: Nonbolded words are voiceless
Bolded words are voiced.

TABLE 5.3 **Beginning and Final /b/ in English**

SOUND AND KEY WORD IN ENGLISH	MAY BE SAID IN THIS WAY	MAY BE DIFFICULT FOR SPEAKERS OF	NOTES
ba̱t	pa̱t	Chinese, Hmong, Vietnamese	/b/ (voiced) may be said more like /p/ (unvoiced).
tu̱b	tup, tu	Arabic, Chinese, Hmong, Korean, Navajo, Spanish, Vietnamese	/b/ is not found in final position; /b/ may be omitted or substituted with /p/ in final position.

PDToolkit

for Words Their Way™ with English Learners

Go to PDToolkit, choose your book, click the Sorts & Games tab, and click on Create Your Own! Or go to Additional Resources and select Pictures for Sorts and Games.

PDToolkit

for Words Their Way™ with English Learners

Go to PDToolkit, choose your book, click the Sorts & Games tab, and search for "Sort 33: /b/ /p/ Focused Picture Sorts to Contrast Beginning Consonants" and for "Sort 101: /-p/ /-b/ Focus on Picture Sorts to Contrast Final Consonants."

syllables. As a result, students from languages with a predominantly open-syllable structure may not distinguish or articulate some final sounds of words. For example, Chinese, Korean, and Spanish speakers may not identify the final consonant sounds of closed syllables or they may add a final sound that they expect to be there (Helman, 2004; Yang, 2005).

To pronounce and spell sounds that are not found in the primary language, students locate a nearby consonant sound in English that is closest to a sound in their primary language. For example, for Spanish, Mandarin, and Cantonese Chinese speakers, English words that end with /n/, /m/, or /ng/ sounds are often confused. While deleting final sounds, students may produce a slight glottal or unreleased sound when they say words that end with a /g/ or /k/, as in the final sound in *dug* or *clock*. This may be heard as a slight /k/ sound and almost like a partial-breath pause.

Table 5.3 provides an example, using the /b/ sound, of how sound differences across languages might make discriminating, pronouncing, and therefore spelling sounds difficult for students from various home languages. The first column presents key words for these sounds. The second column lists how students may say these key words. The third column presents the language backgrounds that might create this contrast with English. The fourth column presents background notes. Table 5.2 showed the manner and point of articulation for these sounds. There are many pictures in the Pictures for Sorts and Games section of the Appendix and on the website that you can use to help your students practice these contrasts, such as *ball, bike, baby, bag, balloon,* and *bath,* with *paint, pan,* and *pear;* or *cab, globe, crab, bib, crib, sub, tub,* and *cube,* with *zip, jeep,* and *cup.* Sorts 33 and 101 on the website also specifically address this difficult contrast.

Table 5.4 points out how sound differences across languages might make differentiating, pronouncing, and therefore spelling /sh/ sounds difficult for students from various home languages. There are many pictures in the Pictures for Sorts and Games section of the Appendix

TABLE 5.4 **Beginning and Final /sh/ in English**

SOUND AND KEY WORD IN ENGLISH	MAY BE SAID IN THIS WAY	MAY BE DIFFICULT FOR SPEAKERS OF	NOTES
she̱ll	chell, jell	Arabic, Chinese, Korean, Spanish, Vietnamese	/sh/ does not exist in all languages. /ch/ substitutes for /sh/ and vice versa.
fi̱sh	fich		

and on the website that you can use to help your students practice these difficult sounds such as *shoe*, *ship*, *shell*, *shirt*, and *shark* along with *trash*, *brush*, *leash*, and *fish*.

Table 5.5 presents some of the more challenging sounds in English, how they may be pronounced, and common spelling errors. Following the introduction of the letter–sound correspondences, the letter name–alphabetic sorts on the website focus on working with these and other challenging sounds.

Vowels and the English Learner

Most languages have between 5 and 7 vowel sounds as well as vowel combinations such as diphthongs (Spanish, Hebrew, and Japanese have 5 vowel sounds; Romanian has 6), but English has 12. This means that many English learners will have a number of additional vowel sounds to master. In terms of spelling those sounds, there are 40 ways in which vowels can be combined in English. For example, the long *a* can be represented in the following ways: *play*, *mail*, *make*, *great*, and *weight*. The Spanish vowels are much more consistent than English across the various dialects and forms of Spanish (e.g., Mexican, Puerto Rican); in English different speakers around the world will pronounce vowels in different ways (e.g., American, British, Indian English), and even regionally as seen in differences in vowels from Vermont to California (Dalbor, 1997).

English learners use the letters from their first language to spell vowels in English. This is what Teresa did when she spelled long *a* with the letter–sound relationships from Spanish, her first language (train = TREIN and place = PLEIS). Figure 5.3 presents the vowel phonemes for American Spanish and English as they are made in the mouth. As noted in Figure 5.3, there are three areas laterally (front, center, and back) and three areas vertically: high with the mouth closed, mid with the mouth slightly open, and low with the mouth open. The five Spanish vowel sounds are underlined. The vowels in blue with arrows beside them are glides that combine two vowels. You can sense the two vowels as you say the vowels in the middles of these words slowly: *bait*, *bite*, *boy*, *how*, and *boat*. Spanish speakers do not have an equivalent for the following vowels in English: short *a* in *bat*, the short *e* in *bet*, the short *i* in *bit*, the short *u* in *but*, or the *oo* in *book*.

When a vowel sound does not exist in Spanish, students match the sounds in English to the closest sounds in Spanish. Table 5.6 presents some comparisons between English vowels and vowels in Spanish. These comparisons explain students' pronunciation and spelling errors.

When students who speak phonetically transparent languages are learning a new set of vowels, they may segment the vowel sound more thoroughly than native English speakers. For example, the long *a* and long *i* of English are diphthongs that involve a movement from one vowel sound to another: short *e* and long *e* for the long *a* and short *o* and long

The vowels in English are often different from the vowels in students' primary languages.

TABLE 5.5	**Examples of Challenging Consonant Sounds for English Learners**

ENGLISH SOUND		MAY BE PRONOUNCED	EXAMPLE SPELLING ERROR
d as in	den	then	DEM (them)
p	peel	beel	BET (pet)
j	joke	choke	GOB (job)
r	rope	(rolled r) rope, wope	WAIPEN (ripen)
v	van	ban	SURBING (serving)
z	zipper	sipper	SIVALAIS (civilize)
sh	shell	chell	CHED (shed)
th	thick	tick	TENK (think)
zh	treasure	treachure	CHESHER (treasure)
final *rd*	hard	har	HAR (hard)
final *st*	toast	tos	TOS (toast)
final *ng*	serving	servin'	SIRVIN (serving)
final *sk*	ask	as	AS (ask)
final *z*	prize	price	PRAES (prize)
final *t*	that	tha	THA (that)
final *mp*	bump	bumpa	BAMPA (bump)

FIGURE 5.3 Vowel Phonemes of General American English and Spanish. The five underlined phonemes exist both in American Spanish and English. The Spanish word examples are written in italics. The phonemes marked in color with an arrow (↑, ←) designate vowels that are glides with two or more sounds.

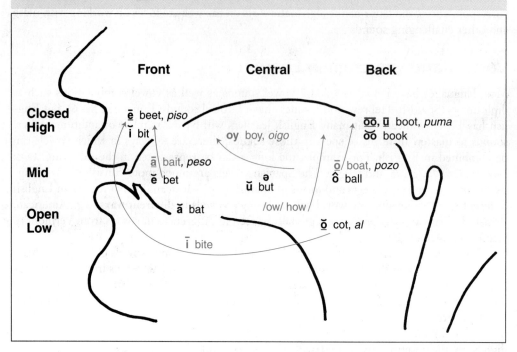

e for the long *i*. This fact may not be evident to native speakers but may show up in the spellings of English language learners. By saying words and sounds slowly as described in the next section, teachers come to understand how English learners analyze the vowels of English.

The Sequence of Word Study Instruction with English Learners

Students in the letter name–alphabetic stage learn the basic letter–sound correspondences for consonants and short vowels. The sequence of word study outlined in Table 5.7 takes into

Go to PDToolkit, choose your book, click the Sorts & Games tab, and select Letter Name–Alphabetic Stage from the Stage filter.

TABLE 5.6 Vowel Sounds in English and Spanish and Examples of Spelling Errors

ENGLISH LETTER AND WORD		COMPARABLE SPANISH LETTER AND WORD		EXAMPLE SPELLING ERROR
/ā/ as in	rake	*e* as in	hecho	CHEK (*shake*)
/ē/	green	*i*	ido	PIC (*peek*)
/ī/	bike	*ai*	aire	BAIT (*bite*)
/ō/	rope	*o*	ocho	FLOUT (*float*)
/o/	top	*a*	ajo	TAP (*top*)
/ū/	June	*u*	usted	FLUT (*flute*)

account how English may be influenced by the sound systems of students' primary languages. The scope and sequence for this stage is divided into three parts: early, middle, and late.

Letter name–alphabetic spellers match the sounds in words to the letters they know that may represent these sounds. Separating the speech stream of words into individual sounds is the focus of word study at this time. Picture sorts for beginning consonant sounds that are common to both English and their home language are the first area of study for early letter name–alphabetic spellers. After students learn beginning consonants, consonant digraphs are introduced with picture sorts. The goal is for students to appreciate that these digraphs make one sound such as /ch/ in the word *chin*. Mastery of these sounds will take some time and should be revisited in the study of word families and short vowels.

Students at the middle of this stage study **word families;** their attention focuses on the onset, or the beginning consonant sound, and the rime, or family (e.g., *b-at* or *b-ell*). Final sounds are emphasized in word study with English learners, beginning with very distinct final sound contrasts (*tan/top*) and proceeding to finer ones (the /d/ and /t/ sounds in *mad/fat*).

▶ **Word Families**

Phonograms or words that share the same rime as in *best, test,* and *rest.*

Parallel to studying word families, students look at English consonant blends and digraphs in words. Words that are difficult to depict in picture sorts are now accessible because students can read words with word family patterns, such as *-an* in *plan* or *-in* in *spin*. Many languages, including Russian, Spanish, and Chinese, do not share English blends and digraphs. English learners benefit from seeing the written words to cue them to differences in articulation among the contrasting sounds of English.

After examining one vowel and its rimes, students compare words across word families to make generalizations about each short vowel—for example, that the *a* in *sad* sounds and feels much the same as the *a* sound in *fan*. In making generalizations about short vowels in English, students become confident that the words *fan, bad, map,* and *pat* sound alike in the middle, especially when these words are sorted next to words like *fin, hid, lip,* and *pit*. Blends and digraphs are again included here and expand the number of words students can spell and read.

In the late letter name stage, students are introduced to the first pattern, the consonant-vowel-consonant (CVC) pattern. This is the first time students have analyzed the syllable structure of English, and from here on, the study of words in English will incorporate all three layers of the orthography: sound, pattern, and meaning. As part of this study, they come to see that words like *spin* and *club* represent the CVC pattern. Final consonant blends and digraphs are studied in words like *fast* and *dish*. At the end of this stage, students sort words by **preconsonantal nasal** endings as they hear and see them in words like *camp, stamp, blend,* and *blink*. Each step along the way, we feature contrasts that are important and useful to English learners as they study the distinctive sounds of English.

▶ **Preconsonantal Nasal**

A nasal sound (/m/, /n/, /ng/) that occurs before a consonant as in *bump* and *sink.*

Components of Literacy Instruction at the Letter Name–Alphabetic Stage

The framework of instruction for letter name–alphabetic spellers continues to build on the five RRWWT literacy activities: Read To, Read With, Write With, Word Study, and Talk With. In this section we outline how these essential literacy activities can be used at this stage. Table 5.7 presents a sequence of word study for English learners at this stage.

Talk With

Talking with students is crucial to language learning. Many of the activities presented in the emergent stage apply to beginning readers as well. Students profit from many opportunities to talk with partners, share in small groups, chant and sing along as a group, and engage in dialogue with others about their questions and new learning. Classroom structures should be set up to give all students time to share ideas and stories. The Sharing Stories routine

TABLE 5.7   **Sequence of Word Study for English Learners in the Letter Name–Alphabetic Stage in English**

FEATURES	EXAMPLES	INSTRUCTIONAL NOTES
Early		
Beginning and ending consonant sounds with pictures	Sort by beginning sounds. log/man/tire/pan ball/call, cup/lip Match pictures with letters and sight words.	Pronunciation of letter names is influenced by the sound contrasts in the primary language (e.g., *very* pronounced *berry*; *zipper* pronounced *sipper*). Final sounds may not be perceived and are omitted in pronunciation and spelling.
Consonant blends and digraphs	Sounds of consonant blends and digraphs are introduced. Picture sorts with *th, sh, ch, wh* Contrasts between substituted and target sounds are made in picture sorts (e.g., *sh/ch*). Picture and word sorts with known words broom/book/rock, truck /table/rain	Consonant blends and digraphs in English may not exist in the students' primary languages (e.g., several languages do not include *s* blends: *sl, sm, st*). Names of the pictures of words that begin with blends and digraphs are often unknown and are used for vocabulary instruction that includes concept sorts and accompanying discussion.
Middle		

Word families and ending sounds	Separate/segment beginning sounds from rimes among word families.
	  sad/man/cat
	  can/cat, jam/sad
	During sorts, student practices pronouncing final sounds of words.
		Ending sounds of CVC words may not be pronounced or may be confused with a similar sound that exists in the primary language.
		
		Final sounds /d/, /t/, /n/ may be omitted or replaced with similar sounds from students' primary languages.

Short vowels sounds and spelling: ă ŏ ĕ ĭ ŭ	Picture sorts to compare and contrast short and long vowel sounds.	Vowel confusions reflect unfamiliarity with English vowels.
Sounds within each vowel	can/cat/cab Picture sorts cat/cake, not/note	Correct spelling may reflect sound–symbol matches in the primary language and not in English
Sounds across vowel—CVC pattern	Compare and contrast short-vowel sounds and patterns. cat/hot/net/sit/cut	Word reading and sight vocabularies may be more advanced than students' understanding of letter–sound correspondences.
Consonant blends and digraphs	Contrast specific blends that are confused in sorting and writing (especially *s* blends) using word sorts with short vowels.	Students may be unfamiliar with final sounds in words if the primary language has mostly open syllables.
Late		
Continued letter–sound associations within and across short vowels	Picture and word sorts that compare and contrast vowel sounds influenced by the final sounds. bar/bat, ball/bat, can/set/hid Sort of final sounds (-ck, -ch, -sh, -th, -st, -ft)	Continue to learn to pronounce and spell ending sounds and difficult beginning sounds. Unfamiliar sounds may be overpronounced; for example, the individual letters of a blend may be sounded out with a vowel, especially the *s* blends spelled out as syllables. (CALIP for *clap*). /r/, /l/, and /w/ may be difficult for English learners to pronounce and substitutions are made based on the closest sounds in their primary language. More difficult beginning and final consonants are learned at this time as sight vocabularies contain more digraphs and blends.
Less frequent and complex consonant blends and digraphs, including preconsonantal nasals	black, catch, bump, stand, sing	Final sounds are still being learned and students substitute similar features; for example, *back* (unvoiced) spelled BAG (voiced), *bump* (unvoiced) as BUMB (voiced). Students with primary languages without ending consonant clusters will often leave one of the letters out.

described in Chapter 4's Activity 4.16 is an excellent way to encourage students to talk. Clearly, when teachers tell short stories to students, students in turn are more likely to tell their own stories.

Concept sorts with pictures and objects are engaging, and while students sort side by side with their classmates, they talk about what they are doing. Before putting away a sort or independent activity, have students explain to classmates what they did.

All creative activities including constructing, doing art, experimenting, and writing should incorporate talking with others. Structure classroom interactions so that students can share what they created with classmates. Thematic areas in the room might include sets for running a restaurant, operating a post office, working in an office, or managing an airport. Literacy props should be included in all sets so students can be shown how to make lists and menus, write letters, answer incoming calls, discuss flight plans, and so forth.

Teachers select key vocabulary words within thematic units and Read To experiences. These words should be discussed and used in lessons systematically so that they become familiar to students. Repeated exposures to key vocabulary words provide a model for students and motivation to use these words in expressing themselves. Post labels and lists of important words along with illustrations in the classroom; this will encourage students to use the words in their writing and artistic activities.

Creative dramatics is a way for students to use physical characterization along with the level of language with which they are comfortable. The repeated enactment of short scenes from a story gives English learners the practice they need to learn vocabulary. For example, groups of three to five students can dramatize one scene from a story with minimal props or rehearsal. The repeated lines of a good story serve as the script, and students can improvise as they use the refrain they remember in the story: "I'll huff and I'll puff, and I'll blow your house in." Some students may just huff and puff, and others may repeat one phrase, "I'll huff," and make the gesture. In creative dramatics all students have a way to participate and to be supported. Language play activities that support phonological awareness are also incorporated in jump rope and clapping games.

Read To

Read To activities provide access to rich language structures developed by real writers. Comprehension and interest are supported by the pictures and the reader's voice. Read To activities allow beginning readers to hear literate language that stimulates thinking and teaches them vocabulary and language structures of English. They can listen to stories that they may not be able to read, and they come to appreciate the phrasing and rhythm of language as they are soothed and challenged intellectually.

For older English learners, the stories they read at an instructional level may not be of intellectual interest or teach them the content vocabulary and information they need to participate in class discussions. Read To activities provide an opportunity to challenge and motivate students to think and to engage them with the content and vocabulary of their grade-level studies.

There are also cultural differences between what students hear and what they experience in their own lives. Folktales from students' home cultures are a way to engage some students with repetitive themes and language that support memory.

Picture books are a springboard for expanded explanations of concepts and vocabulary; the illustrations can clarify the language of the text. The repeated use of vocabulary in meaningful ways makes learning possible for many English learners. Asking students to point to the pictures of their favorite parts in a book is a way for them to participate and for the teacher to model important vocabulary words. Teachers may ask students to show the group the pictures as a way of responding to a question about the text. Students can also draw their own pictures, which can be used to support a beginning conversation. The picture is a prop that helps students explain what they think of a story or have learned from content materials.

Students use pictures in texts to support what they say.

Ideas for literature connections for specific consonants and vowel sounds are included in this chapter's activities section so that teachers can review phonemic awareness and teach letter–sound correspondences through high-quality read-aloud books. To keep close tabs on comprehension, use teaching practices that encourage some form of student response. Monitor comprehension while the reading is ongoing instead of waiting until the end of the reading to see if students are making meaning with the text.

Perhaps the most useful activity for teaching and monitoring comprehension is the Directed Listening–Thinking Activity, the DL-TA. To prepare for the DL-TA, find three or four stopping points in a book where you can pause and ask students what they think is going on and what they believe is going to happen next. The following questions are asked of students in Read To activities for narrative and expository materials. Notice how the questions change according to the materials that are read:

- *Narrative DL-TA:* (1) Predict: "What do you think will happen?" (2) Read to the students to the next stopping point. (3) Check predictions and make a new round of predictions: "What do you think will happen next?"

- *Content DL-TA:* (1) Predict what the text will be about: "What do you know about this topic?" and "What do you want to know?" (2) Read to the next stopping point and check for what was learned: "Did we find out what we wanted to know?" "What did we learn?" (3) Predict again: "What will we learn next?" and "What do we want to know?"

In both types of DL-TAs, comprehension is monitored throughout the reading. Students' discussions of what they hear are a way to teach them to think and question as they read. For students who are not able to communicate much in English, the teacher gives a few choices and students choose among the possibilities.

Read With

Read With activities include tailored reading materials and support reading practices for students.

Read With activities for beginning readers include support reading practices in concert with support reading materials. Support reading practices include choral, echo, repeated, guided, partner, and follow-along reading activities of all kinds. These are described in the activities that follow. Support reading materials include easy rhymes, leveled and decodable texts, dictations, short poems or ditties, and songs.

Personal Readers are used to collect materials that students reread for practice in fluency and word recognition. Rhymes and dictations are the most commonly included texts in Personal Readers with early and middle-level beginning readers.

Dictations are an incredible tool for teachers to use with English learners of all ages at this developmental level. The teacher records on a chart or a page in the Personal Reader what the student dictates as an account of an experience or thought. Numerous activities later in this chapter describe how to collect and use dictations with students.

Why do we take dictations from beginning readers? There are several reasons why Personal Readers contain individual dictations even when many leveled or decodable texts are available. Consider these uses of dictations:

1. *Authorship.* Students compose texts of greater length and coherency than they might have if they were writing on their own. Dictations are a bridge to independent writing and reading.

2. *Creation of interesting materials.* There is an inherent interest in what students themselves create. Dictations are an ideal way to create reading materials for English learners in the beginning reading stage.

3. *Harvest words for word banks.* By rereading their dictations, students acquire a store of words they can recognize automatically, but it is important also to take the words out of

context to examine in isolation. Words that students have learned are written on cards to store in a **word bank** for review over time. These known words can also be used in word study activities such as sorts and word hunts. Word banks can be discontinued when students are in the middle part of the letter name–alphabetic stage and have a sight vocabulary of 150 words or more. Studying word families will add to this number.

4. *Rereading dictations promotes reading fluency and expression.* Because students create the dictations they remember them more easily; the familiar language patterns promote fluency for these beginning readers.

5. *Support in content area studies.* When students dictate about a subject they have been studying in class, they strengthen their understanding of the subject matter.

FIGURE 5.4 Personal Reader with Word Bank

6. *Opportunities for sharing.* Students can reread their dictations to their classmates. With content to share, students' motivation increases and their interest in literacy and new ideas grow.

▶ **Word Banks**

A collection of known sight words students keep for word study.

As can be seen in the illustration in Figure 5.4, Personal Readers can include lists of what students read, sight word lists, and student copies of little books for rereading.

Creating reading materials from students' dictations is also an informal assessment of their oral language resources (Bear & Barone, 1998). When students dictate their language experiences, oral language development works hand in hand with its written production. The Personal Reader Activities in the Activities section of this chapter describe a variety of ways to develop Personal Reader routines. Bilingual dictations are one adaptation of the step-by-step process. For students who are just learning English, bilingual readers that contain dictations written in both the home language and in English are presented with the activities.

Write With

Beginning readers and writers should write every day and often draw pictures to accompany what they write. Move around the room and check in with students as they write to support them as they shape their ideas, and help them as they find the letters for the words. With the support of sound boards (Appendix, pp. 257–260), show students the letters and their sounds. Figure 5.5 shows the sound board for beginning consonants.

In addition to helping students talk about what they want to write, teachers can provide support for Write With activities by suggesting writing frames in which students fill in just one or two words. In this way, reading materials are created because so much of the text is already printed on the page, and there is less of a burden on the students to write. Also, English learners can learn valuable language structures by following the patterned sentences. Some of the language patterns found in picture books are easily

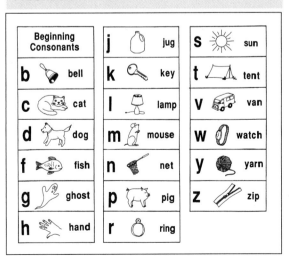

FIGURE 5.5 Sound Board

Beginning Consonants		
b bell	j jug	s sun
c cat	k key	t tent
d dog	l lamp	v van
f fish	m mouse	w watch
g ghost	n net	y yarn
h hand	p pig	z zip
	r ring	

adapted; students enjoy making their own versions of *Brown Bear, Brown Bear* (Martin, 1970) by just changing the animals. More complex patterns to draw on are found in picture books and in poetry guides like Kenneth Koch's *Wishes, Lies and Dreams* (Koch, 1999). A more complex frame is *I used to be . . . , but now I am . . .*

The important point in writing with English learners is to get them to do plenty of it and to focus on meaningful topics. When teachers respect students' bilingual writing, students mature and grow and are able to express themselves in many **registers** as they master standard usage and mechanics. Separate activities geared to writing mechanics can be built from meaningful pieces of writing that you may publish in the class. In editing sessions, students can work on specific features such as capital letters at the beginnings of sentences and ending punctuation.

Reading and writing have a reciprocal relationship. Reading makes students better writers, and their vocabulary and spelling knowledge also grow as they read. Reciprocally, writing improves reading as students become more thoughtful readers. Opportunities to write improve students' orthographic knowledge in reading. Among beginning readers, growth in word recognition substantially improves reading rate—from a word-by-word approach to reading in phrases.

Interactive writing in small groups is a way to teach many composing and spelling skills. The teacher guides the writing lesson on a chart or whiteboard as students dictate or come forward to contribute to the chart writing. Students can be given their own whiteboards or sheets of paper on which to record the developing text. This is more meaningful than copying the sentences later because they are an active part of constructing the message.

Sometimes the student and teacher trade off between writing and dictating. Some writing projects start with students dictating the first two sentences and then taking over the writing themselves. Another quick-write type of activity involves partners passing the writing back and forth to create a short story. These activities are discussed in detail in the Personal Reader activities later in this chapter.

Word Study

Letter name–alphabetic spellers need a steady diet of systematic word study to shepherd them through the sequence of skills outlined in Table 5.7. After you have assessed your students using the spelling inventory described in Chapter 2, you can form developmental groups so that students begin their word study clustered at the level in which they will best learn. Word study with letter name–alphabetic spellers may be built into your small-group guided reading with 10 to 15 minutes per day set aside for word sorts or activities. Or your word study may take place during a "skills" block when all students are engaged in sorting, word hunts, games, and other activities at their assessed levels. However you structure your word study, the following guidelines are important to keep in mind.

1. *Sort for sound before sorting by sight.* Picture sorts during this stage focus attention on the sounds in the words. Student's phonemic awareness will continue to develop throughout the letter name stage as they listen for blends and vowels. Too often, when sorting words, students use visual cues to sort before thinking through the sound similarities among words. For example, when students hunt for words that sound like *cake*, at the beginning they may choose a word like *cents* from their word bank simply because *cents* begins with a *c*.

    Sound sorts are important supports to students learning about vowel sounds. After establishing a solid understanding of the common short vowel families, students can study the more difficult vowel contrasts such as short *e* and short *i*. In English, the sound contrasts between short vowels are subtle and some contrasts are harder than others. When students read through a sort like the one presented in Figure 5.6, they hear themselves and their classmates say the words, and this helps them make generalizations about sounds in English. The visual differences lead students to think about sound differences.

Sidebar notes

▶ **Registers**
The way language systems like prosody, syntax, semantics, and pragmatics present a specific style in social situations for a particular effect. Baby talk, high society, courtroom, and texting registers are just a few examples.

▶ **Interactive Writing**
A shared writing process in which the teacher elicits help in encoding the message from the students.

Sorts and word study activities teach students to make important contrasts among the sounds of consonants and vowels in English.

FIGURE 5.6 Short *o* and Short *a* Word Family Sort

top	sat	?
dot	hat	ball
pot	can	do
mop	mad	

In this book we have structured the sequence of vowel study so that the most difficult contrasts occur after the easier ones.

2. *Students say the words as they sort.* During this stage, articulatory information is quite useful to students. It is also useful for teachers to hear how students pronounce words. Sounds omitted in pronunciation may not be attended to when sorting or writing. Listen for how students say the words and for particular sounds that are hard to pronounce.

3. *Develop routines to identify and teach word meanings over repeated lessons with each new sort.* Sorts begin with naming the pictures or reading the words in the sort. Independently or with the teacher, students set aside words they do not know (and ideally there should just be a few words set aside). These two or three words are revisited after the initial sort. The repeated sorting of the pictures can help students learn all the corresponding words.

   English learners and other students may not know the meanings of words in a sort, yet are able to complete the sort using the visual patterns in the words. If they read the words accurately, it may be difficult to know which meanings they do not know. In their reading of connected texts, students demonstrate through phrasing and expression their understanding of the text and word meanings, but in isolation it is more difficult for teachers to detect the words students may not understand. Throughout the week, use the meanings of several of the words in the sorts. Repeated use in word study activities helps students learn the meanings of many of the words, even words that they can already read.

   As you sort with students, ask them what words they do not know, and choose a few words to study that are unknown and can be taught through repeated uses of the word. Choose words that can be surrounded by conversation. Ask students to use the words in a sentence on a chart or in an individual dictation. Students can also illustrate words with small pictures on the front or back of a word card or in a word study notebook.

Routines for sorting on a weekly basis are presented in Chapter 3

4. *Teach word meanings through multiple exposures.* To plan for multiple exposures, consider these questions: How many times will students hear and use the words that are being taught? Will students hear the words every day? Will the words be used in a made-up sentence or in natural conversation? Are there body movements that can be acted out, or connections made to characters in texts? Can students draw something that incorporates some of the words? Will students have a chance to use the words in a partner or small-group activity? At the letter name level of development, it is important to teach the words that students will frequently use and encounter in their reading.

   Enlist all students as Word Watchers who find ways to teach and learn new vocabulary. Students develop an eye and ear for new words and where they saw and heard the words. What better way to learn about a word than through examples from friends? Second grade students in this stage can write the words on charts with classmates when they hunt for words independently and in small groups.

5. *Pacing word study instruction.* As students work through the numerous sorts in this chapter, choose a level of pacing that fits each group. Three levels of pacing can be considered: introductory, moderate, and fast.

   At the introductory level, the number of categories is reduced and students start with large contrasts. Once the larger contrasts have been made, finer discriminations are presented. For example, with beginning consonants, a large contrast would be to sort pictures that begin with the /b/ and /s/ sounds, compared to a picture sort for the beginning sounds of /b/ and /p/.

   At a moderate pace, students start with large contrasts and more quickly move to two- and three-column sorts. At a fast pace, students already can make the larger contrasts and are ready to begin the finer contrasts needed for English learners.

Word Study Lesson Plan Format

Four steps comprise the word study lesson plan and the many word study sorts presented in the upcoming Activities section incorporate this lesson plan format.

MATERIALS.　Prepare a sort to use for modeling on a table, floor, document camera, or pocket chart. Some teachers enlarge the sort so the pictures and words are easier to see. Also prepare sorts for individual children or partners. These can be copies of the sort for them to cut apart and sort on their own. Some teachers prepare sorts ready for students to use when they gather in their small groups and they may sort along with the teacher during the demonstration.

DEMONSTRATE IN THE GROUP.　The teacher demonstrates the sort to the students and enlists their participation with a teacher-directed sort.

1. Introduce the words or pictures to highlight any vocabulary students might not understand. Name each picture and get students to repeat the words after you: "This is a belt; say belt. Who would wear a belt?"
2. Introduce the categories: "Today we will sort pictures by the beginning sound (or final sound or vowel sound, etc.)." Point out the key word and establish it as the header for the category: "Ball begins with *B*. Listen—ball. We will put other words under here that start with *B*." Show students how to first say the word to sort and then compare it to the first key picture or word; do the same for each column. With word families, you may want to sort the word by the visual pattern and then read down from the top to identify the word.
3. Model how to sort several words in each category and then ask students to help you sort the rest: "Who can find another word to put under *B?*"
4. When students become experienced sorters teachers may use an open sort or student-centered sort. Students are asked to come up with their own categories and then to explain why they sorted as they did.

SORT AND CHECK.　After sorting show students how to check the sort by naming the pictures or words in each category to determine how they are alike, which will also reinforce new vocabulary. This is a good time for students to use the words in the sort in conversations that reinforce new vocabulary. Students can look for words after being given a clue, for instance: "Find a word that is something that might help you get to school. It has wheels." (bus)

REFLECT.　In the reflect step, the teacher helps students listen for sounds or look for patterns as a way to talk about how the words in each category are alike. This discussion can begin with an open-ended question such as, "How are these words alike?"

INDIVIDUAL SORTING.　After the demonstration sort students or student pairs sort a set of word or picture cards, followed by the check and reflect steps. Show students how to cut apart their words or pictures and store them in a baggie or envelope. For identification, students draw colored lines (students should use a different color from others in their group or at their table) down the back of the sorting page before cutting.

Ask students to set up headers with the same key words used in the demonstration sort. They can then work alone or with a partner to sort into categories, naming the words or pictures aloud as they sort. Teaching students to share vocabulary knowledge with each other can be an important support. They should set aside words they cannot name. Ask students to check their sorts and then ask, "Why did you sort the pictures this way? How are these words alike?" Students tell the group why they sorted the way they did.

After sorting instruct students to shuffle or mix up the word cards and store them in a baggie to use the next day. Often the words are in order from the previous sort, and without shuffling, the sort may be too easy. For repeated practice, students sort again at their seats or in centers; enter the sort in their word study notebooks; hunt for related words; play games together; chart collections of related words and pictures for sound, spelling, and meaning; and practice the sort and play word study games at home.

The rest of this chapter outlines numerous activities for use in your word study program: picture and word sorts, multi-use games and activities for working with words and sounds, and Personal Readers.

ACTIVITIES
FOR ENGLISH LEARNERS IN THE LETTER NAME–ALPHABETIC STAGE

Activities are provided for this stage that complement the fundamental endeavors presented as RRWWT. The activities are numbered and organized under the following basic headings: Picture Concept Sorts, Multi-Use Word Study Activities, Working with Words and Sounds, Personal Reader Activities, and Picture and Word Sorts and Related Games.

Picture Concept Sorts

Concept sorts are for learners at all ages if the concepts are interesting and relevant to students. The directions for the first sort, the occupation sort, illustrate in detail how to present sorts. Teaching notes are included for the other picture concept sorts. Be sure to introduce the process of sorting by an easy sort with just two columns: pictures of objects that fit the pattern and those that do not.

Picture concept sorts do not require reading, and students may complete the sort without knowing English. Everyone can participate. Concept sorts are particularly effective with older English learners because they are conceptual. The activities to extend are also adaptable to adult interests and learning needs. Through concept sorts students share their ideas, and through discussions and explicit instruction students learn new content vocabulary.

5.1 Occupation and Tool Concept Picture Sort: Librarian, Construction Worker, Doctor

This sort features a collection of vocabulary words associated with occupations and the tools they use. Students sort objects associated with being a librarian, construction worker, or doctor. The completed sort using the key words should look something like Figure 5.7.

MATERIALS. Make copies of the Occupation and Tool Concept Picture Sort (Sort 10) from the website. Have students cut the figures apart and place them in envelopes or small plastic bags.

FIGURE 5.7 Occupation and Tool Concept Sort

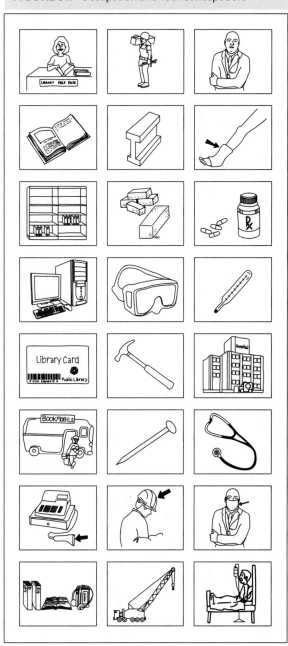

PDToolkit
for Words Their Way™
with English Learners

Go to PDToolkit, choose your book, click the Sorts & Games tab, and search for "Sort 10: Occupation and Tool Concept Picture Sort."

PDToolkit
for Words Their Way™
with English Learners

Go to PDToolkit, choose your book, click the Sorts & Games tab, and search for "Sort 3: Occupations Picture Sort."

PDToolkit
for Words Their Way™
with English Learners

Go to PDToolkit, choose your book, click the Sorts & Games tab, and search for "Sort 11: Matter and Weight Concept Picture Sort: Light, Medium, Heavy." Or click on Create Your Own!

DEMONSTRATE. Review the pictures with the students prior to the actual sort. Students may also review the picture cards with partners before they begin. Choose three or four highly useful unknown pictures to introduce as new vocabulary. Think of things that are likely to be used in classroom conversations or texts when deciding on which words are most important to study. Practice saying the words, acting them out, or using them in student-friendly sentences.

Introduce the key or guide pictures: librarian, construction worker, and doctor. Identify pictures associated with each, such as books, brick, or hospital, and talk about how they fit. "Librarians have many books in the library. Construction workers build with bricks. Doctors help people in a hospital." Use a few examples from each category to demonstrate the sort, explaining why you sorted the way you did through a think-aloud.

SORT, CHECK, AND REFLECT. Students shuffle their pictures and repeat the sort under your supervision. Have students check their sorts by naming the occupation and the pictures in the column underneath.

As a reflection, ask students to explain why they sorted the way they did. Have them make up their own sentences to indicate the connections between the items and occupations; for example, a librarian checks out books. Consider having students draw a picture that shows how an object is related to the occupation. After drawing, students can label the occupation and tools and write a sentence or caption to go with the picture.

EXTEND. There are many activities to accompany this sort that give repeated exposure to the vocabulary and concepts presented. See the Occupations Picture Sort (Sort 3) on the website.

- Students hunt through magazines and newspapers for pictures of people involved in occupations and workplaces along with objects associated with the job. They cut them out and paste them on a poster board with their classmates or create a page of their own—for example, collections of furniture for a furniture store or groceries for a grocery store.
- Students hunt through their word bank and familiar reading materials for words that are related to occupations—for example, *car, mother, book.*
- In pairs or small groups, students research additional occupations. New sorts can be created based on their findings.
- Encourage home and school connections by having students research their parents' or family members' occupations.
- Extend by inviting guest speakers to share the tools from their professions—for example, office staff, car repair, plumbing.
- Provide occupation-related informational texts for students to skim through to add additional items to the list.
- Provide visual dictionaries appropriate for the age group.
- Search online for occupation-related information and pictures.
- The following occupations are examples that students can explore, depending on age and experience: accountant, auto worker, baker, cashier, clergy, construction worker, designer, farmer or other agriculturally related occupation, food and beverage occupation, guard, homemaker, landscaper, medical professions, mining, painter, roofer, soldier, teacher, tile setter, truck driver, upholsterer.

5.2 Matter and Weight Concept Picture Sort: Light, Medium, Heavy Sort Activity

This sort features a collection of vocabulary associated with matter and weight. The pictures can be sorted by weight using the "Goldilocks rule": light, medium/just right, and heavy.

DEMONSTRATE, SORT, AND CHECK. Make copies of Sort 11 on the website, or select a variety of pictures from the Pictures for Sorts and Games beginning on page 262 in the Appendix or on the website. These pictures should represent objects that are light, medium, or heavy. Arrange these pictures on a sorting template using the blank template for sorting on page 331 of the Appendix or on the website. Introduce the guide words and ask students to name the objects that are light, medium/just right, or heavy. Have students work with partners to sort and check.

REFLECT AND EXTEND. After sorting, discuss the weights of the objects—for example, "I know a feather is light because my baby sister can pick it up." Students can add to the list by hunting for magazine pictures that illustrate light, medium/just right, and heavy objects. Students reflect by drawing a picture to illustrate the amount of muscle needed to lift an object. Students extend by thinking of their own examples of comparisons and opposites; for example, a balloon is light and a television is heavy. Encourage home–school connections by having students make a list of examples for each category in their homes.

5.3 Electricity Concept Picture Sort: Uses or Does Not Use Electricity Sort

This sort features a collection of vocabulary words associated with tools that require or do not require electricity. Use Sort 12 on the website or make your own sort using Pictures for Sorts and Games from the Appendix or website.

Discuss the tools and whether or not they require electricity; for example, "A vacuum needs electricity to run because I have to plug it in before I use it."

Multi-Use Word Study Activities

The following activities serve as a foundation for the sorts discussed in this chapter. These activities are integral to word study because they give students the practice they need to learn the principles that underlie the picture and word sorts in this chapter.

5.4 Literature Links

Throughout the activities, literature links are presented. These links are sometimes the center of the activity, and at other times the literature is for the pleasure of the students' ears. This word play reinforces phonemic awareness and phonics instruction. Literature links are also presented in Figure 5.16 (pp. 138–140).

5.5 Build, Blend, Extend

This is an activity to reinforce words studied through sorts and introduce blending as a decoding strategy.

MATERIALS. Make two types of cards from the website—letter cards with initial consonant sounds such as *s* or *f*, and word family cards such as *at* and *ad* for students to manipulate, as in Figure 5.8. Specific letter and word family cards will vary depending on the focus of your lesson. The teacher should have an enlarged set of the cards to demonstrate with during the lesson and students should each have their own set to build, blend, and extend.

PROCEDURES. Words are *built* with letter and family cards; each word is said slowly to *blend* the sounds, and then related words are made in a similar fashion to *extend* learning. For example, the teacher might show the *ip* and *ill* word family cards with a collection of initial sounds such as *s, b, m, l, tr,* and *sl*. The teacher calls out a familiar word like *sip* and asks a student to build the word with the cards. She might then change the beginning sound to /l/ and ask students to blend the sounds together.

FIGURE 5.8 Build, Blend, Extend

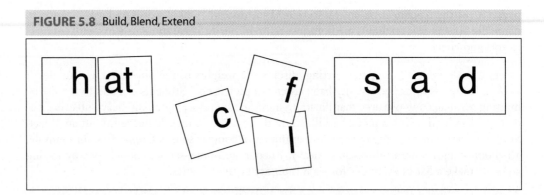

After numerous words have been built with the word families, individual letter cards can be used to help students understand sound contrasts to clarify pronunciation and spelling. For example, after studying the short *a* word families, the contrast between words that end with *t* and *d* can be made (*hat/had*).

After doing the Build, Blend, and Extend activity with the teacher, students in a rotating game format ask each other to make words—for instance, "Make the word *cap.*"

EXTENSION. Extend the activity to consonant blends such as *tr* and *sl* or other sounds that were not part of students' word study sorts. Magnetic letter boards and whiteboards can be used in this activity after the students make words with the cards or as an alternate activity.

5.6 Word and Picture Hunts

Word and picture hunts are the easiest and some of the most enjoyable word study activities. Students simply hunt for words that are related, either by common sounds, spelling patterns, or meanings. Students hunt for words in their word banks or in familiar reading materials. They may hunt for pictures in magazines in the classroom. The words can be written on cards and added to sorts, or pictures and words can be pasted to a bulletin board as a group activity.

5.7 Word Study Notebooks

Word study notebooks (Figure 5.9) are ongoing individual collections of sorts students have completed. In the early part of the letter name–alphabetic stage, the notebooks may be used to paste pictures from students' sorts as culminating activities, for collections of pictures students have drawn, or for words from their word banks that sound alike (e.g., at the beginning, end, or middle). Later in the stage, word study notebooks are a place to write words in categories that have been sorted, including students' collections of word families (*can, fan, ran*), and later for short vowel words across families (*can, bat, nap*). Words that students find in word hunts can also be recorded in the appropriate categories. If students write their sorts in a word study notebook, the words they find in their word hunts are added to the correct columns in the sorts.

FIGURE 5.9 Word Study Notebook

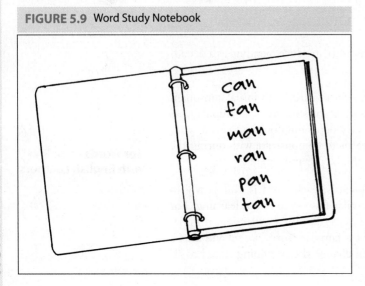

5.8 Word Watchers

English learners and their teachers watch for interesting and important words to learn or teach. Knowledge of word meaning is not taken for granted—teachers ask students what words they do not know, and they encourage students to ask for the meanings of the unknown words they hear or see. When students become self-aware about their comprehension and feel comfortable asking for information, they will be less likely to pass over unknown words, and their vocabulary learning will expand in meaningful ways. The selected words may be common, everyday words or they may be words related to content areas. Picture concept sorting is a good way to introduce vocabulary. English learners can easily participate in concept sorts as they learn new English vocabulary.

5.9 Writing Sorts

Writing sorts are excellent sorts for students from the middle of this stage onward. Instead of using the letters in Build, Blend, Extend, students write the words on their own. The sort begins with the teacher writing the key words on a whiteboard for the students to copy. The teacher or a partner calls out a word and the students write the word underneath the correct key word and column, as in Figure 5.10.

FIGURE 5.10 Example of a Writing Sort

can	stand	stamp
tan	band	camp
plan	hand	
	land	

Working with Words and Sounds

5.10 Collecting Sight Words for My Word Bank

Students enjoy being involved in sight word record-keeping activities. This activity includes a chart to help students practice words they add to their word banks.

Students develop a word bank, or collection of words on cards, that they know at sight. A list of these sight words is kept on a record page with lines spaced appropriately to the age of your group (see example record page on the website). These sight words can come from many places: lists of the sight words your district uses for grade-level benchmarks, words students find hunting through familiar reading materials found in the school, and words in their Personal Readers.

Use the teaching chart in Figure 5.11 to show students how words can be learned. The three steps of the teaching chart show students that reading and knowing the meanings of words are important parts of harvesting sight words.

Words that are recognized quickly and easily as sight words are written onto word cards, or "chips." These words are also written onto a record sheet like the Words in My Word Bank form from the website to help students record and review their sight words. If kept carefully, this record sheet is a way to monitor progress.

The record sheet can be kept in the front of students' Personal Readers and used periodically for students to review these sight words. The teacher records the dates on which students read through their words. After several such sessions, students can check each other as they review sight words in their word banks.

for Words Their Way™ with English Learners

Go to PDToolkit, choose your book, click the Additional Resources tab, and select Words in My Word Bank Chart.

FIGURE 5.11 Teaching Chart to Add Words to the Words in My Word Bank Record Sheet

1. I **read** and **say** the word.

2. I **think** the word.

3. I **know** and **practice** the word.

5.11 Names I Know

The Names I Know activity gives students practice with classmates' names that they know how to read. Say a name and ask students to focus on the beginning sound of the name: "What letter do you hear or feel at the beginning when you say the name?" Model how to write the word and place it on an alphabetic Name Chart or in a pocket chart.

A pocket chart or Velcro board accommodates changes in the class roster and shows various ways to group words when needs arise. A second way to reference names could be a seating chart with the names of the students positioned where each child sits. This is also a good way to help students learn about mapping. Names can also be added to the word bank.

Students hunt for names that begin or end with the same letters as in their own names. Baby naming books hold special fascination for many learners at school and home, especially when there is a new arrival in someone's family.

5.12 Sound Board Activities

Sound boards are used widely during the letter name–alphabetic stage to introduce and review letter–sound correspondences. Students use the sound boards in their word study and in their writing when they look for letter–sound correspondences to spell.

for Words Their Way™ with English Learners

Go to PDToolkit, choose your book, click the Additional Resources tab, and search for "Sound Boards."

MATERIALS. Sound boards for beginning consonants, consonant digraphs and blends, and vowels are found in the Appendix on pages 257–260 and on the website. Enlarge, color, and post these charts at eye level for students to refer to in word study and writing.

Teachers can also make copies of the sound boards students are currently studying and attach them to desks in the reading group area, or have students paste their own copies inside their Personal Readers. Reduce the sound boards on a copy machine to 3 inches by 5 inches (see Figure 5.5).

PROCEDURES. Introduce sounds and pictures for sorting. The sound board is a place to introduce letter–sound correspondences. For example, the following sentence frame introduces the letter *L*: "Let's find the letter *L*. We see the key picture is a picture of a lamp. Let's say lamp—l-l-lamp. What's the first sound? Yes, the word *lamp* begins with the /l/ sound."

This is also a good time to introduce the pictures that will be used for /l/ in sorting, helping English learners develop vocabulary. From here there are any number of sound contrasts and word hunts to pursue. Sound sorts are included in this chapter and in Chapter 4. Extend the sound within the words while showing the pictures to the students.

Sound boards are used to show contrasts to students. For example, after studying the /r/ and /l/ sounds separately, students contrast these sounds at the beginnings and ends of words.

To examine the sounds at the beginning, students use two fingers to point to contrasts as they hear them: "I am going to say two words. If they sound the same, put both fingers on the same letter. If you hear two different sounds, put a finger on each sound. Let's try one. Listen for the beginning sounds. Where will you put your fingers? Ray/rabbit. Yes, both fingers would be on the *r* with the picture of the ring. Now let's try another. Ray/lake. Yes, one finger is on the picture of the ring and the other is on the picture of the lamp." In a short period, the students may make 10 to 12 contrasts.

Personal Reader Activities

Personal Readers are a place for students to store familiar materials that they read on their own or that they use in word study activities. Review the Read With section earlier in this chapter (pp. 120–121) for guidelines on using Personal Readers with English learners.

The activities included here provide instructions on how to collect and read the materials. Four types of Personal Reader entries are presented in Activities 5.13 through 5.17: (1) familiar rhymes, poems, and easy readings; (2) student dictations about personal experiences as illustrated in the Salad Bowl (Activity 5.15); (3) bilingual Personal Readers and dictations; and (4) content dictations to summarize informational material.

For repeated practice, students receive the support they need in partner reading in mixed-ability groups or with a recording. Teach partners, tutors, and parents how to choral read with students. Explain to students that in choral reading, the helping partner reads alongside in a soft voice. When the reading slows with many errors, the helping partner uses a stronger voice. In support reading, the helping partner listens and gives support as needed. We suggest that helping partners wait for three seconds before telling readers the word. In support reading, the reader can tap the helping partner on the arm when assistance is requested. In practice sessions, brainstorm with students what they would do to help a classmate who is having difficulty. These instructions will change with development. Early beginning readers need choral support and sometimes phrase guiding in which the teacher or table partner reads a little ahead when word recognition slows reading to a crawl. These same practices can be used at home; encourage students to teach family members to give them the type of support that has been modeled in class.

5.13* Rhymes and Poems

This activity involves a four-day cycle for using rhymes and poems within Personal Readers. It is important for materials to be short and memorable so students can reread the materials independently after a few practice sessions.

MATERIALS. An easy poem, rhyme, or ditty is selected according to students' instructional levels and the utility of the language pattern. Enlarge the text or type the text in a 26-point font size with double spacing between words and lines. For early beginning readers, the text should range from one or two lines to selections that are several lines long and may be the equivalent of two stanzas. Bilingual texts offer tremendous support to students as they learn English. A book like *¡Pío Peep!* (Ada, Campoy, & Schertle, 2003) has traditional poems from Spanish language cultures that include rhymes and songs with great appeal. A middle letter name speller can read a poem like Sendak's "For September" in *Chicken Soup with Rice* (1991a). Make adjustments according to the developmental level of students. The adjustments are related to the length and complexity of the materials. Transitional readers may also use these materials as they practice fluency and expression.

The materials in the Personal Readers of late beginning and early transitional readers include passages for students to practice phrasal and expressive reading. Two- and three-stanza poems are added to Personal Readers, and the teacher conducts fluency lessons that focus on reading with expression and thinking through the ways comprehension is embedded in the prosodic reading. Examples of instructional materials for fluency and expression include poems from Shel Silverstein, Jack Prelutsky, and from books like *101 Science Poems and Songs for Young Learners* (Goldish, 1999), as well as selections from students' reading series.

PROCEDURES

Day 1. Introduce the poem and read it to students, enjoying the rhythm and rhyme. Read it again, pointing to the words as you speak. Have students recite along with you in a choral fashion. If students need more support have them echo read. You say one line at a time and then students repeat. Then give students their own copy of the poem so they can follow along, pointing to the words as you read together chorally. Discuss the meaning of no more than three or four unknown words. They may also choose words that they found fun to say or that had an interesting meaning.

*Carol Caserta-Henry co-authored this activity in the Nevada REA Personal Reader Project.

Days 2 to 4

1. Reread the poem chorally as students follow along on their own copy. Work on expressive reading according to the mood and tone of the poem using different voices: a happy voice, sad voice, an upset voice, whisper voice, and so forth. When appropriate, dramatize the poem by acting it out or assign lines or stanzas to individual readers for a more dramatic effect as in reader's theater.

2. For early letter name spellers, cut the poem into sentence strips and have the students rebuild it in a pocket chart. Individual copies can also be cut into strips.

3. Go on a word hunt. With a partner, students find words in the poem that fit the sounds or patterns they are studying for word study. Ask students to find high-frequency words and underline words they want to add to their word bank.

5.14 Routine Activities with Personal Reader Selections

The following ideas encourage repeated reading of familiar materials with the dictations and familiar rhymes in students' Personal Readers. These suggestions will help you to develop a repertoire of Personal Reader activities.

1. As you collect contributions to a group experience chart, encourage students to share a sentence that adds a new idea to the chart. A description of this process is presented in Chapter 4 and described in Activity 5.15.

2. As you read chorally, modulate your voice through volume and pacing so that you give students the support they need to reread the materials with modest fluency.

3. Make three copies of each new entry in the Personal Reader: one for the Personal Reader, one for the student to take home, and one as a backup or to use after students cut stories up to rearrange and reread.

4. Allow time for students to read their dictations to two different partners in the small group to improve fluency and rate. Have students keep a tally at the bottom of each page to record every time they read a selection.

5. Develop a checking system for home reading. Family members listen to the student read and then do one of the following: Sign the sheet in the front of the Personal Reader; put their initials on the back of the page read; or make a tick mark on the bottom to show it was reread.

6. As a group, use waxed sticky strips, colored cellophane strips, or highlighters to identify interesting words. Focus on features related to students' development. For example, emergent and early beginning readers focus on high frequency words (*the, is, can, was*) and words with particular beginning consonants.

7. Students use the entries in their Personal Readers to collect sight words for their word banks. Ask students to underline words they know. Check to see if they know the words and then make word cards for each. Sometimes students like to write their own word bank cards. Make a clean set of blank cards for the students. Students can write their own word cards to use at their desks or at home.

8. Unknown words that are not harvested can be deposited in a class word bank, a home for unknown words.

9. Word hunts within the Personal Readers are the most common word study activity with early and middle-level beginning readers. Students should hunt for words that have the same sound as the feature they are studying.

10. Give students two copies of their dictation typed in very large type. Students cut apart the words of one copy and match them to the intact copy, as in Figure 5.12.

FIGURE 5.12 Cut-Up Sentence

5.15 Group or Individual Dictations: Salad Bowl, an Example of Student-Dictated Personal Experience

Salad Bowl is an example of a student language experience activity. In individual and group dictations, students talk about an experience they have had, such as cutting up fruit to make a salad, and new vocabulary is introduced and used. After the language experience with the fruit or vegetables, students dictate statements about the experience that the teacher records. Vary the length of the dictations from one sentence for early letter name–alphabetic spellers to two paragraphs for middle letter name–alphabetic spellers. The steps to follow for this activity encourage memorable dictations and can be adapted for other experiences.

MATERIALS. Vegetables or fruits for the salad. Materials to record students' dictations written on a chart, on an individual page, or typed on a word processor in 26-point font. Salad Bowl is a flexible activity that can include many ways to examine vegetables and fruits.

PROCEDURES

Day 1

- Engage in the experience and take the dictation. In Salad Bowl, the experience is making the salad with students. There are many fruits and vegetables students have not eaten and find new to the touch and taste. Introduce words like *pineapple, sour,* or *crunchy* and encourage students to use them as they discuss the tastes and textures of the food. Create separate groups with specific responsibilities: washing, cutting, dressing, and serving.

- Decide on the length and medium for the dictation. For early beginning readers, consider using a group experience chart and take individual sentence dictations like Ms. Atchison did at the very beginning of this chapter. Keep the overall length to three or four sentences. Bilingual entries can be used to help students transition from a primary language to English. For longer dictations, consider typing the student's account on a word processor. It is easy to make multiple copies from this word-processed version, and volunteers can be taught how to take dictations in readable segments as they work at a word processor.

- You may want to elicit one sentence from each student if the group is small enough. Say each word slowly as you record the students' ideas and then reread the sentence to the student as you point to the words.

- Shape the account into a coherent whole by helping the students sequence their ideas. Parts of the dictation can be edited into standard English as needed if the student can reread the dictation with this slight modification. The editing helps students learn phrasing and vocabulary. You may choose to use a patterned sentence frame such as "Rosa liked the pineapple. Josh liked the bananas. Carl liked the apples." These simple language patterns will make it easier for students to reread the dictation and will reinforce English syntax and vocabulary.

- Make a copy of the dictation for each student and reread it as they follow along. Students can be asked to illustrate their copy. A copy can be added to students' Personal Readers.

- Reread the dictation together several times using choral or echo reading.

Day 2

- Make a copy of the dictation for each student and reread it as they follow along. Students can be asked to illustrate their copy and it can be added to students' Personal Readers.
- Reread the dictation and look for words that have certain features. ("Can you find a word that starts with /f/ or the letter f?") This is the time to decide whether this is a text that the student will be able to reread with support. Adjustments can be made by focusing on a few sentences instead of the whole text, rephrasing a sentence or two in ways that the student will be able to reread.

Day 3. Have students underline words in their dictations that they know by sight and that they want to place in their word banks. The teacher points to words randomly, and words that are recognized quickly are recorded on word cards and record sheets.

Days 3 to 7. Over time, students reread their dictations and other familiar materials in their Personal Readers. Students often reread their selections at the beginning of the day, as well as during small-group reading sessions.

EXTEND

- Read one of the many versions of *Stone Soup* to students. Salad Bowl can be a new version of the classic folktale, a story of resourcefulness and cooperation in which townspeople bring food to a soup that begins with only a stone. Many parts are easy to dramatize without props or preparation.
- Students draw or hunt through newspapers and magazines for pictures of foods to go in a salad.
- Students draw pictures by each line to help support what they are reading.
- Students write about the experience, spelling as best they can.
- A copy of the Personal Reader entry goes home and the student finds someone to read to. Afterward the listeners at home add their initials and date to the bottom of the page.
- A list of possible experiences is presented in Table 5.8. For additional ideas see *Personal Readers for Emergent and Beginning Readers* (Bear, Caserta-Henry, & Venner, 2004).

TABLE 5.8 **Dictation Starters: Experiences That Lead to Group Experience Charts and Individual Dictations**

	ACTIVITIES		
ANIMALS	*To Encourage Talking*	*Food-Related*	*Brief Activities*
Frogs	Favorite music	Cracking nuts	Dissecting flowers
Turtles	Family photographs	Examining and cutting up	Mixing colors
Lizards, snakes	Pictures from weekly magazines	gourds	Playing instruments
Dogs, cats	Concept sorts	Making soup	Going on field trips
Hermit crabs	Flannel board story	Counting seeds	Sharing collections
Birds	Response to a video of a story	Tasting a variety of a food type:	Having worm races
Worms	Response to picture books	apples, potato chips	Conducting science experiments
Spiders	Weather	Tasting spices	Going on nature walks
Rabbits		Comparing and contrasting	Working with clay
Gerbils/hamsters		sweet and sour	Making salt–flour dough animals
Crickets		Making pancakes, pretzels,	Guessing what is in the box
Fish		applesauce, etc.	

Source: Adapted from Bear, Caserta-Henry, and Venner (2004).

FIGURE 5.13 Bilingual Personal Reader Samples

Alma: Hice un color rojo y yellow.

I made the color red and yellow.

Viviana: A mí me gusta hacer diferentes colores.
Y me gusta el color rojo, azul y amarillo.

I like to make different colors.
I like to make red, blue and yellow.

Eduardo: Me gustó hacer los colores, porque se hacían de otro color.

I like to make the colors because they make other colors.

5.16 Bilingual Dictations

Bilingual entries are important additions to Personal Readers that assist students to transfer what they know about literacy into English. The process of taking the dictation is the same as that described in Activity 5.15 except that a translation of what the student has said is written underneath.

Most of us need assistance to collect dictations in other languages and then to translate the words into English. The people who might help take dictations include English language development teachers, parents, school mentors, and literate students from the same language background. As a bridge activity, bilingual dictations are usually brief, and the words chosen and sentence structures are easy.

The examples in Figure 5.13 are from three Spanish-speaking children in a first- and second-grade combination class. After the experience of mixing dyes in water, they dictated these accounts in Spanish. In this case, they also dictated their own translations. Both Eduardo and Alma knew just a little English. Eduardo was a recent arrival and was very limited in his knowledge of English. His dictation in Spanish is illustrative of his age-appropriate language competence in Spanish.

Alma was born in Mexico and attended kindergarten in the United States the previous year. When she dictated in Spanish, she used the English word *yellow* and said later that she did not know the Spanish word for yellow (*amarillo*). This mixing of languages is common and a sign of her learning at school. Viviana was a fluent speaker in Spanish, and though her dictation is concise, she was the most advanced English speaker among the English learners.

5.17 Content Dictations Based on Informational Books and Textbooks

Content dictations are used with older English learners and are a powerful tool for middle and late letter name–alphabetic and early within word pattern stage spellers who find their textbooks too difficult to read and understand. The two- to four-paragraph dictations help to teach students the vocabulary and concepts that underlie their content studies. This technique

ACTIVITIES | LETTER NAME–ALPHABETIC STAGE

FIGURE 5.14 A Content Dictation about Sand Sharks

Sand Sharks

Sand sharks look vicious, but they are not really vicious. Sand sharks mistake humans for prey because they don't have a sense of us. Sand sharks eat squid, other sharks, and shellfish. Sand sharks' teeth are made to hold, not to tear. They hold on with their teeth, and their teeth are not jagged. If their teeth were jagged, the prey could get away. The teeth are circular like pegs. This keeps the prey inside.

extends the use of dictations to transitional reading and within word pattern stage readers who, though they are beginning to read in easy chapter books, still do not read well enough to understand their textbooks. Until there are relevant reading texts written at students' levels, the content dictations make it possible for students to learn the vocabulary and concepts in the text by listening and then summarizing the materials.

Students listen to a selection from their textbooks read to them by the teacher, a tutor, or a table partner. At strategic points, students dictate a summary of what they have heard. The dictations are typed in a 14- to 18-point font for these students and may run over to a second page. In some secondary settings, students have used content dictations to create their own version of the materials, from how-to guides to summaries of key points in the text.

The example in Figure 5.14 is a content dictation based on an informational book about sand sharks. This dictation summarizes what Lucas learned by listening to a reading from the book.

Content dictations are exceptionally useful to help students who cannot read their textbooks at an instructional level. Teachers often need to help students construct coherent dictations. As in all dictations, it is essential that students understand and can reread their dictations.

The length of a dictation reflects what each student can say orally and reread successfully. Lucas was a middle-level beginning reader in the third grade. He reread his dictation several times, and by the third rereading, Lucas read this 75-word dictation in 40 seconds, with no errors, with an excellent rate of 112 words per minute.

Content dictations with older students present a way for them to compose without the burden of writing. The teacher, tutor, or partner can start by taking dictation, and then after a few sentences or a paragraph, turn the physical writing over to the student. After the first few sentences, some of the difficult words have been introduced. You can also move back and forth between dictation and having the students write a sentence.

Picture and Word Sorts and Related Games

5.18 Beginning Consonant Picture Sorts

The beginning consonant picture sorts in this section help students identify and discriminate among more obvious beginning sound contrasts. Students work through a sequence of sorts divided into five groups: (1) /s/, /m/, /b/, /l/; (2) /t/, /p/, /c/, /n/; (3) /d/, /f/, /r/, /g/; (4) /h/, /k/,

/j/, /w/; and (5) /v/, /y/, /z/. The series can be taught at an introductory, moderate, or fast pace, depending on the developmental needs of the group. Beginning consonant picture sorts are Sorts 13–32 on the website. Sort 13 is provided as a sample sort in the Appendix (p. 299).

DEMONSTRATE. Prepare Sort 13 from the website. Copy and cut apart the pictures you will need for the sort. For example, you will begin with a sort contrasting /s/ and /m/. Before doing the teacher-guided sort, hold up each picture card and ask students to give its name. Consider teaching the names of up to five unknown items. Additional unknown items can be set to the side for another time. Proceed through the sort by holding up each picture and sharing your thinking in the following way: "Here is a picture of a sink. Does *sink* sound like *sun* at the beginning or like *monkey?* Right! I'll put *sink* under the card with *S* and the sun on it. Now, you help me sort the rest of these pictures." Continue with the children's help to sort all of the pictures. Model how to isolate, identify, and then categorize the beginning sound in each word.

SORT AND CHECK. Give each student (or pair of students) a set of the pictures to sort. Now have the students repeat the sort under your supervision using the same key pictures as headers. You may want to have students work with partners to mix up the pictures and take turns drawing a card, saying the picture's name out loud and sorting it in the correct column. After sorting, remind students to check their sorts by naming the words in each column to be sure the beginning sounds are the same. A portion of the completed sort should look something like Figure 5.15.

REFLECT. Ask students to reflect on how the words in each column are alike. Have them share their comments with others in the group or ask each other questions about the words. These are excellent ways for students to use English vocabulary in real conversations.

EXTEND. Some students may only need a fast-paced review of consonants, studying four sounds at a time in the sequence suggested here. Others will benefit from a slow pace contrasting two or three sounds at a time and tying in literature links that are outlined in Figure 5.16. Add letter cards or use magnetic letters or write letters on whiteboards to support the phonics being learned in these beginning consonant picture sorts. When students have sorted the pictures several times, they may paste them onto pages, creating beginning sound books. They can also draw pictures of words with these beginning consonant sounds. Students use the familiar reading materials and the word banks described in the Personal Reader activities to hunt for words with the same beginning consonants.

5.19 Mud Puddle Game

In this game two to four players collect picture cards that begin with the /m/ sound (or other designated sound).

MATERIALS. A collection of 30 to 50 picture cards is needed. Just over half of the cards should begin with the /m/ sound, and the rest of the picture cards should represent consonants that have already been studied. You will find 30 /m/ pictures as well as countless others in the Pictures for Sorts and Games in the Appendix and on the website. Each player has a mud puddle, which can be made by cutting out a round piece of brown construction paper.

PROCEDURES. Shuffle the picture cards and place them face down. The first player draws a card from the deck, says the name of the picture, and if the picture name begins with the /m/ sound, places the picture in his or her mud puddle. If the picture does not begin with

FIGURE 5.15 A Sample Beginning Consonant Picture Sort

for Words Their Way™ with English Learners

Go to PDToolkit, choose your book, click the Sorts & Games tab, and search for Sorts 13–32.

for Words Their Way™ with English Learners

Go to PDToolkit, choose your book, click the Additional Resources tab, and select Pictures for Sorts and Games. Or click the Sorts & Games tab, and click Create Your Own!

ACTIVITIES LETTER NAME–ALPHABETIC STAGE

FIGURE 5.16 Literature Links

A

Read *Annie and the Wild Animals* by Jan Brett (1985). In this book, Annie hopes to replace her cat that has gone missing by feeding muffins to the wild animals of the forest. Jan Brett creates additional text by framing each page with the story of the missing cat and the animals yet to appear in the story. Use the story as a springboard to create a classroom book of animals and objects that begin with the short *a* sound as in *Annie* and *animals*, using a variety of letter *a* fonts to frame each page.

B

Read *Brown Bear, Brown Bear, What Do You See?* by Bill Martin (1970). Have students use the pattern in this story to create their own *b* books, such as *Bunny, Bunny, what do you see? I see a button looking at me.*

C

Read *Good-Night, Owl!* by Pat Hutchins (1972). Dramatize *c* sounds such as "cuckoo" and the squirrel c-c-cracking and c-c-crunching nuts. Practice the sound of *c* through the chant *Who Stole the Cookie from the Cookie Jar.* Begin by singing the first line of the song; then in the second line insert the name of one of the students in the classroom, to which that student denies "stealing the cookie" and chooses someone else to accuse of stealing the cookie from the cookie jar. This pattern is repeated until all the children in the classroom have had a turn.

> **Teacher and Class:** Who stole the cookie from the cookie jar?
> **Teacher:** Rosa stole the cookie from the cookie jar.
> **Rosa:** Who me?
> **Class:** Yes you.
> **Rosa:** Couldn't be.
> **Class:** Then who?
> **Rosa:** [Chooses another name] stole the cookie from the cookie jar.

D

Read *A Dark, Dark Tale* by Ruth Brown (1998), and add special emphasis to dark and any other words that begin with /d/.

Teach students a fun and memorable chant for the /d/ sound, *Double double this.* Vocabulary knowledge for the word *double* and some of the *d* words are learned. For articulation, the /d/ and /th/ contrast is a good one. Many students will say the /d/ as a /th/. Return to this ditty when /d/ and /th/ are contrasted later in the series.

> Double double this this,
> Double double that that,
> Double this, double that,
> Double double this that.

Instructions: Hold out your hands as if you are showing someone your favorite ring. As you are saying the chant turn your hands in the following ways: Whenever you say "double" palms should face up, and as you say any other word palms face downward. Practice this hand game until you get very fast at it!

Variations: Exchange any words for *this* and *that.* For example:

> Double double dirty dirty,
> Double double dish dish,
> Double dirty, double dish,
> Double double dirty dish.

E

Read *Never Ride Your Elephant to School* (Johnson, 1995), a hilarious book about taking an elephant to school. Encourage students to think of other problems that an elephant could create.

F

Read and act out the rhyming and repeating text *Four Fur Feet* by Margaret Wise Brown (1993).

G

Read *Flower Garden* by Eve Bunting (2000). With the support of a picture dictionary, have students think of /g/ words to add to this little rhyme:

> Let's go, go, go to the garden
> Where some silly things do grow
> In our /g/, /g/ garden
> There's a (goat, goose, globe, game, or other /g/ word)
> I know!

Read *Little Gorilla* by Ruth Bornstein (1986), a story of a little gorilla loved by all in the jungle, even after Little Gorilla grows up to be Big Gorilla. Following the story, the class can join you in a cheer for Big Gorilla. Cheers are a favorite for students and these cheers can be accompanied with word and letter cards that students hold up.

> Go gorilla, go, go Gorilla, G-O-R-I-L-L-A
> Goooooo, Gorilla!!!

H

Recite *Humpty Dumpty* together and have students find the word that begins with the /h/ sound in *Humpty.* Put this on a chart for reading.

Humpty Dumpty
Humpty Dumpty sat on a wall.
Humpty Dumpty had a great fall.
All the King's horses and all the King's men,
Couldn't put Humpty together again.

FIGURE 5.16 Continued

I

Read *The Icky Bug Alphabet Book* (Pallota, 1993), an informational text on insects and spiders. To tie in the sound of short *i* have students draw pictures of their favorite "icky" bug on a 3-inch by 3-inch piece of paper. Present a variety of pictures and words, with half of the pictures or words beginning with the short *i*. Each time students hear a word that begins the same as *insect*, they show their "icky" bug card.

J

Practice the /j/ sound with two favorite nursery rhymes, *Jack and Jill* and *Jack Be Nimble, Jack Be Quick*. Have students look at the variety of pictures available that illustrate these rhymes, and, of course, have them act the rhymes out!

Jack and Jill went up the hill
To fetch a pail of water.
Jack fell down and broke his crown,
And Jill came tumbling after.

Jack be nimble.
Jack be quick.
Jack jump over the candlestick.

K

Read *Katy No Pocket* (Payne, 1973), a delightful tale about a mother kangaroo who does not have a pocket for her baby Freddy, so she asks other animals how they carry their babies. Have students create their own paper kangaroos with a pocket to collect and store pictures and words that begin with the /k/ sound.

L

Read *Leo the Late Bloomer* by Robert Kraus (1994). Play an oral language game by having students complete the sentence, "Leo likes _____ (things that start with /l/)."

Recite the nursery rhyme *Mary Had a Little Lamb* with students and have them raise both hands each time they say a word that begins with the /l/ sound. Picture cards placed on the easel or on the table will cue students who need vocabulary support.

M

Read *Mud Puddle* by Robert Munsch (2001). After reading the story have students play a game of Mud Puddle, Activity 5.19.

N

Read the story *Noisy Nora* by Rosemary Wells (1973) for a springboard to explore the /n/ sound. With the help of a picture dictionary, guide students to think of "Noisy Nora" words that start with /n/ such as *nail, nurse, nose, newspaper*, and

nest. Then say a word out loud to the group and ask them if it is a "Noisy Nora" word or not.

Play *Nut Butter*, an extension of the Mud Puddle activity presented in Activity 5.19.

O

Read *Old MacDonald Had a Farm* by Carol Jones (1998) or another illustrator. Have students sing along and notice the vowel sounds in E-I-E-I-O. Think of words that start with short and long *o*'s to add to MacDonald's farm.

P

Read one of the Pig Pig books by David McPhail, such as *Pig Pig Gets a Job* (1990). Have students think of words that begin with /p/ that Pig Pig might like to use in his adventures.

Q

Read *Five Little Ducks* by Raffi (1989). Students dramatize both verbally and physically the /q/ sounds as they read "Quack, quack, quack."

Read *Q Is for Duck* (Elting & Folsom, 2005), a guessing game alphabet book. Create other questions related to *q* such as "Why is *q* for money?" (quarter) "Why is *q* for sleeping?" (quilt) "Why is *q* for fairy tale?" (queen) "Why is *q* for library?" (quiet).

R

Practice the /r/ sound in the following nursery rhymes:

Rain on the green grass, and rain on the tree,
rain on the rooftop, but not on me.

If all the raindrops were lemon drops and gum drops,
oh what a rain that would be,
standing outside,
with our mouths open wide.

Row, row, row your boat,
Gently down the stream,
Merrily, merrily, merrily, merrily,
Life is but a dream.

S

Read *The Very Busy Spider* by Eric Carle (1985). Act out what the spider does from the story. Play a variation of Simon Says called "Spider Says," in which students take turns giving directions to the group.

Chant "A sailor went to sea, sea, sea," a favorite /s/ chant:

A sailor went to sea, sea, sea,
To see what he could see, see, see,
But all that he could see, see, see,
Was the bottom of the deep blue sea, sea, sea.

(continued)

FIGURE 5.16 Continued

Students clap with a partner in a crossover manner. Each time they say the word *see* they place a hand on their forehead above their eyes to simulate that they are looking for something.

T

Read *The Teeny Tiny Teacher* (Calmenson, 2002) and accentuate the /t/ sound.

Learn the jump rope chant:

Teddy Bear, Teddy Bear, turn around.
Teddy Bear, Teddy Bear, touch the ground.
Teddy Bear, Teddy Bear, tie your shoe.
Teddy Bear, Teddy Bear, how old are you?
1, 2, 3, 4, . . .

Have students practice this chant as they jump rope or do other exercises.

U

Read *The Ugly Duckling* by Hans Christian Andersen and Jerry Pinkney (1999). Help students hear the short *u* sound in the words *ugly* and *duckling*. Play a listening game where students try to hear whether a word has the short *u* sound in it. They put thumbs up if they hear the sound and thumbs down if it does not have the short *u* sound. For example: *fun*—thumbs up; *ride*—thumbs down.

V

Read and discuss *V Is for Vanishing: An Alphabet of Endangered Animals* by Patricia Mullins (1997). Practice saying and/or act-

ing out lip-tickling /v/ words such as *vanishing, vacuum, vanilla, vase, van, vegetable, vest, vibrate, violin,* and *vulture*.

W

Read *Where the Wild Things Are* by Maurice Sendak (1988), *Watch William Walk* by Ann Jonas (1997), or *Mrs. Wishy Washy* by Joy Cowley (1999). Have students participate in rereadings of the text, and use a whisper voice each time you come to a /w/ word.

X

Investigate the clever ways that *x* has been illustrated in alphabet books, including those listed in the Children's Literature section of the References (designated with "ABC").

Y

Investigate the clever ways that *y* has been illustrated in alphabet books including those listed in the Children's Literature section of the References (designated with "ABC").

Z

Read *My Visit to the Zoo* by Aliki (1999). After reading the book and discussing zoos, have children contribute names of animals they know by adding to the following chant.

There's a /z/, /z/, zebra at the zoo, zoo, zoo.
There's a /l/, /l/, lion at the zoo, zoo, zoo.
There's a /b/, /b/, bear at the zoo, zoo, zoo.
There's a /c/, /c/, camel at the zoo, zoo, zoo.

the /m/ sound the card is placed in the discard pile. The first player to collect eight picture cards wins.

EXTEND. Adapt the Mud Puddles game to a Nut Butter game. An outline of a piece of bread replaces the puddle, and the game is played with a collection of 30 to 50 picture cards. Just over half of the cards should begin with the /n/ sound, and the other picture cards should represent consonants that have already been studied.

5.20 Focused Picture Sorts to Contrast Beginning Consonants

These picture sorts focus on contrasts that most English learners benefit from comparing after the previous sorts. For example, the /b/ and /p/ sort comes after the /p/ /t/ (*pig/tent*) sort. They are presented on the website in Sorts 33–49.

DEMONSTRATE. Prepare Sort 33 from the website. Copy and cut apart the pictures you will need for the sort. For example, you will begin with a sort contrasting /b/ and /p/. Before doing the teacher-guided sort, hold up each picture card and ask students to give its name. Consider teaching the names of up to five unknown items. Additional unknown items can be set to the

PDToolkit
for Words Their Way™
with English Learners

Go to PDToolkit, choose your book, click the Sorts & Games tab, and search for "Sort 33: /b/ /p/ Focused Picture Sorts to Contrast Beginning Consonants."

side for another time. The sort can be demonstrated with pictures in a pocket chart. Proceed through the sort by holding up each picture, and sharing your thinking in the following way: "Here is a picture of a bell. Does *bell* sound like *ball* at the beginning or like *pig?* Right! I'll put *bell* under the card with *Bb* and the ball on it. Now, you help me sort the rest of these pictures." Continue with the children's help to sort all of the pictures. Model how to isolate, identify, and then categorize the beginning sound in each word. Observe how easy or difficult your students find these similar-sounding words. Move quickly or slow down depending on the needs of your students. The final sort will look something like Figure 5.17.

SORT, CHECK, AND REFLECT. The students can then sort their own pictures with a partner. After checking their sorting, students tell each other why they sorted the way they did, as they reflect on the sort.

EXTEND. To extend, students can play board games with these pictures and go on picture hunts through preselected pages from magazines.

5.21 Introduction to Beginning Consonant Digraphs

These picture sorts introduce consonant digraphs by comparing them to the letters they are composed of, for example, sorting words that begin with /c/, /h/, and /ch/, as in Figure 5.18. They are presented on the website in Sorts 50–55.

DEMONSTRATE, SORT, CHECK, AND REFLECT. Demonstrate the sort with students and have them say the words as you show them the sort. Teach students the vocabulary they do not know before conducting the picture sort. Students then sort and check their sorts. When they are finished, students share their reflections about why they sorted the way they did and discuss some of the words they have been using.

EXTEND. The Build, Blend, Extend Activity (see Activity 5.5) makes the contrasts between beginning consonants and digraphs apparent. An extension activity like Bingo (see Activity 4.11) helps students listen for these digraphs after they have worked with word families.

5.22 Introduction to Beginning Consonant Blends

Consonant blends are also introduced in picture sorts but are revisited throughout the stage. Many English learners will find the blends to be new sounds. For example, the Spanish language does not have *s* blends. See Sorts 56–72 on the website. Figure 5.19 is an example.

DEMONSTRATE, SORT, CHECK, AND REFLECT. Demonstrate the sort with students and have them say the words as you work through the sort. Teach students the vocabulary they

FIGURE 5.17 A Picture Sort to Contrast /b/ and /p/

PDToolkit
for Words Their Way™
with English Learners

Go to PDToolkit, choose your book, click the Sorts & Games tab, and search for Sorts 50–55 and Sorts 56–72.

FIGURE 5.18 A Picture Sort to Contrast /c/, /h/, and /ch/

FIGURE 5.19 A Picture Sort to Contrast /sl/, /fl/, and /pl/

do not know before conducting the picture sort, and if there are too many unknown words to learn at once, choose three to five of the most useful to feature.

Next, give students their own materials and have them do the sort on their own or with a partner. When they are finished, students check their sorts, share their reflections about why they sorted the way they did, and discuss some of the words they have been using.

There are too many beginning consonant blend sorts on the website for students to complete all of them; therefore, it is important to pick and choose among the sorts included. Once students learn some of the *s* blends, they will be able to extend their learning to others.

EXTEND. Build, Blend, Extend (Activity 5.5) continues to be an essential activity to teach the new sounds after students have worked with word families. Picture hunts in magazines and drawing pictures are ways for students to practice working with these sounds.

5.23 Focused Picture Sorts to Contrast Beginning Consonant Digraphs and Blends

These picture sorts focus on contrasts that most English learners benefit from comparing because they are complex and closely-related sounds. For example, the /sh/ and /ch/ sounds can be quite difficult for students who do not have both of those sounds in their primary language. These sorts are presented on the website, Sorts 73–86. An example is shown in Figure 5.20.

FIGURE 5.20 A Picture Sort to Contrast /sh/ and /ch/

DEMONSTRATE, SORT, CHECK, AND REFLECT. Demonstrate the sort with students and have them say the words as you work through the sort. Teach students the vocabulary they do not know before conducting the picture sort, and if there are too many unknown words to learn at once, choose three to five of the most useful to feature.

Next, give students their own materials and have them do the sort on their own or with a partner. When they are finished, students check their sorts, share their reflections about why they sorted the way they did, and discuss some of the words they have been using. Encourage students to talk about the "tricky parts" in these sorts, and to share tips for how they learn to differentiate the sounds.

It is not necessary for students to complete all the sorts contrasting digraphs and blends on the website; rather, it is important to pick and choose the sorts that help your students practice sound contrasts that they find difficult based on their primary languages.

EXTEND. Have students create pages in their word study notebooks or create books that compare words with "tricky" beginning sounds.

5.24 Final Consonant Picture Sorts

FIGURE 5.21 Final Consonant Picture Sort for /-b/, /-m/, and /-s/

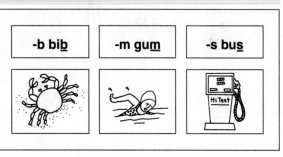

These picture sorts introduce many English learners to sounds they are not accustomed to hearing at the ends of words. Pick and choose the final sounds that students do not pronounce or include in their spelling. English learners may have a hard time discriminating the final sounds of /t/, /d/, /g/, /p/, and /n/ among others. Copy an ending sound sort for each student or pair of students to use. These sorts are presented on the website in Sorts 87–97. An example is shown in Figure 5.21.

DEMONSTRATE, SORT, CHECK, AND REFLECT. Follow the word study lesson plan format outlined on pages 124–125 of this chapter in which you teach vocabulary, model the sort, and have students practice and sort on their own.

REFLECT AND EXTEND. Have students share their reflections about why they sorted the way they did, and discuss some of the words they have been using. Students hunt for pictures or simple words that end with the consonants that represent these ending sounds and add them to their word study notebooks.

5.25 Focused Picture Sorts to Contrast Final Consonants

These sorts build on the previous activity and compare final sounds that are very similar to each other. For example, in the /m/ and /n/ sort (*gum*/*ten*), students practice feeling the differences between words that are easily confused in pronunciation. Often, these sounds differ only in whether they are voiced, as in /d/ and /t/ sounds (*bed*/*net*).

These sorts are presented on the website in Sorts 98–105. Be sure that students are confident with the picture sorts from Activity 5.24 before beginning this series. An example is shown in Figure 5.22.

DEMONSTRATE, SORT, AND CHECK. Follow the word study lesson plan format outlined on pages 124–125 of this chapter in which you teach vocabulary, model the sort, and have students practice and sort on their own. As the teacher, pay special attention to enunciating the final sounds. As students sort and check, be sure they say the words out loud. If they do not pronounce the sounds in their conversational speech, they may have difficulty making these discriminations.

REFLECT. Students explain why they sorted the pictures the way they did. They may comment that these sounds are hard to hear. Show them the shape of your mouth as you say the words and have them practice after you.

EXTEND. Various games, such as Concentration or Go Fish, may be played to reinforce these sounds. Or use the templates on the website to make a game board that includes pictures with tricky ending sounds. Use the pictures from the sorts to place on the board and for the draw pile. Students use a board game piece to move to the sound that matches the one they drew.

5.26 Picture Sorts to Introduce Vowel Sounds

These sorts introduce the short vowel sounds with pictures. They should be fairly easy for most English learners. In this sequence of picture sorts found on the website, Sorts 106–110, students contrast long and short vowel sounds. Copy a vowel sounds sort for each student or pair of students to use. An example is shown in Figure 5.23.

DEMONSTRATE, SORT, CHECK, AND REFLECT. Show students how to compare the short and long vowel sounds represented in these pictures. Use the terms *long* and *short* to describe these vowel sounds. Be sure to introduce the names of pictures they do not recognize. Ask students to help you sort as they listen for the sounds in the middles of these words.

Next, give students their own materials and have them sort on their own or with a partner. As students sort and check, be sure they say the words out loud. If they do not pronounce the sounds in their conversational speech, they may have difficulty making these discriminations. Notice the accuracy and speed with which they sort. Students should explain their sorts to the persons sitting next to them in the group.

EXTEND. Choose books from the literature listed in Figure 5.16 that explore the short vowels. Students can draw pictures of the sounds they hear in these books as entries in their word study notebooks.

for Words Their Way™ with English Learners

Go to PDToolkit, choose your book, click the Sorts & Games tab, and search for Sorts 98–105 and Sorts 106–110.

for Words Their Way™ with English Learners

Go to PDToolkit, choose your book, click the Additional Resources tab, and select Race-track Game Board (left and right) or U Game Board in the Templates section.

FIGURE 5.22 A Picture Sort to Contrast Final /-d/ and /-t/

FIGURE 5.23 Picture Sort to Introduce /ă/ and /ā/

ACTIVITIES · LETTER NAME–ALPHABETIC STAGE

5.27 Same Vowel Family Picture and Word Sorts

Sorts 111–130 on the website present a sequence of same vowel family sorts beginning with a single vowel in which students compare the sounds across vowels. Sorts combine pictures and words at first as in Figure 5.24, and later just words.

DEMONSTRATE, SORT, AND CHECK. Prepare the set of pictures and words for the vowel family sort you will be doing by copying the desired sort from the website. Sort 111 is provided as a sample in the Appendix (p. 303). Before doing the teacher-guided sort, hold up each picture and word card and ask students to give its name. Check that students know the names of pictures and understand the meanings of the words. Consider teaching the names and meanings of up to five unknown items. Additional unknown items can be set aside for another time. Ask students if they notice anything about the words. Ask about the vowel sounds in the middles of the words. Do they all have the same vowel sound?

Introduce the word family symbols and their key pictures on the headers. Model the onset–rime segmentation process involved in isolating and identifying each vowel family; for example, "In *cat* we hear /c/, /at/. In *dad* we hear /d/, /ad/." Demonstrate the sorting process by saying each of the other words and pictures and comparing them each to the guide words. Have your students join in as you continue to model the isolation, identification, and categorization of the vowel family. It is critical that your students say the words out loud and enunciate their sounds rather than simply sorting by the visual pattern present. As you sort, tell students that even though they are now using words, they are to still listen for sounds and not just rely on how words look alike. Remind students to set aside words they do not read accurately or understand. This extra attention is helpful so that English learners can focus on final consonant sounds they are not accustomed to pronouncing.

FIGURE 5.24 Same Vowel Family Picture and Word Sort

REFLECT. In the reflection part of the word study lesson plan format, see if students can generate their own examples of the sounds and word families that are studied.

EXTEND. Build, Blend, Extend (Activity 5.5) is an ideal activity at this time. Students make many words by substituting letters and word families. They see how many words they can make with the -*at* family and how many words they can make by changing just the beginning sound. Gradually, the consonant blends and digraphs are reexamined as students see how the beginning and later the ending blends and digraphs are part of these word families (*cat, brat, chat*).

Students may hunt for words that fit the sound pattern and write them in their word study notebooks.

Continue to use a combination of words and pictures, play Concentration-type games to match words and pictures, and then move on to only words as students' reading and vocabulary grow.

Other extension ideas include the following:

1. Literature links
2. Word hunts
3. Word study notebooks
4. Word Watchers
5. Writing sorts

5.28 Mixed Short Vowel Word Family Sorts

In Sorts 131–139 found on the website, students study short vowels across families. Knowing the families, they concentrate on the sound differences among short vowels, as with *e* and *o* in *net* and *not*. An example of a mixed short vowel word family sort is shown in Figure 5.25.

DEMONSTRATE. Prepare the sort for the mixed short vowel families you will be teaching from the website. (Sort 131 is provided as a sample in the Appendix on page 304.) Before doing the teacher-guided sort, hold up each picture and word card and ask students to give its name. Check that students know the names of pictures and understand the meanings of the words. Consider teaching the names and meanings of up to five unknown items. Additional unknown items can be set aside for another time. Ask your students if they notice anything about the words. Ask about the vowel sounds in the middles of the words. Do they all have the same vowel sound?

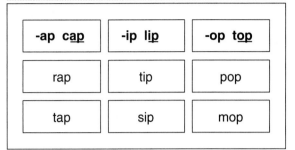

FIGURE 5.25 Mixed Short Vowel Word Family Sort

-ap c<u>ap</u>	-ip l<u>ip</u>	-op t<u>op</u>
rap	tip	pop
tap	sip	mop

Demonstrate the first sort in this series as described in Activity 5.27. Highlight how the words end the same and how the vowels change. Students should find this sort fairly easy and can help you match the words as you sort. It may be possible for many students to move through this series of sorts at a fast pace.

SORT AND CHECK. If this is an easy sort, have pairs of students complete a different sort instead of the same one you modeled. Have the pairs explain their sorts to another pair of students in the group.

REFLECT. Have students discuss their sorts. They will notice that they are all short vowels and that within each sort, the final sounds remain the same.

EXTEND. Games like Go Fish and Bingo are played to practice listening and saying these short vowel words.

5.29 Rhyming Families

This board game challenges students to come up with words that rhyme with the short vowel words on the game board and are different from other players' words.

MATERIALS. Make a follow-the-path game board (see Figure 5.26). You will also need one die or spinner, pieces to move around the board, and a pencil and paper for each player. Write a word from each word family you have been studying in each space on the board. You can also add special spaces such as Roll Again, Go Back Two Spaces, and Write Two Words.

PROCEDURES

1. Spin to determine who goes first. The first player spins and moves the number of places indicated on the spinner. The player reads the word in the space where he or she lands. All players write a rhyming word they know by changing initial letter(s). Players number their words as they go. Play continues until someone reaches the end of the path.

2. Beginning with the player who reaches the end first, each player reads the first word on his or her list. Players who have a word that is different from anyone else's gets to circle the word. If necessary, players should explain to others what the word means. Continue until all words have been compared.

3. Each circle is worth one point; the player who reached the end first receives two extra points. The student with the most points wins the game.

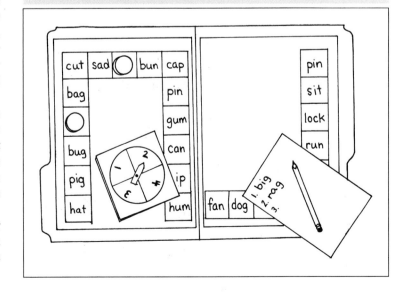

FIGURE 5.26 Game Board for Word Families

VARIATIONS. Label each space on the game board with the rime of a family you have studied (-*at*, -*an*, -*ad*, -*ack*). Use no more than five different rimes and repeat them around the path. Prepare a set of cards that have pictures that correspond to the families. Students move around the board by selecting a picture and moving to the next space it matches. For example, a student with a picture of a hat would move to the next space with -*at* written on it.

Games offer a wonderful opportunity for students to practice word families and interact with classmates. The website contains several game boards that may be used to encourage engagement with these words.

5.30 Focus on Word Sorts to Contrast Final Consonants

Seven sorts on the website (140–147) contrast final consonants. Previously, students contrasted the sounds of final consonants with pictures. Now, with words, students are cued by letters to articulate a difference between contrasting sounds. For example, students sort words that end in *d* from words that end in *t*: *bad, rod, kid, mat, jet, pot, net*. Sort 146 is provided as a sample sort on page 305 of the Appendix.

DEMONSTRATE, SORT, AND CHECK. Show students how to complete the first sort as described in Activity 5.27. Progress through these sorts rapidly. Students say the words as they sort and match written words with key pictures at the top of the columns. Before placing a word in a column, have them say the word being sorted and then the appropriate key word at the top; for example, after matching *jet* to the picture of the bed (*jet–bed*), students then contrast the word *jet* to the key picture *net* (*jet–net*). After following the lesson plan format for the first sort in this series, students can complete the other sorts with partners and record them in their word study notebooks. In small groups, students brainstorm additional words that fit with these sorts.

REFLECT. Students explain why they sorted the way they did. Have them discuss any "tricky" parts to the sort.

EXTEND. To extend, word hunts are particularly effective with these sorts. Students hunt through their readings for words that end with the same sounds and enter them in their word study notebooks, organizing them in columns by ending consonants.

5.31 CVC Short Vowel Word Sorts

These word sorts, numbered 148–157 on the website, compare short vowels beyond word families. Making the generalization from rimes to the short vowel sound is important so that students do not overrely on rhyming in English. This series of sorts begins with easier contrasts and ends with finer contrasts (short *i* and short *e*).

DEMONSTRATE, SORT, AND CHECK. Prepare the short vowel words you will be using by copying the sort from the website for students to use on their own or with a partner. Teachers should be able to predict the words that students can read at sight, which they can then use in the sorts.

Before doing the teacher-guided sort, hold up each word card for students to read. Check that students can both read and understand the meanings of the words. Consider teaching the meanings of up to five unknown items; additional unknown items can be set aside for another time. Ask your students if they notice anything about the words. Ask about the vowel sounds in the middles of the words and the consonants at the ends of the words. Do they all have the same vowel family?

Demonstrate the first sort in a manner similar to that outlined in Activity 5.27. Highlight how the words in this sort have the same vowel but not the same ending sound. Have students say the words along with you as you sort. Help them to pronounce the vowels and ending sounds in the words. Next, have students do the sort on their own or with partners. When they finish, they check their sorts to make sure the words have been correctly sorted. The completed sort should look something like Figure 5.27.

REFLECT. Students observe that the words in each sorted column sound alike in the middle. Students may have difficulty understanding how they sound alike in the middle and yet they end with different sounds. This activity helps them to see the CVC pattern. Students are encouraged to share their questions about this pattern and what might be confusing for them.

EXTEND. In perhaps the final use of word banks, students hunt through their sight words for examples of short vowels and then they begin to examine the sounds and spellings of these words. For example, students hunt for words that have a short *a* sound like in the middle of *cat* and list these words on pages that are later inserted into word study notebooks.

Students play many games with the words from these sorts, including Go Fish, Bingo, and the Racetrack board game that uses the template found on the website. Their word study notebooks should contain pages dedicated to each of the short vowels. As their skills advance, words with beginning and ending blends and digraphs become more frequent as entries in word study notebooks.

This is the time to name the consonant-vowel-consonant (CVC) pattern. Students have many sight words and, having studied short vowels across word families, it is a perfect time to introduce students to their first pattern, CVC.

5.32 Beginning Consonant Digraph and Blend Word Sorts

In Sorts 158–198 on the website students see that digraphs and blends may be seen as one unit. They begin to pronounce them together, without a vowel between the consonants (formerly, the word *split* might have been pronounced "espalitah") and without an ending vowel (formerly, *lump* might have been pronounced "lumpuh").

DEMONSTRATE, SORT, AND CHECK. Refer to the set of consonant digraph and blend sorts formatted on the website. Sort 158 is provided as a sample sort in the Appendix (p. 306). Select the set of words you will work on, and make copies for each student or pair of students. Before doing the teacher-guided sort, hold up each word card and ask students to read it. Check that students can read and understand the meanings of the words. Consider teaching the meanings of up to five unknown items; additional unknown items can be set aside for another time. Ask your students if they notice anything about the words. These words have more letters in them than the simple CVC words. Can students identify the digraphs and consonant blends?

Demonstrate the first sort in a manner similar to that described in Activity 5.23. Highlight how the words include more than one consonant together.

Next, have students complete the sort with partners in small groups. If the students are progressing at a rapid pace, pairs can sort different words that have the same digraphs and blends. When finished, they can read and share their words with other pairs of students.

REFLECT. Have students share their understanding of the short vowel patterned words. Point out that the short vowels follow a CVC pattern when the consonant digraphs and blends are considered as one consonant unit.

EXTEND. Pictures that have the sounds of the consonant digraphs and blends can also be included in these sorts. Have students conduct writing sorts or word hunts with their partners for independent study at their seats.

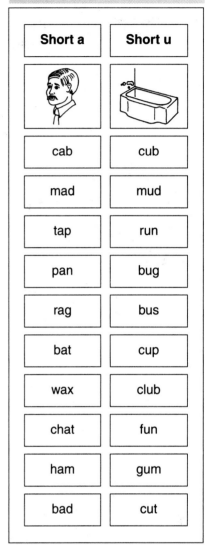

FIGURE 5.27 Sample Short Vowel Word Sort

Short a	Short u
(image)	(image)
cab	cub
mad	mud
tap	run
pan	bug
rag	bus
bat	cup
wax	club
chat	fun
ham	gum
bad	cut

for Words Their Way™ with English Learners

Go to PDToolkit, choose your book, click the Additional Resources tab, and select Racetrack Game Board (left and right) in the Templates section.

for Words Their Way™ with English Learners

Go to PDToolkit, choose your book, click the Sorts & Games tab, and search for Sorts 158–198.

ACTIVITIES | LETTER NAME–ALPHABETIC STAGE

ACTIVITIES | LETTER NAME–ALPHABETIC STAGE

PDToolkit

for Words Their Way™ with English Learners

Go to PDToolkit, choose your book, click the Sorts & Games tab, and search for Sorts 199–212.

5.33 Focused Sorts to Contrast Beginning Consonant Digraphs

These sorts build on the previous activity and compare consonant digraphs that are very similar to each other. For example, in the /sh/ and /ch/ sort, students practice feeling the differences between words that are easily confused in pronunciation. There are often only slight variations in how these sounds are produced in the mouth, as can be seen in Table 5.2 (p. 113).

DEMONSTRATE, SORT, AND CHECK. Sorts 199–212 on the website present consonant digraph contrasts. After selecting the sort you will work on, make a copy for each student or pair of students. Before doing the teacher-guided sort, hold up each word card and ask students to read it. Check that students can read and understand the meanings of the words.

Consider teaching the meanings of up to five unknown items. Ask your students if they notice anything about the words. ("These words all have consonant digraphs like those we have been studying. But now, these digraphs have almost the same sound.") Be aware that some of these digraph sounds may not exist in students' home languages.

Demonstrate the first sort in a manner similar to that described in Activity 5.27. Highlight the digraphs and their respective sounds.

Next, have students complete the sort with partners in small groups. When finished, have them check their sorts together and read their words to other pairs of students.

Students have already studied these sounds, and the pace can be fast if students easily discriminate among the sounds in the sorts in their speech. Some students may not be able to articulate these sound differences clearly, and these sorts help to clarify how the sounds vary. An example is shown in Figure 5.28.

REFLECT. After sorting, have students explain their sorts to table partners. Students may discuss how these sounds are the same in their primary languages.

EXTEND. Word hunts are effective in expanding students' vocabularies and give them practice in how to pronounce these sounds. Students record the words they find in their word study notebooks.

FIGURE 5.28 Contrasting a Beginning Consonant Digraph with a Related Sound

Ff _fish_	th _this_
fin	them
fox	that

PDToolkit

for Words Their Way™ with English Learners

Go to PDToolkit, choose your book, click the Sorts & Games tab, and search for Sorts 213–227.

5.34 Final Consonant Digraph and Blend Word Sorts

Digraphs and blends are studied at the ends of words along with short vowels. The study of these final sounds continues into the next stage when long vowels are studied. The following sorts also include preconsonantal nasals (-_ump_, -_unk_, -_ink_, -_ang_) at the ends of words.

DEMONSTRATE. Select an easy sort from Sorts 213–227 on the website. Have students participate in the demonstration by distributing the word cards that students will use to take turns sorting with the group. An example sort is shown in Figure 5.29.

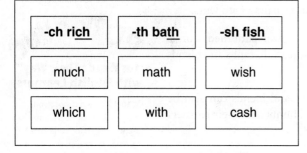

FIGURE 5.29 Final Consonant Digraph and Blend Word Sort

-ch _rich_	-th _bath_	-sh _fish_
much	math	wish
which	with	cash

SORT AND CHECK. Students follow the demonstration by sorting independently. Extending and overpronouncing the final sound is common as students learn how to pronounce the final sounds, sounds that may not exist in their primary languages.

REFLECT. Students explain their sorts and they often comment on how similar the final sounds are. Show students that even words with final blends and digraphs still follow the CVC short vowel pattern.

EXTEND. Students extend these sorts in a number of ways as they sort the words by vowels, by beginning and ending consonant digraphs and blends, by parts of speech, and by meaning. Writing sorts are popular as independent activities as students take turns calling out the words for their partners to record in the correct column.

5.35 Shrimp Camp

In this game, players move around the track and examine words with preconsonantal nasals such as *shrimp, camp,* and *stand.*

MATERIALS. Use the *-imp/-amp/-and* words from previous sorts to play this game, which consist of four playing pieces, racetrack game board found on the website, and a number spinner or a single die to move players around the track.

PROCEDURES. This game for two to four players is played on an oval track divided into 18 spaces. Different words containing preconsonantal nasals are written onto 11 of the spaces. Seven of the spaces are designated for each of the shrimp events: 100-yard dash, one-mile run, triple jump, high jump, hurdle, pole vault, and weightlifting.

For example, *shrimp, camp, stamp, limp, band, tend,* and *stand* could be used on the game board. After the racetrack has been constructed, the game board can be decorated with pictures of actual track events.

1. The person who rolls or spins the highest number goes first. Players and play proceed(s) in a clockwise direction.
2. Playing pieces are placed anywhere on the board.
3. The first player rolls or spins and moves the piece that many spaces. If the player lands on a word space, he or she must read the word. If the word is read correctly, the player earns one point. If the player lands on an event space, he or she must think of a word that is not on the board that contains a preconsonantal nasal. If successful, the player earns two points.
4. Play then proceeds to the next person.
5. The person to earn the most points wins.
6. Set a time limit for this game.

VARIATIONS
1. The person who rolls or spins the highest number goes first. Players and play proceed(s) in a clockwise direction.
2. Playing pieces are placed anywhere on the board.
3. The first player rolls or spins and moves the piece that many spaces. If the player lands on a word space, she or he reads the word and then every player must write a word from the same word family. For example, if a player lands on *shrimp,* players would write an *-imp* word. Each player then reads the word that was written and players who wrote the same word receive 1 point, and players who wrote a different word receive 2 points.
4. If a player lands on an event space, he or she may choose one player and take a point away from that person's score.
5. The player with the most points at the end of the game wins.
6. Set a time limit for this game.

for Words Their Way™ with English Learners

Go to PDToolkit, choose your book, click the Additional Resources tab, and select Racetrack Game Board (left and right) in the Templates section.

ACTIVITIES   LETTER NAME–ALPHABETIC STAGE

Word Study with English Learners in the Within Word Pattern Stage

Ms. Hester's second grade class is bubbling with happy chatter as the students settle in for the day. It is January and the first week back to school after the winter break. She has planned to spend the week reconnecting with the thematic unit the class was working on in December, reviewing their word study lists and revisiting some of the standard literacy block routines and practices.

The classroom is chock-full of books. Bookshelves near Ms. Hester's teaching table hold sets of leveled books to use in her guided reading groups. On one of her bookshelves she has a collection of easy reference materials such as picture dictionaries and alphabet books, as well as laminated cards to illustrate and label specific content areas such as zoo animals, the solar system, colors, weather words, and so on. She asks students to refer to these when they are searching for vocabulary. At the front of the room, three tubs are filled with thematic books related to the current unit of study—matter.

Print is displayed around the room in many ways. One bulletin board announces the class to be "Matter Detectives" and displays pictures and labels of items that are solids, liquids, and gases. Nearby there is a display of related words in a word bank for students to refer to; the display includes *air, water, ice, steam, heavy, light, flow,* and *rise.* Another large bulletin board area displays individual photographs of the students, with their edited writing posted underneath. Labels around the room let students know where classroom materials belong. Charts are displayed all around as well—including alphabet and sound charts, charts of the daily schedule and center rotations, charts of adjectives to use in writing, and charts of directions such as "What to do if you finish early."

Ms. Hester calls together a group of eight children who had been studying long vowel patterns before the winter break. She hands out baggies with word cards inside that feature the long *o* sound as in *rope.* She says, "We've been away from our word study for quite a while now, so let's get our brains warmed up by remembering what we were doing before the break. Sort your words into the three patterns we've discovered so far that make the long *o* sound. If you find a word that doesn't have the /ō/ sound, set it aside."

Ms. Hester writes CVCe, CVVC, and CV on the board. "Find these three cards in your bag to help you set up your columns." She listens to make sure that students are saying the words aloud as they sort. Soon, the table is covered with the words they have sorted—words like *home, vote, stone,* and *globe* under the CVCe column; *boat, coast,* and *loaf* under the CVVC column; and *so* and *no* under the CV column. When students have finished this sort, Mrs. Hester asks them to read their words to partners. "Partners, check to make sure that the words are sorted according to the guide cards!"

Next, students are invited to "think of another way to sort your words." Students mix their words up and make their own categories. One student is sorting her words by whether they start with a single letter, a blend, or a digraph. Another student is counting how many letters each word contains.

When the sorting time is over, Ms. Hester asks the students to replace their words in the baggies and return them to a plastic tub. She takes a few minutes to reflect orally with the group about what they learned from the experience. Students share that it was fun, because they already knew about these word patterns. When asked if their brains are ready to learn more, the group calls out an enthusiastic "Yes!"

This vignette about Ms. Hester's classroom illustrates many key ideas about effective literacy instruction for students at the transitional stage of development. Her classroom is like a greenhouse—she provides the structures, materials, and experiences to nurture students' growing skills. Ms. Hester also holds the expectation that students will soon develop into independent, self-directed readers and writers and provides many experiences to help them in this process. Ms. Hester has set up the physical environment in her classroom with lots of meaningful print and plenty of reading and writing materials for students to access. She knows the developmental levels of her students and plans activities accordingly, building on students' natural enthusiasm and organizing opportunities for students to interact with others.

> Transitional students are becoming independent readers and writers.

This chapter focuses on literacy development and instruction for students at the transitional stage of reading and the within word pattern (WWP) stage of spelling, like many of the students in Ms. Hester's class. We describe how the essential literacy activities of Read To, Read With, Write With, Word Study, and Talk With (RRWWT) work together to provide a cohesive learning environment for English learners. We also share examples of specific word study lessons so you can get a picture of how an effective teacher is explicit, yet still challenges students to think at higher levels.

Literacy Instruction for English Learners in the Transitional/Within Word Pattern Stage

The term *transitional* as used in this chapter refers to the stage of reading development that occurs between the beginning and intermediate levels, as described in Chapter 1 of this book. It is not to be confused with the period of transition that is referred to in the bilingual field when a student moves from instruction in a home language to instruction in English.

Students at the transitional stage of literacy development are beginning to gain fluency in their reading and writing. They recognize a large number of words by sight and can represent all the sounds they hear in words with reasonable letter–sound correspondences. Their advancing skills and extensive knowledge of sight words give them the ability to read longer texts, such as early chapter books, as well as to write more easily. Some words in their writing will be spelled correctly and others will be phonetically close and readable (Bear, Invernizzi, Templeton, & Johnston, 2008; Ehri, 1997).

During the transitional stage of reading students are in the within word pattern stage of spelling. In this stage, students move beyond a reliance on individual sounds as the only decoding tool and begin to look at chunks in words—or their patterns. In their reading, students differentiate between short and long vowel patterns, such as when reading the words *bit* versus *bite*. In their writing, within word pattern spellers begin to mark the long vowel pattern, sometimes incorrectly, such as when they spell *paid* as PADE.

The transitional stage of reading is an especially crucial gateway for English learners as they consolidate their literacy skills. The complexity of phonics patterns can be overwhelming to students who are just learning the meanings of words and have not had as many experiences hearing or reading them. English learners who bring literacy skills from a home language that is much more phonetically regular than English are often shackled to the idea that sounds should be represented in print with more of a one-to-one correspondence to letters. It is important that (1) students have a strong foundation in initial and final consonants, blends, digraphs, and short vowels; (2) they have clear and systematic instruction when moving to more abstract patterns; and (3) new learning builds on what students know. Otherwise, learners are likely to become overloaded and even unsure of how to spell short vowel words.

The following big ideas are important to keep in mind when designing appropriate instruction for English learners at the transitional stage (Díaz-Rico & Weed, 2002; Echevarría, Vogt, & Short, 2008).

Be Pattern Puzzlers

Help students make sense of the ever-more-complex orthographic system of English. What they have learned up to now about the writing system is still true; an additional layer of understanding is just being added. This is growth! Students can become step-by-step "pattern puzzlers," as they work first with comparing short and long sounds and spellings for a specific vowel, and then later as they compare spelling patterns in each vowel as they were doing in Ms. Hester's class with long *o.* Be positive and be systematic. Follow the scope and sequence we have outlined in this book. Take the instructional time needed for students to thoroughly understand the concept you are working with, and always check that you are at your students' developmental levels before moving ahead.

Include Vocabulary Instruction

With expanding reading and writing abilities, the amount and kinds of words that students encounter in their texts will greatly increase. This means that, in addition to learning the process of reading more complex words and sentence structures, students will also face many new vocabulary words. Reading materials and word study activities at this stage become less dependent on picture cues, which in the past have supported students' vocabulary development. It is very important to include explicit vocabulary instruction within literacy activities such as word sorts, concept sorts, and small-group reading instruction. Check for students' understanding of the content and structure words you are using in your lessons by asking them to use the words in a sentence or finding a synonym. Be ready to provide explicit instruction when students do not know common words that you hadn't realized were problematic such as *section* or *source* (Dutro & Helman, 2009).

Wide Reading Supports Oral and Written Language Development

Give students many opportunities to read a wide variety of materials at their instructional levels. Wide reading helps them become more fluent and automatic; it also provides students with frequent encounters with high-frequency words. The more that English learners recognize and practice reading the patterns within words that they are studying, the more they will develop an inner sense for "what looks right." This exposure will also help students build the background knowledge to associate the correct spelling patterns of common **homophones** such as *cheap* and *cheep* that are studied at this stage.

▶ **Homophones**

Words that sound the same but are spelled differently, such as *deer* and *dear.*

    Another benefit of reading lots of easy materials is that it helps English learners to fine-tune distinctions in sound that may have been tricky for them to distinguish aurally. For example, some English learners pronounce the short *i* sound as a long *e* ("seat" for *sit*). With exposure to more and more words in texts, inquisitive readers and spellers now begin to associate spelling patterns with pronunciation differences. Thus, texts support this phonetic awareness.

Sounds Play a Role at the Within Word Pattern Stage

For English learners at the within word pattern stage, sounds continue to play an important role in word study instruction. But discriminating closely related sounds can also become a quagmire for students whose home languages do not have similar sound distinctions. To provide scaffolding for students, consider the following:

1. Help students differentiate closely related sounds in vowel patterns in a low-stress, active manner. Chanting phrases ("I *sit* in my *seat*"), echo reading after a teacher, or doing a dramatic reader's theater are all ways for students to exaggerate word pronunciations and practice hearing and saying the vowel sounds in an enjoyable way.

2. Preassess students' discrimination of vowel sounds so that you are prepared to provide more support if needed. Can students hear the distinctions in contrasting vowel sounds such as in *nest* and *tree*, *ship* and *sheep*? If they cannot, the sorting activity becomes a random guessing game or they become dependent on visual sorting. To avoid this, begin with picture sorts for vowel sound contrasts as a way to assess students' phonological discrimination.

3. When students cannot easily discriminate vowel sounds, find an easier contrast to begin with. For example, if students have difficulty hearing the distinction between the long and short sounds of *a*, it might be wise to start with the long and short sounds of *o* instead. Provide words and pictures to help anchor spelling–sound distinctions. Follow the guidelines in this book to help you predict which sound contrasts may be less difficult for particular students. Ultimately, when confronted with a tricky vowel contrast, provide as much support as possible by using words and pictures together and engaging in lots of modeling and practice.

In the within word pattern stage, students have enough sight words, know enough about sound–symbol correspondences, and understand long and short vowel patterns sufficiently well to attend to sound differences among short vowels. For example, Spanish-speaking students who in the past may have pronounced a word like *hat* more like "hot" will begin to identify the distinction. They also come to recognize that the *a* in *father* may be more like the short *o* sound than the short *a*. The ability to detect subtle sound differences develops at this time for students who speak a regional dialect; students gain proficiency in manipulating language to shift speech styles as they wish. For instance, students may vary their word selection or pronunciation to match the speech of friends or family members. Interestingly, as students progress through the within word pattern stage, changes in their own pronunciation of the vowel sounds are noticeable.

As discussed in the preceding chapter, blends and ending sounds can also require extra support for English learners. Continue to be aware of the relationship between sounds and spelling patterns for transitional students. This is a great time to help students verbalize their understanding of the sound–pattern connection in English words and to compare it to their home languages.

Characteristics of Orthographic Development for English Learners in the Within Word Pattern Stage

for Words Their Way™ with English Learners

Go to PDToolkit, choose your book, click the Videos tab, and watch the videos titled "A Week of Sorting with Second Graders in the Early Within Word Pattern Stage" and "Activities with Fourth Graders in the Within Word Pattern Stage."

During the within word pattern stage of development, students expand on their knowledge of short vowel patterns to experiment with how to spell the long vowel sounds. Students now understand that TRAN does not spell *train*, but they may attempt to spell the long sound by adding a silent *e* to the end, as in TRANE. As students progress through this stage, they explore the varied long vowel patterns, the influence of *r* on vowels, and the spellings of other complex or ambiguous vowel patterns. They also expand on their understanding of digraphs and consonant blends in the study of complex consonants such as the *tch* in *match* or the *thr* in *threw*. By the end of the within word pattern stage, students are working with homophones and homographs and get an introduction to how the meaning layer of the orthography plays a role in spelling. Two sections of video on the website feature students in the within word pattern stage: Ms. Woessner models a week of word study activities with students at the early

FIGURE 6.1 Adriana's Spelling Sample

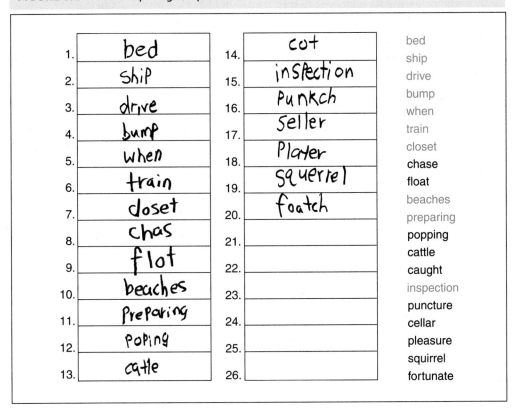

1.	bed	14.	cot	bed
2.	ship	15.	insPection	ship
3.	drive	16.	Punkch	drive
4.	bump	17.	Seller	bump
5.	when	18.	Player	when
6.	train	19.	squerrel	train
7.	closet	20.	foatch	closet
8.	chas	21.		chase
9.	flot	22.		float
10.	beaches	23.		beaches
11.	Preparing	24.		preparing
12.	poping	25.		popping
13.	catle	26.		cattle
				caught
				inspection
				puncture
				cellar
				pleasure
				squirrel
				fortunate

within word pattern stage, and Ms. Roberts models word work at the middle within word pattern stage.

Adriana is a good example of an English learner at the within word pattern stage. Figure 6.1 shows developmental spelling samples from an inventory she was given in class. Adriana correctly spelled all of the short vowel words, including *bump*. When tackling long vowel words, she correctly spelled *train* and *beaches* but spelled *chase* as CHAS and *float* as FLOT. In the multisyllable words on the list, Adriana gave her best guess on words such as SQUER-REL for *squirrel* and CATLE for *cattle*. It is interesting to see how syllables are omitted, as in FOATCH for *fortunate* and PUNKCH for *puncture*. It is also important to note how she may have plugged in a known word for a difficult word: PLAYER for *pleasure*. As a within word pattern speller, it would be important for Adriana to begin a systematic study of long vowel patterns, so she develops a deep understanding of these before moving on to two-syllable word patterns.

The representation of vowel sounds in English is very complex. Although the short vowel sounds may pose some difficulty for English learners because many of their sounds are not present in students' home languages, in general the short vowels represent a one sound to one letter match. When students move into the within word pattern stage of development, they must use more abstract thinking; they not only need to identify the sounds they hear in words, they must also understand and choose from a variety of vowel and consonant patterns that involve silent letters; that is, they are no longer dealing with a one-to-one match.

Within word pattern spellers come to realize several key ideas:

* English has many more vowel sounds than letters. Vowels are used in numerous ways on their own and in combination to represent various sounds.

* There is often more than one possible way to spell a given vowel sound. Even as students learn the logic of "marking" a long vowel with a silent *e* or vowel pair (**plane**, **plain**), they

Representing vowel sounds in English can be very complex for English learners.

need to become familiar with the correct spellings of specific words. For instance, although it would be logical for a student to spell *boat* as BOTE, that would not be correct.

- English has many "oddball" words that do not match the patterns being studied, such as the word *love*, which appears to have a CVCe pattern but no long *o* sound. These words should not be ignored, but rather discussed in the context of how they are different from the norm. Students need to have the support of enough positive examples of the pattern, however, so that they can get a good sense of how vowel and complex consonant patterns work.

- English learners who have literacy experiences in a language that is more phonetically transparent come to understand the qualitative differences between English and their home language. Discussions and comparisons allow students to bring the similarities and differences among languages to a heightened awareness.

The job of students at the within word pattern stage of orthographic development is to understand the whys and hows of patterns involving vowels and complex consonants. Some of the terms describing these patterns are delineated in Table 6.1. This time of transition builds on the sound layer that students have relied on previously and ultimately connects them to the meaning layer that guides advanced spelling.

Sequence of Word Study for the Within Word Pattern Stage

Table 6.2 shows a suggested sequence of word study for English learners at the within word pattern stage. The first two columns outline important features that are studied and give specific examples. The final column highlights aspects of these features that may require special attention or instruction for English learners.

TABLE 6.1 Helpful English Phonics Vocabulary

TERM	WHAT IT IS	EXAMPLE WORDS
Short vowel	A set of sounds the five vowels can represent, typically in closed syllables such as -am, -em, -im, -om, -um.	*cat, bed, him, not, run*
Long vowel	A set of sounds the five vowels can represent, often described as "saying their names."	*play, he, ice, loan, rule*
r-influenced vowel	An *r* that follows a vowel sometimes influences the sound the vowel represents, such as in the word *car*.	*park, her, stir, work, hurt*
Diphthong	Complex sounds in which two vowels glide into each other within the same syllable, for example as represented by *oi/oy* or *ou/ow*.	*join, joy, cloud, cow*
Ambiguous vowel	A vowel sound that is neither long nor short, such as *aw* or *al*, or vowel patterns that stand for more than one sound (e.g., *ough* as in *cough* or *tough*).	*salt, small, draw, fault, fought*
Consonant cluster	A combination of consonants that create blends of two or more sound sequences such as *bl-, str-, -nch, thr-,* or *spl-*.	*shred, three, punch, march, stripe*
Contraction	Two words that have been put together with a letter or letters taken out such as *I'll* (from *I will*).	*can't, won't, hasn't, here's, they'll, she'll, should've*
Homophone	Words that sound alike but have different spellings and different meanings.	*meet/meat, die/dye, by/bye/buy*

TABLE 6.2   Sequence of Word Study for English Learners in the Within Word Pattern Stage

FEATURES	EXAMPLES	INSTRUCTIONAL NOTES
Early		
Short and long sounds of each vowel using pictures	*Cat/cake; desk/cheese; pig/pie; clock/coat; sun/soup*	Sound may not occur in home language, so perceiving its pronunciation is difficult. It is most important that students hear a distinction between the long and short sound, not that their pronunciation of these sounds is exact.
Short and long vowel sounds (CVC/CVCe) in words and pictures	*Mad/made; hot/hose; drum/cute*	See above. Also, students who bring literacy skills from a shallow orthography may have difficulty understanding more complex vowel representations.
Long vowel sounds using the CVCe and CVVC patterns	*Mice, huge, rain, toad*	Different letter patterns spell the same long vowel sounds. In-depth vocabulary is needed to distinguish different spellings for the same pronunciation and to attach an appropriate spelling pattern. Students may attempt to use diphthongs for the long vowel sounds in *a* and *o* (AYTE for *ate*, HOUME for *home*).
Less common long vowel patterns	*Play, chew*—ending vowel or CV *Kind, fold*—VCC *High, right*—VCC (*igh*)	Students who bring literacy skills from a shallow orthography may have difficulty understanding the range and complexity of vowel representations in English.
Middle		
R-influenced vowel patterns	*Far/fare; her/hear; fir/fire; more/work; purr/pure*	Many languages do not have *r*-influenced vowels, so perceiving their pronunciation and attaching the correct spelling pattern is difficult.
Late		
Diphthongs	*Boil, boy; ground, growl*	Vowel sounds may not be combined in this way in students' home languages.
Other ambiguous vowel sounds	*Moon, book; draw, cause; wash; fall; bought*	Sounds may not occur in students' home languages, so perceiving their pronunciation, differentiating them from similar vowel sounds, and attaching the correct spelling patterns are difficult tasks.
Beginning complex consonants and consonant clusters	Silent beginning consonants as in *knife, gnaw, wrist* *Scrape*—triple *r* blends *Three*—consonant digraphs plus *r* blends	These sound and spelling patterns may not exist in students' home languages, which can make attaching spelling patterns more difficult.
Contractions	*Here's, they'll, couldn't*	In-depth vocabulary and verbal flexibility are needed to associate contractions with their longer forms.
Homophones with long vowel patterns	*Plane, plain; meat, meet; write, right; doe, dough; due, do, dew*	In-depth vocabulary is needed to distinguish different spellings for the same pronunciation and to attach an appropriate spelling pattern.
Introduction to two-syllable words	*Afraid, belong*	Spelling two-syllable words increases the cognitive difficulty for students. Unstressed vowels that take on the schwa sound can be especially difficult to represent.
Introduction to inflectional endings with plural and past tense	*Girls (-s), boxes (-es); Cleaned, walked, treated*	Verb forms and plurals may be constructed differently in home languages or these forms may not occur. Perceiving the pronunciation of *-ed* at the end of a word may be difficult.

▶ **Patterns**

The second layer or tier of English orthography in which letter sequences, rather than individual letters themselves, represent vowel sounds.

FIGURE 6.2 Long *a* and Short *a* Pattern Sort

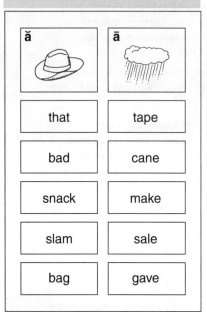

Students first spend time comparing the short and long sounds of each vowel using pictures to make these distinctions. Next, students examine the **patterns** of single-syllable words beginning with the CVC and CVCe patterns. While students begin to look at patterns, instruction also includes continued study of the contrasts between the sound systems of students' home languages and English (e.g., the tendency of some English learners to pronounce a word like *cab* as "cob"). What is important is that students recognize a sound contrast between the sound of the *a* in *cab* and the long *a* in a word like *name*; if they can make this sound difference, then they can also see that there is a spelling difference, a first step to dividing the words by pattern (CVC/CVCe), as in Figure 6.2.

After students are familiar with the sound differences within a vowel, words using the common vowel patterns of CVCe and CVVC are included in the sorts (e.g., *make* versus *paid*). Students spend a significant chunk of time working on these common long vowel patterns with one vowel in depth; when they understand how the short and long patterns differ, their study extends to other vowels. It is hoped that by studying one vowel in depth, perception of the CVCe and CVVC patterns will develop easily and quickly with subsequent vowels.

After students become comfortable with the most common long vowel patterns across all five vowels, they move to exploring less common long vowel patterns such as the ending vowel sounds in *play* and *chew* and VCC patterns such as *kind* and *high*. These diverse sounds and spelling patterns challenge students to continue to grow as "pattern puzzlers." It is the job of the teacher to help English learners see and understand the regularities in the writing system and to build on what students know.

R-INFLUENCED VOWEL PATTERNS. In the middle within word pattern stage, students examine the influence that certain consonants, such as *r*, have on vowel sounds. For instance, *r* changes the sound of the vowel in what should be short vowel words, making it difficult to know how to spell words such as *her*, *first*, *word*, and *turn*. English learners from many languages find the sound of the English *r* hard to pronounce, and this adds to the spelling challenge. *R*-influenced word study activities compare words that contain the *ar*, *er*, *ir*, *or*, and *ur* chunks and their long vowel counterparts, supporting English learners in clarifying their knowledge base relating to this feature. Word study of *r*-influenced vowels continues through the middle and late portions of the within word pattern stage.

DIPHTHONGS. Diphthongs are complex sounds in which two vowel sounds slide into each other within the same syllable, such as in the word *boy* or *cloud*. As students in this stage work to master vowel patterns, diphthongs are an important feature to learn. Students examine the spelling patterns of these sounds and consider how the position of the diphthong within a word influences its spelling, such as in *joy* versus *join*. Because two sounds can be heard in a diphthong, English learners often find them easier to learn.

OTHER AMBIGUOUS VOWEL SOUNDS. Continuing to build on vowel patterns, within word pattern spellers work with "other ambiguous vowel sounds"—sounds that are neither short nor long. These include vowel sounds in words like *book*, *saw*, *caught*, *tall*, and *cough*. Differentiating these sounds from their short and long vowel counterparts and attaching the correct spelling patterns for a variety of words are indeed critical features to master at this stage.

COMPLEX SINGLE-SYLLABLE WORDS. By the later portion of the within word pattern stage of spelling, students take on a deeper analysis of consonant clusters and digraphs. Although students have learned to work with consonant clusters from late in the letter name stage, they now investigate silent beginning consonants such as in *knife* and *gnat*, blends with three letters such as in *scrape* and *stream*, and blends involving digraphs such as *three* and *shrink*. This word work involves multiple layers, as students are asked to discriminate a series of complex consonant sounds (e.g., /s/–/c/–/r/) as well as attach the appropriate vowel pattern (e.g., *ape*) in words like *scrape*. Taking the time to work closely with English learners on these features can serve multiple purposes. First, it helps students explicitly identify the types of clusters possible in English. In many of the students' home languages these complex clusters of consonants simply do not exist. Second, this word work gives students a chance to review both the vowel patterns and the vocabulary of complex single-syllable words such as *shrub* and *strike*. These words use a multiplicity of vowel patterns from short to long to diphthongs and other ambiguous vowel sounds. Working with a variety of complex single-syllable words allows students to put together the sum of their learning about consonants and vowel patterns prior to taking on multisyllable words.

INTRODUCTION TO THE SPELLING–MEANING CONNECTION AND TO TWO-SYLLABLE WORDS. As students become proficient at spelling the vowel patterns and consonant clusters in complex single-syllable words, their word study focus expands. A simple first step in discussing the idea that spelling and meaning are often connected begins with a focus on contractions. Discuss with students the meanings, spellings, and the grammatical usages of contractions. For example, use *isn't* and *is not* in parallel sentences and have students notice the logic of their construction. English learners will need to practice these words orally, understand how each component word contributes to the contraction's meaning, and practice reading and writing contractions in authentic contexts.

Another introduction to the spelling–meaning connection occurs when students investigate homophones, which are word partners that sound the same but are spelled differently, such as *plane* and *plain* or *for*, *four*, and *fore*. Late within word pattern spellers combine their knowledge of vowel patterns with an expanding oral and written vocabulary to begin to understand that what a word means relates to how it is spelled (Templeton, 1983). For example, students come to understand that although *sea* and *see* are pronounced in the same way, only one is correct in the sentence "I want to *see* the movie." Activities to help English learners attach the appropriate spellings to specific words will involve talking explicitly about the meanings of homophones, having lots of opportunities to see these words while reading, illustrating the words, and getting feedback during the writing process.

Late within word pattern spellers have developed a firm foundation in their understanding of a multitude of one-syllable words. Now they prepare to transition into the upper levels of orthographic development and to focus on multisyllable words. This advancement begins with an exploration of high-frequency two-syllable words such as *ago*, *belong*, and *until*. Now that students are comfortable with single-syllable words, these words are not hard to spell.

One final feature addressed at the end of the within word pattern stage is an introduction to plural and past tense inflectional endings such as in *box<u>es</u>* and *clean<u>ed</u>*. Inflectional endings are studied in great depth during the syllables and affixes stage of word study (see Chapter 7), but it is helpful for students in the late within word pattern stage to be introduced to them conceptually with words that do not require any adjustments. For instance, adding *-s*, *-es*, and *-ed* to create words such as *girls*, *wishes*, and *helped* is straightforward and allows English learners to develop a conceptual understanding of the grammatical process.

Studying High-Frequency Words with English Learners

Encouraging English learners to memorize high-frequency words is a tempting way to approach spelling instruction. Many students who have limited oral skills seem to succeed at remembering words visually. In the end, however, this approach does not help students understand the logic of the English writing system, and when students have memorized all they can, they will be left without a road map for their literacy journey. Although some limited time studying high-utility words may be appropriate during the early stages of development, this study should not replace the developmental scope and sequence outlined in this book. Words should be analyzed in systematic ways, by features. This helps students make sense of the writing system and construct categories to support long-term memory. Students must memorize the "oddballs," but must see them as simply that—different from the usual pattern.

. . . .
Components of Literacy Instruction at the Transitional Stage

Students at the transitional stage of reading need many experiences with the essential literacy activities of Read To, Read With, Write With, Word Study, and Talk With to fortify their expanding reading and writing abilities. Here are some suggestions for implementing the essential literacy components with English learners at the transitional stage.

Talk With

At this level, students' oral language skills are advancing, and they are trying out longer, more syntactically complex sentences. If the classroom climate allows them, students will become oral language resources for each other and help one another practice their developing vocabulary and grammar. Teachers can help students to interact orally throughout their literacy activities in many important ways:

- Discuss everything—words, phrases, sentences, lists, poems, stories, books! Help students connect what they say to written language by keeping charts of featured words, poems, directions, dictations, and other notes. Find ways for students to practice the words they are learning in a meaningful context. When working with a large group of students, stop at frequent intervals for partner sharing activities. For example, ask students to turn to the person next to them and "share a time when you felt *productive*."

- Use discussion to check for understanding about the lesson. Ask students to "use that word in a sentence," "share what just happened in the story in your own words," or "tell me how all of those things are alike."

- Now that students can write longer pieces of text, help them develop their ideas ahead of time by talking with fellow students or the teacher. Encourage them to jot down big ideas on a **mind map** or other graphic organizer so they can hold onto these thoughts throughout the writing process.

- Think out loud with students about how speech varies but print remains consistent. As their oral language and literacy skills advance, students begin to be more aware of variations in spoken dialect and connecting those to written language. Students' developing reading proficiency helps them use the support of print to fine-tune their pronunciation. For example, the short *i* and short *e* distinction will become clearer as students learn many written words such as *pen/pin*, *red/rid*, and *beg/big* and attempt to refine their pronunciations.

- Engage in **reader's theater** and other performance and rereading activities to help students focus on expression in reading and speaking.

Read To

Students at the transitional level of reading are finding a greater range of materials to read on their own, but this does not mean you should stop reading *to* them. By listening to stories, nonfiction texts, and other pieces that are too hard for them to read on their own, students learn about unfamiliar topics, hear new vocabulary words and sentence structures, and are motivated to explore an array of reading materials. So for your read-aloud lessons, choose texts that excite, enthrall, and open new doors to students. As you read, be expressive and dramatic, so that students hear fluent models. Pick materials that appeal to students from different cultural backgrounds and to both boys and girls. Inspire your students to become connected personally with books.

▶ **Mind Map**

Starting with a central idea and extending rays outward, a mind map is a visual way of brainstorming and showing connections.

▶ **Reader's Theater**

A simple form of dramatics in which students take roles and read from a script or a story.

The vocabulary in books at this level is becoming more abstract at a rapid pace and is likely to be less familiar than the language of oral conversations. Technical words in nonfiction texts such as *microscopic, decomposition,* or *organism* will demand some visual support and discussion. Even narrative texts use less common words and possibly unfamiliar concepts, such as *previously, annual,* or *loyal*. Preview your read-aloud texts to be sure the vocabulary is at the listening comprehension level of your students. If you doubt that the English learners in class will understand the vocabulary completely, consider providing ways to give extra support. You might preview the content in a small group; provide pictures; find an outlet for students to ask clarifying questions about the material; let students listen to the text on tape after hearing it read aloud; discuss their ideas with peers in their home language; or you may make the decision to select a text that is more connected to students' background experiences and language level.

Read To activities can also be a bridge to creating instructional-level reading materials for students in content dictations, as described in Activity 5.17. If your textbook or content resource material is too difficult for students to read on their own, read it to them. Take time to clarify confusing vocabulary, answer questions, and share visuals relating to the topic. After reading, ask students to dictate to you what they learned from hearing this material. Their dictations can be typed up and used as Read With texts at other times of the day.

Read With

Students at the transitional level are beginning to read easy chapter books; they are reading more fluently in phrases, no longer word by word. Transitional readers need lots of opportunities to read material that is not too hard for them in order to become automatic, rhythmic, and expressive in their reading. Make available to students as many easy-to-read texts as you can.

Schedule multiple opportunities within the school day for students to read on their own, in small teacher-guided groups, and with peers. Even though students can now read a greater range of materials on their own, they still need regular time in small instructional groups at their developmental levels. During these lessons, teachers help students by previewing materials, providing support for vocabulary and more complex decoding skills, developing strategies for comprehension, and assessing that reading materials are at the appropriate level of difficulty.

The transitional stage is a good time for teachers to set up social structures such as **book clubs** (Raphael, Pardo, & Highfield, 2002) within the classroom. Book clubs provide formats for groups of students to read the same texts and discuss them. English learners profit from engaging in these small-group activities because it is less intimidating to speak up in a small group, and it is expected that all members contribute. Reading becomes part of a social interaction, and this is highly motivating. Watch a book club in action in Ms. Nguyen's third grade class on the website. Partner reading activities also give students an opportunity to read material of interest at their levels and to interact with peers about it. Reading skills grow, language is developed and practiced, and motivation to read is enhanced—a winning combination all around!

During Read With activities, have students reread materials aloud, focusing on their pace, expression, and clarity. An improving words-per-minute rate is to be commended, but it is not the only goal. Students should notice and work on clustering together meaningful phrases; they should read at a normal pace; and their intonation should match the text's meaning. For instance, in the phrase "down the dark, scary hallway" there would be a slight pause between *dark* and *scary*, and the phrase might be read in a low or trembling manner. There are numerous ways for students to reread materials aloud for a meaningful purpose such as in reader's theater, where students use a short text as a dramatic reading; through the shared reading of poetry from group charts or overhead projections, especially if they will have an occasion to read the poem for an audience; in **author's chair**, where students have opportunities to read their personal writing to other students; and by practicing and reading simple picture books to younger students in a "big buddy" type relationship. Students can also be asked to reread some of these materials to family members at home for homework.

Provide vocabulary support for the texts you read aloud in class.

microscope

▶ **Book Clubs**
In-class structures in which groups of students select, read, and discuss books.

for Words Their Way™ with English Learners

Go to PDToolkit, choose your book, click the Videos tab, and watch the video titled "A Look into a Third-Grade Classroom Literacy Environment."

▶ **Author's Chair**
A format in which students present their own writing in class.

FIGURE 6.3 Writing Samples Tell about Language Development

We went to another one cars-cars that crash.

▶ **Writer's Workshop**

A time in class for students to focus on various aspects of the writing process, including prewriting, drafting, writing, revising, sharing, and publishing.

Write With

As in all stages of spelling development, students' unedited writing shows teachers their understanding of the orthographic system, as in the example shown in Figure 6.3. With advancing abilities to put more down in writing with less effort, the writing of students at the within word pattern level also gives teachers a window into their proficiency with the syntax and vocabulary of English. In other words, by looking at students' first-draft writing, teachers can get a good idea of what spelling features, sentence structures, and words students need to work on next. Based on common needs within the classroom, teachers can set up minilessons for individuals and small groups of students to address these goals. These lessons will be highly effective for students, because they focus on students' current understandings and confusions.

Write With time will progress along a couple of avenues. First, students should be encouraged to write freely in journals, personal narratives, notetaking, and so on. In many of these cases, content will override form, and students should not feel the pressure of "having to write it correctly." The message of what students are saying should be valued unconditionally. Processes such as **writer's workshop,** in which students work through a series of steps from prewriting through final editing and publishing, can be used with students on selected writing projects. Feedback from peers and teachers about the message and voice of the writing will help students see themselves as writers and value the importance of what they have to share while also attending to mastering the conventions of good writing.

Write With activities should also involve explicit instruction in the structures of specific writing forms such as letters, essays, stories, and reports. By using support strategies—modeling, providing visuals, guided practice, graphic organizers, and the like—teachers provide a scaffold for students to follow at first and then to expand on as their skills and understandings grow. Explicit guidelines allow English learners to be successful at writing projects even as they are developing oral and written language proficiency.

Word Study

Use the results of your developmental spelling assessments (see Chapter 2) to identify and cluster students into instructional groups. As the year progresses, continue to informally assess students and adjust groupings according to students' development. When you have identified students who are at the within word pattern stage, look at their spelling carefully to place them at the early, middle, or late stage and also to inform yourself about the features within this stage that they are using correctly and those they are just beginning to try out. The activities presented later in this chapter progress from early to late in this stage and can be selected according to the needs of your specific groups of students. The suggestions outlined next are general enough to apply to students throughout the within word pattern stage.

BUILD A CURIOSITY FOR WORD LEARNING. The increasing complexity of the orthographic system through the within word pattern stage might tempt you as a teacher to throw up your hands and say, "English spelling is very confusing!" This response will provoke overwhelming feelings of confusion in your students, too. Instead, consider fostering a climate of confidence and curiosity about words in your classroom. Let your students know that you will be their guide on a journey of discovery as they learn about the wide range of patterns in the writing system, moving from simple to more complex. Frame your word study lessons around the idea that all students are "pattern puzzlers" who explore words to look for commonalities and variations. Marvel at the abundance of interesting patterns you find, and talk about the oddballs that do not seem to fit. Learn with your students, and enjoy this adventure!

CONNECT THE PATTERNS BEING LEARNED TO THEIR SOUNDS. It is important for English learners to continue to work with pictures, to say words aloud as they sort, and not just to memorize visual patterns. Connecting words in print and speech allows word study to support oral language development and aids in deeper learning. Sounds and patterns go together, and speaking words helps learners to read and spell words.

DEVELOP A CONSISTENT AND COMPREHENSIVE ROUTINE FOR WORD SORTS. As you work with students in their instructional-level word study groups, follow a set format characterized by the terms *demonstrate*, *sort*, *check*, *reflect*, and *extend*. Ensure that the words or pictures are known, and only teach a small number of unknown words at a time. Teaching three to five new words is usually sufficient. Demonstrate and talk through the sort with the group the first time through. Then students sort on their own or with a partner under your supervision. Have students check their sorts with you or with peers before putting them away. Take the time to share reflections about what was learned in the sort. Extend the sort throughout the week using techniques described in Chapter 3, such as word hunts, speed sorts, no-peeking and writing sorts, and related games.

INTEGRATE PHONICS, SPELLING, AND VOCABULARY LEARNING. With increasingly complex vowel patterns to explore at this stage, there may be a tendency to focus only on the forms or structures of words. It is easy to get so intrigued by the ways that vowel sounds get expressed, such as the long *u* sound in *tune*, *cruise*, *clue*, *brew*, *food*, and *through*, that the meanings of these words may be assumed or overlooked. English learners need to know not only *how* the writing system operates but also what the words *mean*. Word study should not be attempted with unknown words unless meaningful vocabulary instruction is included. Set up procedures to ensure that students understand the words being used in sorts and games.

Check their background knowledge, teach them to self-monitor their comprehension and ask clarifying questions about words they do not know, use the words in sentences and other meaningful contexts, and have them set aside words they do not know before sorting. You might have students add small drawings on the fronts or backs of word cards to capture the meanings of the words (see Figure 6.4.) For an example of how to teach vocabulary in a word study lesson, watch Ms. Woessner in the long and short *u* lesson on the website.

FIGURE 6.4 Add Illustrations to Word Cards

tail | chain | frame

HELP STUDENTS LEARN AND APPLY ACADEMIC VOCABULARY FROM CONTENT AREA STUDIES. As students transition from the "learning to read" stage to the "learning from reading" stage, the importance of academic language takes on even greater prominence. Students are required to understand a growing body of technical vocabulary in their textbooks and reference materials. Word study activities such as the concept sorts included later in the Activities section can help students learn new academic vocabulary and apply it to their classroom units of study. After you have tried out some of the concept sorts in this book, consider the following approaches:

- Develop your own concept sorts based on the thematic units or content area studies in your classroom. Create cards with related words that students can read or pictures for words that are too difficult for them to decode. Conduct open and closed sorts using these cards.
- Use a pocket chart, bulletin board, or chart paper to create vocabulary word banks related to the key content words in the unit of study. Find pictures to clarify these terms, or ask student volunteers to illustrate them.
- Help students create personal dictionaries with vocabulary from content area studies. These can be used as a reference for the pronunciations, meanings, and spellings of important words.
- Include nonfiction reading materials at the students' instructional levels relating to the content area you are studying.
- Make connections to what students are reading. Have students discuss interesting words that come up in their daily reading, and connect these to word study lessons or concept sorts.

PDToolkit

for Words Their Way™ with English Learners

Go to PDToolkit, choose your book, click the Videos tab, and watch the video titled "A Week of Sorting with Second Graders in the Early Within Word Pattern Stage."

- Include writing projects that ask students to use specific vocabulary words relating to key concepts. On some occasions, you may want to provide frame sentences for students to build on such as "Electricity can make (*name of thing*) (*action*)." For example, "Electricity can make refrigerators get cold."

PDToolkit

for Words Their Way™ with English Learners

Go to PDToolkit, choose your book, click the Videos tab, and watch the video titled "Activities with Fourth Graders in the Within Word Pattern Stage."

MAKE THE MOST OF WORD STUDY NOTEBOOKS. Word study notebooks are mentioned throughout this book (see Chapters 3, 5, and 7). At the within word pattern stage, word study notebooks serve several purposes: to document or reflect on a learning activity, to categorize and keep lists of related words, or to use as a reference tool for spelling patterns and vocabulary. Create word study notebooks by adding lined paper to a three-pronged paper folder or using a single-subject composition book. Add tabs for different activities, such as "Reflections," "My Sorts," "Homophones," or "Vocabulary Words." Include the categories that fit with your word study lessons and students' needs. Add new pages or tabs as needed. For an example of students writing sorts in their word study notebooks as in Figure 6.5, see the lesson by Ms. Roberts on the website.

Make the word study notebook a working document and reference source. Bring it out for word study activities, and reflect on it at the close of your daily lesson. Use the notebook to list words that follow specific patterns as students discover them throughout the day and during word hunts. Encourage students to "look it up" in their word study notebook if they have questions about spelling patterns or vocabulary. Just as you and your students at the within word pattern stage are explorers on a learning adventure, let the word study notebook be your travel log to record the journey!

The preceding general ideas have presented a framework for the specific lessons you will use with your within word pattern spellers in word study. The rest of this chapter describes numerous specific sorts and games sequenced from least to most difficult for English learners at the within word pattern stage of development. These activities can be used to guide students into the world of complex vowel and consonant patterns while also helping them negotiate the increasing demands of content area study. Participating in these activities helps your students transition into a more advanced understanding of words that will frame their literacy development into the future.

FIGURE 6.5 Using a Word Study Notebook to Document Sorts

ACTIVITIES
FOR ENGLISH LEARNERS IN THE WITHIN WORD PATTERN STAGE

Throughout the following sorts and activities, students will have many opportunities to work with words and pictures that may be new to them. Sorts and other activities are sequenced according to early, middle, or late within-word pattern. Table 6.2 is a good reference for this sequence.

The series of sorts described in the activities section that follows are listed as Sorts 228–261 on the website that accompanies this book. To use the sorts in class, you will need to print them out from the website and make multiple copies for student use or have students access the interactive sorts on the website. To include additional pictures in your sorts, find the appropriate pictures that are laid out alphabetically in the Pictures for Sorts and Games section of the Appendix (pp. 262–297), copy them, and add them to your sort or go to the Create Your Own section of the website.

for Words Their Way™ with English Learners

Go to PDToolkit, choose your book, click the Sorts & Games tab, and select Within Word Pattern Stage from the Stage filter.

for Words Their Way™ with English Learners

Go to PDToolkit, choose your book, click the Additional Resources tab, and select Pictures for Sorts and Games. Or click the Sorts & Games tab and click Create Your Own!

Teaching New Words

The following ideas should be helpful in teaching new vocabulary as you sort and play.

MATERIALS. Depending on the sort or game involved, plan to have multiple copies of the words and pictures. They should be cut apart and placed in separate envelopes for student use. Students might be assigned to cut these up when they first come in so that they are ready for sorting later. At times you will want students to have their word study notebooks available to keep track of words, or you may ask them to create a personal picture dictionary. Other support materials that are helpful include commercially produced picture dictionaries, simple encyclopedias, topical reference materials, and reference cards (often sold as laminated pages with pictures and labels).

PROCEDURES. As you begin to work with a group of students in a word study activity, set the context for how the words or pictures are related. For example, if all of the words relate to a thematic unit, such as the community, introduce the words by letting students know the connection. If the words are not related by content but rather by a spelling pattern or grammatical feature, encourage students to be "pattern detectives" to see how the words are similar. You will not use all of the following steps in any one lesson, but consider the ideas as a resource list for your vocabulary instruction.

1. As a group, read through the set of picture or word cards in the sort or game. If students do not know how to read a certain word or do not know its meaning, set it aside for the time being.
2. Select a limited number of new vocabulary words to teach in a given lesson; three to five is usually a good number. Choose useful and important words that students will work with in their ongoing academic work and content area studies.
3. Identify the new vocabulary words or pictures, say the names out loud, and have students repeat them. Use the words in simple sentences.
4. Ask students to try using the new words in sentences or to say what they know about the words.
5. Encourage students to translate the words or pictures into their home languages. Let them discuss an unknown term with fellow students who may not understand it yet.
6. When possible, find pictures of the words that are unknown. This book has numerous simple pictures in the Appendix to use for reference. You may also want to expand your library of picture cards, picture dictionaries, reference charts or cards, and simple informational texts to use as support materials.
7. Let students practice saying and using the new words with partners or in small groups before doing the sort or game.

VARIATIONS. If you want to teach a bigger group of new words or pictures, consider some active games such as those presented in Chapter 4 in the Games Using Concept Picture Sorts section (p. 89).

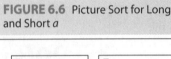

Go to PDToolkit, choose your book, click the Sorts & Games tab, and search for "Sort 228: Picture Sort Contrasting Short and Long Sound of *a*."

Word Study Activities at the Early Within Word Pattern Stage

6.1 Picture Sorts Contrasting the Short and Long Sounds of *a, o, u, i,* and *e*

FIGURE 6.6 Picture Sort for Long and Short *a*

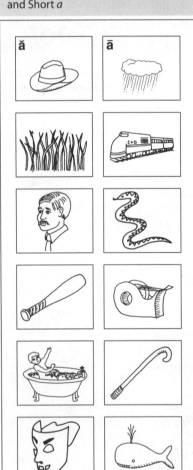

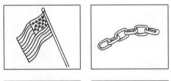
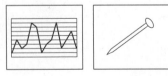

This series of five picture sorts draws students' attention to the short and long sounds of each of the vowels. The first sort will be described here in detail and the others should be done in a similar fashion. The letter *a* is a good vowel to start with for English learners. The short *e* sound is a very difficult sound to produce and differentiate for many English learners so it is saved for last. Using these picture sorts will ensure that students are really hearing the differences between the long and short sounds, as opposed to relying on letter cues.

DEMONSTRATE. Prepare Sort 228 from the website—short *a* and long *a*. Copy a sort page for each student or pair of students. Before doing the teacher-guided sort, hold up each picture card and ask students to give its name. Consider teaching the names of up to five unknown items. Additional unknown items can be set aside for another time. Set up *hat* and *rain* as the guide pictures at the top of your columns. Proceed through the sort by holding up each picture, and sharing your thinking in the following way:

> Here is a picture of a snake . . . Snn—aaaa—kk; I hear the letter *a* say its name in the middle. When we hear a vowel say its name in the middle, we call it a long vowel sound. I hear a long *a* in the middle of *snake. Snake* has the same sound as *rain* in the middle, so I will put it under the picture of rain. This is a picture of a bat. Bb–aaa–tt has a short *a* in the middle—the /ă/ sound like in the middle of the word *hat*. I'll put *bat* under *hat* because they both have the /ă/ sound, the short *a* sound in the middle. Now, you help me sort the rest of these pictures.

Continue with the students' help to sort all of the pictures. Model how to divide words into individual phonemes to isolate, identify, and then categorize the medial vowel sound in each word. If students do not pronounce the vowel sounds exactly as you do, don't worry. What is important is that they differentiate between the short and long sounds. Refined pronunciation will come with time.

When all the pictures have been sorted, check the sort. Name all of the pictures in each column and check to make sure they all have the same vowel sound in the middle. Ask, "Do all of these words sound alike in the middle? Do we need to move any?" The sort should look like Figure 6.6.

SORT, CHECK, AND REFLECT. Give each student (or pair of students) a copy of the set of pictures for guided practice. Now have the students repeat the sort under your supervision using the same key pictures as column headers. You may want to have students work with partners to mix up the pictures and take turns drawing a card, saying its name out loud, and sorting it in the correct column. More fluent English-speaking partners can supply the vocabulary for English learners. After sorting, remind students to check their sort by naming the words in each column to be sure the vowel sounds are the same. Ask them to reflect about how the words in each column are alike. Have them share their comments with others in the group. What did they find easy or difficult about this sort?

EXTEND. Give each student a plastic bag or envelope in which to store the pictures for independent sorting over several days by themselves or with a partner. As they sort, ask students to separate a word into its individual sounds and to explain why they placed a particular picture in a column. Have them restate the sounds of the vowels on which they are working.

Follow the same procedures for picture sorts contrasting the short and long sounds of *o*, *u*, *i*, and *e*. These sorts are outlined on the website (Sorts 228–232).

PDToolkit
for Words Their Way™ with English Learners

Go to PDToolkit, choose your book, click the Sorts & Games tab, and search for Sorts 228–232.

6.2 Concept Sort: Community

Make copies of the community concept sort from the website (Sort 233), cut the cards apart, and place them in envelopes or small plastic bags. To help keep multiple sets organized, consider using various colors of paper or scribbling with a colored marker on the back of each card so that it can easily be reorganized if multiple copies get mixed up.

PDToolkit
for Words Their Way™ with English Learners

Go to PDToolkit, choose your book, click the Sorts & Games tab, and search for "Sort 233: Community Concept Sort."

DEMONSTRATE. This sort features a collection of vocabulary words associated with communities. Introduce the key words (guide cards) as in Figure 6.7 and ask students to name places, persons, and objects in a community to activate their prior knowledge. Use several words from each category to demonstrate the sort, explaining your rationale through a think-aloud. For example, you may pick *factory*, *harvest*, and *drawbridge* to discuss together. In which environment does each item belong? Review all of the picture and word cards with the students to make sure they can both read and understand the meaning of each term. You may also want to have students review the picture and word cards with a partner. The completed sort should look something like the one listed as Sort 233 on the website.

FIGURE 6.7 The Community: An Example Concept Sort

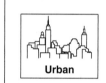

Urban · Rural · Waterway

After sorting, discuss how the places and objects relate to each other within a concept: "A farmer stores grain in a silo." Some words such as *barge* and *irrigation* may be unknown to students. Provide outlets for students to learn the meanings of these words, such as in explicit lessons, by asking classmates and teachers, or by using picture dictionaries, informational texts, and online reference materials.

SORT, CHECK, AND REFLECT. Students should shuffle their cards and repeat the sort under your supervision. Have them check their sorts by explaining their rationales to partners or to you. Encourage students to reflect by asking them to write a few sentences or draw a picture about one or all of the communities. For picture reflections, individual items can be labeled with the names of items from the sort.

EXTEND. Have the students work in pairs or small groups to create a detailed illustration of their own or a nearby community, identifying parts of the community presented in the sort and adding components that were not represented but could be included in the sort.

6.3 Word Sort Contrasting Short and Long Sounds of *a*, *o*, *u*, and *i*

This set of four sorts directs students' attention to the CVC and CVCe spelling patterns for the short and long sounds of *a*, *o*, *u*, and *i*; *e* is not included because there are so few words that have the pattern. Some of these will be included in a later sort. See Sorts 236–239 on the website. Several pictures are included in these sorts to ensure that students are focusing on sound differences, as opposed to relying only on letter cues.

DEMONSTRATE. Prepare Sort 236 from the website. Before doing the teacher-guided sort, hold up each picture and word card and ask students to give its name. Check that students

PDToolkit
for Words Their Way™ with English Learners

Go to PDToolkit, choose your book, click the Sorts & Games tab, and search for Sorts 236–239.

FIGURE 6.8 Word Sort Contrasting Short and Long Sounds of *a*

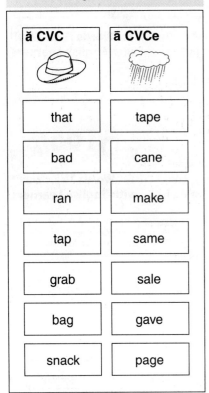

ă CVC	ā CVCe
that	tape
bad	cane
ran	make
tap	same
grab	sale
bag	gave
snack	page

know the names of pictures and understand the meanings of the words. Consider teaching the names and meanings of up to five unknown items. Additional unknown items can be set aside for another time. Ask your students if they notice anything about the words (they all have an *a* in them). Ask about the vowel sounds in the middles of the words. "Do they all have the same vowel sound?"

Introduce the short ă and the long ā symbols and their key pictures on the headers. Model the phoneme segmentation process involved in isolating and identifying each vowel sound—for example, "In *hat* we hear /h/–/ă/–/t/. In *rain* we hear /r/–/ā/–/n/." Demonstrate the sorting process by saying each of the other words and pictures and comparing them each to the guide words. Have your students join in as you continue to model the isolation, identification, and categorization of the medial vowel sound. It is critical that your students say the words out loud and segment their sounds rather than simply sorting by the visual pattern present. The sort should look like Figure 6.8; it is also outlined in full on the website.

When you are finished sorting, ask the students how the words in each column are alike and how they are different from the other words. Check the sort by naming all of the pictures and words in each column to make sure they all have the same vowel sound in the middle. "Do all of these words sound alike in the middle? Do we need to move any? What do we notice about the spellings of the words?" Add the CVC and CVCe cards to the top of the appropriate column and talk about how the C stands for any number of consonants (single, blend, or digraph) and the V for a vowel. Encourage students to discuss the role that the silent *e* has in creating the long vowel sound.

SORT, CHECK, AND REFLECT. Give each student or pair of students a copy of the sort for guided practice. Now have the students repeat the sort under your supervision, using the same key pictures as column headers. Tell your students to say each word aloud as they sort. You may want to have students work with partners to mix up the words and take turns drawing a card, saying its name out loud and sorting it into the correct column. After sorting, remind students to check their sorts by naming the words in each column to be sure the sounds are the same in the middle. If a student does not notice a mistake, provide guidance by saying, "One of these doesn't fit. See if you can hear which one as I read them all." Then read each word card, being careful to enunciate each vowel sound clearly. Ask students to reflect on how the words and pictures in each column are alike. Have them share their comments with others in the group. You might have students write how the words in one column are alike and how they are different from the words in the other. What did they find easy or difficult about this sort?

EXTEND. Have students store their words and pictures in an envelope or plastic bag so they can reuse them throughout the week in individual and partner sorts. Students should repeat this sort several times. See the list of routines for word sorting in Chapter 3 to plan follow-up activities to the basic sorting lesson. It is important to introduce the no-peeking sort now that students are working with visual patterns. Model it before sending students off to do it with partners. After sorting words across the week students can now be assessed by calling out six to ten words for a short spelling test or assessment on a whiteboard.

Follow the same directions to contrast long and short *o*, *u*, and *i* sounds by using Sorts 237–239 on the website.

6.4 Word Sorts Contrasting Spelling Patterns for Long *a* and *o*

This sort focuses on two common long vowel patterns, CVCe and CVVC. This sort supports students in learning the most common patterns that create the long vowel sound.

DEMONSTRATE. Prepare Sort 240 on the website, "Word Sorts Contrasting Spelling Patterns for Long *a*." Follow the procedures described before to check that students can read and understand the words. Teach a small number of words that are new to students. Ask your students if they notice anything about the words (they all have an *a* in them). Ask about the vowel sounds in the middles of the words. "Do they all have the same vowel sound?"

Introduce the CVCe and CVVC column header cards. Ask students to tell you what these letters stand for and to think of example words. Model the process of looking at one of the long vowel words and labeling its components: "*Make* has a consonant, a vowel, another consonant, and the letter *e*. So, *make* follows the CVCe pattern. *Paid* has a consonant, vowel, another vowel, and a final consonant. So, *paid* follows the CVVC pattern." Demonstrate the sorting process by analyzing each of the other words and comparing them to the header cards. Have students join in as you continue to model this process. Note that a blend or digraph can also be considered as a consonant in this pattern (e.g., *claim* = CVVC). It is critical that your students say the words out loud even as they look for visual patterns for sorting. The completed sort should look like Figure 6.9.

When you are finished sorting, ask the students how the words in each column are alike and how they are different from the other words. Check the sort by rereading the words aloud and visually noticing the spelling patterns. "Do all of these words follow the CVCe or CVVC pattern? Do we need to move any?"

SORT, CHECK, AND REFLECT. Give each student or pair of students a copy of the sort for guided practice. Now have the students repeat the sort under your supervision, using the same column headers. Tell your students to say each word aloud as they sort. You may want to have students work with partners to mix up the words and take turns drawing a card, saying its name out loud and sorting it in the correct column. After sorting, remind students to check their sorts by naming the words in each column and reviewing the spelling patterns. If a student does not notice a mistake, provide guidance by saying, "One of these doesn't fit. See if you can notice the spelling pattern that is different." Ask students to reflect on how the words in each column are alike. Have them share their comments with others in the group. You might have students write how the words in one column are alike and how they are different from the words in the other. What did they find easy or difficult about this sort?

EXTEND. Have students store their words in an envelope or plastic bag so they can reuse them throughout the week in individual and partner sorts. Students can also go on a word hunt to find long *a* words that match the CVCe and CVVC patterns to add to their word study notebooks.

Use the same directions for the long *o* sound, using Sort 241 on the website.

6.5 Word Sort Contrasting Sounds and Spelling Patterns for Long *a* and *o*

This sort starts by differentiating words with the long *a* or long *o* sound and then asks students to notice the spelling patterns across both long vowels. It is a good review and provides an opportunity for students to reflect on what they are learning with the CVCe and CVVC patterns.

DEMONSTRATE. Prepare Sort 242 from the website. Follow the procedures described before to check that students can read and understand the words. Teach a small number of words that are new to students. Set up *nail* and *goat* as the guide words at the top of your columns. Demonstrate the sorting process by saying each of the words and comparing them to the guide words: "Does *take* sound like *nail* or *goat* in the middle?" Have your students join in as you continue to model the isolation, identification, and categorization of the medial vowel

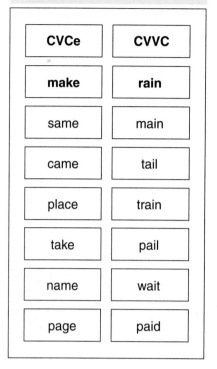

FIGURE 6.9 Word Sort Contrasting Spelling Patterns for Long *a*

CVCe	CVVC
make	**rain**
same	main
came	tail
place	train
take	pail
name	wait
page	paid

PDToolkit

for Words Their Way™ with English Learners

Go to PDToolkit, choose your book, click the Sorts & Games tab, and search for "Sort 240: Word Sort Contrasting Spelling Patterns for Long *a* (CVCe and CVVC)" and "Sort 241: Word Sort Contrasting Spelling Patterns for Long *o* (CVCe and CVVC)."

PDToolkit

for Words Their Way™ with English Learners

Go to PDToolkit, choose your book, click the Sorts & Games tab, and search for "Sort 242: Word Sort Contrasting Sounds and Spelling Patterns for Long *a* and *o*."

ACTIVITIES | WITHIN WORD PATTERN STAGE

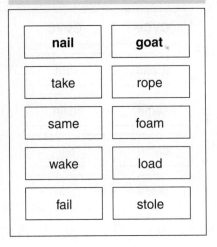

nail	goat
take	rope
same	foam
wake	load
fail	stole

sound. It is critical that your students say the words out loud and segment their sounds rather than simply sorting by the visual pattern present.

When you finish sorting (Figure 6.10), ask the students how the words in each column are alike and how they are different from the other words. Check the sort by naming all of the words in each column to make sure they all have the same vowel sound in the middle. "Do all of these words sound alike in the middle? Do we need to move any? What do we notice about the spelling of the words?"

SORT, CHECK, AND REFLECT. Give each student or pair of students a copy of the sort for guided practice. Now have the students repeat the sort under your supervision using the same key words as column headers. Tell your students to say each word aloud as they sort. You may want to have students work with partners to mix up the words and take turns drawing a card, saying its name out loud and sorting it in the correct column. After sorting, remind students to check their sorts by naming the words in each column to be sure the sounds are the same in the middle. If a student does not notice a mistake, provide guidance by saying, "One of these doesn't fit. See if you can hear which one as I read them all." Then read each word card, being careful to enunciate each vowel sound clearly. Ask students to reflect on how the words in each column are alike.

EXTEND. In the second part of this sort, ask students to subdivide each of the columns in their sort by the spelling patterns for the words, as in Figure 6.11. Use the CVCe and CVVC header cards under each long vowel to sort the words according to spelling pattern. Your completed sort will look something like Sort 242 on the website.

When you are finished sorting, ask the students how the words in each column are similar to and different from the other words. Encourage students to write this sort into a page of their word study notebook and add to it as they find more related words.

PDToolkit

for Words Their Way™ with English Learners

Go to PDToolkit, choose your book, click the Sorts & Games tab, and search for "Sort 243: CVCe/CVVC Word Sort with Long *a*, *o* and *e*."

6.6 CVCe/CVVC Word Sort with Long *a*, *o*, and *e*

This sort asks students to separate long vowel words into the spelling patterns of CVCe or CVVC. Because three different vowels are used, students are guided to generalize the pattern into larger contexts.

DEMONSTRATE. Prepare the set of long CVCe and CVVC words for Sort 243 on the website. Follow the procedures described before to check that students can read and understand the words. Teach a small number of words that are new to students. Set up *nose* and *soap* as the guide words at the top of your columns. Ask students to tell you which column the CVCe card goes with and which column is for CVVC words. Demonstrate the sorting process by saying each of the words and comparing them to the guide words: "Does *globe* have the CVCe pattern like *nose* or the CVVC pattern like *goat*?" Have your students join in as you continue to model the identification and categorization of the correct pattern. It is critical that your students say the words out loud even as they visually discern the pattern.

When you are finished sorting (Figure 6.12), ask the students how the words in each column are alike and how they are different from the other words. The completed sort should look something like the outline for Sort 243 on the website. Check the sort by naming all of the

FIGURE 6.11 Extended Word Sort for Long *a* and Long *o*

nail		goat	
CVCe	**CVVC**	**CVCe**	**CVVC**
take	fail	rope	foam
same	maid	stole	load
wake	trail	broke	loaf
cape	braid	chose	coast

words in each column and visually reviewing their spelling patterns. "Do all of these words have the same spelling pattern? Do we need to move any? What do we notice about the sounds in the words?"

SORT, CHECK, AND REFLECT. Give each student or pair of students a copy of the sort for guided practice. Now have the students repeat the sort under your supervision using the same key words as column headers. Tell your students to say each word aloud as they sort. You may want to have students work with partners to mix up the words and take turns drawing a card, saying its name out loud and sorting it in the correct column. After sorting, remind students to check their sorts by naming the words in each column to be sure the spelling patterns are the same. If a student does not notice a mistake, guide him or her to it by saying, "One of these doesn't fit. Which one looks like it doesn't have the same spelling pattern?" Ask students to reflect on how the words in each column are alike.

EXTEND. This is an excellent opportunity to have students go on a word hunt to find other CVCe and CVVC words with the long sounds of *a*, *e*, and *o*. If students find words with these patterns that do not have the long sound, such as *said*, discuss them and put them into an "oddball" category. Students may write this sort and other found words into their word study notebooks.

6.7 Word Sort Contrasting Spelling Patterns for Long *i*

This sort works on two common patterns for the long *i* sound: CVCe (as in *like*) and CV (as in *by* or *tie*).

DEMONSTRATE. Prepare the set of long *i* words to use with Sort 244 on the website. Follow the procedures described before to check that students can read and understand the words. Teach a few words that are new to students. Ask your students if they notice any common feature in all the words (they all have a long *i* sound in them). Ask if the same letter represents that sound in all the words.

Place the CVCe and CV header cards at the tops of the columns, along with the guide words *like*, *by*, and *tie*. Note that *-y* and *-ie* both can make the long *i* sound and might be described as a CV (consonant-vowel) pattern. Proceed through the sort by looking at the long vowel words one at a time and labeling their patterns as you have done in previous sorts, such as Activity 6.4. Have your students join in as you continue to model this process. The completed sort should look something like Figure 6.13 (also see Sort 244 from the website).

When you are finished sorting, ask the students how the words in each column are alike and how they are different from the other words. Check the sort by rereading the words aloud and visually noticing the spelling patterns. "Do all of these words follow the CVCe or CV pattern? Do we need to move any?"

SORT, CHECK, AND REFLECT. Give each student or pair of students a copy of the sort for guided practice. Now have the students repeat the sorting, checking, and reflecting under your supervision.

EXTEND. Have students store their words in an envelope or plastic bag so they can reuse them throughout the week in individual and partner sorts. Students can also go on a word hunt to find long *i* words that match the CVCe and CV patterns to add to their word study notebooks.

6.8 Leaves on a Tree Game

In this game, two players compare visual long *e* vowel patterns.

FIGURE 6.12 CVCe/CVVC Word Sort with Long *a, o,* and *e*

CVCe	CVVC
nose	soap
globe	boat
cake	seat
these	brain

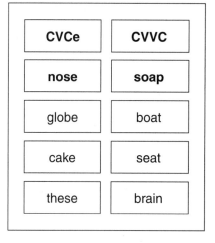

PDToolkit
for Words Their Way™ with English Learners

Go to PDToolkit, choose your book, click the Sorts & Games tab, and search for "Sort 244: Word Sort Contrasting Spelling Patterns for Long *i* (CVCe and CV)."

FIGURE 6.13 Word Sort Contrasting Spelling Patterns for Long *i*

CVCe	CV
like	by, tie
write	my
five	sky
size	lie

MATERIALS. You will need two paper or cardboard trees without leaves, ten construction paper leaves, and word cards representing the long *e* vowel pattern—for example:

e	e-e	ea	ee	ie
he	eve	bean	seek	chief
be	scene	reach	sheet	field
me	theme	steal	cheek	piece
she	these	teach	deep	thief
		steam	sleep	niece
		plead	queen	grief
		beast	creep	brief
		feast	greed	shriek

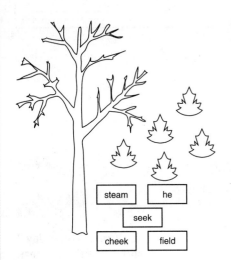

PROCEDURES

1. One player shuffles and deals five cards and five leaves to each player.
2. Remaining cards are placed face down for the draw pile.
3. Each player puts down pairs that match by pattern. For example, *reach/steal* would be a pair, but *eve/chief* would not. Each time a pair is laid down, the player puts one leaf on his or her tree.
4. The dealer goes first, saying a word from his or her hand and asking if the second player has a card with the same pattern.
5. If player 2 has a card that matches the pattern, player 1 gets a leaf; if not, player 1 must draw a card. If the player draws a card that matches any word in his or her hand, the pair can be discarded, and a leaf is earned. Player 2 proceeds in the same manner.
6. The first player earning five leaves wins. A player who uses all the cards in his or her hand before earning five leaves must draw a card before the other player's turn.

VARIATIONS. After earning all five leaves, a player must correctly pronounce his or her words. If a word is mispronounced, the player loses a leaf and the game continues.

▊6.9▊ Word Sort Contrasting Spelling Patterns for Long *u*

This sort works on two common patterns for the long *u* sound: CVCe (as in *use*), and CVVC (as in *fruit* or *food*).

DEMONSTRATE. Prepare the set of long *u* words to use with Sort 245 on the website. Follow the procedures described before to check that students can read and understand the words. Teach a small number of words that are new to students. Ask your students whether they notice anything in common for all the words—which is a trick question this time, because some of the words that make the long *u* sound do not have a *u*. They have a double *o* instead. Ask whether all the words have the same vowel sound. Help them hear that the *oo* in *food* is the same sound as in *fruit*.

Place the CVCe and CVVC header cards at the tops of the columns, along with the guide words *use*, *fruit*, and *food*. Note that *oo* and *ui* both can represent the long *u* sound and might be described as a CVVC pattern. Proceed through the sort by looking at the long vowel words one at a time and labeling their patterns as you have done in previous sorts. Have your students join in as you continue to model this process.

Students may want to include the words *juice*, *bruise*, and *cruise* in the column of CVCe words, because each ends with an *e*. If this comes up, you can explain that the *e* ending these

PDToolkit

for Words Their Way™ with English Learners

Go to PDToolkit, choose your book, click the Sorts & Games tab, and search for "Sort 245: Word Sort Contrasting Spelling Patterns for Long *u* (CVCe and CVVC)."

words is not the same kind of silent *e* that makes a vowel "say its name." The *e* at the end of *cruise* and *bruise* tells us that the *s* is pronounced like a /z/ instead of an /s/; the *e* at the end of *juice* tells us to pronounce the *c* with an /s/ sound. The vowel patterns in these words are CVVC. When you are finished sorting, ask the students how the words in each column are alike and how they are different from the other column. The completed sort should look something like Figure 6.14 (also see Sort 245 on the website). Check the sort by rereading the words aloud and visually noticing the spelling patterns. "Do all of these words follow the CVCe or CVVC pattern? Do we need to move any?"

Now sort by these patterns as well: *u-e, ui, oo*.

SORT, CHECK, AND REFLECT. Give each student or pair of students a copy of the sort for guided practice. Now have the students repeat the sorting, checking, and reflecting under your supervision.

EXTEND. Have students store their words in an envelope or plastic bag so they can reuse them throughout the week in individual and partner sorts. Encourage students to chant the words so the long *u* sound in all of these patterns is reinforced. For added practice, ask students to do a speed sort to see how fast they can go.

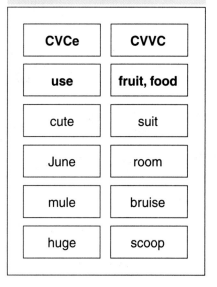

FIGURE 6.14 Word Sort Contrasting Spelling Patterns for Long *u*

CVCe	CVVC
use	fruit, food
cute	suit
June	room
mule	bruise
huge	scoop

6.10 Concept Sort: Matter

Make copies of the matter concept sort (Sort 234 on the website), cut them apart, and place them in envelopes or small plastic bags. To help keep multiple sets organized, consider using various colors of paper or scribbling with different colored markers on the back of each card so that it can easily be reorganized if multiple copies get mixed up.

DEMONSTRATE. This sort features a collection of vocabulary words associated with matter and can be used when your class is studying this science topic. Introduce the key words (guide cards) as in Figure 6.15 and ask students to tell you what they know about solids, liquids, and gases to activate their prior knowledge. Use several words from each category to demonstrate the sort, explaining your rationale through a think-aloud. For example, you may pick *ice, water,* and *air* to review together. How does each item represent its category? Review all of the picture and word cards with the students to make sure they can both read and understand the meaning of each term. You may also want to have students review the picture and word cards with partners. Then work your way through the sort as a group. The completed sort should look something like the outline of Sort 234 on the website.

After sorting, discuss the similarities within each category and the differences among the categories. For example: "Statue and steel are similar because they both take up space and hold their own shape. Ice and steam are different because ice is a solid—it takes up space and holds its own shape, whereas steam is a gas because it does not hold its own shape and it takes the shape of its container." The vocabulary words found in the solid and liquid categories may be understood without too much difficulty but should be reviewed to be sure. Students may experience more difficulty with the concept of gas and will likely need support to understand some of the more abstract terms. Provide outlets for students to learn the meanings of these words, such as in explicit lessons, by asking classmates and teachers, or by using picture dictionaries, informational texts, and online reference materials.

SORT, CHECK, AND REFLECT. Students should shuffle their cards and repeat the sort under your supervision. Have them check their sorts by explaining their rationales to partners or the teacher. Encourage students to reflect by asking them to draw a picture of a solid, liquid, or gas. The example may or may not be from the actual sort.

PDToolkit
for Words Their Way™
with English Learners

Go to PDToolkit, choose your book, click the Sorts & Games tab, and search for "Sort 234: Matter Concept Sort."

FIGURE 6.15 Matter Concept Sort

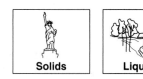

Solids **Liquids** **Gas**

ACTIVITIES WITHIN WORD PATTERN STAGE

EXTEND. Create a classroom chart for each state of matter: solid, liquid, and gas. Add to the chart over time by finding examples of each from the surrounding environment. For example, a student may ask to include hamburger, grill, and propane: "I ate a hamburger which my dad cooked on the propane grill—hamburger and grill are examples of a solid, and propane is an example of a gas."

6.11 Word Sort with *a-e, ai, ay*

This sort adds the *ay* spelling pattern to students' repertoires of long *a* words.

DEMONSTRATE. Prepare Sort 246 on the website. Follow the procedures described before to check that students can read and understand the words. Teach a small number of words that are new to students. Ask your students if they notice anything in common about the words (they all have an *a* in them). Ask about the middle vowel sounds in the words. Do they all have the same vowel sound?

Show students the *a-e, ai,* and *ay* header cards. Remind students that they have worked previously with long vowel patterns that follow the CVCe and CVVC patterns. In this sort, you will be adding a new pattern for long *a* words—*ay*. Show the guide words for each column and match them to the corresponding pattern—*name* with *a-e, rain* with *ai,* and *day* with *ay*. Model the process of looking at one of the long vowel words and figuring out which pattern it belongs with: "*Make* has a consonant, a vowel, another consonant, and the letter *e*. So, *make* follows the *a-e* pattern. *Paid* follows the *ai* pattern. *Play* follows the *ay* pattern." Demonstrate the sorting process by analyzing each of the other words and comparing them to the header cards. Have your students join in as you continue to model this process. It is critical that your students say the words out loud even as they look for visual patterns for sorting. The completed sort should look something like Figure 6.16 (also see Sort 246 on the website).

FIGURE 6.16 Word Sort with *a-e, ai,* and *ay*

a-e	ai	ay
name	rain	day
make	paid	may
late	mail	play
blame	main	way

When you are finished sorting, ask the students how the words in each column are alike and how they are different from the other words. What ideas do they have about why some words are spelled with *ai* whereas others are spelled with *ay*? Check the sort by rereading the words aloud and visually noticing the spelling patterns. "Does each column of words match the pattern of its header? Do we need to move any?"

SORT, CHECK, AND REFLECT. Give each student or pair of students a copy of the sort for guided practice. Now have the students repeat the sorting, checking, and reflecting under your supervision.

EXTEND. Have students store their words in an envelope or plastic bag so they can reuse them throughout the week in individual and partner sorts. Students can also go on a word hunt to find words with *ay* to add to the list of long *a* words in their word study notebooks.

6.12 Word Sort with *o-e, oa, ow*

This sort adds the *ow* spelling pattern to students' repertoires of long *o* words.

DEMONSTRATE. Prepare Sort 247 on the website. Follow the procedures described before to check that students can read and understand the words. Teach a small number of words that are new to students. Ask your students if they notice anything in common about the words (they all have an *o* in them). "Do all of the words have the same vowel sound?"

Show students the *o-e, oa,* and *ow* header cards. Remind students that they have worked previously with long vowel patterns that follow the CVCe and CVVC patterns. In this sort, you will be adding a new pattern for long *o* words—*ow*. Show the guide words for each column and match them to the corresponding pattern—*bone* with *o-e*, *soap* with *oa*, and *low* with *ow*. Model the process of looking at one of the long vowel words and figuring out which pattern it belongs with: "*Home* has a consonant, a vowel, another consonant, and the letter *e*. So, *home* follows the *o-e* pattern. *Roam* follows the *oa* pattern. *Grow* follows the *ow* pattern." Demonstrate the sorting process by analyzing each of the other words and comparing them to the header cards. Have your students join in as you continue to model this process. It is critical that your students say the words out loud even as they look for visual patterns for sorting.

When you finish sorting, ask the students how the words in each column are alike and how they differ from the other columns. The completed sort should look something like Figure 6.17 (see also Sort 247 on the website). Check the sort by rereading the words aloud and visually noticing the spelling patterns. "Does each column's words match the pattern of its header? Do we need to move any?"

SORT, CHECK, AND REFLECT. Give each student or pair of students a copy of the sort for guided practice. Now have the students repeat the sorting, checking, and reflecting under your supervision.

EXTEND. Have students store their words in an envelope or plastic bag so they can reuse them throughout the week in individual and partner sorts. Students can also go on a word hunt to find words with *ow* to add to the list of long *o* words in the word study notebooks.

6.13 Word Sort with *u-e, ew, ue*

This sort adds the *ew* and *ue* spelling patterns to students' repertoires of long *u* words.

DEMONSTRATE. Prepare the set of long *u* words to use with Sort 248 on the website. Follow the procedures described before to check that students can read and understand the words. Teach a small number of words that are new to students. "Do all of the words have the same vowel letters? Do all of the words have the same vowel sound?"

Show students the *u-e, ew,* and *ue* header cards. Remind students that they have worked previously with long vowel patterns that follow the CVCe and CVVC patterns. In this sort, you will be adding two new patterns for long *u* words—*ew* and *ue*. Show the guide words for each column and match them to the corresponding pattern—*tube* with *u-e*, *new* with *ew*, and *blue* with *ue*. Model the process of looking at one of the long vowel words and figuring out which pattern it belongs with: "*Rule* has a consonant, a vowel, another consonant, and the letter *e*. So, *rule* follows the *u-e* pattern. *Few* follows the *ew* pattern. *True* follows the *ue* pattern." Demonstrate the sorting process by analyzing each of the other words and comparing them to the header cards. Have your students join in as you continue to work through this process. It is critical that your students say the words out loud even as they look for visual patterns for sorting.

When you are finished sorting, ask the students how the words in each column are alike and how they are different from the other columns. The completed sort should look something like Figure 6.18 (see also Sort 248 on the website). Check the sort by rereading the words aloud and visually noticing the spelling patterns. "Does each column of words match the pattern of its header? Do we need to move any?"

FIGURE 6.17 Word Sort with *o-e, oa,* and *ow*

o-e	oa	ow
bone	soap	low
close	road	grow
wrote	float	slow
home	toast	show

PDToolkit
for Words Their Way™
with English Learners

Go to PDToolkit, choose your book, click the Sorts & Games tab, and search for "Sort 248: Word Sort with *u-e, ew, ue*."

FIGURE 6.18 Word Sort with *u-e, ew,* and *ue*

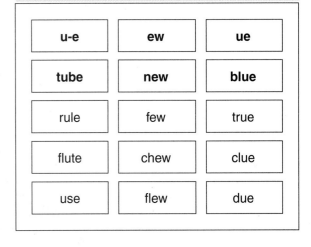

u-e	ew	ue
tube	new	blue
rule	few	true
flute	chew	clue
use	flew	due

ACTIVITIES | WITHIN WORD PATTERN STAGE

SORT, CHECK AND REFLECT. Give each student or pair of students a copy of the sort for guided practice. Now have the students repeat the sorting, checking, and reflecting under your supervision.

EXTEND. Have students store their words in an envelope or plastic bag so they can reuse them throughout the week in individual and partner sorts. Students can also go on a word hunt to find words with *ew* and *ue* patterns to add to the list of long *u* words in their word study notebooks.

6.14 Word Sort with *i-e, igh, y*

This sort adds the *igh* spelling pattern to students' repertoires of long *i* words.

DEMONSTRATE. Prepare Sort 249 on the website. Follow the procedures described before to check that students can read and understand the words. Teach a small number of words that are new to students. "Do all of the words have the same vowel letters? Do all of the words have the same vowel sound?"

Show students the *i-e, igh,* and *y* header cards. Remind students that they have worked previously with long vowel patterns that follow the CVCe and CV patterns. In this sort, you will be adding a new pattern for long *i* words—*igh*. Show the guide words for each column and match them to the corresponding pattern—*line* with *i-e, high* with *igh,* and *my* with *y*. Model the process of looking at one of the long vowel words and figuring out which pattern it belongs with: "*Like* has a consonant, a vowel, another consonant, and the letter *e*. So, *like* follows the *i-e* pattern. *Might* follows the *igh* pattern. *By* follows the *y* pattern." Demonstrate the sorting process by analyzing each of the other words and comparing them to the header cards. Have your students join in as you continue to work through each word. It is critical that your students say the words out loud even as they look for visual patterns for sorting.

When you are finished sorting, ask the students how the words in each column are alike and how they are different from the other columns. The completed sort should look something like Figure 6.19 (see also Sort 249 on the website). Check the sort by rereading the words aloud and visually noticing the spelling patterns. "Does each column of words follow the pattern of its header? Do we need to move any?"

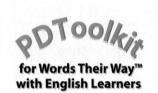

FIGURE 6.19 Word Sort with *i-e, igh,* and *y*

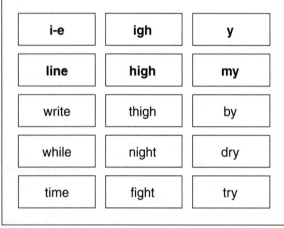

i-e	igh	y
line	high	my
write	thigh	by
while	night	dry
time	fight	try

SORT, CHECK, AND REFLECT. Give each student or pair of students a copy of the sort for guided practice. Now have the students repeat the sorting, checking, and reflecting under your supervision.

EXTEND. Have students store their words in an envelope or plastic bag so they can reuse them throughout the week in individual and partner sorts. Students can also go on a word hunt to find words with *igh* patterns to add to the list of long *i* words in their word study notebooks.

6.15 Star Light, Star Bright Game

In this game, two players compare long *i* vowel pattern words.

MATERIALS. Print the "Night Sky" game board from the website and color the squares yellow, green, blue, and red. You will also need a collection of at least 24 words with long *i* vowel patterns written on yellow, green, blue, and red paper or tag board stars. Designate a space at one end as the starting point and a space at the other end as the finish line. A number spinner or a single die is used to move players along the path. Here is a list of words you may want to include on the word cards:

i-e	ie	y	igh
like	pie	sky	high
nice	tie	fly	light
ride	lie	try	night
time	die	my	bright
white		spy	flight
mile		spry	sight
pride		dry	right
slice		cry	fright
strive			might
glide			

PROCEDURES

1. Each player rolls the die or spins the spinner to see who goes first. The player with the highest roll or spin will start, and play proceeds in a clockwise manner.
2. Shuffle the word cards and place them face down on the game board.
3. The first player draws a card, reads the word, and designates the vowel pattern. If the player reads the word correctly and identifies the vowel pattern, he or she moves to the first colored space that matches the color of the word card.
4. The winner is the first one to get to the end of the path.

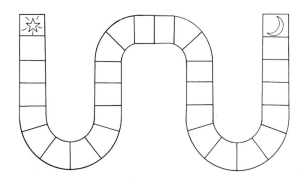

VARIATION

1. Each player rolls the die or spins the spinner to see who goes first. The player with the highest roll or spin will start, and play proceeds in a clockwise manner.
2. The second player draws a card from the stack of words placed face down. The player reads the word aloud to the first player who must spell the word aloud. If the player spells the word correctly, he or she moves to the first colored space that matches the color of the word card.
3. The winner is the first one to get to the end of the path.

Note: This game board can be used for any vowel patterns as long as the word cards are color-coded.

6.16 Homophone Personal Picture Dictionaries

This activity will take place over time and helps students create personal reference books of homophones that can be used for many purposes.

MATERIALS. Use composition folders with paper or make construction paper notebooks with at least one page for each letter of the alphabet. Make copies of the example homophone word list that follows. Students can also add to their homophone dictionaries as they find words in their reading. Have pens, markers, and other art materials available for students to use as they illustrate their homophone picture dictionaries.

PROCEDURES. Write the words *no* and *know* on chart paper for students to see. Ask them to read both of the words. Do they sound the same? Do they mean the same thing? How do we know when to use which word? Tell students that these words are homophones; they sound the same but have different meanings. What we mean to say when using one of these words helps us know how to spell it correctly. Write a sentence using *no* and another using *know*. Discuss the meaning of the word in each sentence. Have students make up their own sentences orally using these words.

Remind students that they have been studying lots of vowel patterns. Sometimes, there is more than one pattern to express a certain vowel sound; for instance, *ai* and *a-e* both make the long *a* sound. Because of different spelling patterns, many homophones can be formed. Share homophone pairs such as *tail/tale*, *maid/made*, *sail/sale*, and *plain/plane*. Discuss the meanings of these pairs, and ask students to use them in a sentence. Finally, ask students to choose one of the homophone pairs to write and illustrate in their personal homophone picture dictionary. The words should be written on the appropriate letter page according to their first letters.

Continue coming back to the picture dictionary over time, exploring other patterns that create homophones. Use the following homophones to have students match words that sound the same

die	dye	bear	bare	pour	pore
eye	I	ate	eight	cheap	cheep
one	won	great	grate	sun	son
add	ad	not	knot	sale	sail
male	mail	brows	browse	high	hi
four	for	made	maid	meet	meat
boar	bore	we	wee	cell	sell
board	bored	in	inn	jeans	genes
ant	aunt	passed	past	tied	tide
plane	plain	stake	steak	led	lead
pray	prey	heal	heel	role	roll
dear	deer	praise	prays	poll	pole

aisle	I'll	isle	too	two	to

Focus on specific homophone pairs for vocabulary and spelling development in ongoing lessons. Encourage students to note homophones they discover, write them in their dictionary, and illustrate them during free time. Refer to students' homophone picture dictionaries when spelling confusions arise among words.

VARIATIONS AND EXTENSIONS. Use the example homophone list as a resource to make larger cards for games such as Rummy, Go Fish, and Concentration. Share the book *If You Were a Homonym or a Homophone* (Loewen, 2007) to see a range of homonyms and homophones used and explained in a colorful format. Read books that feature jokes using homophones such as *The King Who Rained* (Gwynne, 1988), *How Much Can a Bare Bear Bear?* (Cleary & Gable, 2005), and *The Moose Is in the Mousse* (Scheunemann, 2002). See whether students can make up their own homophone word plays, and construct a class book of their individual pages.

6.17 Find the Gold Game

This board game reviews long vowel words that follow the VCC pattern such as *find* and *gold*. Make a literature connection by playing this game after you have read *That's What Leprechauns Do* by Eve Bunting (2005), about three mischievous leprechauns who must dig up their pot of gold before the rainbow comes to point it out.

MATERIALS

1. Prepare the game board and word card page for this activity from the website. Here are samples of the words:

find	blind	gold	fold	post	stroll	wild
kind	grind	cold	roll	sold	volt	wind
child	hind	hold	scold	bold	jolt	told
climb	sign	most	bolt	colt	poll	ghost
mind	bind	old	folk	host	scroll	mold

PDToolkit

for Words Their Way™ with English Learners

Go to PDToolkit, choose your book, click the Sorts & Games tab, and search for "Find the Gold Game."

2. You will need a spinner with numbers 1 through 4, playing pieces to move around the board, and a pencil and small piece of paper for each player.

PROCEDURES

1. After reading *That's What Leprechauns Do* and sorting words with the VCC pattern, players move to the game board and place game markers at the start position.
2. One player spins and moves that number of spaces on the board.
3. The player reads the word on the space. A player moves back a space if he or she reads the word incorrectly. Students "add a piece of gold to their pot" by drawing a circle on their note paper and writing in a word that rhymes from the game board.
4. Players take turns. The winner is the player who reaches the finish line first or who has the greatest number of gold pieces.

VARIATIONS

1. Players can move two or three times around the board.
2. Students hunt for these words or words that follow the same patterns in other texts and record them on a rainbow.

Word Study Activities at the Middle Within Word Pattern Stage

6.18 Word Sort with Long Vowel *r* Words

This sort examines words with *r* that retain their long vowel sound.

DEMONSTRATE. Prepare the set of long vowel *r* words for Sort 250 on the website. Follow the procedures described before to check that students can read and understand the words. Teach a small number of words that are new to students. Set up *a, e, i, o,* and *u* as the guide letters at the top of your columns. Demonstrate the sorting process by saying each of the words and comparing them to the guide letters. "Does *care* have the long *a* pattern or another long vowel sound?" Have your students join in as you continue to model the identification and categorization of the correct long vowel sound and place the word in the appropriate column. It is critical that your students say the words out loud even as they visually discern the letters in the words. The completed sort should look something like Figure 6.20 (see also Sort 250 on the website).

When you are finished sorting, ask the students what makes the words in each column alike. Check the sort by naming all of the words in each column and visually reviewing their spelling patterns. "Do the words in each column have the same vowel sound? Do we need to move any? What do we notice about the spelling patterns in the words?"

SORT, CHECK, AND REFLECT. Give each student or pair of students a copy of the sort for guided practice. Now have the students repeat the sorting, checking, and reflecting under your supervision using the same vowel letters as column headers.

EXTEND. Have students brainstorm other words that rhyme with the words in this sort. Do the words they thought of follow the same spelling patterns?

6.19 R-Influenced Word Sort

In this sort, *r*-influenced words using all five vowels are explored for sound differences.

PDToolkit

for Words Their Way™ with English Learners

Go to PDToolkit, choose your book, click the Sorts & Games tab, and search for "Sort 250: Word Sort with Long Vowel *r* Words."

ACTIVITIES WITHIN WORD PATTERN STAGE

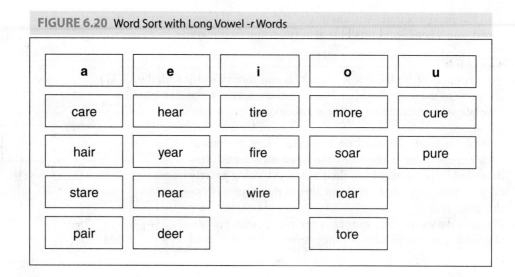

FIGURE 6.20 Word Sort with Long Vowel -r Words

a	e	i	o	u
care	hear	tire	more	cure
hair	year	fire	soar	pure
stare	near	wire	roar	
pair	deer		tore	

PDToolkit

for Words Their Way™ with English Learners

Go to PDToolkit, choose your book, click the Sorts & Games tab, and search for "Sort 251: R-Influenced Word Sort."

DEMONSTRATE. Prepare the set of *r*-influenced words for Sort 251 on the website. Follow the procedures previously described to check that students are able to read and understand the words. Teach a small number of words that are new to students. Set up *ar, er, ir, or,* and *ur* as the guide patterns at the top of your columns. Demonstrate the sorting process by saying each of the words and comparing them to the guide patterns. "What pattern does the word *car* have? Yes, the *ar* pattern." Have your students join in as you continue to model the identification and categorization of the correct *r*-influenced pattern, placing the word in the appropriate column. It is critical that your students say the words out loud even as they visually discern the letters in the words.

When you are finished sorting, ask the students what makes the words in each column similar. The completed sort should look something like Figure 6.21 (see also Sort 251 on the website). Check the sort by naming all of the words in each column and visually reviewing their spelling patterns. "Do the words in each column have the same spelling pattern? Do we need to move any? What do we notice about the sounds in the words?" Discuss with students the fact that when the *r* combines with some of the vowels, it is so strong that the words sound alike. The /er/ sounds in *er, ir,* and *ur* words sound just the same. This makes spelling them more difficult.

SORT, CHECK, AND REFLECT. Give each student or pair of students a copy of the sort for guided practice. Now have the students repeat the sorting, checking, and reflecting under your supervision using the same letter patterns as column headers.

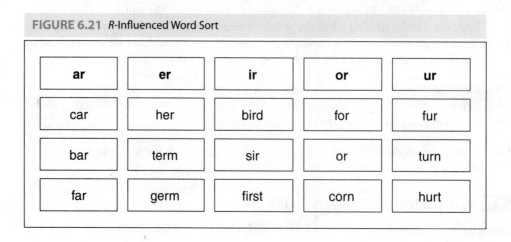

FIGURE 6.21 *R*-Influenced Word Sort

ar	er	ir	or	ur
car	her	bird	for	fur
bar	term	sir	or	turn
far	germ	first	corn	hurt

EXTEND. Pronouncing and spelling *r*-influenced words can be quite a challenge for many English learners. Provide lots of opportunities for students to review the sorts and practice reading and spelling the words. Encourage students to work with partners, reading each other the *r*-influenced words and predicting the spelling pattern without looking.

6.20 Her First Word Turn Game: The Spellings of *er*

This Tic-Tac-Toe variation explores the variety of spelling patterns for the /er/ sound.

MATERIALS. You will need a stack of cards with words printed on them that have the /er/ sound. Write the words you are studying on cards, or print out the word card page for this activity from the website. Here is a list of suggested words:

Her: herd, perch, fern, germ, clerk, term, per, jerk
First: bird, chirp, girl, dirt, shirt, third, birth, firm, stir, fir, thirst, squirt, swirl, whirl, twirl
Word: work, worm, world, worth, worse
Turn: burn, hurt, curl, purr, burst, church, churn, curb, hurl, burr, blurt, lurch, lurk, spur, surf

Each student will need scratch paper and a pencil to make a personal *Her First Word Turn* (tic-tac-toe) board.

PROCEDURES
1. Place the /er/ word cards in a small bag or tub and mix them up.
2. Each student makes a Tic-Tac-Toe grid and writes one of the words *her, first, word,* or *turn* in each of the spaces. The student may begin on *her* or any of the other words, but should write each word in sequence without skipping or repeating. For example, a student may choose to begin on the word *turn* but should then write the remaining words in sequence as in *turn, her, first, word, turn, her, first, word, turn.*
3. One student is the "caller," or students take turns with this job. The caller pulls a card out of the bag, reads it to the group, and spells it. Students looks at their game boards for a word that has the same /er/ spelling and put an X on it. If more than one word works, they choose the best match to help them make three in a row. If students no longer have a word that matches the spelling pattern of the called word, they do nothing.
4. The first person to get three in a row across, down, or diagonally wins.
5. Make another game board and play again!

VARIATIONS. Instead of getting three in a row, play until all of the words on the board are crossed out. Or try playing Her First Word Turn without spelling. See whether students can figure out the spelling patterns of the called words without first hearing the words spelled.

her	first	word
turn	her	first
word	turn	her

turn	her	first
word	turn	her
first	word	turn

Word Study Activities at the Late Within Word Pattern Stage

6.21 Word Sort with Diphthongs

This sort features the diphthongs *oi/oy* and *ou/ow*. Diphthongs are vowel sounds that glide from one position to another within the same syllable.

DEMONSTRATE. Prepare Sort 252 on the website. Follow the procedures described before to check that students can read and understand the words. Teach a small number of words that are new to students. Set up *oi, oy, ou,* and *ow* as the guide patterns at the top of your

ACTIVITIES   WITHIN WORD PATTERN STAGE

FIGURE 6.22 Word Sort with Diphthongs

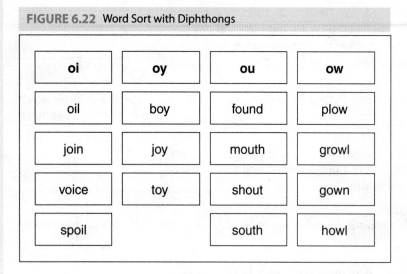

oi	oy	ou	ow
oil	boy	found	plow
join	joy	mouth	growl
voice	toy	shout	gown
spoil		south	howl

columns. Demonstrate the sorting process by naming each of the words and comparing them to the guide patterns. "What pattern does the word *oil* have? Yes, the *oi* pattern." Have your students join in as you continue to model the identification and categorization of each correct diphthong spelling, placing the words in the appropriate columns. It is critical that your students say the words out loud even as they visually discern the letters in the words.

When you are finished sorting, ask the students what makes the words in each column similar. The completed sort should look something like Figure 6.22 (see also Sort 252 on the website). Check the sort by naming all of the words in each column and visually reviewing their spelling patterns. "Do the words in each column have the same spelling pattern? Do we need to move any? What do we notice about the sounds in the words?" Discuss with students the fact that the *oi* and *oy* have the same sound, and *ou* and *ow* do, too. Why do students think the letters might be different for different words?

SORT, CHECK, AND REFLECT. Give each student or pair of students a copy of the sort for guided practice. Now have the students repeat the sorting, checking, and reflecting under your supervision, using the same letter patterns as column headers.

EXTEND. Provide additional opportunities for students to review the sort and practice reading and spelling the words. Go on a word hunt to find further examples of words with these spellings. Do *ou* and *ow* always get pronounced as a diphthong?

6.22 Word Sort with Ambiguous Vowel Sounds

This sort contrasts an array of related open vowel sounds similar to the *a* in *draw*. The sort features the spelling patterns short *o*, *aw*, *au*, *al*, *w + a*, and *ough*.

DEMONSTRATE. Prepare the set of ambiguous vowel words for Sort 253 on the website. Follow the procedures described before to check that students can read and understand the words. Teach a small number of words that are new to students. Set up *o*, *aw*, *au*, *al*, *w + a*, and *ough* as the guide patterns at the top of your columns. Demonstrate the sorting process by naming each of the words and comparing them to the guide patterns. "What pattern does the word *cloth* have? Yes, the short *o* pattern." Have your students join in as you continue to model the identification and categorization of the correct ambiguous vowel spelling, placing the words in the appropriate column. This is a difficult sort because of the variety of spelling patterns and the similarity among the sounds in the words. It is critical that your students say the words out loud even as they visually discern the letters in the words. The completed sort should look something like Figure 6.23 (see also Sort 253 on the website).

When you are finished sorting, ask the students what makes the words in each column similar. Check the sort by naming all of the words in each column and visually reviewing their spelling patterns. "Do the words in each column have the same spelling pattern? Do we need to move any? What do we notice about the sounds in the words?" Think aloud with the group about what is tricky in spelling these words.

SORT, CHECK, AND REFLECT. Give each student or pair of students a copy of the sort for guided practice. Now have the students repeat the sorting, checking, and reflecting under your supervision, using the same letter patterns as column headers.

EXTEND. Provide numerous opportunities for students to review the sort and practice reading and spelling the words. Go on a word hunt to find further examples of words with these

PDToolkit
for Words Their Way™
with English Learners

Go to PDToolkit, choose your book, click the Sorts & Games tab, and search for "Sort 253: Word Sort with Ambiguous Vowel Sounds."

FIGURE 6.23 Word Sort with Ambiguous Vowel Sounds

o	aw	au	al	w + a	ough
golf	draw	pause	tall	wash	ought
cloth	law	sauce	small	want	bought
toss	yawn	taught	salt	watch	fought

spellings. Create lists of rhyming words to put in word study notebooks so that students have a chance to review common spelling patterns.

6.23 Ambiguous Vowel Sound: Jeopardy

This guessing game helps students learn and practice words with ambiguous vowel sounds. Students have to guess the right word based on a clue, so it is also a good way to get vocabulary practice.

MATERIALS. You will need dice, a game board, and clue cards. A poster board or open file folder is divided into five columns with three boxes each (Figure 6.24). A clue card worth 100, 200, or 300 points is placed on each space. Cards should be color coded or labeled by their category so they are placed in the appropriate column.

Following is a list of possible words and point values for you to get started.

FIGURE 6.24 Example Jeopardy Game Board

aw	w + a	ough	au	oo
100	100	100	100	100
200	200	200	200	200
300	300	300	300	300

Figure 6.25 shows their positions on the game board. You can add new words to this game over time, but remember to find words that are concrete, so that English learners can predict them from short clues. The words should also represent an ambiguous vowel word that they have worked with in the past.

Answers for clue cards:

aw
100: A baby moves this way.
200: A loud cry or scream, like a goose might make.
300: This means to melt.

w + a
100: Something you wear to tell time.
200: This means to hit, like you would a fly.
300: This means to trade things, like friends might do.

ough
100: You spent money. You _____ things.
200: They had a fight yesterday. They _____.
300: When you are sick you might sneeze or _____.

FIGURE 6.25 Words Used in Sample Jeopardy Game

Point Value	aw	w + a	ough	au	oo
100	crawl	watch	bought	caught	book
200	squawk	swat	fought	fault	wood
300	thaw	swap	cough	launch	hood

au

100: When they threw the ball to him, he _____ it.

200: When someone is to blame, it is his or her _____.

300: What is done to make a rocket take off.

oo

100: Something to read.

200: We get this from the trunks of trees.

300: This part of your jacket covers the head.

PROCEDURES

1. One player is the game host. The others roll the dice to determine who goes first.
2. The game begins when the first player picks a category and an amount for the host to read, for example, "I'll take *aw* for 100." The host reads the clue and the player must respond by phrasing a question and spelling the word, as in the following example:

Host: "A baby moves this way."
Player: "What is crawl? *c-r-a-w-l.*"

3. If correct, the player receives the card. This player chooses another clue. (A player can only have two consecutive turns.) If the player misses, the player to the left may answer.
4. The game continues until all the clue cards are read and won, or left unanswered. Players add their points, and the one with the highest number of points wins.
5. Depending on the English proficiency level of your students, adjust the difficulty level of words and clues.

6.24 Word Sort with *spr, str, scr*

This sort is the first to examine complex consonant clusters with students. Explicit attention to and practice with blends such as *spr, str,* and *scr* help English learners to discriminate and represent these sounds more effectively.

DEMONSTRATE. Prepare Sort 254 on the website. Before doing the teacher-guided sort, ask students to read the words aloud and check to see that they know the meanings of the words. Because many of the words sound very similar to each other (e.g., *scrap* and *scrape*), students may need extra support in the pronunciation aspect of this new learning. Make saying these words fun—like working with tongue twisters. Consider teaching up to five unknown terms. Additional unknown items can be set aside for another time. Set up *spr, str,* and *scr* as the guide patterns at the top of your columns. Demonstrate the sorting process by discussing each of the key words and comparing them to the guide patterns. "What cluster does the word *spray* have? Yes, the *spr* cluster." Have your students join in as you continue to model the identification and categorization of the correct consonant cluster, placing the words in the appropriate columns. This is a difficult sort because of the similarity among the sounds in the words. Keep the mood playful and supportive. It is critical that your students say the words out loud even as they visually discern the letters in the words. The completed sort should look something like Figure 6.26 (see also Sort 254 on the website).

When you are finished sorting, ask students to compare the words in each column. Check the sort by naming all of the words in each column and visually reviewing their spelling patterns. Make the checking fun by chanting or adding rhythm to the rereading of the words. "Do the words in each column have the same consonant cluster? Do we need to move any? What do we notice about the sounds in the words?" Think aloud with the group about what is tricky in spelling these words.

SORT, CHECK, AND REFLECT. Give each student or pair of students a copy of the sort for guided practice. Now have the students repeat the sorting, checking, and reflecting under your supervision using the same letter patterns as column headers.

EXTEND. Have students make up fun tongue-twister sentences using several words from this sort such as "I *scratch* and *scream* crossing the *strong stream*." Can they say the sentence quickly several times?

FIGURE 6.26 Word Sort with *spr, str,* and *scr*

spr	str	scr
spray	strap	scrape
spring	stray	screen

6.25 Word Sort with *squ, thr, shr*

This sort continues to examine complex consonant clusters with students, in the format of Activity 6.24, but this time with the blends *squ, thr,* and *shr*.

DEMONSTRATE. Prepare the set of *squ, thr,* and *shr* words for Sort 255 on the website. Before doing the teacher-guided sort, ask students to read the words aloud and check to see that they know the meanings of the words. Because these words contain blends that are complex or may not exist in students' home languages, extra support and practice may be called for here. Keep the atmosphere light and supportive—don't fixate on minor pronunciation problems. First check to see whether students can read and understand the meanings of the words. Consider teaching up to five unknown terms. Additional unknown items can be set aside for another time. Set up *squ, thr,* and *shr* as the guide patterns at the top of your columns. Demonstrate the sorting process as described in Activity 6.24. The completed sort should look something like Figure 6.27 (see also Sort 255 on the website). When you are finished sorting, check the sort as described in Activity 6.24.

for Words Their Way™ with English Learners

Go to PDToolkit, choose your book, click the Sorts & Games tab, and search for "Sort 255: Word Sort with *squ, thr, shr*."

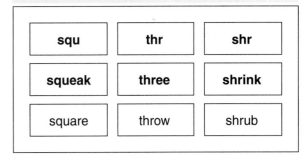

FIGURE 6.27 Word Sort with *squ, thr,* and *shr*

squ	thr	shr
squeak	three	shrink
square	throw	shrub

SORT, CHECK, AND REFLECT. Give each student or pair of students a copy of the sort for guided practice. Now have the students repeat the sorting, checking, and reflecting under your supervision.

EXTEND. Have students illustrate some of the interesting words in this sort, such as *squish* or *shriek*. Collect their illustrations to create a class book or wall display.

6.26 Triple Threat Racetrack Game

In this game, two players match words in their hand with words on the track. This is a great way to examine triple *r* blends and digraphs with *r* blends.

MATERIALS. Make the Triple Threat Racetrack game board from the website or use the Racetrack game board template to write your own words on (see Figure 6.28). Reproduce the

for Words Their Way™ with English Learners

Go to PDToolkit, choose your book, click the Sorts & Games tab, and search for "Triple Threat Racetrack Game."

FIGURE 6.28 Racetrack Game Board

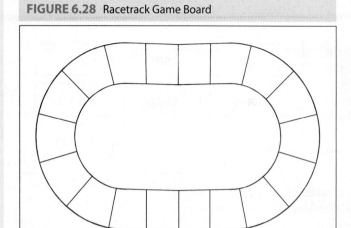

two sides of this game board. Triple *r* blend words might include *stripe, scream, scrape, stream, spring, threat, thread, through, sprout, sprint, threw, throat, string, street, struck, strand, strict, strike, phrase, shrimp, thrill, spray, scram, screech,* and *screw.* You will also need to print out the page of word cards that share the same beginning consonant cluster patterns as the game board words. A number spinner or a single die is used to move players around the track.

PROCEDURES

1. Shuffle the word cards and deal six to each player. Turn the rest face down to become the deck.
2. Playing pieces are placed anywhere on the board and moved according to the number spinner or die.
3. When players land on a space, they read the word and then look for words in their hand that have the same pattern. For example, a player who lands on *scream* may pull *screech* and *screw* from his hand to put in the winning pile. A player who lands on a space with a star can choose a pattern to lay down.
4. The cards placed in the winning pile are replaced by drawing the same number from the deck before play passes to the next player.
5. A player who has no match for the pattern must draw a card anyway.
6. The game is over when there are no more cards to play. The winner is the player with the most word cards in his or her lay-down pile.

6.27 Word Sort with Endings *dge, ge*

This sort examines words that end with the final /j/, spelled with *dge* or *ge*. Students learn how specific letters such as *r, l,* and *n,* as well as the vowel sounds in these words, influence their spellings.

PDToolkit

for Words Their Way™ with English Learners

Go to PDToolkit, choose your book, click the Sorts & Games tab, and search for "Sort 256: Word Sort with Endings *dge* and *ge.*"

DEMONSTRATE. Prepare Sort 256 on the website. Before doing the teacher-guided sort, ask students to read the words aloud and check to see that they know the meanings of the words. Many of the words may not be familiar to English learners (e.g., *surge* and *bulge*), so students may need extra support in learning the vocabulary. Consider teaching up to five unknown terms. Additional unknown items can be set aside for another time. Set up *dge, ge,* and *r, l, n + ge* as the guide patterns at the top of your columns. Demonstrate the sorting process by discussing each of the key words and comparing them to the guide patterns. "What ending does the word *dodge* have? Yes, the *dge* cluster." Have your students join in as you continue to model each identification and categorization of the correct ending spelling pattern, placing the words in the appropriate columns. It is critical that your students say the words out loud even as they visually discern the letters in the words. This helps them articulate the *r, l,* or *n* sound in addition to the /j/ that they all end with. The completed sort should look something like Figure 6.29 (see also Sort 256 on the website).

When you finish sorting, ask the students to compare the words in each column. "Do the words in each column have the same consonant cluster? Do we need to move any? What do we notice about the sounds in the words?" Next, ask the students to consider the vowel sound in each word: "What do you notice about the vowel sounds in the *ge* column? Why do you think these words have a long vowel sound? Do the words in the *dge* column have a long or a short sound? Why do you think there is a *d* in their ending spelling patterns? How are the words in the *r,*

FIGURE 6.29 Word Sort with Endings *dge* and *ge*

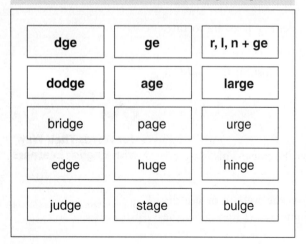

dge	ge	r, l, n + ge
dodge	age	large
bridge	page	urge
edge	huge	hinge
judge	stage	bulge

l, n + ge column the same or different?" ("When you hear a short vowel sound, use *dge*, unless you hear an *r*, *l*, or *n* before it.")

SORT, CHECK, AND REFLECT. Give each student or pair of students a copy of the sort for guided practice. Now have the students repeat the sorting, checking, and reflecting under your supervision, using the same letter patterns as column headers.

EXTEND. These interesting words can be used for vocabulary development activities and as cards in word study board games.

6.28 Word Sort with Endings *tch, ch*

This sort examines words that end with the final /ch/ sound, spelled with *tch* or *ch*. As in the previous sort, students learn how specific letters such as *r*, *l*, and *n*, as well as the vowel sounds in these words influence their spelling.

DEMONSTRATE. Prepare Sort 257 on the website. Before doing the teacher-guided sort, ask students to read the words aloud and check to see that they know the meanings of the words. Many of the words may not be familiar to English learners (e.g., *clutch* and *pouch*), so students may need extra support in learning the vocabulary. Teach a small number of words that are new to students. Set up *tch*, *ch*, and *r*, *l*, *n + ch* as the guide patterns at the top of your columns. Demonstrate the sorting process by discussing each of the key words and comparing them to the guide patterns. "What ending does the word *catch* have? Yes, the *tch* cluster." Have your students join in as you continue to model the identification and categorization of the correct spelling pattern, placing the words in the appropriate columns. It is important that your students say the words out loud even as they visually discern the letters in the words. This helps them articulate the *r*, *l*, or *n* sound in addition to the /ch/ that the words end with. The completed sort should look something like Figure 6.30 (see also Sort 257 on the website).

When you are finished sorting, ask the students to compare the words in each column. "Do the words in each column have the same spelling pattern? Do we need to move any? What do we notice about the sounds in the words?" Next, ask the students to consider the vowel sound in each word: "What do you notice about the vowel sounds in the *tch* column? Why do you think these words have a short vowel sound? Do the words in the *ch* column have a long or a short sound? If we think that they should have a long vowel sound, which words would be 'oddballs'? What about the words in the *r*, *l*, *n + ch* column? What vowel sound do they have? Why do you think this is so?"

SORT, CHECK, AND REFLECT. Give each student or pair of students a copy of the sort for guided practice. Now have the students repeat the sorting, checking, and reflecting under your supervision using the same letter patterns as column headers.

EXTEND. Encourage students to quiz each other on the meanings and spellings of these interesting words. Have students practice the sort over time to gain fluency.

6.29 Introduction to Two-Syllable Words

This sort gives a peek into the world of multisyllable words by exploring some of the most high-frequency two-syllable words. It is a first opportunity to discuss the "uh" or schwa sound that occurs in unaccented syllables.

DEMONSTRATE. Prepare Sort 258 on the website. Before doing the teacher-guided sort, ask students to read the words aloud and check that they know the meanings. These words are

for Words Their Way™ with English Learners

Go to PDToolkit, choose your book, click the Sorts & Games tab, and search for "Sort 257: Word Sort with Endings *tch* and *ch*."

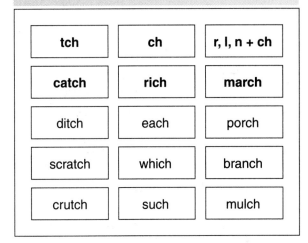

FIGURE 6.30 Word Sort with Endings *tch* and *ch*

tch	ch	r, l, n + ch
catch	**rich**	**march**
ditch	each	porch
scratch	which	branch
crutch	such	mulch

for Words Their Way™ with English Learners

Go to PDToolkit, choose your book, click the Sorts & Games tab, and search for "Sort 258: Word Sort with Two-Syllable Words."

ACTIVITIES WITHIN WORD PATTERN STAGE

FIGURE 6.31 Word Sort with Two-Syllable Words

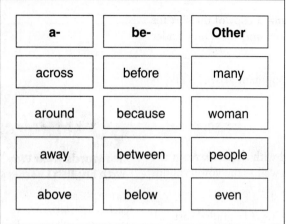

a-	be-	Other
across	before	many
around	because	woman
away	between	people
above	below	even

very common and highly used, so if any are unknown, consider taking the time to teach them. Tell students that now that they have learned so much about all kinds of one-syllable words, they are ready to start exploring longer words. You might say, "Today we are going to work with longer words. The words we are using are all around the room—on our signs, in our books, and in your writing. I have seen many of you have trouble spelling some of these words. Let's see why." Set up *a-*, *be-*, and *Other* as the guide cards at the top of your columns. Demonstrate the sorting process by naming the words and comparing each to the guide cards: "What letter does the word *across* start with? Yes, the *a*. What about the word *really*? That doesn't start with *a-* or *be-*, so let's put it in the *Other* column." Have your students join in as you continue to model the identification and categorization of the beginning letter, and place the word in the appropriate column. The completed sort should look something like Figure 6.31 (see also Sort 258 on the website).

When you finish sorting, ask students to check the sort by naming all of the words in each column and making sure they are in the correct column. "Have you ever had trouble spelling any of these words? What has been tricky for you?" Reread the *a-* words with the group, and ask them to notice the first sound they hear: "The 'uh' sound happens because it is not in the strong syllable. Sometimes it is hard to know how to spell that 'uh' sound." Ask students if they notice any "uh" sounds in the other columns of words. What can they do to help spell these words in the future?

SORT, CHECK, AND REFLECT. Give each student or pair of students a copy of the sort for guided practice. Now have the students repeat the sorting, checking, and reflecting under your supervision using the same column headers.

EXTEND. Provide numerous opportunities for students to review the sort and practice reading and spelling the words. Encourage students to write these high-frequency words in their word study notebooks or personal dictionaries. These are also good words to include on a classroom word wall.

6.30 Word Sort with Contractions

This sort explores common contractions and the words that work together to create their meanings. It serves as an initial foray into the world of the spelling–meaning connection.

DEMONSTRATE. Prepare Sort 259 on the website. You might introduce this sort by asking students to use some of the following words in a sentence: *don't*, *isn't*, *you're*, and *I'll*. You can model by saying something like, "I'll be going to the store on my way home from school today." As students contribute sentences, think aloud about which two words are put together to create the contraction they are using: "*I'll* comes from the two words *I* and *will*. So instead of *I'll*, we could also say, '*I will* be going to the store on my way home from school today.'" Explain to students that you will be working today on words like these, called contractions. Contractions are two words that have been put together, with a letter or letters taken out. An apostrophe has been added to show where the letter(s) are missing. Students will have likely heard and worked with contractions before, but this may be the first time that they have explored their spelling–meaning connections in depth.

Share the headers *not*, *are*, *is*, and *will*. Now, discuss each of the key words to show how they connect with one of the headers: "*Don't* means do not. It belongs in the *not* column." Demonstrate the sorting process by naming the words and comparing each to the guide cards: "What two words make up *you're*? Yes, *you* and *are*. *You're* goes under the *are* column." Have your students join in as you continue to model the identification and categorization of

the contractions with their component word, and place the contraction in the appropriate column. The completed sort should look something like Figure 6.32 (see also Sort 259 on the website). When you finish sorting, ask students to check the sort by naming all of the words in each column and making sure they are in the correct column. Have students point out where the letter is missing in each contraction and what the component words are.

SORT, CHECK, AND REFLECT. Give each student or pair of students a copy of the sort for guided practice. Have the students repeat the sorting, checking, and reflecting under your supervision using the same column headers.

FIGURE 6.32 Word Sort with Contractions

not	are	is	will
don't	you're	he's	I'll
can't	we're	it's	we'll
isn't	they're	that's	you'll

EXTEND. Give students numerous opportunities to review the sort and practice reading and spelling the words. Share the book *If You Were a Contraction* (Shaskan, 2009) to see a range of contractions used and explained in a colorful format. Encourage students to write these contractions in their word study notebooks or personal dictionaries. For oral language development, practice using the contractions in storytelling or writing.

6.31 Concept Sort: Ecosystems

This sort features a collection of vocabulary words associated with ecosystems. It is a good example of how sorting connects to other content areas and will help students develop academic vocabulary related to a unit of study in science.

DEMONSTRATE. Prepare Sort 235 on the website. Introduce the key words (guide cards) as on Figure 6.33 and ask students to name any plants and animals that may live in ponds, oceans, and deserts to activate their prior knowledge. Use several words from each category to demonstrate the sort, explaining your rationale through a think-aloud. For example, you may pick *sagebrush*, *seaweed*, and *reeds* as plants that live in different ecosystems. Review all of the picture and word cards with the students to make sure they can both read and understand the meaning of each term. You may also want to have students review the picture and word cards with partners. The completed sort should look something like Sort 235 on the website.

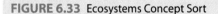

FIGURE 6.33 Ecosystems Concept Sort

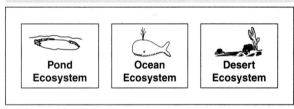

| Pond Ecosystem | Ocean Ecosystem | Desert Ecosystem |

After sorting, discuss the relationships between the plants and animals in each of the ecosystems: "A frog sits on a lily pad waiting to catch a dragonfly as it flies by." The words will range in difficulty based on their abstractness and on students' background knowledge. Much of the vocabulary should be reinforced in ongoing activities related to your hands-on study of this science unit. Provide outlets for students to learn the meanings of these words, such as in explicit lessons, by asking classmates and teachers, and by using picture dictionaries, informational texts, and online reference materials.

SORT, CHECK, AND REFLECT. Students should shuffle their cards and repeat the sort under your supervision. Have them check their sorts by explaining their rationale to a partner or the teacher. Encourage students to reflect by drawing a picture of one or all of the ecosystems, labeling each concept, and writing a few sentences that describe the ecosystem(s).

EXTEND. Have students work in pairs or small groups to research additional plants and animals and create food chains or food webs for each of the ecosystems.

PDToolkit

for Words Their Way™ with English Learners

Go to PDToolkit, choose your book, click the Sorts & Games tab, and search for "Sort 235: Ecosystems Concept Sort."

ACTIVITIES WITHIN WORD PATTERN STAGE

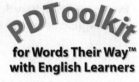

for Words Their Way™ with English Learners

Go to PDToolkit, choose your book, click the Sorts & Games tab, and search for "Sort 260: Word Sort for Plural Endings."

FIGURE 6.34 Word Sort for Plural Endings

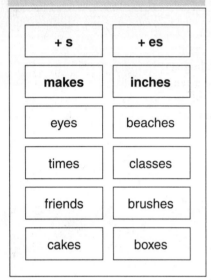

+ s	+ es
makes	**inches**
eyes	beaches
times	classes
friends	brushes
cakes	boxes

6.32 Word Sort for Plural Endings

This sort is an introduction to how *-s* and *-es* are added to words to create plurals. It serves as a foundation for sorts that will be conducted in later stages.

DEMONSTRATE. Prepare Sort 260 on the website. Play some language games with students to make plural words orally: "Today we will be working with words that mean more than one. For instance, *trees* means more than one tree. I'll say a word, and you tell me how to say more than one of it. Ready? Car; paint; name; fox, witch." If students have any trouble making plurals, work with them orally before beginning the sort. Next, ask students to read the words in this sort aloud and check to see that they know the meanings of the words. Consider teaching up to five unknown terms. Additional unknown items can be set aside for another time. Set up *+s* and *+es* as the guide patterns at the top of your columns. Demonstrate the sorting process by discussing the key words and comparing each to the guide patterns: "You'll have to think carefully about each word and how it is spelled before it becomes more than one." Work with a whiteboard to show students the original word and its plural if students are confused. Have your students join in as you identify and categorize each of the words as to whether an *-s* or *-es* has been added. It is important that your students say the words out loud even as they visually discern the letters in the words. This helps them hear the words that have one or two syllables. The completed sort should look something like Figure 6.34 (see also Sort 260 on the website).

When you are finished sorting, ask the students to compare the words in each column. "Which words needed *-es* to be added? Why? When was only *-s* needed?" Reread the sort as you check the words, and notice how many syllables each word has. "Are words like *friends* and *tests* harder to say because they are only one syllable?"

SORT, CHECK, AND REFLECT. Give each student or pair of students a copy of the sort for guided practice. Now have the students repeat the sorting, checking, and reflecting under your supervision using the same column headers.

EXTEND. Have students go on a word hunt for plural words. How many words can they find or think of? What else do they learn about adding *-s* or *-es* to words?

6.33 Word Sort for Past Tense Endings

This sort is an introduction to how *-ed* is added to words to show that something has already happened. It is modeled with simple forms and serves as a foundation for sorts that will be conducted in later stages.

DEMONSTRATE. Prepare Sort 261 on the website. Play some language games with students to help them understand the concept of past tense: "Today we will be working with words that tell you that something has already happened. For instance, *rained* means it already happened. I'll say a word, and you change the word to mean that it already happened. Ready? Plant, paint, show, help, start." If students have any trouble putting words into the past tense, work with them orally before beginning the sort. Next, ask students to read the words in this sort aloud and check to see that they know the meanings of the words. Consider teaching up to five unknown terms. Additional unknown items can be set aside for another time. Set up /d/, /id/, and /t/ as the guide patterns at the top of your columns. Tell students that when you add *-ed* to a word to make it the past, it can be pronounced in different ways: "Today you will be comparing the different sounds that *-ed* makes." Demonstrate the sorting process by discussing the key words and comparing each to the guide patterns: "*Mailed* means that something has already been put in the mail. What does the *-ed* sound like in *mailed*? Right, it sounds like a /d/. It goes under the card with the /d/ sound." Have your students join in as you identify and categorize each of the words as to what sound the *-ed* makes. It is important that your students say the words out loud so they can accurately identify the sound. Listen carefully and help your students if they mispronounce the words. The completed sort should look something like Figure 6.35 (see also Sort 261 on the website).

When you are finished sorting, ask the students to reread the words in each column. Did they all get placed in the correct sound column?

SORT, CHECK, AND REFLECT. Give each student or pair of students a copy of the sort for guided practice. Now have the students repeat the sorting, checking, and reflecting under your supervision, using the same column headers.

EXTEND. Have students go on a word hunt for other words that mean something has already happened. How many words can they find or think of?

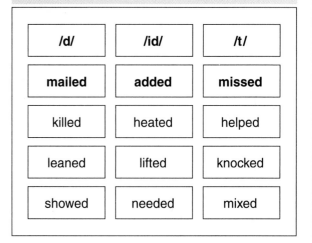

FIGURE 6.35 Word Sort for Past Tense Endings

/d/	/id/	/t/
mailed	**added**	**missed**
killed	heated	helped
leaned	lifted	knocked
showed	needed	mixed

Word Study with English Learners in the Syllables and Affixes Stage

Ms. Thompson's fourth grade class is well organized and emanates a sense of purpose. Student desks are clustered into table groups, and there is an open floor space for community meetings. Tubs of books are everywhere you turn: this way, a bookshelf filled with chapter books, including collections of mysteries and series such as The Boxcar Children and Cam Jansen; that way, bins of nonfiction books labeled with a content area such as U.S. History and Government, Famous People, Math, or Land Animals.

The bulletin boards hold useful directions and reference materials for students. On one bulletin board there is a word wall with academic vocabulary that students often misspell such as *issue, source,* and *procedure.* Another wall houses a math word bank that displays vocabulary words related to the math curriculum; the letter *D* is represented by the words *difference, division, decimal,* and *deposit.* Various charts capture previous group brainstorms, such as "Choosing new books," "When to abandon a book," and "Possible topics for writing a letter." Easy-to-read charts outline when each of the book clubs will meet and who is working at each center on Monday, Tuesday, Wednesday, and Thursday.

During literacy center time Ms. Thompson's multilingual and multiethnic class is active but not chaotic. Four students are working at the state history center, using resource materials to write the text for their individual state books. Three students are playing a word study game together on the floor area. Six students are at an independent reading center, either reading to themselves or completing entries in their reading response journals. Two students are cooperatively engaged in reading on a computer, and four other students are listening to books on tape at tape players around the room. Ms. Thompson knows it is important for English learners to have repeated opportunities to come back to interesting texts as they build their oral language skills, so she has many books available on tape or on the computer, along with a number of listening stations around the room.

On the rug in the meeting area, Ms. Thompson and a group of six English learners are gathered around a small chart stand with paper. The group is brainstorming words related to families, the topic of today's reading text. There are many common words on the list already, such as *brother, sister, mom, dad,* and *grandma.* Now the group is moving into more complex words and concepts, such as *stepsister, stepbrother,* and *stepfather.* The students are asking questions, and Ms. Thompson helps them to clarify their understanding of these relationships.

After brainstorming a list of about 25 family-related words, Ms. Thompson moves to her word study focus of the day—the use of the plural *s* versus *'s* for the possessive. She begins with a teacher-led word sort using the key words *mothers* and *mother's.* The group discusses in which column *aunts, brother's, cousins,* and other words belong, as in Figure 7.1. Ms. Thompson asks students whether they can use the words in a sentence and helps them understand the role of the apostrophe in changing a word's meaning.

When the word sort is done, the students get out their book for the day. It is a nonfiction text about families written at a late second grade level, which is the students' instructional reading level. She walks them through the book, noting some of the key vocabulary. Students point out to her that there are one or two family-related words that are missing from the group's brainstorming chart, so these are added to the list. The group is guided to make predictions and then read the first five pages and stop for a brief discussion to check for understanding. In this way, Ms. Thompson provides practice time for her students to read at their instructional level while supporting their language development and comprehension of the text. By explicitly working with the plural and possessive *s*, she integrates grammar, spelling, and vocabulary development into the language arts lesson.

FIGURE 7.1 Charting Plural *s* versus Possessive *'s*

mothers	mother's
aunts	brother's
cousins	father's
sisters	
sons	

Ms. Thompson's lesson models many of the guiding principles we have focused on throughout this book. Students receive explicit and systematic instruction during discussions of content-related words with teacher support. The teacher uses reading materials at students' instructional levels and provides opportunities for guided practice in reading and sorting within a supportive small-group context that engages students within a learning community. Ms. Thompson helps students make connections in numerous ways—by writing their oral language on chart paper, by helping them connect the schema for family words in English, by matching a word study lesson to the theme of the book being read, and by eliciting their background knowledge during brainstorming. Finally, she provides opportunities for the active construction of knowledge when students participate in sorting the family words, coming up with their own sentences and having time to talk in a small-group setting.

This chapter takes an in-depth look at helpful support strategies, the characteristics of development, and the content of instruction for English learners at the intermediate level of reading and the syllables and affixes stage of spelling. We describe how the essential literacy activities of Read To, Read With, Write With, Word Study, and Talk With (RRWWT) work together to provide a cohesive learning environment for English learners. We share examples of word study conversations so you can get a picture of how an effective teacher can be explicit and still challenge students to think at higher levels. Ideas for organizing word study activities that accommodate students from a range of developmental levels within a single classroom are also presented. The chapter concludes with dozens of hands-on sorts, games, and activities to use with your students as they progress through the syllables and affixes stage of word knowledge in English.

Literacy Instruction for English Learners in the Syllables and Affixes Stage

Students in the syllables and affixes stage may be mature in age and social skills while operating at earlier literacy levels. They may be ready to quickly translate their previous literate experiences into English, or they may be confounded by academic vocabulary and content that are totally unfamiliar. It will be important for you to keep a host of factors in mind as you design lessons for your students: developmental spelling level, previous literacy experiences in another language, oral language proficiency in English, level of background knowledge about the content of the material, and social maturity. The following ideas will guide you in designing appropriate instruction for English learners at the upper levels:

Adapt and tailor lessons to students' background knowledge and experiences.

1. Cluster students into word study groups based on the results of their developmental spelling inventories. Do not assume that age or grade level equals achievement level.

2. Find out who your students are. What languages do they speak at home? What literacy skills do they have in their first language? What background experiences do they have that relate to the content of the lesson? What do current language proficiency tests show about students' oral language skills in English? Use this knowledge to adapt your lessons and tailor questions to individual students as you go.

3. Although you may need to simplify instruction to address the language and literacy levels of your students, try to do so with materials that match the social maturity of your students.

4. Be as explicit as needed in your word study instruction. English learners do not have a large reservoir of vocabulary words to pull from during lessons. Provide lists and simple dictionaries for them to reference as you work together. Help them by using student-friendly definitions that can be connected to new vocabulary. See the *Longman Dictionary of American English* (Pearson/Longman, 2008) for a good example.

5. Make every lesson a language-learning event. Move from what students can say to putting it into writing. Incorporate daily opportunities for talking about words and texts. Assume that much of the vocabulary in your lesson will need to be taught and worked with. Oral discussions about words are critical so that students are bathed in language—they hear it spoken and use it to share experiences, discuss issues, ask questions, and make connections during their literacy lessons.

6. Place meaning-making at the center of each literacy lesson, even if you are focusing on a skill. Help students to self-monitor and speak up when they do not understand what is going on.

7. Connect spelling, vocabulary, and grammar study. Words that are featured in word study must also become vocabulary words, used and analyzed in conversational speech and connected to text as a part of the lesson.

8. Don't overemphasize pronunciation. Students at the upper levels of word study understand distinctions in letter–sound correspondences, even if they cannot pronounce them perfectly. Pronunciation will continue to be refined by students' interactions with printed materials over time.

9. Give extra support to students who have more limited English language skills. This may include working with a partner, having a peer translator, or seeing physical examples of projects.

Characteristics of Orthographic Development for English Learners in the Syllables and Affixes Stage

Students with more advanced word knowledge in English are ready to learn about the *deep characteristics* of English orthography. As Venezky (1999) expressed it about English spelling, "Visual identity of word parts takes precedence over letter–sound similarity" (p. 197). Students who have learned similar deep orthographies have a supportive mind-set for learning how English orthography works. On the other hand, students who are literate in a home language that is highly regular phonetically may find this orthographic complexity surprising and confusing. Making connections and comparisons between other writing systems and English can be very helpful to both sets of students at this time.

▶ **Morphemes**

The smallest meaningful units in words. The word *walked* has two morphemes—*walk* and *ed* (signaling past tense).

▶ **Affixes**

Most commonly, suffixes or prefixes that are attached to base words or word roots, such as the prefix *pre-* as an affix in *predict*.

▶ **Open Syllable**

A syllable that ends with a vowel as in *pilot, reason*.

▶ **Syllable Juncture**

The point where two syllables meet such as between *u* and *p* in *super* or between *p* and *p* in *supper*.

Inflectional endings such as *-s, -ed,* and *-ing* are used to indicate plurals and verb tense but do not change the meaning of the word.

A fundamental aspect of intermediate students' developmental word knowledge is learning about morphology, the processes by which meaningful word parts, called **morphemes,** combine, such as when we put *un-* + *break* + *-able* together to form *unbreakable.* These morphemes include base words, prefixes, and suffixes; prefixes and suffixes are collectively referred to as **affixes.** Importantly, understanding these processes will support students' spelling *and* vocabulary development. Two related but distinct areas of spelling are also explored at this level: (1) spelling conventions concerning the way syllables join—for example, whether consonants are doubled or left alone, as in *sun/sunny* or *dine/diner,* or whether a final *y* changes to *i* before adding a suffix, as in *supply/supplier;* and (2) spelling patterns in accented and unaccented syllables, for example, *curtain* and *table*.

Because of the aspects of word structure that students explore at this phase, we refer to students' word knowledge at the intermediate phase of literacy development as the syllables and affixes stage. Table 7.1 outlines the sequence of word study for English learners at this stage. The first two columns share important features that are studied and examples of those features. The final column highlights aspects of this study that may be difficult for students learning English.

Some of the components of Table 7.1 are not new for learners at this phase. What is new is applying this understanding, developed through the earlier examination of one-syllable words, to two-syllable words.

Syllable Juncture and Inflectional Endings

Consonant doubling is a fundamental process in spelling words of more than one syllable in English. Study the words that have been sorted into two categories in Figure 7.2. Note the difference in the vowel sound between *diner* and *dinner, super* and *supper,* and *hoping* and *hopping.* What else do you notice? In the second column two consonants come after the short vowel. The first syllable in words like *su per* is described as **open** and the pattern of where the two syllables come together (the **syllable juncture**) is abbreviated as VCV (*super*). The first syllable of words like *sup per* is described as closed and the syllable juncture pattern is VCCV (*supper*). Knowing how open (CV) and closed (CVC) syllables work in English will help spellers know when to double and readers know how to break words into syllables and pronounce the vowel. Because many languages, such as Spanish, do not have double letters that work this way, it needs to be addressed explicitly through word sorts such as Figure 7.2.

Students first explore the conventions of consonant doubling—when you do and when you don't—in the context of adding simple inflectional suffixes such as *-s, -ed,* and *-ing* to base words. Students' learning builds on their within word pattern understanding of long and short vowel patterns in single-syllable words. Students learn that whether you double a consonant or drop a final silent *e* depends on the vowel pattern in the base word—is it short or long? In the case of *hop,* a CVC pattern, the final consonant is doubled to keep the vowel short and closed as in *hop-ping.* In the case of *hope,* a CVCe pattern, the *e* is dropped before adding *-ing* and the first syllable retains its long vowel sound. In other patterns (CVCC, CVVC), there is no change: *land* + *-ing* = *landing; soak* + *-ing* = *soaking* because there is no danger of the first syllable becoming open.

Students whose first language derived from Latin may already be familiar with these types of morphological processes of word formation—adding prefixes and suffixes. For instance, in Spanish *-ir* is dropped from *vivir* and *-iendo* is added to change *live* to *living.* Extending this knowledge to English should be easier than learning it from scratch. It is important, however, to determine whether English inflectional suffixes are perceptible to students. For many English learners, it is initially difficult to perceive auditorally the *-ed* suffix, much less discriminate among the three different ways in which it can be pronounced: /t/ as in *hoped;* /id/ as in *wanted;* /d/ as in *climbed.* For this reason we have included many activities in this chapter to support students' oral language development in the context of word study.

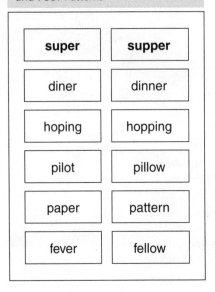

FIGURE 7.2 Exploring the VCV and VCCV Patterns

super	**supper**
diner	dinner
hoping	hopping
pilot	pillow
paper	pattern
fever	fellow

TABLE 7.1 **Sequence of Word Study for English Learners in the Syllables and Affixes Stage**

FEATURES TO STUDY	EXAMPLES	INSTRUCTIONAL NOTES
Early		
Plural endings -s and -es	plants /s/; dogs /z/; places /ez/ wishes—es after sh, ch, ss, and x parties—change y to i + es	Plurals may be formed differently in students' home language. Perceiving and producing the pronunciations of -s and -es at the end of a word may be difficult.
Unusual plurals	knife/knives; mouse/mice; goose/geese	Learning the small subset of nouns, verbs, and adjectives that involve an internal sound/spelling change.
Compound words	downtown, bookworm	Morphology in the home language may not involve compounding.
Inflectional ending/ suffix -ing	running—short vowel + double consonant standing—short vowel, no change writing—long vowel, e-drop dreaming—double vowel, no change	Verb forms may be constructed differently in students' home language, or this form may not occur. Perceiving the pronunciation of -ing at the end of a word is difficult. Spelling changes in the base word add a layer of complexity to the process.
Inflectional ending/ suffix -ed	talked /t/; begged /d/; shouted /id/ wanted—short vowel, no change hopped—short vowel + double consonant hoped—long vowel, e-drop dreamed—double vowel, no change	Past tense may be constructed differently in students' home language. Perceiving and producing the pronunciations of -ed may be difficult. Spelling changes in the base word add a layer of complexity to the process.
Ambiguous vowels in one-syllable words	paw, fault, thought	Sounds may not occur in the home language, so perceiving their differences in pronunciation and attaching the correct spelling pattern is difficult.
Middle		
Open and closed syllable patterns: V/CV vs. VC/CV	silent vs. happen, basket	Students' home language may not signal change in pronunciation through spelling; English signals long or short vowel through number of consonants at the syllable juncture that follows the vowel.
Familiar vowel patterns in accented syllables	painter, awake; ninety, delight; alone, soapy	Different pronunciations of accented and unaccented syllables. Students may use vowel sound instead of schwa in unaccented syllables.
Less familiar and ambiguous vowels in accented syllables	fountain, powder; employ, embroider	Sounds may not occur in students' home language, so perceiving their pronunciations and attaching the correct spelling patterns become difficult.
Final unaccented syllables -er, -or, -ar	mother, doctor, sugar	The r-influenced vowel does not provide clue to spelling.
Less frequent one-syllable homophones Two-syllable homophones	aisle/isle; cruise/crews allowed/aloud; principle/principal	In-depth vocabulary needed to distinguish different spellings for same pronunciation and to attach appropriate spelling patterns.
Less frequent one-syllable homographs Two-syllable homographs	bow; wound present/present; object/object	In-depth vocabulary needed to interpret correct pronunciation for words with the same spelling.
Special consonants in two-syllable words: hard and soft c and g wr, kn, gh	circle vs. correct, gentle vs. garden writing, kneecap, daughter, laughter	Same letters have different sounds.

(continued)

TABLE 7.1 **Continued**

FEATURES TO STUDY	EXAMPLES	INSTRUCTIONAL NOTES
Late		
Simple prefixes and base words and how they influence word meaning: *re-* (again), *un-* (not), *dis-* (opposite, not), *mis-* (wrong)	*redo, remake; unhappy, unwrap; dislike, disagree; misbehave, misspell*	Morphology in students' home language may not occur by combining different morphemes., but rather by tonal changes. In addition, morphology in home language may not be signaled by spelling/orthography.
Simple suffixes and base words and how they influence word meaning: comparatives *-er/-est*, Change *y* to *i* before suffix: *-ier/-iest*	*calmer/calmest* *happy/happier/happiest*	Comparatives must be both understood conceptually and then distinguished aurally. These forms may be constructed differently in students' home language.
-y, -ly	*cloudy, slowly*	These forms may be represented or constructed differently in students' home language.

Compare word formation in English to students' home languages.

Syllables and affixes spellers investigate and review vowel patterns they have previously studied, now within the accented syllable of a longer word. Ambiguous vowels that are neither long nor short (i.e., *spoiled, destroy, surround, daughter*) may continue to need attention for some students beyond the within word pattern stage. *Accent* refers to the amount of emphasis or stress applied to the syllables within a word. In English more words are accented on the first syllable than on the second whereas in many other languages the accent is on the second. Sorting words by the stressed syllable can both review vowel patterns and fine-tune pronunciation for students mastering English. Show students how accent is indicated in the dictionaries they are using (sometimes with accent marks and sometimes with bolded letters). Sorting students' names by where the accent falls can be an engaging way to introduce students to the role of accent. Try shifting where the accent falls so students can see how it affects the pronunciation. Is it **Da**vid or Da**vid**?

By the middle of the stage students are exploring final unaccented syllables such as ə + *l* in *table, sandal,* and *nickel.* Note how this final syllable is spelled three different ways but pronounced the same in each case. The schwa sound (symbolized by ə and usually pronounced "uh") is the most common vowel sound in English and occurs in nearly all words of more than one syllable (*residential* = /re zə 'den shəl/) yet it does not exist as a vowel sound in many other languages.

Explore Meaning

Another topic of study that begins in the within word pattern stage but should continue into the syllables and affixes stage is that of homophones (words that sound alike but are spelled differently and have different meanings like *bear* and *bare*) and homographs (words spelled the same but with different pronunciations and different meanings like *wind* or *live*). Now is the time to study less frequent one-syllable homophones, two-syllable homophones, and homographs such as **pre**sent/pre**sent**. Given the sound and spelling similarities among these words it is critical that English learners have many opportunities to engage in language experiences and build strong vocabularies as they study these words (Jacobson, Lapp, & Flood, 2007).

In the late syllables and affixes stage intermediate students develop their understanding of the morphological processes that underlie word formation in English as they begin to study simple prefixes and suffixes that change the meanings of base words in straightforward ways, such as how *un-* changes *able* to *unable*, and suffixes that change a word's part of speech, such as how adding *-ly* to the adjective *slow* changes it to an adverb. This sets the groundwork for an in-depth and systematic exploration of the spelling–meaning connection that is the focus of the derivational relations stage. Students' awareness and understanding of how morphemes contribute to word meaning becomes a powerful base for more advanced spelling knowledge and lays the foundation for their understanding of the critical role of Greek and Latin word parts in English.

This period also invites an exploration of cognates among languages—words that come from the same root and have a meaningful connection across languages. For example, consider the words *airport* and *aeropuerto* or *tecnología* and *technology*. Cognates allow students to make connections to other languages they know and provide a tool for hypothesizing the meanings of new words (Nagy, García, Durgunoglu, & Hancin-Bhatt, 1993). You may want to start a chart or bulletin board in your classroom for cognates.

FIGURE 7.3 Supporting English Learners in Word Analysis

> **reporter**
>
> To ensure that students are given a strong foundation of examples in putting word parts together, provide them with these opportunities:
>
> 1. Begin with teacher-guided sorts that include a thorough discussion of vocabulary issues, and make time for students to ask questions. With experience students can be asked to do more open sorts where they come up with categories and generalizations themselves.
>
> 2. Provide opportunities for students to partner with proficient English speakers to support their oral language and vocabulary development.
>
> 3. Have students say the words aloud, and frequently check for understanding.
>
> 4. Repeat sorts until students are able to do them quickly and accurately.
>
> 5. Have students record their words and word meanings in a word study notebook for future reference.
>
> 6. When students have internalized a wide variety of base words and affixes, plan learning activities for them to hunt for additional examples independently or in small groups.

Instructional Implications

Many students come from countries or cultures in which classroom instruction is primarily direct and lecture based, with a strong emphasis on memorization. These students need time to learn and negotiate the more socially interactive contexts characteristic of so many American classrooms. The implications for analytic word study, however, are critical. At first, we immerse students in numerous clear examples of regular word construction. In addition, it is important to provide explicit instruction for students, when appropriate, to help them understand the logic of word structure. After many guided experiences with sorts, introduce more open-ended questions (what do you notice about these words) and then provide opportunities for students to explore and search for patterns on their own. Figure 7.3 offers suggestions for instructing students who are learning English and need support in understanding how English words are constructed.

Components of Literacy Instruction at the Syllables and Affixes Stage

At the intermediate level of literacy learning, we continue to provide a "balanced diet" of Read To, Read With, Write With, Word Study, and Talk With essential literacy activities, although at this level the activities will look different from those in the early grades.

Talk With

English learners at all ages need many opportunities to engage in instructional conversations, and this is still the case at the upper levels of literacy development (Saunders & Goldenberg, 1999). Students at the syllables and affixes stage will be presented with challenging content area vocabulary and complex written texts at school. Provide outlets for students to dialogue with peers and instructors every day. Talk With activities can be integrated throughout the day, separately or as part of the other four essential literacy activities. For example, stop while reading a text aloud to have students make predictions about the content, share personal connections, comment on interesting words, or ask questions. If students share with a partner or in small groups, more students will get a chance to speak.

Read With activities also provide an important venue for integrating conversation. Have students share their impressions of what they are reading with fellow students in book clubs (Raphael, Pardo, & Highfield, 2002) or other structured group formats. Provide English learners with a graphic organizer or other notetaking guide as a reference to use as they speak to the group. Teachers will not only help develop students' verbal abilities, but they will also get important informal assessment information from discussing students' reading with them in a small-group setting. Getting students to talk in such activities as reader's theater and sharing book reviews are also good ways to connect Talk With and Read With activities.

Write With can become a socially interactive event if students are allowed to read their drafts to others, provide or request feedback, or present their finished writing aloud to the group. Students can be encouraged to suggest interesting words, ask thoughtful questions about a peer's writing, or create translations to make a bilingual book. Speaking and writing are activities that support each other for those developing literacy skills in a new language. Encourage students to write before sharing and discuss with others before writing.

Opportunities to integrate talking into word study are outlined in great detail later in this chapter. In word study lessons students examine word meanings with partners, talk about what they sort, play games, go on word hunts, build and take apart words, brainstorm word derivations, and discuss interesting or tricky words. All of these activities get students talking and learning together. In addition, Word Study activities become key times to analyze and discuss content area words that are critical so that students understand the curriculum in their classroom. For instance, before having English learners read about the solar system they will profit from discussing and trying out words such as *rotation, gravity, orbit,* and *atmosphere.* Concept sorts that, for instance, contrast warm-blooded and cold-blooded animals will help students integrate what they are learning in a content area with their study of new words. Table 7.2, Thinking Ahead in Vocabulary and Word Study, provides additional examples of how to engage students in vocabulary study that reaches beyond their current developmental level, so they become acquainted with more complex words and grammatical structures to come.

Read To

Reading aloud to students at the upper levels can serve a number of purposes. It is a good way to share content information that may be too difficult for your students to read independently. You can connect your read-aloud text to a thematic unit you are studying and include schema-building discussion activities such as charting, listing, or sorting the information that has been presented. A read-aloud session is also a good way to present, clarify, and discuss new vocabulary with students. Learning a term like *magnetism* or *compassion* may be facilitated by a book that illustrates its meaning and provides a gateway to discussion.

Reading to students lets them hear a fluent and expressive reader and presents words that are not common in conversational language. English learners need as many opportunities as possible to listen to a variety of words used in context, as long as they are able to comprehend what is being said. Books on CD or tape are helpful, but even better is a real teacher who can help clarify words that are not understood. Books on computer or presented in electronic form may also provide students with the ability to have words repeated or clarified as many times as needed.

TABLE 7.2   **Thinking Ahead in Vocabulary and Word Study**

Errors Made by Syllables and Affixes Spellers / Correct Spelling

VILAGE / village

CONFADANCE / confidence

VISABEL / visible

CORESPOND / correspond

ENFASIZE / emphasize

IRESPONSIBLE / irresponsible

STUDENTS IN THE NEXT STAGE ...	SO IN THE INTERMEDIATE READERS/SYLLABLES AND AFFIXES SPELLERS STAGE ...
Learn Greek and Latin roots	Teachers point out roots to students in academic content
Understand less frequent prefixes and suffixes (*anti-, per-, pre-, inter-, -ion*)	Students refer to lists of these prefixes and suffixes with definitions
Study polysyllabic words and find the meaning relationships among words	Teachers provide support in lessons in which two or more related words are brainstormed (*declare/declaration/declarative*)
Read polysyllabic words	Teachers demonstrate how to examine polysyllabic words in whole-group lessons
Learn the meanings of many new words	Students develop semantic webs and diagrams of related words
Read polysyllabic words with ease	Teachers read to students so that they hear the vocabulary they will need to read on their own

As for all students, read-aloud time provides motivation for expanding into unknown and exciting texts and to reinforce the interpersonal relationship between teacher and students. If your classroom has a wide variation in the listening comprehension levels of your students, you may need to tailor your text to a vocabulary level that most students will understand. Provide support for students with limited English proficiency in some of the following ways: Allow bilingual peers to fill students in about details in the book, meet with students before or after reading to answer their questions about what has been read, offer books on tape for them to review, provide printed or recorded versions in their home language for reading or listening, or find simpler books related to the theme to read to them at a different time of the day or to discuss with an available volunteer.

Read With

Students at the intermediate level of literacy development are now reading silently in longer texts on their own. They need to have lots of time to read material that is not too difficult to decode or comprehend. After assessing your students, form groups with similar needs in terms of reading level and vocabulary development. Find engaging texts that support your goals for the students, offering choices when possible. Books on the same subject or theme but at various reading levels are important resources that allow students to read at their instructional levels. Structure time throughout the week to meet with the groups to scaffold vocabulary development, discuss the text, and partner read for oral practice. You can listen in as students read together or pull students out periodically to assess whether the text is at their instructional level (93% or better accuracy, with good comprehension).

If you have students in your upper-grade classroom who are still beginning or transitional readers, you will want to meet with them in teacher-led instructional reading groups on a daily basis. To do this, you may try to enlist any teaching help available from support personnel

(ESL, literacy, or resource teachers), volunteers from the community or university, students' families, or elsewhere.

Write With

Students at the intermediate literacy level are now able to write longer pieces with greater fluency. They have the stamina to participate in the writing process, from rough drafts to final editing. They are able to revise their work based on teacher or peer feedback. Writing With projects at this stage will likely focus on expanding repertoire or genre, developing voice and style, and using increasingly descriptive vocabulary. Example activities include expository content area reports, letters, and personal or fictional stories.

English learners at this stage need guidance in a number of ways during Write With time. Some support strategies may be presented to the class as a whole, such as when you provide models for various writing genres, discuss how writers express their voice, or expand students' written vocabularies. For example, you may lead a group lesson in how to write a consumer letter by posting a chart-sized model for the class and having students write their own letters based on products they use. You may also have the whole class participate in an activity to brainstorm other ways to say *nice*, *happy*, or *said*, as in Figure 7.4. These lists of words can be posted on the wall or printed on large cards for students to refer to during writing. Another activity that develops written vocabulary is to have students take a number of descriptive words and place them on a continuum so that they can see subtle variations in meaning. For example, consider the following words: *mad, upset, angry, irritated, bothered, infuriated, aggravated,* and *incensed*. Help students discuss how they might arrange these words from least to most strongly felt. They can save their lists in a word study notebook or on a chart in class.

On other occasions, it will work better to conduct small-group minilessons with students who can use help in specific areas. You will discover these needs by examining students' unedited writing or as you work with them in your instructional reading groups. English learners may make grammatical errors in their writing because they are learning English syntax or because they are representing the structure of their home language in their English writing. For example, Ms. Phillips noticed that several students in her class were omitting *do* or *did* in their questions, such as in "How you get to school?" This signaled to her a grammatical error that she could take time to clarify and practice correctly in a small group. Unedited writing is a wonderful informal assessment showing how to guide students' oral and written language development.

English learners will find it helpful to have reference materials close at hand, so consider helping students create a writer's notebook or expanding their word study notebook to include vocabulary lists, personalized dictionaries or thesauruses, and/or lists of synonyms, antonyms, homophones, or cognates. The notebook might also contain a personal list of writing ideas or story starters that the student can draw from over the course of the year.

As in other instructional activities, English learners need opportunities to talk about their writing both as they develop ideas and after they have created a first draft. Writing conferences with the teacher and in peer groups allow students to engage in meaningful conversations about words, sentences, and whole pieces of text. Conferences also help students learn new words to express ideas while providing a forum for contributing their insights to others' work.

FIGURE 7.4 Other Words for *said*

asked	blurted
replied	begged
added	answered
shouted	admitted
whispered	yelled
agreed	piped in
demanded	mumbled
cried	

Word Study

After assessing students using the Elementary Spelling Inventory (Appendix, p. 251), form groups of students who cluster at similar developmental levels as described in Chapter 2. Spelling lists and word study instruction should be based on the features that students are using but confusing in their assessment. To make your classroom organization manageable, you may need to work with groups that span a range of levels at one time, tailoring words and activities to students' specific needs. For instance, Mr. O'Brien was able to cluster his fifth graders into three groups for word study: a late syllables and affixes group, an early syllables and affixes group, and a middle within word pattern group. He also had two late letter name–alphabetic students who were newer to English reading; he asked them to be part of the within word pattern group but provided differentiated word lists and support for them within that group.

Fostering a Climate for Word Learning

While working in word study groups, students will do the sorts and activities described throughout this book and in other *Words Their Way*™ publications. In addition to these small-group and individualized activities, there are many ways to foster an interest in words with the class as a whole. Talk with students about interesting words in the books they are reading and listening to. Make a place for interesting words on your classroom walls and in word study notebooks. Make connections to words that tie into students' home languages or relate to their lives, hobbies, and activities. Use the academic words from your content area studies to create concept sorts about topics such as polygons or the human skeleton, as in Figure 7.5. Create a **semantic map** for the conceptual ideas and vocabulary you are studying, such as *immigration* in Figure 7.6. Investigate blended words such as *smog* (*smoke + fog*), clipped words such as *gas* (*gasoline*) and *Internet* (*inter-network*), or abbreviations and acronyms such as PC (*personal computer*). What other examples can they think of? Find creative ways to study idioms like "apple of my eye"; when explicit, these discussions will give English learners a greater understanding of the subtleties in the language. Use texts that include **codeswitching,** such as Gary Soto's Chato series (Soto, 1997, 2004), to delve into the richness of words in different languages. For an extended range of ideas on building academic vocabulary with older students, see *Vocabulary Their Way*™: *Word Study with Middle and Secondary Students* (Templeton, Bear, Invernizzi, & Johnston, 2010).

Students' spelling lists should be based on their developmental levels. Polysyllabic theme words that relate to your content area study can be used in reading, discussions, and added to a vocabulary section of their word study notebooks, but should not be used as spelling words.

▶ **Semantic Map**
A concept map that visually outlines relationships for a conceptual idea.

▶ **Codeswitching**
Moving between two or more languages or dialects in a conversation when people have more than one language in common.

FIGURE 7.5 Concept Sort for the Human Skeleton

The Human Skeleton	
Limbs	**Core**
metacarpals	spine
femur	skull
fibula	rib cage
humerus	pelvis

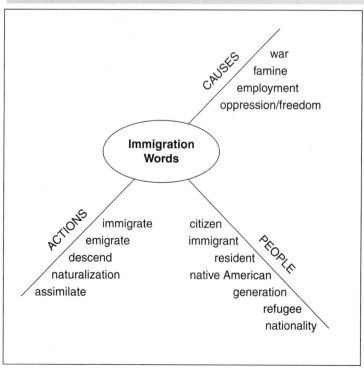

FIGURE 7.6 Semantic Map for Immigration Words

Students become excited about word study when the teacher models an inquiring stance. Show students that you wonder about where words come from, what the logic is behind a certain spelling, or how English compares with students' home languages. Explore how the vocabulary from your unit of study may share meaningful word parts, such as *cycle*, *bicycle*, *tricycle*, and *motorcycle*. Even though students may not yet be spelling these words correctly, this exploration will set a foundation for future word work.

Walking through Words with Students

"Walk through words" with students both in your developmental groups and, from time to time, on a classwide basis. As noted in the sequence outlined in Table 7.1, students in the late syllables and affixes stage are ready to examine the most concrete and frequently occurring prefixes and suffixes. In this chapter we offer a first example of a teacher introducing how the concept of morphemes—prefixes, suffixes, bases, and word roots—works within words. We begin with two of the most straightforward prefixes (*un-* and *re-*) and walk through how they combine with concrete, well-understood base words. Walking through words with derivational affixes and Latin and Greek roots is described as part of Chapter 8's discussion of derivational relations.

In "walking through words" the teacher joins a written or visual representation of words and elements to an oral conversation/discussion with the students and then involves the students in talking about their understandings. This allows the teacher the opportunity to respond as necessary to confirm, clarify, or extend, as shown in the accompanying lesson on the prefixes *re-* and *un-*.

- Writing the word *do* on the overhead, the teacher says, "I wonder: When you *do* a chore, what does that mean? [Students respond.] Yes, like cleaning up after you and your friends make sandwiches. If it's still a mess after you finish, though, we say you will have to *re*do that chore. [Adds the prefix *re-* to the base word *do*.]"

- Writing the word *make* on the overhead, the teacher continues, "If your mother tells you to *make* your bed and she doesn't like how you've made it, she'll have you *re*make the bed. [Adds the prefix *re-* to *make*.]"

- "If you *fill* a glass with water, what does that mean? [Students respond.] If you are very thirsty and want to put more water in the glass, we can say you will [pause briefly, waiting to see if students will apply *re-* to *fill*]. Excellent! Yes, we say you *re*fill your glass."

  If students respond with something like "You put more water in it" rather than saying *refill*, the teacher may in turn answer, "That's right. Now, remember when we said you *re*make your bed if it isn't done right? So, another way of saying you put more water in your glass when you *fill* it again is to say you . . . [pause for the students to respond]." With this additional clarification, students usually will reply "refill." If they still do not, however, the teacher goes ahead and supplies the correct word: "Just like when you *make* your bed but your mother tells you to do it again, you *re*make it. So if you fill your glass and need to do it again, we say you *re*fill it."

- The teacher helps students pull together the understandings from each of her examples to realize what *re-* means: She writes the words *do*, *make*, and *fill* on another transparency. Pointing to each word as she says it, she continues: "Let's go back over what we did when we said we had to *do*, *make*, or *fill* something again. When we had to *do* the chore again, we had to [pause]. That's right! We had to *re*do it. [Adds *re-* to *do*.] When we had to *make* our bed again, we had to . . ." and so forth.

  On the overhead, the teacher writes the sentence *Johnny had to rewrite his paper*. She asks the students to read the sentence with her; she pauses at the word *rewrite* to see if the students will identify it. If they have difficulty, she covers the prefix *re-* to see if they know the base. She then uncovers the prefix; they finish reading the sentence. She asks the students, "So, what do you think Johnny had to do . . . ? How do you know? So, whenever we see the word part *re-* added to a word, what do you think it will mean?" If the students are uncertain or hesitant to respond, the teacher says, "The word part *re-* will mean 'to do again.' We call word parts like *re-* that are added at the beginning of a word *prefixes*. We will be learning about other prefixes over the next several days."

- The teacher has students write the words and their meanings in their word study notebooks. She provides the model based on what she has written on the transparency:

  redo = "to do again"
  remake = "to make again"
  refill = "to fill again"
  The prefix *re-* means "to do again."

- The next day the teacher reviews the *re-* prefix with students, drawing out their explanations. She then introduces the prefix *un-* (meaning "not" or "taking away") in the same fashion, using the words *happy, wrap, do,* and *selfish.*

  unhappy = "not happy"
  unwrap = "taking away the wrap"
  undo = "taking away what was done"
  unselfish = "not selfish"

ACTIVITIES
FOR ENGLISH LEARNERS IN THE SYLLABLES AND AFFIXES STAGE

The following activities are sequenced according to *early, middle,* or *late* syllables and affixes stage. Table 7.1 is a good reference for this sequence. The sorts described in this activities section are listed as Sorts 262–278 on the website. After locating the sort or game page on the website you can print it and make the appropriate number of copies for student use. Not all sorts needed for this stage are described here but these will give you an idea of how to conduct sorting lessons. Sorts should be introduced in small groups and then students should re-sort, record sorts, work with partners, and do word hunts across the week as described in Chapter 3.

for Words Their Way™ with English Learners

Go to PDToolkit, choose your book, click the Sorts & Games tab, and select Syllables and Affixes Stage from the Stage filter.

Word Study Activities at the Early Syllables and Affixes Stage

7.1 Plural Endings: Adding -es

DEMONSTRATE. Prepare the set of plural words to use with Sort 262 on the website. Be sure the students can read the words and know the meaning of each. Remind students that to make a word plural either *-s* or *-es* is added. Sort the words first by these two column headers, as in Figure 7.7. Students will need to think about the base word in order to make this distinction. Because all of the words end in *-es* we recommend underlining the base word. Read the words in columns and point out that adding *-es* also adds another syllable. This additional syllable makes these words fairly easy to spell.

Push the words that simply added *-s* to the side and request students to focus on the words that are left. Ask them if there is anything they notice about the words. Point out the base words and focus students' attention on the last one or two letters. Model the next step of the sort by placing *catches, ashes, mixes,* and *crosses* into separate categories. Create headers for these if you want by underlining the *ch* in *reaches,* the *sh* in *rushes,* and so on, or by creating headers like the ones shown for Sort 262 on the website. After completing the sort as shown, ask

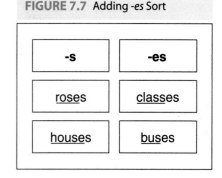

FIGURE 7.7 Adding -es Sort

-s	-es
<u>roses</u>	<u>classes</u>
<u>houses</u>	<u>buses</u>

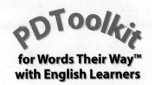

students how the words in each column are alike. Help students articulate a rule (Add -*es* to words that end in *ch*, *sh*, *x*, and *s*.) and note it on a class chart. Because adding -*es* to make a word plural adds another syllable /əz/ to the word, students do not have too much problem spelling the plural form.

EXTEND. Give students transfer words to practice applying the rules: *switch, horse, glass, tray, choice, peach, flame, fox, mess, shape, lunch, sandwich, grade, wish, guess, glove.*

7.2 Language in Use: Plural Ending Word Hunt

Students may find it difficult to hear and spell the ending sound in plural nouns and in verbs. This activity is an opportunity for students to work on plural formation in a directed way.

PROCEDURES

1. Students find 10 nouns each from texts they are using in class, picture dictionaries, their word study notebooks, or from environmental print. Remind them that a noun is often something you can touch—like an object or an animal. Give them examples such as *dog, bird, paper,* or *toy.*

2. Students write the nouns on small cards. On one side write the singular form (e.g., *truck*); on the other side write what it would be if there were more than one (e.g., *trucks*).

| boxes | trucks | hats | benches |

3. Students check their cards with a partner to make sure they are correct. They can also check with a teacher if necessary.

4. Students practice saying the words aloud, so they can hear the difference between the name for one and more than one.

5. Play games with the cards, such as sorting them by -*s*, -*es*, or other categories; matching words that go together such as school items, animals, or another category; "winning" cards by using them correctly in a sentence; or any other activity that encourages students to use the plural words in conversation and notice their features.

7.3 Unusual Plurals: Go Fish

Have students play this classic card game after sorting words with unusual plurals. Use 22 to 26 cards for two players; add more cards for three or four players.

MATERIALS. Create a deck of cards by cutting cardstock into pieces approximately 2 inches by 3 inches. Print one word per card from the following list of unusual plural nouns and their singular partners:

> *wife, wives, leaf, leaves, loaf, loaves, life, lives, wolf, wolves, knife, knives, half, halves, calf, calves, shelf, shelves, elf, elves, yourself, yourselves, scarf, scarves, foot, feet, man, men, woman, women, mouse, mice, tooth, teeth, goose, geese, deer, deer, sheep, sheep, fish, fish, child, children*

PROCEDURES. Five cards are dealt to each player and the remaining cards are placed in the middle as a draw pile. The first player asks any other player for a match to his or her hand: "I have *leaf*. Do you have *leaves*?" A player may also request the singular word, such as "I have *geese*. Do you have *goose*?" A player who is uncertain of the singular or plural word to request may ask for assistance from another student.

If the player receives the requested card, he or she puts the pair down and asks for another card. If the requested card is not matched, the other player tells the first player to "Go fish," which means to take a card from the draw pile. The first player's turn is over when he or she can no longer make a match.

Play continues around the circle until one player runs out of cards. Points can be awarded to the first person to go out and to the person who has the most matching cards.

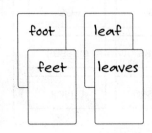

7.4 Compound Words

DEMONSTRATE. Prepare compound words for Sort 263 from the website. This sort features compound words that are fairly common and concrete for English learners. Show your students all the words and ask whether they see some parts that are related. They may notice *day* in *daylight*, *birthday*, and *someday*. Ask them to sort these words into categories based on the common components: *day*, *side*, *book*, *play*, or *mail*. Be ready to model two or three categories and sort a few words into each if necessary. Review the term *compound words* with your students and help them develop their own definition based on the words they see in the sort. After sorting, discuss the meanings of some of the words and how the meaning relates to the two words that make up the compound: *A bookcase is a place to store your books. Birthday is the day of your birth.* Some compound words cannot be interpreted literally. A *scrapbook* is not for scraps. Ask students to investigate the meanings of words they do not understand. The completed sort should look something like Sort 263 on the website.

FIGURE 7.8 Studying Compound Words

SORT, CHECK, AND REFLECT. Have students shuffle their words and repeat the sort under your supervision, as in Figure 7.8. Have them check their sorts by looking for or underlining the word part that is shared by all of the words in each column. Encourage the students to reflect by asking them to define the term *compound word* in their own way.

EXTEND. Have students think of other compound words such as those using *light*, *down*, *some*, or *self* (e.g., *lighthouse*, *flashlight*, *downtown*, *downstairs*, *someone*, *something*, *myself*, *herself*).

for Words Their Way™ with English Learners

Go to PDToolkit, choose your book, click the Sorts & Games tab, and search for "Sort 263: Compound Words."

7.5 Adding *-ing* to Words with VC and VCC Patterns

DEMONSTRATE. Prepare the words for Sort 264 on the website. Students should find these words easy to read, but it is helpful if they say the words aloud to themselves before beginning the sort. Assist with pronunciation questions as needed. Put up the headers VC and VCC. Pull out the base words and have the students help you sort them into two categories starting with *let* and *call*, as in Figure 7.9. Explain to the students that these are called *base words*. Ask whether there is anything they notice about all the base words: They all have one vowel that is usually short. Some end in one consonant (*let* = CVC) and some end in two (*call* = CVCC). They are all verbs. Then match the *-ing* form of the word to each base word. Ask the students what happens to the base word *let* when the *-ing* is added. Repeat with several more words in the column. Say the term "doubling" and explain that when a base word ends in one vowel and one consonant we must double the final consonant before adding *-ing*. Put the header Double above *letting*. Then ask students what they notice about the *-ing* words in the other column. Guide them to notice that the *-ing* was just added without any change because there are already two consonants after the vowel. Add the header No Change, as in Figure 7.10. The completed sort should look something like Sort 264 on the website.

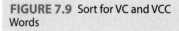

for Words Their Way™ with English Learners

Go to PDToolkit, choose your book, click the Sorts & Games tab, and search for "Sort 264: Adding *-ing* to Words with VC and VCC Patterns."

SORT, CHECK, AND REFLECT. After modeling the sort with the group, have students repeat the sorting under your supervision using the same column headers and key words. Tell them to check their sorts by looking for the pattern in each column. Encourage reflection by asking them how the words in each column are alike and what they have learned about adding *-ing* to base words. Have the students put the rule into their own words. You may want to write down this rule on chart paper and post it for reference. Leave space for the additional rules and revisions that will develop over the weeks to come.

FIGURE 7.9 Sort for VC and VCC Words

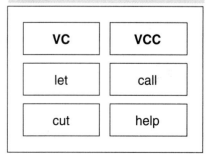

VC	VCC
let	call
cut	help

FIGURE 7.10 Adding *-ing* to VC and VCC words

VC	Double	VCC	No Change
let	letting	call	calling
cut	cutting	think	thinking

EXTEND. Students should repeat this sort several times and work with the words using some of the weekly word study routines described in Chapter 3: buddy sorts, blind sorts, writing sorts, and timed sorts. Word hunts will turn up lots of words that can be added to these categories but students will find many words that do not fit either of them. Tell them to add these words to a third column (oddballs) and challenge students to try to discover the rule that governs these other words in anticipation of the sort for next week.

Students might be encouraged to share contrasting sentences (orally or in writing) for the base word and its *-ing* form. For example, I <u>plan</u> to go to the beach. I have been <u>planning</u> my trip all month. Ask students to share sentences using the *-ing* form and also what they notice about their sentences (using *-ing* as a verb often requires helping verbs such as *am, have been, was,* and so on).

Give students additional words and ask them to apply the rule. Some suggested transfer words are *rest, hunt, swim, kick, stir, mop, run, quit, wish, sit, guess,* and *smell.*

7.6 Adding *-ing* to Words with VCe and VVC Patterns

DEMONSTRATE. Prepare the set of words for Sort 265 on the website. Introduce it in a manner similar to the sort for Activity 7.5. Ask students what happens to the base word *like* when *-ing* is added. Look at the other words under the VCe column to see how the *e* is dropped in each word. Say the term "*e*-Drop" and put it at the top of the column. Explain that a base word ending in silent *e* drops the *e* before adding *-ing.* Guide them to notice that *-ing* was just added without any change to the VVC words. See Figure 7.11. The completed sort should look something like Sort 265 on the website.

SORT, CHECK, REFLECT, AND EXTEND. Students should repeat the sort using the same column headers and key words. Encourage the students to reflect by asking them how the words in each column are alike and what they have learned about adding *-ing* to base words. Review what they learned in the previous sort and add to the chart. Give students additional words and ask them to apply the rule. Some suggested transfer words are *ride, need, close, use, eat, smile, vote, meet, mail, clean, turn,* and *speak.*

FIGURE 7.11 Adding *-ing* to VCe and VVC Words

VCe	e-Drop	VCC	No Change
like	liking	rain	raining

7.7 Adding *-ed* to Words with Double, *e*-Drop, and No Change

DEMONSTRATE, SORT, CHECK, AND REFLECT. Prepare the set of words to use with Sort 266 on the website. You might begin this sort by asking your students to spell *hopped* and then *hoped.* Ask them to justify why they spelled as they did. Explain that students often have trouble with these words and that the sort for this week will help them learn and remember the rules that govern the addition of *-ed* just as they did for *-ing.* Begin with a teacher-directed sort using the headers *hopped* and *hoped* and proceed in a manner similar to that of Activity 7.5. You may want your students to underline the base word to help them identify the pattern, especially in words like *hoped* and *moved.* Help the students see that the rules are similar to the rules for adding *-ing* and can be summed up as "double, *e*-drop, or no change." Talk about the fact that adding *-ed* means that something has already happened and that words such as these

PDToolkit

for Words Their Way™ with English Learners

Go to PDToolkit, choose your book, click the Sorts & Games tab, and search for "Sort 265: Adding *-ing* to Words with VCe and VVC Patterns."

PDToolkit

for Words Their Way™ with English Learners

Go to PDToolkit, choose your book, click the Sorts & Games tab, and search for "Sort 266: Adding *-ed* to Words with Double, *e*-Drop, and No Change."

are said to be in the "past tense." Have students use some example words in a sentence to check for understanding of meaning.

EXTEND. Also challenge your students to sort these words by the sound of the -*ed* ending, as shown here. No headers should be provided for this sort but are indicated here for clarity. Ask students if there is anything they can discover about the words in each column. They might notice that certain consonants precede certain sounds (*p* before /t/, *d* and *t* before /əd/) and that the words in the last column have added a syllable to the base word.

e-Drop	Double	No Change
traded	hugged	asked
	slipped	

/t/	/d/	/əd/
asked	hugged	hated
walked	rhymed	spotted
picked	fanned	floated
slipped	rained	twisted
cooked	jailed	traded
	mailed	
	poured	
	begged	
	named	
	phoned	
	sneezed	
	shaved	
	slammed	

Ask students to apply their knowledge by adding -*ed* to additional words: *dream, march, plan, nod, step, drop, save, close, like, live, tame, beg, clean, wave, boil, clip, scoop, pet, talk, climb, snap, melt, score, shout, wait,* and *help.*

7.8 Language in Use: Present and Past Tense

Talk with your students about the concept of actions taking place in the present or the past. Brainstorm a list of what they did yesterday, and write these words on a chart: *ate, walked, saw, fixed, helped, rode,* and so on, as in Figure 7.12. Circle the words on the chart that end with -*ed*. As they know from the previous lesson, adding -*ed* is one way to show that something happened in the past. Ask students to change the words into actions that they might be doing today—*eat, walk, dress,* or *study,* for example. Note any difficulties that arise for students so that you can support them in the future.

To close the lesson, do a group sort of past tense versus other -*ed* words. With a list of words such as *walked, rented, bed, named, shred, worked, seaweed,* and so on, have students decide which of the words refer to events in the past and which do not.

7.9 Unusual Past Tense: Card Games

After charting past tense words in Activity 7.8, review your brainstormed list to find the words that do not end in -*ed* (e.g., *ate, rode*). If you did not already brainstorm a list, ask students to talk about what they have done in the past week. Write down any past tense verbs they mention. Remind students that we often show that something already happened by adding -*ed*. There are also many words in English that indicate the past in unusual ways. Create word cards from the unusual past tense list that follows. Introduce the word cards

FIGURE 7.12 Past Tense Chart

ate
walked
saw
fixed
helped
rode

ACTIVITIES SYLLABLES AND AFFIXES STAGE

in this lesson, and ask students to use the words in a sentence. Clarify the meanings of any unknown words.

begin	began	blow	blew	buy	bought	bring	brought
drink	drank	go	went	have	had	hold	held
meet	met	say	said	speak	spoke	teach	taught
win	won	find	found	wear	wore	send	sent
see	saw	grow	grew	ride	rode	sell	sold
feed	fed	pay	paid	run	ran	leave	left

The cards can be used in a variety of games including the following:

- *Concentration.* Turn the cards face down and take turns searching for present tense and past tense matches such as *run–ran.*
- *Go Fish.* See Activity 7.3 for a description.

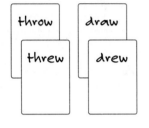

EXTEND. English has many irregular verbs, so students might set aside a part of their word study notebook to keep track of them and add others over time. For a complete list check the Internet, such as the site www.englishpage.com/irregularverbs/irregularverbs.html. As more and more words are added to students' lists, challenge them to come up with ways to sort the pairs into categories that reflect how they change from present to past. For instance, *blow–blew, grow–grew, know–knew, throw–threw,* and *draw–drew* all change the vowel sound to *-ew.*

Word Study Activities at the Middle Syllables and Affixes Stage

7.10 Syllable Juncture in VCV and VCCV (Doublet) Patterns

DEMONSTRATE. Prepare the set of VCV and VCCV words for Sort 267 on the website. You might introduce this lesson by requesting your students to spell *hoping* and *hopping.* Ask them to tell you why they spelled the words as they did. Assure them that the sort you are doing will help them understand what is going on with such words. Resist the temptation to explain to students what is taking place in these words. They will learn so much more if they are allowed to figure this out as you work through the sort. Tell students that you will be looking at patterns in a different way and introduce the headers VCV and VCCV, reminding them that V stands for vowel and C for consonant. Put the key words *hoping* and *hopping* under the headers. Label and underline letters in these key words: VCV represents the *o, p,* and *i* in *hoping* and VCCV represents the *o, p, p,* and *i* in *hopping.* Notice that one or more letters—or no letters—can come on either side of the juncture. Model how to sort several more of the word cards and then begin to involve your students in the sorting process. Show the group one of the word cards and ask students where it should be placed. Continue with their help to sort all the words into columns under each header, as in Figure 7.13. The completed sort should look something like Sort 267 on the website.

Now read down each column of words and ask your students to listen to the vowel sound in the first syllable. They should notice that in each word of the VCV column the vowel is long. Explain that these first syllables end with a long vowel sound that is called *open.* You might demonstrate how to break the word

FIGURE 7.13 Syllable Juncture in VCV and VCCV Patterns

VCV	VCCV
hoping	**hopping**
writer	pepper
moment	sunny
music	foggy

apart by drawing a line between the two syllables as in *ho/ping*. Remind them that they have studied open syllables in words such as *go, row,* and *blue.* Next read the other column to find that the vowel is short in the first syllable. Again you might draw a line between the syllables (*hop/ping*) and explain that these syllables are called *closed* because they end with a consonant.

SORT, CHECK, AND REFLECT. Now have students repeat the sort under your supervision. To reinforce the idea of the syllables, you might ask students to draw a line between them. They could also divide the words into syllables on small whiteboards or in their word study notebooks. Have them check their sorts by looking for the pattern in each column. Encourage the students to reflect by asking them how the words in each column are alike and what they have learned. Help the students to articulate a generalization such as *A syllable that ends in a vowel usually has a long vowel sound, and a syllable that ends in a consonant usually has a short vowel sound.*

7.11 More Syllable Juncture in VCV and VCCV Patterns

DEMONSTRATE. Prepare the set of VCV and VCCV words for Sort 268 on the website. This sort reinforces the patterns from the previous sort but adds words that have different consonants at the juncture (e.g., *carpet*) in addition to words with the same consonants at the juncture or "doublets" (e.g., *funny*). Introduce the sort in a manner similar to that of Activity 7.10, but this time ask students to notice what is different about the consonants among the VCCV words (some are doublets and some are different). Set up the column headers and key words, and model several of the words. Guide students to notice how many consonants there are at the syllable juncture. If there are two, are they both the same or are they different? Think aloud as you sort the words with student help. After students are comfortable with the patterns, have them do the sort on their own or with a partner. Your final sort will look something like Figure 7.14, Sort 268 on the website.

PDToolkit
for Words Their Way™ with English Learners

Go to PDToolkit, choose your book, click the Sorts & Games tab, and search for "Sort 268: More Syllable Juncture in VCV and VCCV Patterns."

EXTEND. Students should work with the words using some of the weekly routines that have been previously outlined, such as writing them in their word study notebooks, using them in card games, or going on word hunts. A word hunt will turn up many words as well as oddballs that are open syllables but do not have a long vowel sound. Have them put oddballs into a fourth column and keep them handy for further reference.

7.12 Accented Syllables: Jeopardy Game

This is a favorite game that can be adapted to many spelling features. In this version, a small group of students recall and spell words that follow familiar long vowel patterns in accented syllables. Students have to guess the right word based on a clue, so it is also a good way to get vocabulary practice.

MATERIALS. You will need dice, a game board, and clue cards. A poster board or open file folder is divided into five columns with four boxes each. A clue card worth 100, 200, 300, or 400 points is placed on each space—cards should be color coded or labeled by their category so they are placed in the appropriate column. A list of possible words and point values follows that will help you get started. You can add new words to this game over time, but remember to find words that are concrete, so that English learners can predict them from short clues. The words should also represent the given long vowel sound in an accented syllable.

FIGURE 7.14 More Syllable Juncture in VCV and VCCV Patterns

VCV	VCCV Doublet	VCCV Different
defend	funny	carpet
baby	common	signal
stolen	mammal	basket
robot	office	dentist
flavor	tennis	infant
pirate	sudden	enjoy
final		capture
		twenty

Point Value	Long a	Long e	Long i	Long o	Long u
100	today	fifteen	ninety	remote	perfume
200	mistake	reader	polite	lonely	pollute
300	rainbow	repeat	decide	toaster	shampoo
400	escape	compete	surprise	hopeful	toothache

Answers for clue cards:

Long *a*
100: The past is yesterday, the present is _____.
200: It is wrong; it is a _____.
300: A big arch of colors in the sky.
400: When the house caught on fire, the people ran to _____.

Long *e*
100: The number after 14.
200: Look at your book list. You are a good _____!
300: To do it again.
400: To try to win against others.

Long *i*
100: 60, 70, 80, _____.
200: To have good manners is to be _____.
300: To make a decision.
400: At the party, they jumped out and yelled, "_____!"

Long *o*
100: Use this to change the channel on the TV.
200: By yourself and feeling sad.
300: Use this to brown your bread.
400: Feeling like it will all work out.

Long *u*
100: To smell good, women use _____.
200: To dirty the water or land.
300: Use this to clean your hair.
400: A pain in your mouth.

PROCEDURES

1. One player is the game host. The others roll the dice to determine who goes first.
2. The game begins when the first player picks a category and an amount for the host to read, for example, "I'll take Long *o* for 100." The host reads the clue and the player must respond by phrasing a question and spelling the word, as in the following example:

   Host: "The past is yesterday, the present is _____."
   Player: "What is today? *t-o-d-a-y*."

3. The player receives the card if the answer is correct and then chooses another clue. (A player can only have two consecutive turns.) If the player misses, the player to the left may answer.
4. The game continues until all the clue cards are read and won or left unanswered. Players add their points, and the one with the highest number of points wins.

5. Depending on the English proficiency levels of your students, adjust the difficulty level of words and clues.

7.13 Less Familiar and Ambiguous Vowels in Accented Syllables

DEMONSTRATE. Prepare the set of words for Sort 269 on the website. This sort includes a collection of words whose vowel sounds are neither long nor short in the stressed syllable of a two-syllable word. Many of these words have diphthongs, in which the vowel sound "slides" from one sound into another, such as the "ow" sound in *house*. We have combined six types of ambiguous vowels into this sort. It is recommended that if your students have difficulty with these patterns you should pull the individual contrasts out for them to study in more depth.

Begin by reading the words together and discussing their meanings as needed. Show students the bold headers, and put these at the top of your sorting columns. Help students to notice the letter patterns in each word, and say the word out loud as you sort it into the correct column. After several examples, give students responsibility for finding the right column for each new word. Your finished sort will look something like Figure 7.15, Sort 269 on the website.

SORT, CHECK, AND REFLECT. After modeling this sort, have students repeat it under your supervision. Request them to check their sorts by looking for the pattern in each column. Ask students to notice that the focus pattern is part of the accented syllable, such as in *enjoy*. Encourage them to say the words in a chant-like manner to highlight the accented syllable or to tap their leg or make a hand movement on the strong syllable as they read their finished sorts.

EXTEND. If you find that your students need more practice on these ambiguous vowel sorts, have them go on a word hunt for additional words to add to the sort. You can focus on specific patterns that are difficult for your students. With these other words, you can also encourage students to do two sorts: (1) to sort by vowel pattern and (2) to sort based on whether the word is accented on the first or second syllable.

7.14 Final Unaccented Syllables *-er, -or, -ar*

DEMONSTRATE. Prepare the word cards for Sort 270 on the website. You might begin this sort with a short spelling test in which you ask students to spell three words: *enter, doctor,* and *polar*. Discuss the problem spellers face when they can hear the sound in the final unaccented

PDToolkit
for Words Their Way™
with English Learners

Go to PDToolkit, choose your book, click the Sorts & Games tab, and search for "Sort 269: Less Familiar and Ambiguous Vowels in Accented Syllables."

PDToolkit
for Words Their Way™
with English Learners

Go to PDToolkit, choose your book, click the Sorts & Games tab, and search for "Sort 270: Final Unaccented Syllables *-er, -or, -ar.*"

ACTIVITIES   SYLLABLES AND AFFIXES STAGE

FIGURE 7.15 Less Familiar and Ambiguous Vowels in Accented Syllables

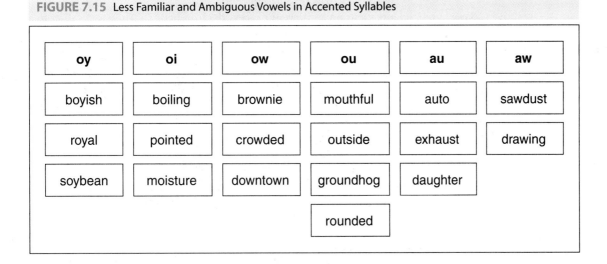

oy	**oi**	**ow**	**ou**	**au**	**aw**
boyish	boiling	brownie	mouthful	auto	sawdust
royal	pointed	crowded	outside	exhaust	drawing
soybean	moisture	downtown	groundhog	daughter	
			rounded		

FIGURE 7.16 Final Unaccented Syllables -er, -or, -ar

-er	-or	-ar
power	error	lunar
either	flavor	cheddar
under	tutor	pillar
slipper	humor	polar

syllable but are not sure how to spell it. Show students the words for this sort and read them aloud together. Talk about how the final sound is exactly the same but may be spelled in several ways. Ask them to hypothesize about which one is most common. What words do they know that end with this sound? Proceed with a teacher-directed sort that will end up looking something like Sort 270 on the website. Also see Figure 7.16. Again review the idea of accent or stress by reading the columns of words and noticing that the final syllables in these words are unaccented. Show students how they can use the dictionary to check the way pronunciation of the unaccented syllable is represented.

SORT, CHECK, AND REFLECT. After modeling this sort, have students repeat it under your supervision. Let them practice reading and pronouncing the words. Discuss the fact that despite different spellings, the words all sound the same at the end.

EXTEND. After completing this sort, ask students to find other words that end in unaccented -er, -or, and -ar. Which pattern is the most common? You can also challenge students to sort the words they find by parts of speech. They will find many adjectives and nouns that will help get them ready for the next sort.

7.15 Language in Use: Agents and Comparatives Word Building Activity

This word building activity highlights how words change to agents (i.e., people or objects that do things) or comparatives (e.g., *fast–faster*) when -er, -or, and -ar are added. In the second phase of the activity, the transformed words can be sorted in several ways.

PROCEDURES

PDToolkit
for Words Their Way™
with English Learners

Go to PDToolkit, choose your book, click the Sorts & Games tab, and search for "Sort 271: Agents and Comparatives."

1. Prepare the word cards for Sort 271 on the website. Begin this activity by writing the word *teach* on the board. Ask students to talk about what it means to teach. Now add -er to make *teacher*. How has the meaning of the word changed? Do the same with some additional words such as *farmer, hunter,* and *dreamer*. What kinds of words are created when the -er ending is added? Help students understand that these words represent people who do things. Point out that the words can be created by adding -er, -or, and -ar to some words in English. Ask students if they can think of any words that describe a person who does something. Write these words on a group chart.

   Now have students focus on a different process that can happen when we add -er to a word. Demonstrate by adding -er to *old* to make it *older*. What happened? Try again with *harder, softer,* and *slower*. Discuss with students that these adjectives, or describing words, have now become words that can be compared, or comparative adjectives.

2. Pass out a set of the word cards to each student (the bolded headers should not be included at this point). Ask students to pair up the words that have been transformed with an -er, -or, or –ar, such as *fast–faster*. When all the words have been paired, ask students to reread them and think about their meanings. Discuss the meanings of any words that are unknown.

   Guide students to look at the spellings of the words. What has been added to change the words into an agent or comparative? What changes needed to occur in the base words in some cases? Remind students about the rules they learned when they studied about other endings: Sometimes it is necessary to double consonants or drop an *e*, and at other times the ending can be added with no change. With the base words close at hand, ask students to notice the changes that occur when -er, -or, and -ar are added.

3. Have students put away the base words from their pairings. Now it is time to sort! In the first round, ask students to sort the words by whether they represent people who do things or words that compare. Provide the column headers for these categories. Once sorted, ask students to sort again by whether an *-er, -or,* or *-ar* has been added. The completed sort should look something like this:

People Who Do Things			Words to Compare
teacher	educator	beggar	faster
walker	actor		larger
rider	sailor		younger
jogger			smaller
drummer			hotter
shopper			older
juggler			shorter
diner			
leader			

4. Finally, sort the words by how the ending is added. Does the change require doubling a letter, dropping an *e*, or simply adding the ending (no change)? The completed sort should look something like this:

Double	e-Drop	No Change
beggar	educator	teacher
hotter	larger	walker
shopper	rider	sailor
jogger	juggler	leader
drummer	diner	faster
		younger
		smaller
		older
		shorter
		actor

The words in this sort can be transcribed into students' word study notebooks and added to as new samples are discovered.

7.16 Homophones

DEMONSTRATE, SORT, AND REFLECT. The 24 words in Sort 272 on the website will likely be a vocabulary challenge to your students and you may want to split them into two groups to work on over time. Homophones are tricky—the words sound alike, but the meaning tells how they should be spelled. Use a simple example of a homophone such as *eye/I* to introduce the topic. Homophones sound alike but mean different things. Take the time to discuss the word meanings in this sort so you are sure that students understand them. Quick drawings, visuals, or using the words in a clarifying sentence may be helpful. For example, you might say, "I like to put a bouquet of flowers on my table to make it colorful. Another kind of flour is what I use when I make a cake." (Draw a vase of flowers and a sack of flour.) If there are too many unknown words, either put some aside or take another day to learn the words before doing this matching sort.

PDToolkit
for Words Their Way™
with English Learners

Go to PDToolkit, choose your book, click the Sorts & Games tab, and search for "Sort 272: Homophones."

No column headers are needed because the sorting activity consists of matching word pairs or triplets. Present a pair of words like *principle* and *principal*. Ask students what they notice about them. (They sound alike but are spelled differently.) If students do not know the term, say "homophone." Continue to pair up words and to talk about what the words mean. Students will typically know one homophone better than the other, but by pairing them up to compare spelling and by discussing their meanings the new words will become more familiar.

Ask students for ideas about how certain spellings can be remembered: *There* has the little word *here* as in "here and there." One of the *s*'s deserted in the *desert* and so on.

EXTEND. Draw small pictures on word cards or in word study notebooks to stimulate memory for the meaning of a word (e.g., draw a strawberry for *berry* and a tombstone for *bury*). Also have students use these words in sentences. Pairs of students might be assigned two to three words and asked to compose sentences. These can be shared with each other orally or made into a group book to be illustrated.

The sorting cards can also be used in a Memory or Concentration game—just remember to remove one of each of the triplets before doing it as a pairing activity.

for Words Their Way™ with English Learners

Go to PDToolkit, choose your book, click the Sorts & Games tab, and search for "Sort 273: Homographs."

7.17 Homographs

DEMONSTRATE, SORT, CHECK, AND REFLECT. In the homographs for Sort 273 on the website, the accented syllable is in bold type. Stressed syllables can also be marked with accent marks or underlined. As with Activity 7.16, you are likely to challenge your students' vocabularies with these words, so take the time needed to clarify and discuss their meanings well. If there are too many new words, set some aside for another day.

Begin by writing a sentence such as *He will permit you to have a permit.* Ask students what they notice about the words *per mit'* and *per'mit.* They should note that the words are spelled the same but sound slightly different. Review with students words that are spelled the same but pronounced differently such as *tear, live,* and *read* and introduce the term *homograph,* meaning "same writing" or "same spelling." (You might point out how this term is related to *homophone,* which means "same sound.") Remind students about how some words are nouns and others verbs. As a review, have students brainstorm a few examples of each in the group. Go back to the *permit* sentence and ask students to identify the part of speech for each word and place them under the headers Noun (**per**mit) and Verb (per**mit**). Proceed in a similar manner with each set of words. Use them in sentences or invite students to do so and then sort them under the headings. Make sure that the words are being pronounced aloud as they are sorted and not just examined visually. The completed sort should look something like Sort 273 on the website. Also see Figure 7.17. When all of the words have been sorted, read down each column, placing extra emphasis on the accented syllable. Ask students what they notice. (The nouns are accented on the first syllable and the verbs on the second syllable.)

FIGURE 7.17 Homographs

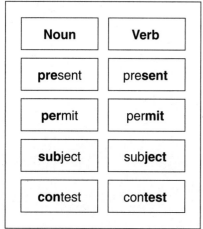

Noun	Verb
present	pre**sent**
permit	per**mit**
subject	sub**ject**
contest	con**test**

EXTEND. Students should return to these words several times to practice pronouncing and sorting them and to discuss their meanings. When working with partners, students should be careful to pronounce the words clearly and perhaps use them in sentences before asking their buddies to sort them by accented syllable. Ask students to work together to create sentences for these words and to record some of these sentences in their word study notebooks. They might also draw small pictures as described for homophones in Activity 7.16.

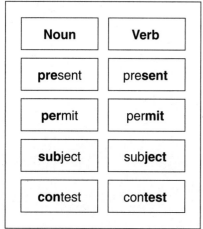

for Words Their Way™ with English Learners

Go to PDToolkit, choose your book, click the Sorts & Games tab, and search for "Sort 274: Spanish and English Hard and Soft *g* and *c*."

7.18 Spanish and English Hard and Soft *g* and *c*

DEMONSTRATE. This double set of sorts, found as Sort 274 on the website, has many possibilities, so consider using it over several days. If you have students who speak Spanish, it will provide the opportunity for them to build on vocabulary and spelling patterns in their home language. If your English-learning students don't speak Spanish, consider using the words as examples of cognates between languages and ask students to brainstorm examples of cognates between their personal home languages and English.

To begin, take the set of words in English and the set in Spanish and spread them out on a table. If you like, you can have the two sets color coded so it is clear which words go with each language. Ask students whether they see any similarities between any of the words. Do they see any words that are spelled almost the same? Have them look for pairs such as *celebrar–celebrate*. Encourage students to share the meanings of the words and their pronunciations if they can. Continue matching the words with their cognates and sharing and discussing the words.

Once the words have been paired up, ask students whether they notice anything about the beginning sounds of *c* and *g*. Read some of the words together and notice that the *c* sometimes represents a soft sound as in *center* and sometimes a hard sound as in *curve*. Also, *g* sometimes stands for the soft sound as in *giant* and the hard sound as in *goal*. Create four header labels for hard and soft *g* and *c*. Using the header labels, sort one or two of the *c* words by whether each word represents the hard or soft sound. Tell students they will now be sorting the words in this way on their own.

SORT, CHECK, AND REFLECT. Depending on the circumstances of your classroom, you can have the students sort either the English words only, the Spanish words only, or all of the words from both sorts. You be the judge of how to best support the success of your English learners on this task. The completed sort if done in English will look something like the following:

Soft c	Soft g	Hard c	Hard g
circus	giant	canoe	goal
celebrate	geography	calendar	guide
cemetery	general	calm	gorilla
center	generous	curve	garage
ceremony		control	gasoline
cycle			

The completed sort if done in Spanish will look something like the following:

Soft c	Soft g	Hard c	Hard g
circo	gigante	canoa	gol
celebrar	geografía	calendario	guía
cementerio	general	calma	gorila
centro	generoso	curva	garaje
ceremonia		control	gasolina
ciclo			

Next (whether you are doing the sort in English, Spanish, or both), combine all of the soft *c* and soft *g* words. Ask students if they notice anything about the vowels in these words. Repeat this with the hard *c* and hard *g* words. Suggest that they try sorting the words by the second letter in each word. The final sort will reveal that the hard and soft sounds in both English and Spanish are related to the vowel that follows. Underline or highlight one example of each kind of vowel that follows the *c* or *g* to use as a key word for each column. The sort in English will look something like the following:

Soft g and Soft c			Hard g and Hard c		
center	circus	cycle	garage	gorilla	curve
celebrate	giant		gasoline	control	guide
cemetery			calendar	goal	
ceremony			calm		
generous			canoe		
general					
geography					

The sort in Spanish will look something like the following:

Soft g and Soft c			Hard g and Hard c		
centro	circo		garaje	gol	curva
celebrar	gigante		gasolina	control	guía
cementerio	ciclo		calendario	gorila	
generoso			calma		
ceremonia			canoa		
geografía					
general					

Students may notice that Spanish does not use the *y* in the same way to create the soft sound in *c* and *g* words.

Encourage reflections by asking the students how the words in each column are alike and how they are different from the other words. Help students formulate a generalization that goes something like this: The letters *c* and *g* are usually soft when followed by *e*, *i*, and *y* and hard when followed by *a*, *o*, or *u*.

EXTEND. Students should repeat these sorts several times and record them in their word study notebooks. They may also want to create a section in their notebook for Spanish word sorts or cognates. Many additional *c* and *g* words can be found to add to their lists that may or may not be cognates. Let them explore which ones are and which ones aren't.

Word Study Activities at the Late Syllables and Affixes Stage

7.19 Prefixes (*re-, un-*)

DEMONSTRATE. Prepare the set of prefixes for Sort 275 on the website. See the example of how to "walk through words" with students on pages 204–205 of this chapter. For teacher-directed modeling, hand out the sheet of words to the students or display a list of words on an overhead or interactive whiteboard. Ask them what they notice about the words and get ideas about how the words can be sorted. Students might note that the words all contain smaller words and remind them of the term *base words* that was used in the study of inflected endings. Put up the column headers and key words and then sort the rest of the words. During this first sort the oddballs *under* and *reading* might be unconsciously included under *re-* and *un-*. The words are there to help students see that these letters do not always spell a meaningful prefix added to a meaningful base word. Praise students if they notice this on the first sort.

After the sort discuss the word meanings with students. What do they notice about all of the words under the *re-* column? Start with *reuse*. Ask students for the base word. Explain that a prefix has been added to the base word and that it changes the meaning of the word. Ask students what *reuse* means. (To use something over again, as in *We had to reuse the party hats at every birthday.*) Repeat this with the other words under *re-*, talking about the meaning of each word. *Repay* means to pay again. *Recount* means to count again, and so on. The word *reading* does not mean to do something again and should be transferred to the oddballs. Then explain that a prefix has a meaning of its own and ask them what *re-* means in all the words. (It means to do something again.) Repeat this with the words in the *un-* column to determine that the prefix means "not" in words such as *unbroken* or *unkind* but something more like "the opposite of" in words like *untie* and *uncover*. *Under* will be moved to the oddballs because it does not have a prefix or base word and does not mean the opposite of anything. Students might be asked to write the meaning of the prefix on the headers (for example, *re-* = again). The completed sort should look something like Sort 275 on the website.

"Repay" means to pay again.

SORT, CHECK, AND REFLECT. Students should repeat this sort several times and work with the words using some of the weekly routines, such as writing them in their word study notebooks, word hunts, or using words in sentences. When students write these words in their word study notebooks, they might be asked to underline and write the meaning of each prefix.

EXTEND. Word hunts will turn up lots of words that begin with *re-* and *un-*, including more oddballs that look like they might have a prefix until the meaning and base word are considered. Word hunts will also reveal other subtle variations in meaning for the prefix *re-* as well as words with no clear base words. While studying these prefixes, you can also encourage students to see how these morphemic changes take place in their home languages. For example, in Spanish *re-* has a similar meaning and is used in words like *repasar* (review) or *representar* (represent). In Spanish, *un-* often takes the form of *des-* such as in *desafortunado* (unlucky) or *deshacer* (undo).

7.20 Prefixes (*dis-, mis-*)

DEMONSTRATE. As in Activity 7.19, help students see spelling–meaning connections in the words of this sort, which you will find as Sort 276 on the website. You might begin by asking students how to spell the word *misspell* (a word that is often misspelled). Have them speculate about why there are two *s*'s in the word. If students come up with an explanation, talk it through with them. If they look confused, divide the word between *mis-* and *-spell*, and ask them if one of those pieces looks like a whole word. Then, encourage them to look at the rest of the words in the sort. Do they see other whole words preceded by *mis-* or *dis-*? Remind them what a prefix means, and tell them that today you will be working with two new prefixes.

Sort the words into two columns under the headers. The completed sort should look something like Sort 276 on the website. When the words have been sorted, discuss the meaning of each word in the *dis-* column. Help students discover that *dis-* means "the opposite of." Next, examine the *mis-* words. Help them determine that *mis-* means to do something "wrongly."

Have students examine the words *dishes*, *missed*, and *mishmash*. They should be able to see that in those three words there is no base word whose meaning is changed by the prefix. Create an oddball category for them. After discussing the prefix meanings and how the prefixes change the meanings of the base words, revisit the word *misspell*. Ask students again about the spelling of the word. Can they explain to you that one *s* is part of the prefix and the other is part of the base word, so both must be there?

EXTEND. As in the previous sort, students can investigate cognates for prefixes in other languages such as Spanish. Have them use a bilingual dictionary to see if they come up with a common way to express the concept of *mis-* or *dis-*. Activities 7.19 and 7.20 can also be put together as a larger collection of words for students to use in speed sorts alone or with a partner. Encourage word analysis skills by having students look up words in the dictionary that begin with *mis-*, *dis-*, *re-*, and *un-* to see if they can find out how the prefix changes a given word's meaning.

7.21 Comparatives *-er* and *-est*

**for Words Their Way™
with English Learners**

Go to PDToolkit, choose your book, click the Sorts & Games tab, and search for "Sort 277: Comparatives *-er* and *-est*."

DEMONSTRATE, SORT, AND CHECK. Prepare the comparative word cards for Sort 277 on the website. Introduce this sort by discussing the term *suffix*, a part that is added to the end of a word. Practice adding *-er* and *-est* to some words orally first, such as asking what happens when you add *-er* to *brave*. To *close*? What do they mean? How is the suffix *-est* different from *-er*? How are the words *braver* and *bravest* different in meaning? *Closer* and *closest*? Act out the terms to dramatize meaning differences. Other words to help you discuss meaning might also include *calmer/calmest*, *hotter/hottest*, and *weaker/weakest*. To provide visual support, write some base words such as *calm*, *hot*, and *weak* on the board and show how the endings are added to create the related word. Now sort the cards in this word sort by *-er* and *-est* and talk about the meanings of the words and what the suffix does to the base word. (When comparing two things *-er* is used. When comparing more than two use *-est*.) Ask students to underline the base words to highlight the fact that in words like *happier* or *happiest* the *y* has been changed. Sort any words that fall into that category under *-ier* and *-iest*. Ask the students to form a generalization that covers these words and remind them of previous sorts. (When a word ends in *y* change the *y* to *i* before adding *-er* or *-est*.) The completed sort should look something like Sort 277 on the website.

EXTEND. To review the rules involved in adding suffixes, sort the words as shown here:

Double	e-Drop	Change y to i	No Change
hotter	finer	happier	faster
bigger	nicer	luckier	cleaner
		angrier	longer
		earlier	
		fancier	
		funnier	

To help students transfer their understanding of these rules to new words, ask them to add *-er* and *-est* to these words: *few*, *wet*, *close*, *pretty*.

7.22 Suffixes *-y*, *-ly*, and *-ily*

**for Words Their Way™
with English Learners**

Go to PDToolkit, choose your book, click the Sorts & Games tab, and search for "Sort 278: Suffixes *-y*, *-ly*, and *-ily*."

DEMONSTRATE, SORT, CHECK, AND REFLECT. Prepare the suffix word cards for Sort 278 on the website. This sort builds on some of the ideas in Activity 7.19. Remind students that suffixes are added to the ends of words and that they change the meaning. "Today you will be looking at the suffixes *-y*, *-ly*, and *-ily*." Present some base words orally first, such as *rain* and *cloud*. What happens when *-y* is added to these words? Help them come to the understanding that *-y* turns a noun like *sun* into an adjective that means "like the sun" or "having sun." Now discuss how adding *-ly* or *-ily* to words such as *slow* or *happy* changes their meanings. These suffixes turn adjectives (that describe words) into adverbs (that describe the manner in which something is done).

Before beginning the sort go through the word cards and discuss the meanings of the words and how the suffixes affect the meaning. Once students have a good sense of what the words mean and the role of the endings, demonstrate the sort to the group. Encourage students to participate as you sort the words into columns for *-y*, *-ly*, and *-ily*. The completed sort should look something like Sort 278 on the website.

Have students repeat the sort using the same column headers and key words. To reinforce the idea of base words you might suggest underlining them. Remind students of how *happy* was changed in previous sorts to make the words *happier* and *happiest*. The same procedure is followed here—words that end in *y* change to *i* before an ending is added. Have students write in the base word for the *-ily* words because they cannot simply underline it. Encourage the students to reflect by asking them how the words in each column are alike and what they have learned about adding *-y* and *-ly* to base words.

EXTEND AND REVIEW. To review parts of speech create frame sentences such as *The weather today is _____* and *He worked _____*. Use such sentences to test words for their part of speech. Ask students to find words that describe the noun *weather* and the verb *work*.

Review with students how to add *-ing* and *-ed* to words like *beg*. Ask them to find two words in the sort that also had to double letters before adding a suffix (*runny, funny*). Point out that the word *bad* does not have to double before adding *-ly*. Review how to form the plural of words like *party* and *baby* (change the *y* to *i* and add *es*) and how to make the past tense of words like *carry* and *fly* (change the *y* to *i* and add *ed*). Ask them to find words in the sort that also had to change the *y* to *i* (such as *easily*). Help them articulate a new rule about adding *-ly* to words that end in *y*.

Give students transfer words to practice applying the rules. Ask them to add *-y* or *-ly* to these base words: *fog* (*foggy*), *snow* (*snowy*), *wind* (*windy*), *chop* (*choppy*), *rock* (*rocky*), *point* (*pointy*), *soap* (*soapy*), *great* (*greatly*), *fair* (*fairly*), *deep* (*deeply*), *real* (*really*), *noisy* (*noisily*), *hungry* (*hungrily*).

7.23 Taking Words Apart

This activity builds on numerous experiences with the inflectional endings *-s*, *-es*, *-ed*, and *-ing* and the simple prefixes and suffixes such as *re-*, *un-*, *dis-*, *mis-*, *-er*, *-est*, *-ier*, *-iest*, *-y*, *-ly*, and *-ily* presented in this chapter. "Take Apart" helps your students begin to systematically look into words and to separate base words from their affixes as they encounter new words in their reading and word study.

DEMONSTRATE. Prepare a set of word cards based on Sort 279 on the website. Introduce the process of "Take Apart" by asking students, "What parts do you see in this word? Do you see prefixes or suffixes that we can remove? Let's take it apart." Begin with a simple word such as *combed*. Say the word in a meaningful sentence such as *Yesterday, I combed my hair.* Write *combed* in the first column on the board. Say aloud, "I see an ending that could be pulled off of the word: *-ed*." Write *comb* in a second column and provide an example sentence such as *I comb my hair when it gets messy.*

Have students examine words from the sort such as *stepped, missed, filling*, and *dishes*. Ask whether they see a part of the word that could be removed. Write the complex word on the board in the first column and the simpler word next to it after the affix has been removed. As needed, discuss the fact that if a consonant has been doubled when an affix was added, the extra consonant may need to be pulled off as well (*stepped > step*) or an *e* or *y* that has been changed may also need to be adjusted (*hoping > hope; pennies > penny*). Have students write the complex and simple word in their word study notebooks along with you.

Next, move on to harder words with simple prefixes and suffixes as well as inflected endings (*uncovered*). Provide support as needed for students to identify the affixes that may be pulled off the complex word.

SORT, CHECK, AND REFLECT. Now have students repeat the procedure under your supervision. Provide a copy of Sort 279 from the website for each student or pair of students. Conduct an open sort first. Have students group the words according to what they see as they take the words apart. Next, have students write the complex word in a column of their word

PDToolkit
for Words Their Way™
with English Learners

Go to PDToolkit, choose your book, click the Sorts & Games tab, and search for "Sort 279: Taking Words Apart."

study notebook and then the word stripped of affixes in the second column. Have students go on a word hunt for additional words they can take apart, and add two novel words to their lists. Bring the group together and share reflections about the process of taking words apart.

EXTEND. Take apart activities may also be conducted in reverse, starting with a simple word such as *step, comb, miss, call,* or *learn.* For a helpful list of verbs, check out the English Club at www.englishclub.com/vocabulary/index.htm. Have students add inflected endings and simple prefixes or suffixes to words, decide if they make sense, and share them with friends. Students can write these words in their word study notebooks and create possible definitions for them.

7.24 Cover Your Bases Game

In this game students study easy base words and add affixes and related words to them.

**for Words Their Way™
with English Learners**

Go to PDToolkit, choose your book, click the Sorts & Games tab, and search for "Cover Your Bases Game."

MATERIALS. You will need a copy of the baseball game card from the website for each student and a sand clock or timer for the group. Print the base words and cut them apart into small word cards:

> **Base word cards:** *like, see, make, call, look, think, work, cake, help, tell, give, ask, read, form, move, cut, drip, lock, stop, plan, tap, let, owe, rule, rain, feel, load, wait, walk, play, paint, hate, fan, taste, spot, slip, forget*

Provide a stack of small, blank word cards to write related words.

PROCEDURES

1. Model ways to add affixes to base words. Here are four examples you can write on the overhead or whiteboard:

fan	rule	feel	call
fanned	rules	feels	calling
fanning	ruler	feelings	called
fans	ruled	unfeeling	calls
	ruling		recall
	rulings		recalling
	unruly		

2. Choose a method to determine order of play. For example, players draw from the collection of base words and the student with the word earliest alphabetically goes first.
3. The first player's base word is placed in front of the group.
4. Players have 30 seconds or one or two turns of the sand clock to write all the words they can think of that contain this base.
5. Go around the group to share words. Fellow players check to see that the invented words represent real words and are spelled correctly.
6. Players lay their words on the bases of their playing boards. If they have come up with four or more related words, they score a "home run" and can give themselves a point.
7. Players clear the word cards off the playing boards to prepare for a new round. Move on to the base word that was drawn by the next player, and repeat steps 3 through 6.
8. Continue until each player's base word card has been played.
9. The player with the most home run points at the end wins.

VARIATIONS AND EXTENSIONS

1. Words and their relations are recorded by students in their word study notebooks.
2. Sort by prefixes and suffixes, past/present tense, singular/plural.
3. In one or two turns of the same clock, players search dictionaries and word study books and write down new base words. A new round of play is made with these new words.
4. Write prefixes and suffixes on word cards and have students combine them with base words.
5. Include in the game directions a list of prefixes and suffixes for players to refer to as they play.
6. Students use the words in sentences.
7. Make a game board with the bases. Students land on a base and have to use the word in a sentence. Explore the multiple meanings of words.

8

Word Study with English Learners in the Derivational Relations Stage

In her sixth grade class, Danielle Hudson meets with her native-speaking and English-learning students whose spelling knowledge suggests that they are skilled, proficient readers. She knows that English learners in particular at this phase may need more in-depth exploration of derivational or morphological relationships among words. This is often the case with native speakers at this level as well. She includes a systematic investigation of a number of English/Spanish cognates over the course of the school year—words from English and Spanish that share the same or similar spellings and the same or similar meanings. Her ongoing objectives are to (1) maintain her native-Spanish-speaking students' facility with understanding academic Spanish, (2) help her native-English-speaking students learn some Spanish, and (3) facilitate the types of conversation about language that lead to in-depth understanding of important concepts in core academic and content area academic vocabulary. In her math instruction, for example, when addressing geometric figures she includes both English and Spanish terms:

polygon	polígono
pentagon	pentágono
hexagon	hexágono
quadrilateral	cuadrilátero

She has already addressed a number of Greek and Latin word roots in her reading/language arts instruction and the English/Spanish cognates that include them, so by directing her students' attention to these meaningful parts in the math vocabulary cognates, she is reinforcing both conceptual *and* morphological understanding.

When focusing on fractions, Ms. Hudson pairs the following English and Spanish cognates:

common denominator	denominador común
proper fraction	fracción propia
improper fraction	fracción impropia
equivalent fractions	fracciones equivalentes

All students notice the different order of the words in each pair, and Ms. Hudson uses the academic vocabulary of grammar to discuss the difference. In English, adjectives come before the nouns they modify; in Spanish, they come after. With her derivational-level students, Ms. Hudson explores the pair *equivalent fractions / fracciones equivalentes:* The noun is plural. Do adjectives in both English and Spanish represent the plural? Or just one of the languages? As students discuss this, Ms. Hudson writes two other cognate pairs that represent concepts addressed earlier in the year: *congruent figures/figuras congruentes* and *compatible numbers/números compatibles.* These pairs confirm what the students were discussing: The spelling of Spanish adjectives shows plurality, whereas the spelling of English adjectives doesn't. With her derivational students, Ms. Hudson explores more systematically the relationships between words in English and Spanish that are not at first glance cognates—*resultado* and *outcome*, for example, and *addition* and *suma*. Students usually expect *sum* and *suma* to mean exactly the same thing, and when they don't that can be frustrating. Teachers can show them, however, that these cognates are still in the same conceptual ballpark: Ms. Hudson explains to her students how both *addition* and *suma* represent the same process or operation in math. The English cognate of *suma*—*sum*—has a more specific meaning, referring to the result of that operation, the *answer* to the problem. This meaning, though, is "close enough" for Ms. Hudson's native-Spanish-speaking students to learn this more specific meaning of *sum*. And the Spanish cognate of *sum*—*suma*—is close enough for Ms. Hudson's native-English-speaking students to learn the more general meaning of *suma*.

This chapter builds on the strategies we presented in Chapter 7 and extends the content of upper-level instruction to in-depth explorations of the derivational morphological relationships among words.

Literacy Instruction for English Learners in the Derivational Relations Stage

For advanced learners, we will continue to be mindful of the following considerations in designing appropriate instruction for English learners:

1. Continue to connect spelling, vocabulary, and grammar study.

2. Explore idiomatic language and expressions in more depth. Encourage students to share idiomatic expressions from their home language, if they are comfortable doing so, and discuss how the connotations of these expressions correspond to those of English expressions.

3. As with students at earlier proficiency levels, don't overemphasize pronunciation. Even native English speakers at this level often have difficulty with the higher-order phonological patterns that polysyllabic and derivationally complex words reflect (Nippold, 2007; Templeton, 2004). It also is not uncommon for highly educated adults who have learned English as a second language and speak and write it well to mispronounce some forms of derivationally related words—for example, *internaytional* rather than *internashional*; *inevitable* rather than *inevitable*.

Characteristics of Orthographic Development for English Learners in the Derivational Relations Stage

Even native English speakers who are advanced in their word knowledge are often not explicitly aware of the deep, meaning-based aspects of English spelling. At this advanced level, making connections and comparisons between other writing systems and English can be very helpful to both English-learning and native-English-speaking students as well.

Chapter 7 presented the basics of morphological analysis. Derivational-level students may continue in their development by investigating the types of patterns presented in Table 8.1. Recall that understanding these processes will support students' spelling *and* vocabulary development. Students probe further the relationship between spelling and meaning as they learn additional prefixes and suffixes and explore in more depth the Greco-Latin component of the language. Although there are not as many students at the advanced phase in the upper elementary grades, teachers like Ms. Hudson will find it helpful to know the content of word study at this level because there is some overlap with word study for syllables and affixes spellers, and it spotlights the pathway on which students are heading.

Spelling–meaning exploration also helps develop students' understanding of English syntax and grammar. As students explore spelling–meaning relationships, we point out how adding certain suffixes—such as *-ity* to *similar*—changes the part of speech from the base word to the derived word. In addition to *-ity*, there are a number of other **derivational suffixes** that have this effect: *-ly, -y, -ment, -al, -ion/-tion/-ation*. Derivational suffixes are the "workhorses" of morphology, allowing us to *derive* several additional words from a single **base word** or **word root.** When we help students to understand the meanings of these derivational suffixes and how they affect the bases to which they are attached, we simultaneously build students' awareness of syntax and relationships among words. For languages that do not have a Greek and Latin component and therefore do not share many cognates with English—Asian languages, for example—it is especially important to focus on the processes of suffixation in English: first, as was addressed in Chapter 7, inflectional suffixes such as *-ed* in *stopped* and next, derivational suffixes such as *-ment* in *government*. These suffixes occur so often that they become a visual "hook" for English learners. By exploring how suffixes affect the base words to which they are attached and how they usually change the part of speech of the word, students not only learn the structure of English, but also develop a foundation for learning the Greek and Latin component of English. As Corson (1997) points out, learning the specialist vocabulary that is constructed from Greek and Latin roots then becomes easier. This occurs through two instructional emphases: First, point out words that are visually similar in structure—and therefore similar in meaning. Second, help students learn to analyze words in order to locate their meaningful parts—prefixes, suffixes, and bases and word roots.

The Greco-Latin component of English includes word roots, those parts of words to which affixes may be added but which cannot stand alone as words. For example, *tract* in *attraction* and *spect* in *inspection* are the roots in these words and are the foundation for families of related words that share these roots: *tract* (meaning "to draw or pull") is at the heart of the words *retract, traction,* and *subtract; spect* (meaning "to look") yields a family of words that includes *inspect, retrospect,* and *spectacle.* Many English learners, particularly those whose first language is Spanish, will notice the visual/spelling similarity between roots in English and in their home language, such as *foto/photo* and *dictador/dictator.* They will, in other words, have discovered **cognates,** those words from different languages that share the same or similar spellings and the same or similar meanings. In this respect, students whose home language includes Latin and Greek roots among the most frequently occurring words in their language may have an "edge" over native-English-speaking students (Hiebert & Lubliner, 2008): The spellings of these roots in English and many other languages are similar, so a native-Spanish-speaking student reading an English science text, for example, may recognize the root in *arboretum (arbor)* because of its similarity to *árbol,* the frequently occurring word for "tree" in Spanish.

As students advance in word study at this level, they are able to consider a number of features of words simultaneously and in greater depth than earlier in development: meaning, spelling, sound, and the history of words and processes that apply to them. The purpose of exploring a bit of history is to provide students with explanations for how meaning, spelling, and sound interact. The phenomenon of absorbed prefixes, for example, illustrates this interaction. As presented in Table 8.1, the spelling of the prefix *in-* may change to *il-, im-,* and *ir-.* This spelling change is not random, but rather reflects a process of language change that has occurred over time. Because of the significant role that morphology plays in determining the meanings of words in English, much of the critically important core academic vocabulary

▶ **Derivational Suffixes**

Suffixes added to base words or roots that affect meaning (*break* > *breakable*) or the part of speech (*similar* > *similarity*).

▶ **Base Word**

A word to which prefixes or suffixes are added. For example, *found* is the base word of *unfounded.*

▶ **Word Root**

A morpheme, not necessarily standing as a word on its own, that is often combined with other roots or affixes to form words. For example, *spect* is the root in *inspect.*

▶ **Cognates**

Similar words shared by different languages that also share the same or similar spellings and the same or similar meanings. For example, English *alarm* and Spanish *alarma* are cognates.

TABLE 8.1

Sequence of Word Study in the Derivational Relations Stage

Consonant and Vowel Alternations

1. Consonant Alternations

silent/sounded	sign/signal, condemn/condemnation, soften/soft	/k/ to /s/	critic/criticize, political/politicize
/t/ to /sh/	connect/connection, select/ selection	/s/ to /sh/	prejudice/prejudicial, office/official
/k/ to /sh/	music/musician, magic/magician		

2. Vowel Alternations

Long to short	crime/criminal, ignite/ignition, humane/humanity
Long to schwa	compete/competition, define/definition, gene/genetic,
Schwa to short	local/locality, legal/legality, metal/metallic

3. Suffix Study
Explore the addition of -sion, -tion, -ian to basewords.

Greek and Latin Word Elements

1. Start with Greek number prefixes mono- (one), di- (two), tri- (three), and move to the Greek roots tele (far, distant), therm (heat), photo (light), and astr (star).

2. Move to frequent Latin roots with the aim of gaining a working understanding of a few frequently occurring roots with relatively concrete and constant meanings: tract (draw, pull), spect (look), port (carry), dict (to say), rupt (to break), and scrib (to write).

3. Explore additional Latin and Greek prefixes, building on those already taught at the syllables and affixes stage.

Prefix	Meaning	Prefix	Meaning
inter-	between	sub-	under
intra-	within	pre-	before
super-	over; greater	anti-	against
counter-	opposing	demi-	half
ex-	out	semi-	half
fore-	before	quadr-	four
post-	after	pent-	five
pro-	in front of, forward		

4. Explore common Greek suffixes

Suffix	Meaning
-crat/-cracy	rule: democracy—rule by the demos, people
-emia	condition of the blood: leukemia—the blood has too many white (leuk) blood cells
-ician	specialist in: dietician
-ine	chemical substance: chlorine, Benzedrine
-ism/-ist	belief in; one who believes: communism/communist, capitalism/capitalist
-logy/-logist	science of; scientist: geology—science of the earth, studying the earth; geologist—one who studies the earth
-pathy/-path	disease; one who suffers from a disease: sociopath—someone with a personality disorder
-phobia	abnormal fear: claustrophobia—fear of being closed in or shut in (claus)

Predictable Spelling Changes in Consonants and Vowels

1. /t/ to /sh/	permit/permission, transmit/transmission
2. /t/ to /s/	silent/silence
3. /d/ to /zh/	explode/explosion, decide/decision
4. /sh/ to /s/	ferocious/ferocity, precocious/precocity
5. Long to short	vain/vanity, receive/reception, retain/retention
6. Long to schwa	explain/explanation, exclaim/exclamation

Advanced Suffix Study

1. -able/-ible	respectable, favorable versus visible, audible
2. -ant/-ance	fragrant/fragrance, dominant/dominance
-ent/-ence	dependent/dependence, florescent/florescence
3. Consonant doubling and accent	occurred, permitted versus traveled, benefited

Absorbed Prefixes

1. Prefix + base word	in + mobile = immobile; ad + count = account
2. Prefix + word root	ad + cept = accept, in + mune = immune

and the content-specific academic vocabulary that English learners need to acquire may be learned through focusing on these meaningful elements. Researchers refer to this emphasis on processes of word formation in English as *generative* vocabulary instruction, because understanding these processes will *generate* student learning about thousands of words they will encounter in their instructional and independent reading (Stahl & Nagy, 2006; Templeton et al., 2010).

Components of Literacy Instruction at the Derivational Relations Stage

At the upper levels of literacy learning, Read To, Read With, Write With, Word Study, and Talk With continue to be the touchstones of our essential literacy activities. In particular, Read To should not be given short shrift at this level, as too often happens. It is essential that students hear the language from different subject matter areas read to them. Informational texts, usually apart from textbooks, have a rhythm and flow to the language of the particular subject area, as well as a specialized vocabulary that is invaluable to hear and experience through the voice of a knowledgeable teacher.

Word study continues to involve lots of focused discussion on concepts and on the words that represent those concepts. For instance, before having English learners read about ancient civilizations, a word study of political words and their relationships such as *democracy, oligarchy, monarchy, patriarchy, matriarchy, hierarchy, dynasty, empire*, and *tyranny* will support their conceptual preparation and vocabulary development for the upcoming content. In addition, discussion anchors students' exploration of higher-order morphological processes such as absorbed prefixes and advanced word root aspects. As at earlier levels, students may keep vocabulary notebooks that include observations and information about words and their morphological and semantic relatives. The notebook might also contain a personal list of "golden lines"—sentences that contain words that really "grab" the students and illustrations of words and phrases used effectively and powerfully. At this level students have the potential to draw on a wide range of reference materials, both printed and online, that focus on words and their origins. Derivational-level students will explore cognates more extensively, as well as etymology or word histories. Figure 8.1 contains a list of resources that are particularly helpful for this level of study.

Word Study

The Elementary Spelling Inventory will differentiate your syllables and affixes students from your derivational relational students, but if you need further information about some students or simply want to confirm this initial assessment you should administer the Upper-Level Spelling Inventory from the website. Grouping for word study is more of a challenge at the middle grades, although varying scheduling configurations are possible. Although some English/language arts classes are more homogenous, most are not, and taking the time to differentiate instruction appropriately can have significant payoffs. To make your classroom organization manageable, you may need to work with groups that span a range of levels at one time, tailoring words and activities to students' specific needs. For instance, in two of her seventh grade English classes Kelly Rubero was able to cluster her students into two groups for word study: one syllables and affixes group and one derivational group.

ACCOMMODATIONS. What happens when a teacher needs to scaffold derivational material for students who are working at the syllables and affixes level of word study? Figure 8.2 provides examples of how you can support students who may need a "boost" to comfortably work with the advanced reading materials and difficult academic vocabulary presented at this level.

for Words Their Way™ with English Learners

Go to PDToolkit, choose your book, click the Assessment Tools tab, and select Assessment Materials to see the Upper-Level Spelling Inventory.

FIGURE 8.1 Resources for Upper-Level Word Exploration

Ayers, D. M. (1986). *English words from Latin and Greek elements* (2nd ed.; revised by Thomas Worthen). Tucson: The University of Arizona Press.

Crutchfield, R. *English vocabulary quick reference: A comprehensive dictionary arranged by word roots.* Leesburg, VA: LexaDyne Publishing.

Danner, H., & Noel, R. (1996). *Discover it! A better vocabulary the better way.* Occoquan, VA: Imprimis.

Kennedy, J. (1996). *Word stems: A dictionary.* New York: Soho Press.

Moore, B., & Moore, M. (1997). *NTC's dictionary of Latin and Greek origins: A comprehensive guide to the classical origins of English words.* Chicago: NTC Publishing Group.

www.onelook.com A comprehensive dictionary website. Most of the major, well-respected dictionaries are available; the link to the *American Heritage Dictionary* also includes an additional link to a dictionary of Indo-European Roots, which greatly simplifies etymological searches for you and your students. The onelook.com site also features excellent search capabilities that allow you to search for words that contain specific roots and affixes, spelling patterns, words as they occur in specific phrases (very helpful for English learners—see Chapter 7), and words that relate to a particular concept.

www.americancorpus.org The *Corpus of American English,* created by Michael Davies, is an invaluable online resource for locating related words in English. It requires that you register, but registration is free. It may be used to search for the occurrence of words in different contexts—for example, spoken language, magazines, fiction, and academic texts.

www.etymonline.com Very useful for exploring word histories, this site includes much of the etymological information you would find in the Oxford English Dictionary.

http://translate.reference.com/translate This site provides, for any word in English, words in a number of other languages that have the same or similar meaning. It is an excellent resource for finding cognates.

www.wordsmith.org You may subscribe for free and receive a new word in your inbox every day. Words follow a theme each week, and the categories of words discussed in this book—for example *toponyms, eponyms, sesquipedalian* words, and more—will be represented.

www.verbivore.com/rllink.htm An especially good site for wordplay and word consciousness, with innumerable links to excellent and informative language and word sites.

Longman Dictionaries (Pearson). Longman publishes the most comprehensive group of dictionaries appropriate for English learners and bilingual students. Dictionaries for different beginning levels of English proficiency on up are available.

Longman's *Dictionary of Contemporary English* is available online at www.ldoceonline.com

Spanish Print Resources

Davies, M. (2006). *A frequency dictionary of Spanish: Core vocabulary for learners.* New York: Routledge.

Nash, R. (1997). *NTC's dictionary of Spanish cognates thematically organized.* Chicago: NTC Publishing Group.

FIGURE 8.2 Accommodations to Support Derivational Relations Materials

- To support students who cannot read the advanced level texts, students read from book sets of easier materials, read along to the books on tape, and view related videos on the subject.
- To support students who cannot read the vocabulary easily (e.g., *constitution, supersaturate, convenient, metamorphosis*) the teacher charts the words and conducts a concept sort. Students record their words in the vocabulary sections of their word study notebooks.
- To learn difficult vocabulary in grades 6 to 12, students require a variety of oral and written support, including support from partners.
- To learn to write vocabulary and content words accurately, students check their writing with an alphabetized list of content words from the unit of study.

FOSTERING A CLIMATE FOR WORD LEARNING. While working in word study groups, students will do the sorts and activities described throughout this book and in other Words Their Way publications. In addition to these developmental group activities, there are many ways to foster an interest in words with the class as a whole. Identify and discuss the important and interesting words in the common texts students are reading and referencing. Make a place for interesting words and etymology charts on your classroom walls and in word study notebooks. Point out and discuss words that tie into students' home languages and connect to their interests. Investigate specialty words such as acronyms (e.g., AIDS: Acquired Immune Deficiency Syndrome); clipped words such as *gas* (from *gasoline*); eponyms that are derived from a person's name (e.g., *Molotov cocktail, Frisbee*); "portmanteau" or blended words that combine the sounds and meanings of two words (e.g., *camcorder* from *camera* and *recorder*); or abbreviations (e.g., ASAP: "as soon as possible"). What other examples can they think of? Find creative ways to work with idioms like "a piece of cake"; when explicit, these discussions will give English learners a greater understanding of the subtleties in the language. Use texts that include codeswitching, such as *The House on Mango Street* (Cisneros, 1984) to delve into the connection between word use and a person's identity.

There is significant potential at this level for extending students' word consciousness, particularly their appreciation for how words are used and how they came to have their current meanings. They can explore and understand how the original, more concrete meaning that resulted from combining word parts evolved into a more abstract meaning—for example, *analyze* literally means "loosen" (*-lyze*) "up" (*ana-*).

Word Study Conversations: "Walking through Words" with Students

Teachers guide students' exploration of words and in doing so provide the academic language about words that students will appropriate and use in their own explorations. In this section, examples are provided of how teachers walk through aspects of the scope and sequence presented in Table 8.1: spelling–meaning connections, Greek and Latin word roots, cognates, absorbed prefixes, and student "frequently asked questions" that usually emerge as they explore words at the derivational level.

THE SPELLING–MEANING CONNECTION. Attention to the spelling–meaning connection is especially important because spelling helps English learners become aware of the morphology of the language. Meaningful units, or morphemes, are usually spelled consistently, despite changes in sound. Because of this consistency, they become visual cues that help students notice important meaning elements in English such as prefixes, suffixes, base words, and word roots.

The teacher writes the following words on the overhead:

nation
national

She asks the students, "Are these words similar in meaning?" She gets the students to discuss the relationships and encourages them to use each of the words in a sentence.

The teacher then points out, "When we add the suffix *-al* to the base word *nation*, do you notice how the sound of the base word *nation* changes?" She encourages the students to talk about how it changes. If necessary, she will point out that the sound that the letter *a* stands for changes, from a long *a* sound in *nation* to a short *a* sound in *national*. She comments, "But notice that we don't *spell* these sounds with different letters, do we?"

Next, she writes the following words on the overhead:

human
humanity

Again she asks the students, "Are these words similar in meaning?" She continues, "When we add the suffix *-ity* to the base word *human*, do you notice how the sound of the base word *human* changes?" Again, she encourages the students to discuss how it changes; if necessary, she points out how the sound that the letter *a* stands for changes from a schwa sound in *human* to a short *a* in *humanity*. The accent also shifts from the first syllable to the second.

The teacher summarizes the spelling–meaning connection as follows: "This is a very important thing about the way we spell most words in English. While every *sound* isn't spelled with its own letter all of the time, words that share similar *meanings* are *spelled* similarly."

WORD ROOTS. The teacher reminds the students that they have discussed base words, prefixes, and suffixes. She continues, "There is another very important word part that we will learn about today, called a word root. If you remove all of the prefixes and suffixes from a word and what remains is no longer a word, you have discovered what we call the word root.

"For example, let's look at the word *inspect* [writes *inspect* on the board]. When you *inspect* something, what does that mean?" It is fairly easy to draw out the students' ideas about the word because it is one that they know. "How about *inspection?*" Again, the students are able to discuss this word fairly easily.

"Good! Now, let's find the word root in each of these words. The word *inspect* has the prefix *in-*, meaning 'into.' When we take it off, what's left? Right! *Spect*. Now, is *spect* a word? No, it isn't. It is the word *root*, and it has a meaning. As we'll learn, word roots come from Latin and Greek and occur in thousands of words in English. The word root *spect* comes from a Latin word that means 'to look.' So when we put the prefix *in*, meaning 'into,' and the word root *spect*, meaning 'look,' together, we get a verb meaning 'to look into'—and that is what you've already said *inspect* means!

"How about the word *inspection?* Do you see a word root in it? Right! We take off the prefix *in*, meaning 'into,' and the suffix *-ion*, meaning 'the act of,' and we find *spect* again. Now put the word parts back together: *-ion*, meaning 'the act of,' plus *spect*, meaning 'look,' and *in-*, meaning 'into.' *Inspection* literally means 'the act of looking into.' And isn't that what happens in an *inspection?* The *-ion* has also changed the verb *inspect* to a noun—*inspection.*

"We will be learning the most important word roots in English and thinking about how they combine with prefixes and suffixes. Your understanding of this process of combination will help you learn new words in your reading and help your spelling as well."

COGNATE INSTRUCTION. The vignette at the beginning of this chapter illustrates how one teacher included Spanish and English cognates in her math instruction. Cognates are words in different languages whose spelling is the same or almost identical and which represent the same or similar concepts. We begin to explore cognates when we address Greek and Latin word roots in our instruction. Seeing how these Greek and Latin elements occur in languages other than English helps students truly appreciate to an even greater degree the generative potential of these elements (Templeton et al., 2010). We first directly teach about cognates, explore their structures, and thereby lay the groundwork for their inclusion in much of our subsequent vocabulary instruction. This degree of attention is important for English-learning and native-English-speaking students alike. Cognate exploration is particularly fruitful in science and math instruction (Hiebert & Bravo, 2010; Templeton et al., 2010), where the meanings in respective languages are identical or quite close—for example *observe/observar, hypothesis/hipótesis, identify/identificar, discover/descubrir,* or *concept/concepto.*

Begin instruction with cognates that are spelled the same—for example *doctor, admirable,* and *hospital* in English and Spanish—or nearly the same in two languages—for example, English and Spanish *complete/completar, instruction/instruccion,* and *ambitious/ambicioso.* Cognates may first be matched by "stacking" them, one beneath the other, so that the examination of their similarities is most obvious:

office	initial	generous
oficina	inicial	generoso

Additional sorts may be conducted within and between forms in different languages. For example, base and derived forms in Spanish and English may be sorted as follows:

abbreviate	elevate	declare
abreviar	elevar	declarar

Derived forms may be matched, and suffixes may be compared:

abbreviation	elevation	imitation
abreviación	elevación	imitación

Instruction then explores cognates whose spelling is "close enough" that they are recognizable, such as the following examples:

courage	escuela	hour	state
coraje	school	hora	estado

An Example Cognate Lesson. For the first few lessons in which cognates are examined, a structured lesson is advisable (Templeton et al., 2010). To illustrate, here's how Khaled Akkeh set up one of his first lessons addressing cognates. Using an online multilingual dictionary (http://translate.reference.com/translate), Mr. Akkeh selected the following words:

television	*computer*	*telephone*
téléviseur (French)	ordinateur (French)	téléphone (French)
televisión (Spanish)	ordenador (Spanish)	teléfono (Spanish)
televisietoestel (Dutch)	computer (Dutch)	telefoon (Dutch)
televizyon (Turkish)	bilgisayar (Turkish)	telefon (Turkish)
televisi (Indonesian)	komputer (Indonesian)	telepon (Indonesian)

He then set up his students' exploration. On the interactive whiteboard, Mr. Akkeh displayed a picture of a telephone, a television, and a computer. The English name for each appeared beneath each picture. He asked his students if they knew the name for *telephone* in a language other than English. His Spanish-speaking students suggested *teléfono*, and a student from Indonesia suggested *telepon*.

"Thank you! Let's take *teléfono*—how is that spelled?" As students call out the spelling, Mr. Akkeh writes it underneath *telephone*. If they do not mention the *diacrítico* or accent mark, he stops after spelling the word and wonders aloud about something missing. Students who are at intermediate-level Spanish literacy usually will mention the accent; if not, he adds it and asks what it tells us about pronouncing *teléfono* (the accent or stress is on the second syllable).

"Now, how about *telepon*?" He also writes it under *telephone*. "Now let's think about *television*. What are some other words for *television*?" And so it continues.

After students have suggested other words, Mr. Akkeh displays the following words, telling the students that some are from Spanish, some from French, others from Indonesian, and still others from Dutch or Turkish. The letter following each word stands for the language from which it comes (an option is to turn to a map to indicate the location of the major countries in which these languages are spoken):

téléviseur-F	ordenador-S	computer-D	televisi-I
telefon-T	telefoon-D	bilgisayar-T	televisietoestel-D
televisión-S	telepon-I	televizyon-T	komputer-I
teléfono-S	ordinateur-F	téléphone-F	

"Let's see which of these you've already suggested." As students call the Spanish and Indonesian words out, Mr. Akkeh draws a line through each:

téléviseur	~~ordenador~~	computer	~~televisi~~
telefon	telefoon	bilgisayar	televisietoestel
~~televisión~~	~~telepon~~	televizyon	~~komputer~~
~~teléfono~~	ordinateur	téléphone	

"Now turn to a partner and decide where the remaining words go. It will be interesting to see if we have any words left that we're unsure about!" After a couple of minutes, Mr. Akkeh asks the students to volunteer the remaining words; on the whiteboard, the students see each word then move to the column underneath the pictures of the computer, telephone, or television. *Bilgisayar* is the one left over.

"As we look down the *telephone* column, what do you notice about these words?" Mr. Akkeh then responds as appropriate to the students' observations, discussing with them the similar letters and different sounds. Pointing to *televisietoestel*, he asks them if they have a clue to its meaning even though they may be uncertain of its pronunciation, and why. They discuss how English and Dutch *computer* is the same and Indonesian *komputer* is very nearly the same, but how Spanish and French have *ordenador* and *ordinateur*, very different-looking words from *computer*. The students agree, however, that *ordenador* and *ordinateur* look similar; Mr. Akkeh wonders aloud if they might have something to do with "ordering" or "organizing data and information—maybe that's where the similar spellings came from." Two students volunteer to look into that on an online translation site.

"And what about the Turkish word for computer? You know, I was really fascinated by that. Just for fun, I typed in *bilgi* on a translation website, and it turns out to be a word by itself in Turkish, and it refers to knowledge, learning, information, and data. I typed in the rest of the word for *computer—sayar—*and a similar-looking word popped up that has to do with counting and numbering. Putting these meanings together, like a compound word in English, we get the meaning related to counting or numbering knowledge, learning, information, and data.

"We've agreed that most of our words for telephone, television, and computer look more alike than different. Words with similar spellings and similar meanings in different languages are called cognates. Turn to a partner and talk about how cognates may be helpful to you when you're learning another language."

What had Mr. Akkeh tried to do in this beginning lesson on cognates? He knows that a number of his students, including those in the early intermediate stage of English proficiency, will not be picking up on everything that he and other students are discussing. He does have a wide range of language competence and background knowledge represented in this class, and he has structured his lesson to capitalize on that. He has used pictures, chosen enough cognates that are clearly similar, provided for student and whole-class discussion, and included some examples—*ordenador/ordinateur* and *bilgisayar*—that are appropriate for his more advanced students as well as serving to pique the curiosity of the rest of his class. He has also modeled how to think about cognates that are different—why *ordenador/ordinateur* appear different from *computer*.

For frequently occurring words that mean the same thing but are spelled quite differently, the Spanish form usually contains the Latin or Greek root whereas the English form does not. The Latin or Greek roots do occur, however, in less frequently occurring English words that are themselves important academic vocabulary terms. For example, *vacía/empty* are clearly not cognates, but there are less frequent words in English that are spelled similarly to the Spanish form: *vacate*, *evacuate*, and *vacuum*. The Spanish word for ground—*tierra*—contains a root spelled similarly to the root in *territory*, *subterranean*, and *terrestrial*.

Even when cognates exist, the use of the cognate in each respective language may be somewhat different. For students learning the academic vocabulary of an additional language, it is important to be aware of this fact. When a translation website or a text in a specific language uses a word that is not an exact or close match, for example English *taxonomy* versus French *systématique*, that is a rich opportunity for growing a deeper understanding of each word. Students may attend to their use in context to see the different shades of meaning that they have in their respective languages. In a science unit, for example, the English word that means "slow movement of land along a fault" is *creep*, whereas the Spanish word is *arrastrar*. In English, the similar form *arrest* means not only what often happens to suspected criminals but also to slow and stop the movement of something. This is not the same meaning as "creep" but is similar in terms of the core concept of "to slow, stop" in both English and Spanish. Over time, in other words, teachers can help students get a sense of different nuances of meaning between languages as well as how a cognate in one language may have a more specific, more general, or more nuanced meaning than its counterpart in another language.

Languages with Few English Cognates. What about languages that do not have English cognates—for example, Hmong, Chinese, Vietnamese, and Korean? The key is first to help these students think about language in general and what it does. Almost all languages do the same sorts of things—for example, use words and phrases that once had quite literal meanings that, over time, became extended metaphorically. All languages evolve, all languages have etymologies or word histories, and the writing systems of most languages carry within them keys and insights into these legacies. So in addition to the word-specific strategies and activities we have discussed, teachers may build on students' understanding of their own spoken and written language and then extend these understandings to English. This type of reflection on language and its relationship to meaning is the type of metacognitive activity that is essential for learning a new language—and it benefits native-English-speaking students as well. It is not uncommon for students to be hesitant to talk about their own language; in such situations ask an adult member of the language community to visit the class and share. For example, Sara Jones wanted her students, some of whom spoke a dialect of Chinese at home, to become aware of how very different writing systems still are able to express meaning visually, just as English does through the connection between spelling and meaning. She invited one of her student's uncles, Chang Wei, a speaker of Cantonese Chinese at home, to "team teach" with her.

First, Ms. Jones reminded her students of the spelling–meaning connection, writing the following word pairs on the whiteboard and underlining the spellings in each pair that are shared:

com<u>pose</u>	com<u>pet</u>e	<u>sign</u>
com<u>posi</u>tion	com<u>peti</u>tion	<u>sign</u>ature

Chang then wrote several Chinese words on the whiteboard, underlying the character that they share in common. Figure 8.3 illustrates two of the words, *television* and *movie*. He explained how the first character in each means "electricity." He then briefly shared with them some other examples of "word formation" in Chinese, and Ms. Jones concluded their team presentation by pointing out that both English and Chinese spelling have visual patterns that correspond to meaning and that readers in both languages can learn to look for these common visual patterns when they run into unfamiliar words. They may recognize a pattern that is familiar and may provide a clue to the new word.

Recently formed words in languages quite different from English, such as Korean and Japanese, often have very similar pronunciations to the English versions. This is particularly true in words having to do with technological innovation. On a translation website, for example, students could compare how *television* or *computer* is pronounced in Chinese, Japanese, and Korean.

ABSORBED PREFIXES. It was mentioned earlier that the spelling of the prefix *in-* may change to *il-*, *im-*, and *ir-*. Why did this occur? When *in-* was first affixed to a word in Roman times—such as to *mediate* to mean "not mediated," it was pronounced "inmediate." It's difficult to say "inmediate" rapidly, however, because of the switch from the nasal /n/ sound of the prefix to the nasal /m/ sound at the beginning of *mediate*. Speakers of Latin during Roman times had the same difficulty, so what happened over time as people used such words is that the /n/ sound in the prefix became slurred or absorbed into the /m/ sound at the beginning of the word to which it was attached. Eventually, spelling changed to reflect this sound change. The spelling of *in-* also changed to *ir-* when it was attached to words that began with *r* (because *i<u>r</u>relevant* is easier to pronounce than *i<u>n</u>relevant*) and to *il-* when attached to words that began with *l* (because *i<u>l</u>legible* is easier to pronounce than *i<u>n</u>legible*).

FIGURE 8.3 Visual Meaning Patterns in Chinese

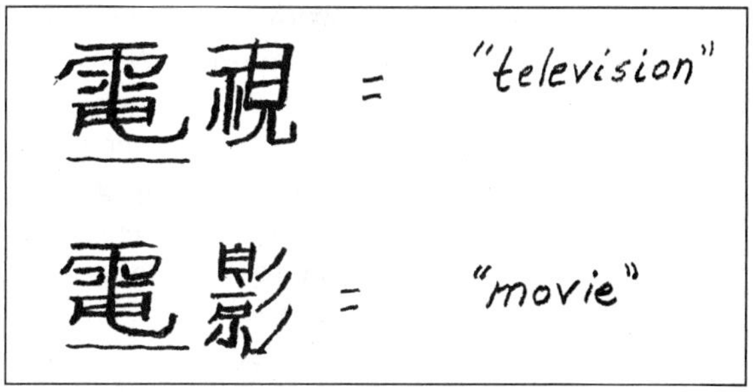

電視 = "television"

電影 = "movie"

STUDENTS' "FREQUENTLY ASKED QUESTIONS" ABOUT WORDS. As upper-level students explore the logic of English words, they inevitably ask questions about apparent "exceptions"—spellings or features that don't seem to fit their expectations. Here are their most frequently occurring questions and the explanations you may offer:

Why Are There Different Prefixes and Roots for the Same Meanings? Take *un-* and *in-*, for example. Why do some words have the prefix *un-* and others have the prefix *in-?* Actually, both prefixes started out the same because they came from the same ancient language, Indo-European, spoken about 5,000 B.C.E. As the years went by, some sounds changed, and eventually people who lived in Northern Europe said *un-*, whereas people in Southern and Western Europe said *in-*. Old English used *un-*, whereas *in-* came from Latin and entered the English language hundreds of years later.

Many words and word elements passed from Greek into Latin, and the Latin forms are more common in present-day English. A number of words and elements from Greek, however, have passed directly into English—and this is usually why two or more roots or two or more prefixes exist for the same core meaning. Often the meaning is pretty concrete. Even though the Greek prefix *mono-* and the Latin prefix *uni-* look quite different, they both mean "one" and the meanings of many words that contain them are obvious. Other times, although the underlying meaning of a Greek and a Latin root is still there, the root will have taken on a different connotation in the words that contain it. For example, the concept of "old" is represented by the Greek root *paleo* (*paleontology*) and the Latin roots *sen* and *veter* (*senile*; *veteran*). Words in which *paleo* occurs usually have to do with science, whereas words in which *sen* and *veter* occur have to do more with describing people. The Latin root for "mother" is *matr/mater* (*matricide*, *maternal*) and *metr* in Greek (*metropolis*). The Latin root literally refers to "mother" whereas the Greek usage is more metaphorical, conveying the idea of a city as "mother."

What Happens When the Meaningful Elements in a Word Don't Seem to Add Up? As students are learning how different word roots function within words, they inevitably encounter what appear to be exceptions: words whose component morphemes don't seem to add up to a word that makes sense in the context in which it occurs. One student was perplexed by the word *circumspect* in the sentence, *We're a breed of teenage girls who have been taught to be too circumspect*. She had learned that *spect* means "look" and *circum* means "around," but when she plugged that meaning back into the sentence, it didn't seem to make sense: *Teenage girls who have been taught to look around too much*. Her teacher, Sara Jones, explained that hundreds of years ago the original meaning was, literally, "to look around," to be "watchful on all sides." Ms. Jones then helped the student understand that being "watchful on all sides" is another way of being cautious and careful—the modern meaning of *circumspect*—and this meaning fits much better in the sentence. When we model this way of thinking about words we help our students develop a sensitivity to words that goes well beyond the particular word being analyzed.

Why Does the Spelling Sometimes Change in Related Words? As students come to appreciate the power of the spelling–meaning connection in generating an understanding of many words, they also encounter exceptions. The root *vis* means "to see" in *vision* and *visible* but changes to *vid* in *video* and *provide* (literally, "to see forward"). The root *scrib* means "to write" in *scribble* and *transcribe* but changes to *script* in *scripture* and *inscription*. Why is there a change in spelling of the root? The explanation is similar to that for absorbed prefixes (p. 235): When word parts are combined, changes frequently occur where they come together. In Latin, when certain endings were added to a base or word root the pronunciation of the base or root would change, and the spelling usually changed as well to represent this change in pronunciation. Students can get a feel for this when you ask them to try pronouncing *scribture* or *inscribtion* rapidly several times. They can hear and feel how the /b/ sound becomes a /p/ sound as it combines with or blends into the /sh/ sound that begins the suffix. Over time, the spelling of the root changed to reflect this change in sound. These examples of walking through words with students show how you can teach directly about word meaning and structure in the classroom. Throughout this process, teachers check for understanding in a number of ways, including writing, classroom reference charts, students' notebooks, and the application of these and other strategies to learn new words independently.

Now that we have presented some overarching ideas of how to organize and introduce word study with your class, it is time to share the specific word sorts and activities that you will use at the upper levels of development. The rest of this chapter outlines a number of specific sorts and games sequenced from least to most difficult for English learners at the derivational relations stage. These activities can be used in teacher-directed, guided, and independent activities with students.

ACTIVITIES
FOR ENGLISH LEARNERS IN THE DERIVATIONAL RELATIONS STAGE

8.1 Adding *-ion*, No Spelling Change

DEMONSTRATE, SORT, AND REFLECT. Prepare the set of words for Sort 280 on the website. Introduce this sort by displaying a transparency of the words on an overhead or hand out a sheet of words to the students. Spend some time sharing what students know about the meaning of each of the words in the sort. Ask them what they notice about the words, and get ideas about how the words can be sorted. Students will likely notice that the words can be matched up with one word being contained in another, which also adds *-ion*. Point out the pair *prevent/prevention*. Discuss how the meaning of the word is changed when *-ion* is added. When we *prevent* something, we are performing an action. A *prevention* is the result of our action, a "thing." Encourage them to put the meanings into their own words as they discuss what happens when we put *-ion* onto base words. Scaffold their understandings of the following: Putting *-ion* on a base word results in a word that means "the act or result" of the meaning of the base word. For example, if you *predict* that a team will win a game you have made a *prediction*; the act of subtracting one number from another is called the process of *subtraction*.

Once students have noted the base word/suffixed word distinction, discuss the pronunciation of the base + *-ion* pattern. What happens to the sound of *t* when it is added to the base words? Thinking of the meaning relationship shared by the base word and its derivative can help students remember the spelling, despite the sound change. The completed sort should look something like Sort 280 on the website. See also Figure 8.4.

FIGURE 8.4 Adding *-ion*, No Spelling Change

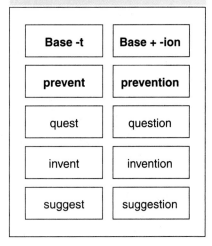

Base -t	Base + -ion
prevent	**prevention**
quest	question
invent	invention
suggest	suggestion

EXTEND. Note that sometimes words ending in two consonants add *-ation* as in *adaptation* and *condemnation*. These are easy to spell because we can clearly hear the "ation." In spelling, a common confusion primarily at the syllables and affixes stage but also at the derivational relations stage is the treatment of *-ion*. Students often remember the various spellings but are uncertain about when to use a particular one and whether and how it affects the spelling of the base word. The next sort will examine another application of this feature.

8.2 Adding *-ion*, *e*-Drop, and Spelling Change

DEMONSTRATE, SORT, AND REFLECT. Ask the students to notice how the words in this sort are related. What similarities do they see? Does this look similar to a sort they have previously done? Discuss the meanings of the words and how they may be used in sentences. How does *celebrate* change when it becomes *celebration*? (It changes from a verb to a noun.) Sort the words together so that each base matches up with its suffixed form—its **derivative**—and

**PDToolkit
for Words Their Way™
with English Learners**

Go to PDToolkit, choose your book, click the Sorts & Games tab, and search for "Sort 280: Adding *-ion*, No Spelling Change."

▶ **Derivative**

A word that has been formed or adapted from another, such as *electricity* from *electric*.

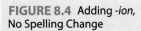

ACTIVITIES DERIVATIONAL RELATIONS STAGE

**for Words Their Way™
with English Learners**

Go to PDToolkit, choose your
book, click the Sorts & Games
tab, and search for "Sort 281:
Adding *-ion*, e-Drop and Spelling
Change."

meanings are clarified and contextualized for students (this is an appropriate place in word study at the derivational level to begin to use the term *derivative*). The completed sort should look something like Sort 281 on the website. Guide students to compare the words in the first column to those in the second. What happens to the word when the *-ion* is added? (*e*-drop) Try creating some new *-ion* words with the bases *vacate*, *relate*, *rotate*, *narrate*, and *imitate*.

EXTEND. Students can be encouraged to go on word hunts to look for words that end in *-ion*. They will find some that fit into the categories that have been studied and others that will have new patterns such as *production*, *permission*, and *explosion*. This may whet their appetites for exploring words with related affixation patterns.

8.3 Vowel Alternation: Long to Short

The focus in Sort 282 on the website is the constancy of spelling despite a change in pronunciation of the vowel from the base to its derivative.

**for Words Their Way™
with English Learners**

Go to PDToolkit, choose your
book, click the Sorts & Games
tab, and search for "Sort 282:
Vowel Alternation: Long to
Short."

DEMONSTRATE, SORT, AND REFLECT. Ask the students how they might sort the words. They will probably notice that some are base words. Suggest that they sort the words into base words and related suffixed or derived words. Discuss the meanings of the base words and derived words as you sort. For instance, how are *wise* and *wisdom* related? What about *decide* and *decision?* Clarify and contextualize the meanings of any words students are unsure of. The completed sort should look something like Sort 282 on the website.

Once the related words have been matched up, ask the students if the vowel sounds in the accented syllables of the word pairs change. (Yes, they do.) Does the spelling of the vowel change? (No.) Remind the students that this is because the words are related in meaning; this is the spelling–meaning connection. For many English learners, some of the short vowel sounds can be especially difficult to distinguish. As you review these paired words, if you find that students need additional, explicit instruction, consider using a highlighter pen to mark the vowel sounds you are discussing. You may also want to help students read the focus words in a dramatic voice, accentuating the vowel sound in question.

8.4 Vowel Alternation: Long to Short/Schwa

DEMONSTRATE, SORT, AND REFLECT. Prepare the word cards for Sort 283 on the website. The words in this sort help students contrast the long/short vowel alternation pattern with a schwa. We know that a good many spelling errors at this level are in the unaccented syllables of words, so that is why these spelling–meaning patterns are helpful to study. Importantly, this sort will help students attend to accent within words.

Introduce the sort by asking the students if they've ever had to stop and think about how to spell a particular word, such as *competition* or *invitation*. Tell them that thinking of a related word may provide a clue. For example, thinking of the base word *compete* will help with *competition*; thinking of the base word *invite* may help with *invitation*. Tell them that thinking of these spelling–meaning patterns is what they are going to explore in this sort.

Work with students to match up each base word with its derivative. As you do, discuss and clarify word meanings and pronunciations. Explore students' familiarity with the words, and if you find there are too many to learn in one day, work with only a few of the words on the first day. After the words are paired up, have students listen for the vowel alternation. Remind them that in the previous sort they noticed how some derivatives changed from a long to a short vowel. In this sort, some of the derivatives also take on the schwa or "uh" sound. Distinguishing these sounds, especially the schwa sound, may be very difficult for your students. Use a greater level of explicitness and directness if you find that your students cannot hear these differences without your support.

If students do not notice the different types of vowel alternation on their own, ask them to compare the pair *produce/production* with *compete/competition*. In *produce/production*, do they hear how the long *u* in *produce* changes to a short *u* in *production?* Does the long *e* in *compete*

**for Words Their Way™
with English Learners**

Go to PDToolkit, choose your
book, click the Sorts & Games
tab, and search for "Sort 283:
Vowel Alternation: Long to
Short/Schwa."

change to a short *e* in *competition*? Not exactly? In *production*, the second syllable is clearly accented—in other words, it gets most of the "oomph" when we say the word. In *competition*, is the second syllable clearly accented? Not really. Because of this fact—it is not accented—the vowel sound in the second syllable of *competition* sounds like an unaccented short *u* sound (the schwa); there's no "oomph" behind it. How might they remember how it is spelled? (By thinking of *compete*.) In most unaccented or least accented syllables the vowel sound is also unaccented, becoming a schwa. The completed sort should look something like Figure 8.5.

Students may notice that the word *cycle* is spelled with a *y* but becomes a short *i* sound in the word *cyclical*. This is because the *y* is alternating from a long *i* sound.

EXTEND. Use these words to jumpstart your vocabulary discussions. Find out which words hold particular connection or interest for your students and work with them in greater depth. What related words can you think of? Can they be featured in students' writing? Are there any cognates in students' home languages (examples in Spanish from this list include *preference/preferencia*, *invitation/invitación*, *cycle/ciclo*, and *photograph/fotografía*)? Build on your students' background experiences and curiosity and see where this exploration takes you!

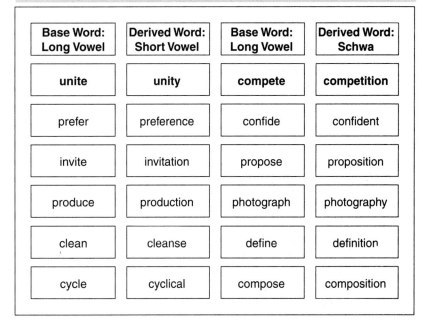

FIGURE 8.5 Vowel Alternation: Long to Short/Schwa

Base Word: Long Vowel	Derived Word: Short Vowel	Base Word: Long Vowel	Derived Word: Schwa
unite	unity	compete	competition
prefer	preference	confide	confident
invite	invitation	propose	proposition
produce	production	photograph	photography
clean	cleanse	define	definition
cycle	cyclical	compose	composition

8.5 Greek Roots *graph, tele*

DEMONSTRATE, SORT, AND REFLECT. Prepare the Greek roots cards for Sort 284 on the website. Tell the students that a large number of words contain Greek roots and that these roots usually have a pretty consistent or constant meaning. Most often they do not occur by themselves as words, though on occasion some of them may do so. We want students to think directly about the meaning of each of these elements and to examine, discuss, and understand how these word parts combine to result in the meaning of a word. When they combine with other Greek elements, the resulting word meanings often become decipherable. We encourage you to review the format outlined in the overview of this chapter as an example of how to explicitly "walk through" the words in these meaning-based sorts.

Tell the students that learning the meanings of a number of these roots and understanding how they combine to create words will be extremely helpful to the students in figuring out and learning new vocabulary through their reading as well as in helping them with occasional spelling errors. Begin by writing the familiar words *television* and *telephone* on the board or overhead. Ask students if they see a smaller word within *television*? (*vision*) How about *telephone*? (*phone*) Then tell them that the word part or root *tele* comes from Greek and means "distant." When it combines with *vision*, it literally means "vision from a distance." Discuss why this is, literally, what television is and does—it delivers vision from a distance (cable, satellite, antenna). Next, discuss how *phone* in *telephone* actually comes from a Greek word that means "sound." When it combines with *tele*, it literally means "sound from a distance."

Have the students sort the words by whether they contain *tele* or *graph*. Note that *telegraph* can go in either column or in between because it contains both parts. The completed sort should look something like Sort 284 on the website. Have students review all of the *tele* words. Discuss how the meaning of each results from the combination of *tele* with another

PDToolkit
for Words Their Way™
with English Learners

Go to PDToolkit, choose your book, click the Sorts & Games tab, and search for "Sort 284: Greek Roots *graph, tele*."

ACTIVITIES   DERIVATIONAL RELATIONS STAGE

word. Elicit definitions and explanations from the students, though you may need to scaffold their explanations for particular words. For example, *telegraph* contains another word that came from Greek—*graph*, which means "writing." They have probably heard about the *telegraph* but perhaps not thought about the fact that it was, literally, "writing from a distance." As for *telescope*, tell them that *scope* is also a word that originally came from Greek and means "target" or "aim"; what, then, does *telescope* literally mean? Encourage students to contribute their ideas to how *tele* contributes to the total meaning of each individual word, such as in *telecommunication*, *telecast*, and *telethon*.

Next, look over the *graph* words. Discuss *photography*—literally "writing with light"—because there usually is at least one student who understands the process by which photography works. If not, this may be a good time to mention the process briefly; for example, the lens lets in light that is "written" onto film or a disk (as with a digital camera). A reference book of Greek and Latin word parts will help you and your students find out more about the meanings of these elements, and this will contribute to your investigations and discussions. Another good practice is to photocopy a table of Greek word roots and place it in the students' word study notebooks for ready reference.

8.6 Greek Roots *photo, auto*

DEMONSTRATE, SORT, AND REFLECT. Prepare the Greek root cards for Sort 285 on the website. This sort offers additional opportunities to explore Greek elements, this time in words that contain *auto*, meaning "self," and *photo*, which means "light." Remind students that learning the meanings of a number of these roots and understanding how they combine to create words will be extremely helpful in figuring out and learning new vocabulary through their reading as well as in helping them with occasional spelling errors.

Work with the students to sort the words into two columns—*photo* and *auto*—as you read and practice saying them aloud. Say that after the words are sorted, you will discuss what "light" and "self" might have to do with the meaning of each of the words. The completed sort should look something like Sort 285 on the website.

Now work through each column, examining the word parts. For example, *photo* and *graph* come from the Greek roots for "light" and "write," respectively, as discussed in the previous sort. Make connections to how *tele*, meaning "distant," can help us understand that telephoto lenses are used to take pictures from far away. Photocopiers use light to make copies of documents, and so on. In this way, proceed through the rest of the *photo* words.

For the *auto* column, ask students to think about how the idea of "self" relates to the word meanings. A camera with *autofocus* does the focusing by itself. An *autobiography* is written by a person about him- or herself. An *automobile* is powered by itself, unlike a cart that requires animals to pull it along. Use these words to discuss how to break apart words to get at their meanings. For unfamiliar words, have students discuss what the meaning might be, based on their inferences from the combination of the word parts. When in doubt, pull out a reference book on Greek and Latin elements for you and your students to use in exploring the meanings of word parts. Discuss how the meanings of the Greek combining forms work to result in the overall meaning of each word.

EXTEND. How many of these words have cognates in your students' home languages? As you walk through the words, ask students if any look similar to words they have seen in other languages. For instance, some of your students may notice that words such as *photography* and *automobile* have similar meanings and spellings in Spanish (*fotografía*, *automóvil*). Encourage students to note these cognates in their word study notebooks.

8.7 Latin Roots *spect, port*

DEMONSTRATE, SORT, AND REFLECT. Prepare the Latin root words for Sort 286 on the website. Because this is a beginning sort for Latin word roots, you may wish to begin by walking the students through two or three words, explaining how the elements combine to produce the meaning of the word. (We have outlined a possible teacher script about "walking through words" earlier in this chapter on pages 231–232 that can help you structure your lesson.)

The meanings of the Latin roots in this sort are fairly straightforward, as are the meanings of most of the words in which they combine with other affixes and roots. As with the Greek roots or combining forms in the previous two sorts, these Latin roots occur with some frequency in printed materials from the intermediate grades onward. Remember that for students from Latinate language backgrounds, there may be numerous opportunities for students to connect these words to cognates in their home languages.

Begin by writing the words *inspect* and *transport* on the board or overhead. Ask the students to explain the meaning of *inspect* and use it in a sentence. Then tell them that the word is made up of the Latin root *spect*, which means "to look at," and the prefix *in-* meaning "into." Now think about it: Given their explanation and definition of *inspect*, do they see that putting these word parts together literally means "to look into" something? Repeat this process with *transport*. Have them discuss what the word means and then show them that the word comes from the Latin root *port*, which means "to carry," and the prefix *trans-*, meaning "across." Now think about it: Given their explanation and definition of *transport*, do they see that putting the root *port* together with the prefix *trans-* literally means "carrying across"? (You may mention *import* as well here. Tell them the prefix *im-* means "in, into." Is it clear how *transport* and *import* are related?)

After the introduction, have students sort the words according to the root in each. The completed sort should look something like the word list below (Sort 286 on the website).

spect	port
inspect	transport
perspective	deport
retrospective	import
spectator	exporter
circumspect	report
respect	portfolio
suspect	heliport
spectacle	portable
spectacular	airport
spectrum	carport
unsuspecting	portal
prospect	transportation

Follow up by discussing with students how they think the word parts combine to produce the meaning of each word. You may want to "walk through" some words with students after they sort and discuss them, such as *perspective*—"look through." When you talk about your *perspective* on an issue or on life, you are actually talking about how you have *looked through* that issue. Or you may discuss *prospect*—"look forward." Point out to the students that for most words that appear to contain word roots, they can best analyze the meaning by beginning at the ends of the words. Reflect on how you analyzed the words *inspect* and *transport*.

EXTEND. Several words offer possibilities for generating additional derived words by adding *-ion* or *-ation*. Have students see how many derived words they can generate, first discussing whether the derived words really exist or not, and then checking the dictionary for confirmation. For example, *inspection* or *inspectation? Importation* or *importion?*

8.8 Root Webs

Teachers can use root webs (Figure 8.6) to illustrate how words can be generated from a single root through the addition of affixes (Padak, Newton, Rasinski, & Newton, 2008; Templeton

FIGURE 8.6 Root Web for *gress*—"move"

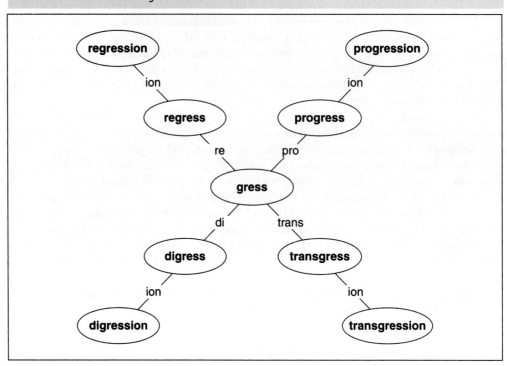

et al., 2010). On the whiteboard, draw several ovals. Particular affixes may be added to the connections, as shown in Figure 8.6 (or in sample graphic organizers included on the website). As students progress in their understanding of roots and their combinations, they can work in pairs or small groups to see how many words can be generated.

You may also use the idea of the root web as a graphic organizer for a unit of study. Figure 8.7 shows an elaborated graphic organizer—the basic graphic organizer that includes most important words or concepts to be addressed in a unit on the Renaissance, with the addition of Spanish cognates.

FIGURE 8.7 Major Concepts/Vocabulary in Renaissance Unit

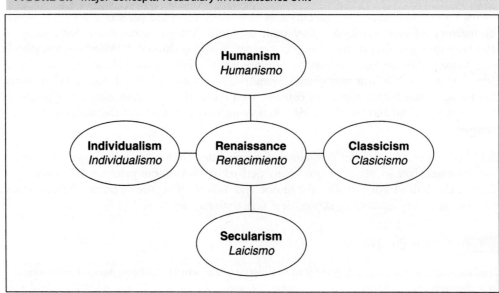

8.9 Cognate Games

MATERIALS. Make a copy of the sorting grid of cognates (Sort 287 on the website) and cut the pieces apart. If you would like to have students do this sort independently following the guided activity, make additional copies for them to cut apart.

PROCEDURES. Start by showing students the picture cards for this sort along with the English labels for them. Match the words to pictures and spread them out on a table or floor area. Ask students if they know the names of these things in a language besides English. As students respond, listen to see if any of the words they share sound similar to the English versions. If a word does, ask the student to repeat it slowly and, if possible, to help you write it down.

Explain to students that words with similar spellings and meanings across languages are called cognates. Today you will be sorting some words that are cognates with English. Even though they are written in other languages, they shouldn't be too difficult to figure out. Now bring out the other word cards, and see if students can tell you which picture they go with. If students recognize the words in another language, or if you do, help students practice pronouncing them. The words are written in many other languages, including Spanish, Italian, German, French, Norwegian, and Dutch. The completed sort should look something like Sort 287 on the website.

Once the sort has been completed, encourage students to share what they notice about the words and reflect on how cognates may be helpful to them as they learn new languages. They may want to go on an Internet or library hunt to find other cognates for *bank, music, train, park, telephone,* and *computer.* They may also want to try to find cognates for other simple words like *museum, university,* or *tourist.*

VARIATIONS. Using the picture cards from the Appendix of this book, give a key word picture to a pair of students and have them research on the Internet, in reference materials, or from multilingual speakers in the class or community how many cognates they can find for the word. Create a classroom dictionary of cognates or a word wall of cognates to which students can add.

train

tren

treno

trem

PDToolkit

for Words Their Way™ with English Learners

Go to PDToolkit, choose your book, click the Sorts & Games tab, and search for "Sort 287: Cognate Sort."

8.10 From Spanish to English, a Dictionary Word Hunt

The purpose of this activity is to expand vocabularies by finding relations among languages. We present a version for Spanish, but it may be adapted to other Latinate languages as well.

MATERIALS. You will need a Spanish–English dictionary for each student or partnership. Find a version that is fairly simple or designed for students.

PROCEDURES

1. With a Spanish–English dictionary find words in Spanish that remind you of words in English. Briefly note the definition or a synonym.
2. With an English dictionary, find words that share the same root or affix. Write these related words into your word study notebooks.
3. Use a Spanish dictionary to find related words with the same meaning, such as *night–noche.*

Here are some sample entries on a class chart of related words that students collected in this activity.

Spanish (Translation)	English Relations	Spanish Relations
presumir *(boast)*	presume, presumption, presumptuous	presumido, presunción
extenso *(extensive)*	extend, extension	extensivo, extender
nocturno *(nightly)*	nocturnal, nocturne	noche, noctámbulo
polvo *(powder)*	pulverize (from Latin *pulvis,* dust)	polvillo, polvorear

8.11 Adding Suffixes: Vowel Alternation, Accented to Unaccented

DEMONSTRATE, SORT, AND REFLECT. Prepare the word cards for Sort 288 on the website. This sort continues students' exploration of how vowel sounds may alternate across related words while the spelling remains constant. Students' examination of this type of pattern is very productive because it continues to build a spelling–meaning strategy: If you are uncertain about the spelling of a particular word, thinking of a related word may provide a clue.

Have students match up each base word with its derived word. The completed sort should look something like Sort 288 on the website. See also Figure 8.8. Using *combine* and *combination* as examples, discuss how accent affects each word. In *combine*, is the last syllable accented? (Yes.) What happens to that syllable when the suffix *-ation* is added? (It becomes unstressed.) If they were uncertain about the spelling of the /in/ syllable in the middle of *combination*, thinking of the word *combine* might help them because they can clearly hear the vowel sound in the second syllable of *combine* and they know how to spell that sound. Because words that are related in spelling are often related in meaning as well, the stressed syllable in *combine* provides a clue to the spelling of the schwa sound in *combination*. Also take the time to discuss the related meanings of the word pair. What is *combine*, and what is *combination*? How can the base word inform students about a derived word's meaning?

Discuss the rest of the word pairs in this same manner. You may also present a misspelling such as CONFADENT, for example, and ask students which word would clear up the spelling of the schwa sound, and why.

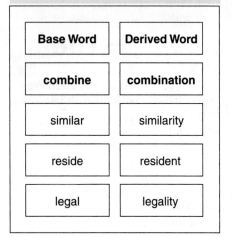

FIGURE 8.8 Adding Suffixes: Vowel Alternation, Accented to Unaccented

Base Word	Derived Word
combine	combination
similar	similarity
reside	resident
legal	legality

EXTEND. Provide many opportunities for students to revisit this sort with partners to practice pronouncing, comparing, and looking for related words. Encourage students to write translations of words that are similar in their home language such as *combinación/ combination*, *vacación/vacation*, and *residente/resident*.

8.12 Adding Suffix *-ity*: Vowel Alternation, Schwa to Short

DEMONSTRATE, SORT, AND REFLECT. Prepare the word cards for Sort 289 on the website. Students first dealt with *-ity* in the previous sort and discussed its effect on the pronunciation of the word to which it is affixed. The derivational suffix *-ity* (state, quality) is very productive, and for that reason its effect on words is examined further in this sort. In this sort, the unaccented final syllable in each base word, *al* becomes accented when *-ity* is affixed.

Ask the students how they might sort the words. By now, an obvious suggestion is to put the *-ity* words together in one column and their related words in the other column. Match the words with derivational partners. The completed sort should look something like Figure 8.9.

Ask the students to look at the first few word pairs. What do they notice when *-ity* is added? If they do not mention that they have worked with words ending in *-ity* in an earlier sort, remind them of this and mention some of those word pairs (for example, *legal/legality*, *similar/similarity*). Remind students that words related in spelling are often related in meaning as well, which is the case with these words. For example, the stressed syllable in *personality* provides a clue to the spelling of the schwa sound in *personal*. Also take the time to discuss the related meanings of the word pair. What is *personal*, and what is *personality*? How can the relationships between word parts inform students about a derived word's meaning?

Discuss the rest of the word pairs in this same manner. You may also present a misspelling such as MUSICUL, for example, and ask students which word would clear up the spelling of the schwa sound, and why.

EXTEND. Encourage students to revisit this sort with partners to practice reviewing their meanings and pronunciations. Have them find other words that relate, such as *person, personality, personal, persons, interpersonal, craftsperson, impersonator, personify,* and *salesperson.* This will help students understand that once they learn one new word, they may have a good sense about the meanings of many more as well!

FIGURE 8.9 Sort for *-ity*

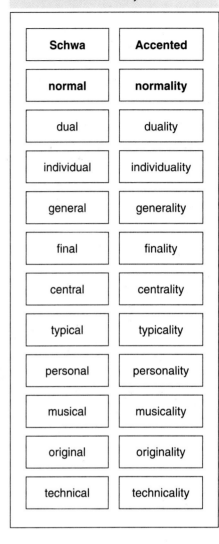

Schwa	Accented
normal	**normality**
dual	duality
individual	individuality
general	generality
final	finality
central	centrality
typical	typicality
personal	personality
musical	musicality
original	originality
technical	technicality

APPENDIX

This Appendix consists of eight sections. The first section contains the materials you will need for assessments. Most of the Appendix consists of pictures, sorts, lists, and materials that you can use to create your own sets of picture and word cards for the basic sorting activities described throughout the book. The final section summarizes what media has been integrated into each chapter and where to find it in the text and on the Web.

Assessment Materials for Chapter 2

Primary Spelling Inventory

Directions. This is a brief spelling assessment to understand the word knowledge students bring to their reading and spelling. This assessment can be administered multiple times over a year to monitor progress and plan instruction. The words in this inventory are ordered in terms of their relative difficulty. Follow the directions agreed on in your school. If you use the inventory independently, consider calling out just 8 words in kindergarten, 15 words in first grade, and the entire list for students in other grades.

Administer the Spelling Inventory. Call the words as you would for any spelling test. Use the words in a sentence to be sure your children know the exact word, but be aware that this can also be confusing to young spellers, and you may not choose to use the sentences at all or only in the case of some words. Assure your students that this is not for a grade but to help you plan better for their needs. Seat the children to minimize copying or test the children in small groups (recommended for kindergarten and early first grade).

Possible Script. "I am going to ask you to spell some words. Spell them the best you can. Some of the words will be easy to spell; some may be difficult. When you do not know how to spell a word, spell it the best you can; write down all the sounds you feel and hear."

Score and Analyze Spelling with a Feature Guide. Copy a feature guide for each student. For each word, check the features that are spelled correctly. Write in substitutions if you wish. Do not count reversed letters as errors but note them in the boxes. Give credit for features even when other letters might be added. (FANE for *fan* still has a final N and a short A and student should get credit for those features.) Add an additional point in the "words spelled correctly" column if the entire word is correct. Total the number of points under each feature and word, and enter the totals at the top of the page. The total score can be compared over time. If less than the total list was called out, *adjust the totals.*

Study the bottom row for the accuracy of spelling for particular features. *Consider starting the student's instruction in the first place where the student missed more than one feature in a column.* A student who gets only two or three of the seven short vowels needs a lot of work on that feature. If the child does not get any points for a feature, it is beyond his or her instructional range and earlier features need to be addressed first.

To determine what stage a student is in, follow this column to the top row and match the feature to a gradation within a stage: early, middle, or late. Staple the student's paper to the feature guide. See Chapter 2 for further instructions on administration and interpretation.

Classroom Composite and Classroom Organization Chart. Make one copy of the classroom composite form on the website. Arrange students' feature guides from highest total points to lowest total points before transferring the numbers from the bottom row of each student's feature guide to this classroom composite. To view students' needs and to form groups for instruction, *highlight* students who make *more than one error* on a particular feature.

The Spelling-by-Stage Classroom Organization Chart on the website is another tool to organize word study groups. Write students' names under the stage and then organize word study/reading groups for differentiated instruction choosing activities from the instructional chapters, Chapters 4 through 8.

PDToolkit

for Words Their Way™ with English Learners

Go to PDToolkit, choose your book, click the Assessment Tools tab, and select Assessment Materials to see the Primary Spelling Inventory Classroom Composite and the Spelling-by-Stage Classroom Organization Chart.

Sentences to Use with the Primary Spelling Inventory

1. fan	I use a fan on a hot day. *fan*
2. pet	I have a pet cat. *pet*
3. dig	He will dig a hole in the sand. *dig*
4. rob	The bad man will rob a bank. *rob*
5. hope	I hope you have a good day. *hope*
6. wait	You will need to wait in line. *wait*
7. gum	I chew some gum. *gum*
8. sled	I play with a sled in the snow. *sled*
(You may stop here for kindergarten unless a child has spelled five words correctly.)	
9. stick	I poke the hole with a stick. *stick*
10. shine	He cleaned his shoe to make it shine. *shine*
11. dream	I had a funny dream last night. *dream*
12. blade	The blade of the knife was very sharp. *blade*
13. coach	The coach is the head of the team. *coach*
14. fright	She had a fright on Halloween. *fright*
15. chewed	The dog chewed the bone until it was gone. *chewed*
(You may stop here for first grade unless a child has spelled 10 words correctly.)	
16. crawl	You will get dirty if you crawl under the bed. *crawl*
17. wishes	In fairy tales wishes come true. *wishes*
18. thorn	The rose bush has a sharp thorn. *thorn*
19. shouted	They shouted at the barking dog. *shouted*
20. spoil	The food will spoil if it sits out too long. *spoil*
21. growl	The dog will growl if you bother him. *growl*
22. third	I was the third person in line. *third*
23. camped	We camped down by the river. *camped*
24. tries	He tries hard every day to finish his work. *tries*
25. clapping	The audience was clapping after the program. *clapping*
26. riding	They are riding their bikes to the park today. *riding*

Feature Guide for Primary Spelling Inventory

Student's Name _____ Teacher _____ Grade _____ Date _____

Words Spelled Correctly: ____ / 26   Feature Points: ____ / 56   Total: ____ / 82   Spelling Stage: _____

SPELLING STAGES →	EMERGENT		LETTER NAME–ALPHABETIC			WITHIN WORD PATTERN		SYLLABLES AND AFFIXES		
	LATE		EARLY — MIDDLE	LATE	LATE	EARLY — MIDDLE	MIDDLE	LATE — EARLY		
Features →	Consonants Initial	Final	Short Vowels	Digraphs	Blends	Long Vowel Patterns	Other Vowels	Inflected Endings	Feature Points	Words Spelled Correctly
1. fan	f	n	a							
2. pet	p	t	e							
3. dig	d	g	i							
4. rob	r	b	o							
5. hope	h	p				o-e				
6. wait	w	t				ai				
7. gum	g	m	u							
8. sled			e		sl					
9. stick			i		st					
10. shine				sh		i-e				
11. dream					dr	ea				
12. blade					bl	a-e				
13. coach				-ch		oa				
14. fright					fr	igh				
15. chewed				ch			ew	-ed		
16. crawl					cr		aw			
17. wishes				-sh				-es		
18. thorn				th			or			
19. shouted				sh			ou	-ed		
20. spoil							oi			
21. growl							ow			
22. third				th			ir			
23. camped								-ed		
24. tries					tr			-ies		
25. clapping								-pping		
26. riding								-ding		
Totals	/7	/7	/7	/7	/7	/7	/7	/7	/ 56	/ 26

Elementary Spelling Inventory

Directions. This is a brief spelling assessment to understand the word knowledge students bring to their reading and spelling. This assessment can be administered multiple times over a year to monitor progress and plan instruction. The words in this inventory are ordered in terms of their relative difficulty. Follow the directions agreed on in your school. If you use the inventory independently, consider discontinuing the inventory when students misspell 8 of the first 10 words. This means that there are probably enough errors to determine a stage of spelling. Students who spell more than half the words correctly may be asked to spell words on a more advanced inventory at another time.

Possible Script. "I am going to ask you to spell some words. Spell them the best you can. Some of the words will be easy to spell; some may be difficult. When you do not know how to spell a word, spell it the best you can; write down all the sounds you feel and hear."

Students should know that this is not a test, and that they can help you plan their learning if they do their best. Students are not to study this inventory beforehand. Say the word once, read the sentence, and then say the word again.

Score and Analyze Spelling with a Feature Guide. Copy a feature guide for each student. For each word, check the features that are spelled correctly. Write in substitutions if you wish. Add an additional point in the "words spelled correctly" column if the word is correct. Do not count reversed letters as errors but note them in the boxes.

Total the number of points under each feature and across each word; this is a check for accuracy. The total score can be compared over time. If less than the total list was called out, *adjust the totals.*

Study the bottom row for the accuracy of spelling for particular features. *Consider starting the student's instruction in the first place where the student missed more than one feature in a column.*

To determine what stage a student is in, follow this column to the top row and match the feature to a gradation within a stage: early, middle, or late. Staple the student's paper to the feature guide. See Chapter 2 for further instructions on administration and interpretation.

Classroom Composite and Classroom Organization Chart. Make one copy of the classroom composite form on the website. Arrange students' feature guides from highest total points to lowest total points before transferring the numbers from the bottom row of each student's feature guide to this classroom composite. To view students' needs and to form groups for instruction, *highlight* students who make *more than one error* on a particular feature.

The Spelling-by-Stage Classroom Organization Chart on the website is another tool to organize word study groups. Write students' names under the stage and then organize word study/reading groups for differentiated instruction choosing activities from the instuctional chapters, Chapters 4 through 8.

PDToolkit

for Words Their Way™ with English Learners

Go to PDToolkit, choose your book, click the Assessment Tools tab, and select Assessment Materials to see the Elementary Spelling Inventory Classroom Composite and the Spelling-by-Stage Classroom Organization Chart.

Sentences to Use with Elementary Spelling Inventory

1.	bed	I hopped out of bed this morning. *bed*
2.	ship	The ship sailed around the island. *ship*
3.	when	When will you come back? *when*
4.	lump	He had a lump on his head after he fell. *lump*
5.	float	I can float on the water with my new raft. *float*
6.	train	I rode the train to the next town. *train*
7.	place	I found a new place to put my books. *place*
8.	drive	I learned to drive a car. *drive*
9.	bright	The light is very bright. *bright*
10.	shopping	She went shopping at the mall. *shopping*
11.	spoil	The food will spoil if it is not kept cool. *spoil*
12.	serving	The restaurant is serving dinner tonight. *serving*
13.	chewed	The dog chewed the bone until it was gone. *chewed*
14.	carries	She carries apples in her basket. *carries*
15.	marched	We marched in the parade. *marched*
16.	shower	The shower in the bathroom was very hot. *shower*
17.	bottle	The father fed his baby with a bottle. *bottle*
18.	favor	He did his brother a favor by taking out the trash. *favor*
19.	ripen	The fruit will ripen over the next few days. *ripen*
20.	cellar	I went down to the cellar for the can of paint. *cellar*
21.	pleasure	It was a pleasure to listen to the choir sing. *pleasure*
22.	fortunate	It was fortunate that the driver had snow tires during the snowstorm. *fortunate*
23.	confident	I am confident that we can win the game. *confident*
24.	civilize	They had the idea that they could civilize the forest. *civilize*
25.	opposition	The coach said the opposition would give us a tough game. *opposition*

Feature Guide for Elementary Spelling Inventory

Student's Name _____ Teacher _____ Grade _____ Date _____

Words Spelled Correctly: _____ / 25   Feature Points: _____ / 62   Total: _____ / 87   Spelling Stage: _____

| SPELLING STAGES → | EMERGENT LATE | LETTER NAME—ALPHABETIC | | | | WITHIN WORD PATTERN | | | SYLLABLES AND AFFIXES | | | DERIVATIONAL RELATIONS | | | |
| | | EARLY | MIDDLE | MIDDLE | LATE | EARLY | MIDDLE | LATE | EARLY | MIDDLE | EARLY | MIDDLE | | |
Features →	Consonants Initial	Consonants Final	Short Vowels	Digraphs	Blends	Long Vowels	Other Vowels	Inflected Endings	Syllable Junctures	Unaccented Final Syllables	Harder Suffixes	Bases or Roots	Feature Points	Words Spelled Correctly
1. bed	b	d	e											
2. ship		p		sh										
3. when			e	wh										
4. lump	l		u		mp									
5. float		t			fl	oa								
6. train		n			tr	ai								
7. place					pl	a-e								
8. drive		v			dr	i-e								
9. bright					br	igh								
10. shopping			o	sh				pping						
11. spoil					sp		oi							
12. serving							er	ving						
13. chewed				ch			ew	ed						
14. carries							ar	ies	rr					
15. marched				ch			ar	ed						
16. shower				sh			ow			er				
17. bottle									tt	le				
18. favor									v	or				
19. ripen									p	en				
20. cellar									ll	ar				
21. pleasure											ure	pleas		
22. fortunate							or				ate	fortun		
23. confident											ent	confid		
24. civilize											ize	civil		
25. opposition											tion	pos		
Totals	/ 7		/ 5	/ 6	/ 7	/ 5	/ 7	/ 5	/ 5	/ 5	/ 5	/ 5	/ 62	/ 25

Picture Spelling Inventory

This 20-word picture spelling inventory supports English learners with visual cues to help them know what word to spell (Bear, 1995). This inventory begins with emergent spelling and has spelling words that probe for students' knowledge from emergent through the middle of the syllables and affixes stage of spelling.

Directions. Say the word and show the picture. Say the word again. "I am going to show you a picture. Please spell the word. Spell the word the best you can. Say the word after me and write down all the sounds that you hear." Use characterization that might be useful, such as driving a tractor, blowing a whistle.

PICTURE SPELLING INVENTORY

Feature Guide for Picture Spelling Inventory

Directions: Check the features that are present in each student's spelling. In the bottom row, total the features spelled correctly. Note the first column of features in which the student missed more than one feature. Check the spelling stage that summarizes the student's development. Begin instruction on the features needed.

Student's Name _____   Teacher _____   Grade _____   Date _____

SPELLING STAGES →

Features →	Beginning Consonants (EMERGENT LATE)	Final Consonants (EARLY)	Short Vowels (MIDDLE)	Consonant Digraphs & Trigraphs (LATE)	Consonant Blends (EARLY)	Long Vowel Patterns	Other Vowel Patterns (MIDDLE)	Inflected Endings, Unaccented Syllables, & Consonant Doubling (LATE)	Feature Points (EARLY)	Words Spelled Correctly (MIDDLE)
1. bed	b	d	e							
2. lip	l	p	i							
3. drum		m	u		dr					
4. belt			e		-lt					
5. ring	r		i		-ng					
6. cake	c	k				a-e				
7. witch	w			-tch						
8. thumb			u	th	-mb					
9. wheel		l		wh		ee				
10. train		n			tr	ai				
11. knife		f			kn	i-e				
12. chair				ch		ai				
13. whale				wh		a-e				
14. heart	h	t					ear			
15. cheese		s				ee-e				
16. jacket	j		a		-ck			et		
17. tractor			a		-ct			or		
18. window					-nd		ow			
19. zipper	z							er pp		
20. whistle				wh				le		
Circle cells with more than 1 error.	(8)	(9)	(8)	(6)	(9)	(7)	(2)	(5)	(54)	(20)

SPELLING STAGES:

☐ EARLY ☐ MIDDLE
☐ LATE ☐ EMERGENT
☐ LETTER NAME–ALPHABETIC
☐ WITHIN-WORD PATTERN
☐ SYLLABLES & AFFIXES

Words Spelled Correctly: /20
Feature Points: /54
Total: /74

Sound Boards and Alphabets

Sound Board for Beginning Consonants and Digraphs

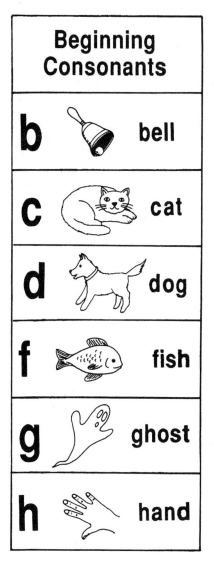

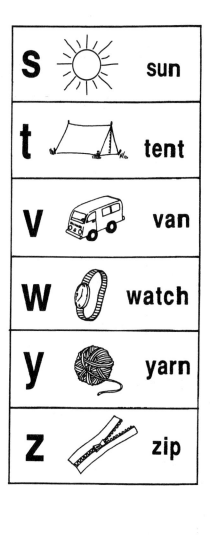

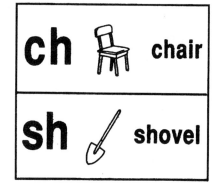

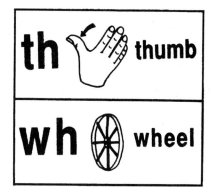

Sound Board for Beginning Blends

Beginning Blends	br broom	sc scooter
bl block	cr crab	sk skate
cl cloud	dr drum	sm smile
fl flag	fr frog	sn snail
gl glasses	gr grapes	sp spider
sl slide	pr present	st star
pl 2+1=3 plus	tr tree	sw swing
tw twins	qu quilt	

Sound Board for Long and Short Vowels

Short Vowels	Long Vowels	
a cat	**a** cake	**a** tray
		a rain
e bed	**e** feet	**e** leaf
i pig	**i** kite	**i** light
o sock	**o** bone	**o** soap
u cup	**u** tube	

Bilingual Picture Alphabet—English/Spanish

Bilingual Picture Alphabet English/Spanish	**Aa** airplane *avión*	**Bb** boat *barco*
Cc car *coche*	**Dd** dice *dados*	**Ee** elephant *elefante*
Ff fire *fuego*	**Gg** goose *ganso*	**Hh** hay *heno*
Ii igloo *iglú*	**Jj** jug *jarro*	**Kk** kayak *kayac*
Ll lion *león*	**Mm** map *mapa*	**Nn** nest *nido*
Oo oval *óvalo*	**Pp** pig *puerco*	**Qq** quiet *quieto*
Rr rat *ratón*	**Ss** sun *sol*	**Tt** turtle *tortuga*
Uu uniform *uniforme*	**Vv** violin *violín*	**Ww** walkie-talkie *walki-talki*
Xx xylophone *xilófono*	**Yy** yo-yo *yo-yo*	**Zz** zoo *zoo*

Sample Alphabets with Various Scripts

English Alphabet

Aa Bb Cc Dd Ee
Ff Gg Hh Ii Jj Kk
Ll Mm Nn Oo Pp
Qq Rr Ss Tt Uu
Vv Ww Xx Yy Zz

Thai Consonants

ก ข ฃ ค ฅ ฆ ง
จ ฉ ช ซ ฌ ญ ฎ
ฏ ฐ ฑ ฒ ณ ด ต
ถ ท ธ น บ ป ผ
ฝ พ ฟ ภ ม ย ร
ล ว ศ ษ ส ห ฬ อ ฮ

Russian Alphabet

Аа Бб Вв Гг Дд Ее Ёё
Жж Зз Ии Йй Кк Лл Мм
Нн Оо Пп Рр Сс Тт Уу
Фф Хх Цц Чч Шш Щщ
Ъъ ы ь Ээ Юю Яя

Arabic Alphabet

أ 'Alif	ب Baa'	ت Taa'	ث Thaa'
ج Jiim	ح H'aa'	خ Xaa'	د Daal
ذ Thaal	ر Raa'	ز Zaay	س Siin
ش Shiin	ص Saad	ض Daad	ط Taa'
ظ Th:aa'	ع 'Ayn	غ Ghayn	ف Faa'
ق Qaaf	ك Kaaf	ل Laam	م Miim
ن Nuun	ه Haa'	و Waaw	ي Yau'

Pictures for Sorts and Games

The pictures in this section of the Appendix can be copied on cardstock or glued to cardstock to create a set of pictures for sorting or vocabulary activities. The pictures are organized alphabetically and have been referred to throughout the book chapters. The pictures may be used to create additional sorts, as materials in various games, and for activities appropriate to the teacher's individual needs. A word list of the pictures is included in the Word Lists of Pictures in Book with Translations beginning on p. 309 of this Appendix. This also includes translations of the picture words into Spanish, Arabic, Chinese, Korean, Hmong, and Vietnamese.

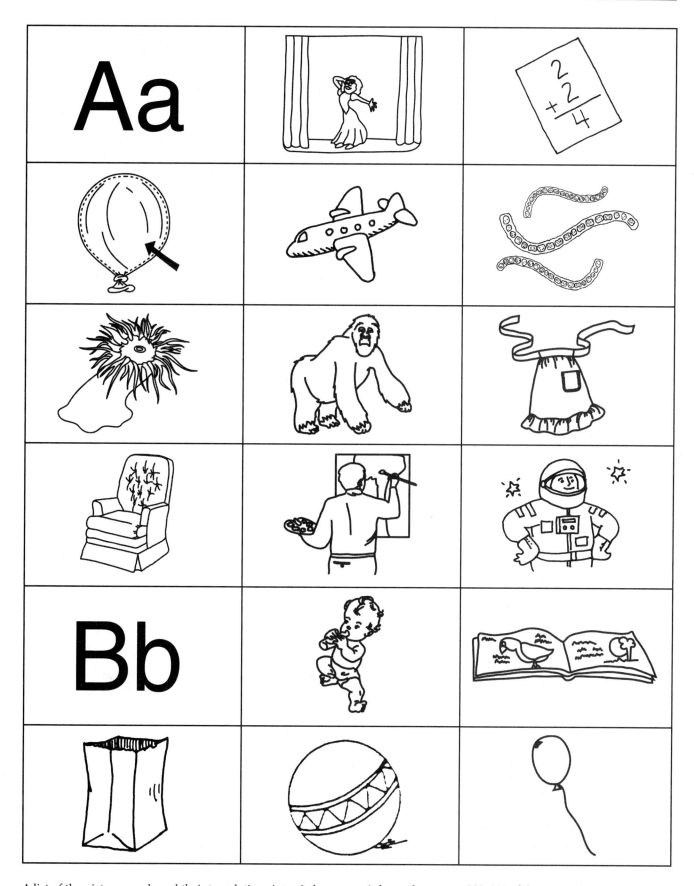

A list of the picture words and their translations into six languages is located on pages 309–330 of the Appendix.

A list of the picture words and their translations into six languages is located on pages 309–330 of the Appendix.

A list of the picture words and their translations into six languages is located on pages 309–330 of the Appendix.

A list of the picture words and their translations into six languages is located on pages 309–330 of the Appendix.

A list of the picture words and their translations into six languages is located on pages 309–330 of the Appendix.

A list of the picture words and their translations into six languages is located on pages 309–330 of the Appendix.

A list of the picture words and their translations into six languages is located on pages 309–330 of the Appendix.

A list of the picture words and their translations into six languages is located on pages 309–330 of the Appendix.

A list of the picture words and their translations into six languages is located on pages 309–330 of the Appendix.

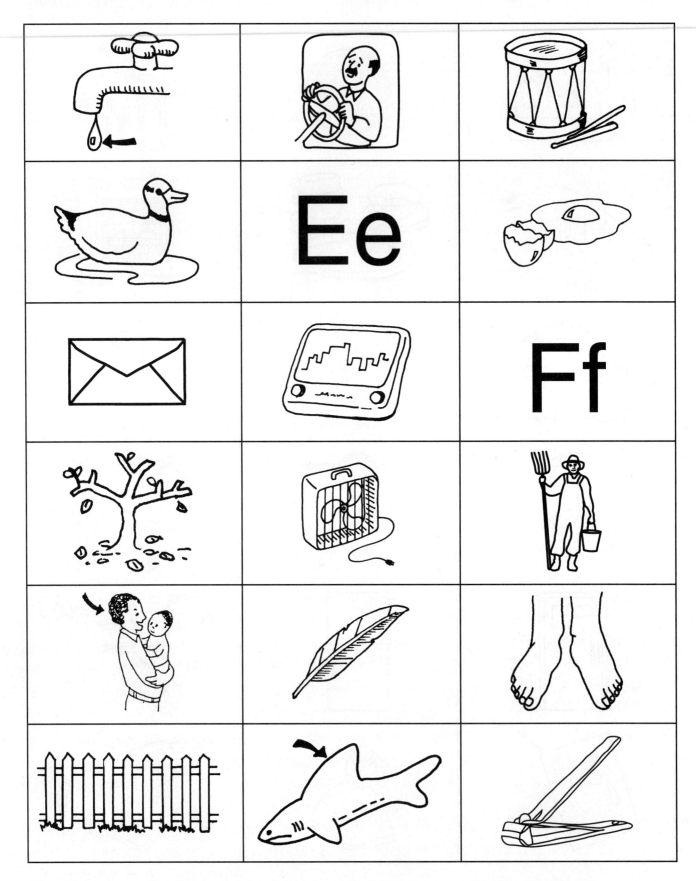

A list of the picture words and their translations into six languages is located on pages 309–330 of the Appendix.

A list of the picture words and their translations into six languages is located on pages 309–330 of the Appendix.

Gg

A list of the picture words and their translations into six languages is located on pages 309–330 of the Appendix.

A list of the picture words and their translations into six languages is located on pages 309–330 of the Appendix.

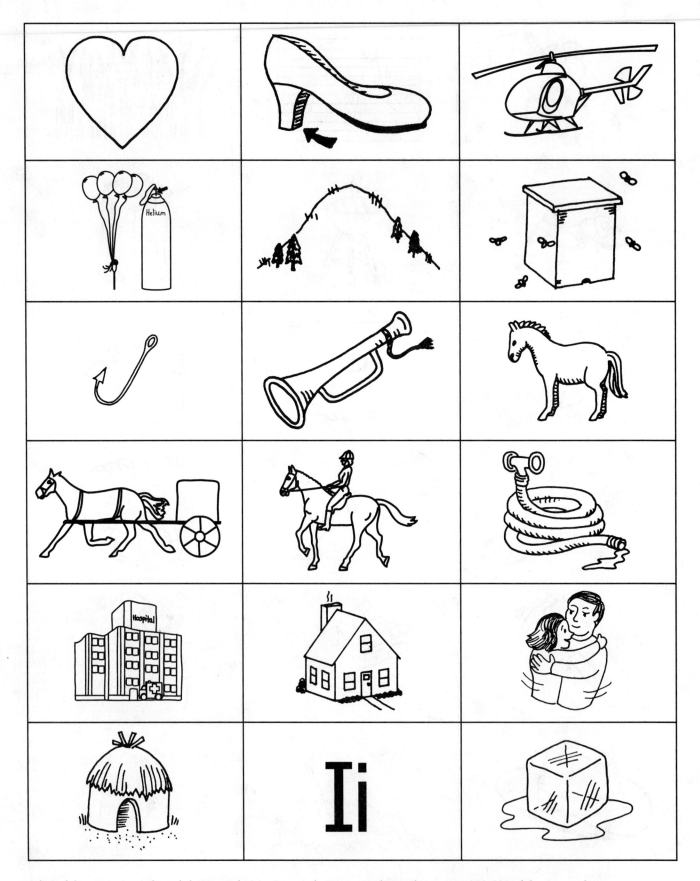

A list of the picture words and their translations into six languages is located on pages 309–330 of the Appendix.

A list of the picture words and their translations into six languages is located on pages 309–330 of the Appendix.

A list of the picture words and their translations into six languages is located on pages 309–330 of the Appendix.

A list of the picture words and their translations into six languages is located on pages 309–330 of the Appendix.

A list of the picture words and their translations into six languages is located on pages 309–330 of the Appendix.

A list of the picture words and their translations into six languages is located on pages 309–330 of the Appendix.

A list of the picture words and their translations into six languages is located on pages 309–330 of the Appendix.

A list of the picture words and their translations into six languages is located on pages 309–330 of the Appendix.

A list of the picture words and their translations into six languages is located on pages 309–330 of the Appendix.

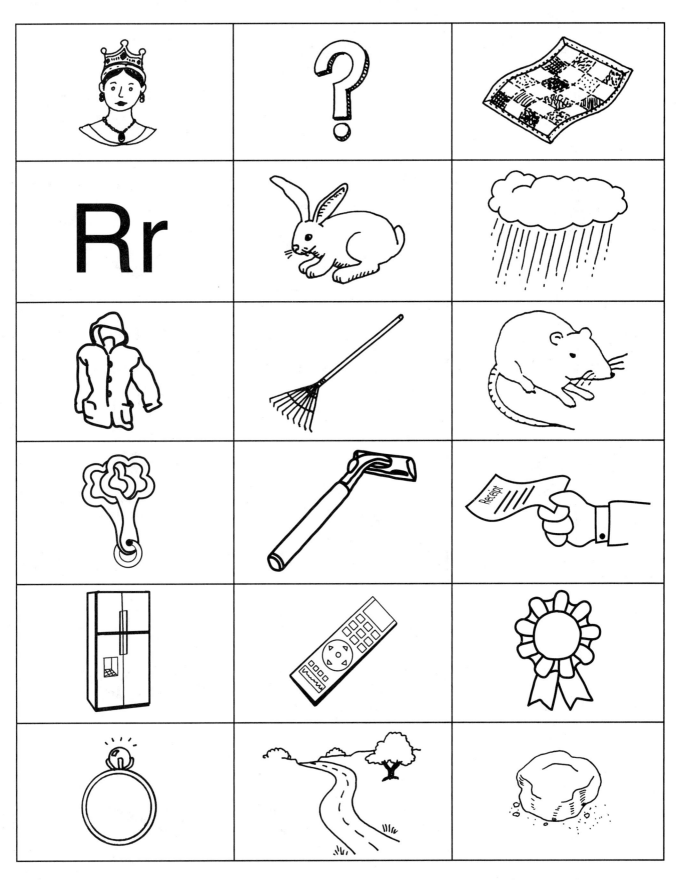

A list of the picture words and their translations into six languages is located on pages 309–330 of the Appendix.

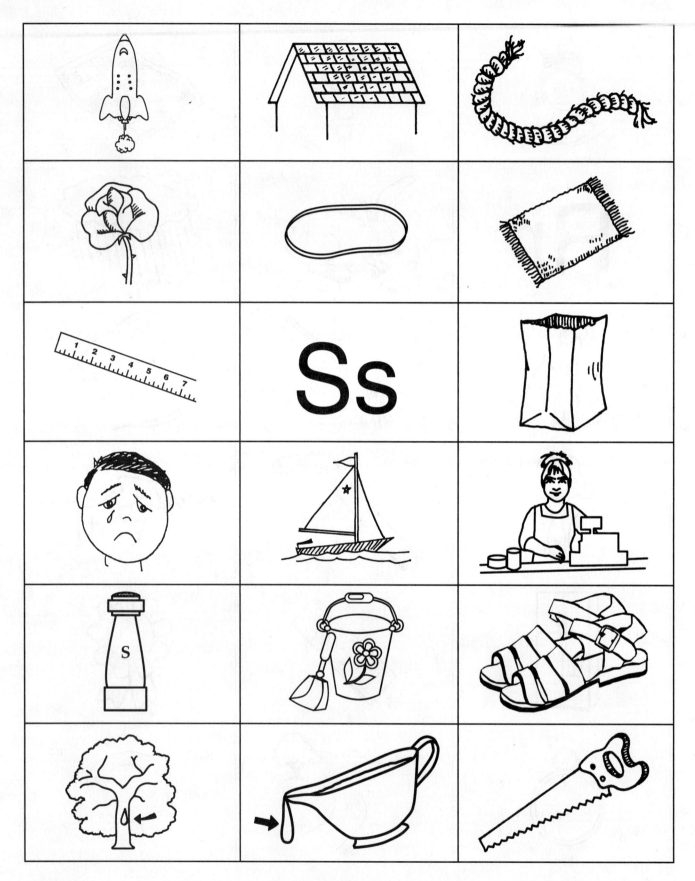

A list of the picture words and their translations into six languages is located on pages 309–330 of the Appendix.

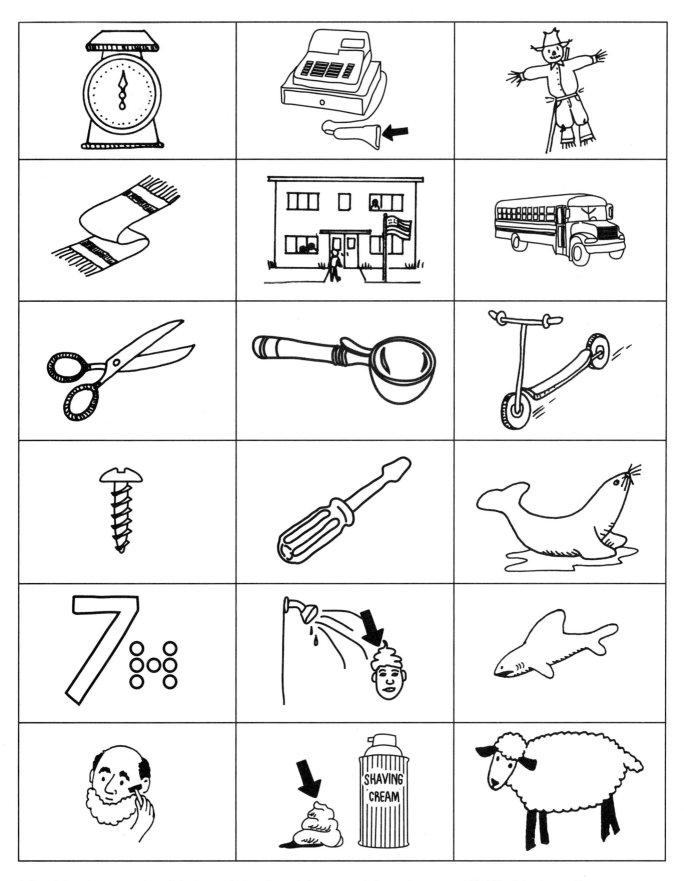

A list of the picture words and their translations into six languages is located on pages 309–330 of the Appendix.

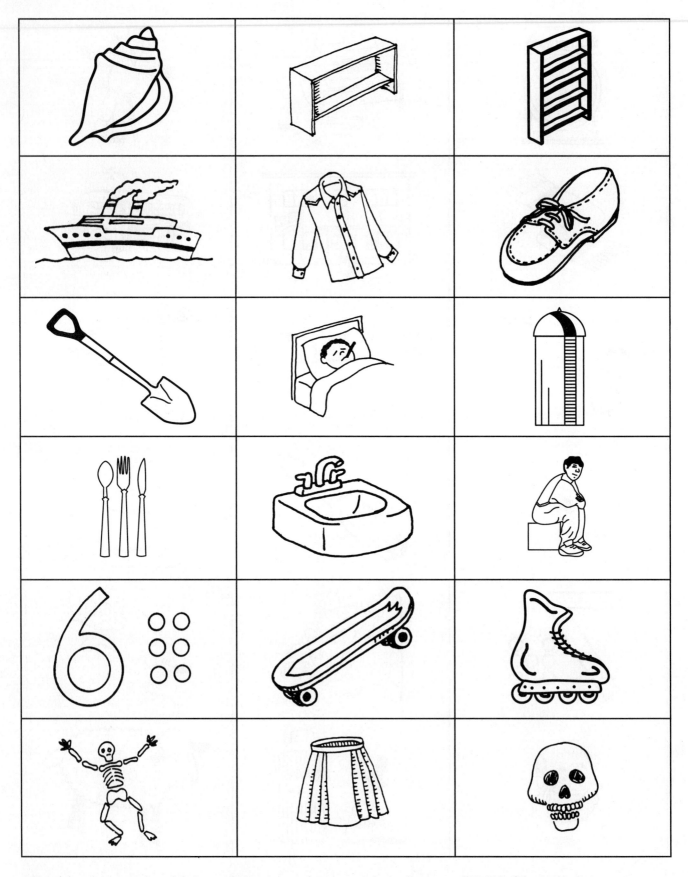

A list of the picture words and their translations into six languages is located on pages 309–330 of the Appendix.

A list of the picture words and their translations into six languages is located on pages 309–330 of the Appendix.

A list of the picture words and their translations into six languages is located on pages 309–330 of the Appendix.

A list of the picture words and their translations into six languages is located on pages 309–330 of the Appendix.

A list of the picture words and their translations into six languages is located on **pages 309–330** of the Appendix.

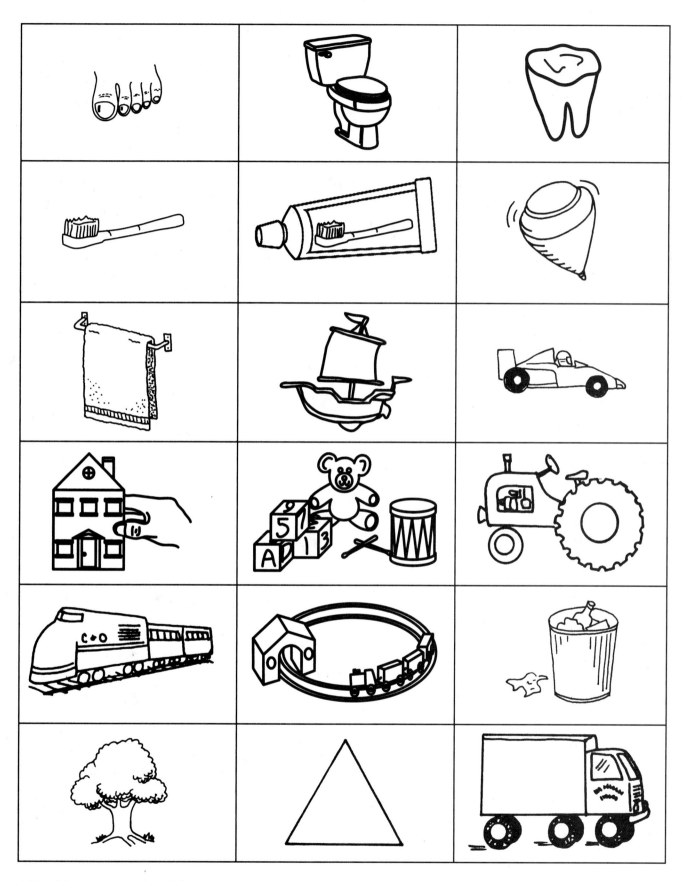

A list of the picture words and their translations into six languages is located on pages 309–330 of the Appendix.

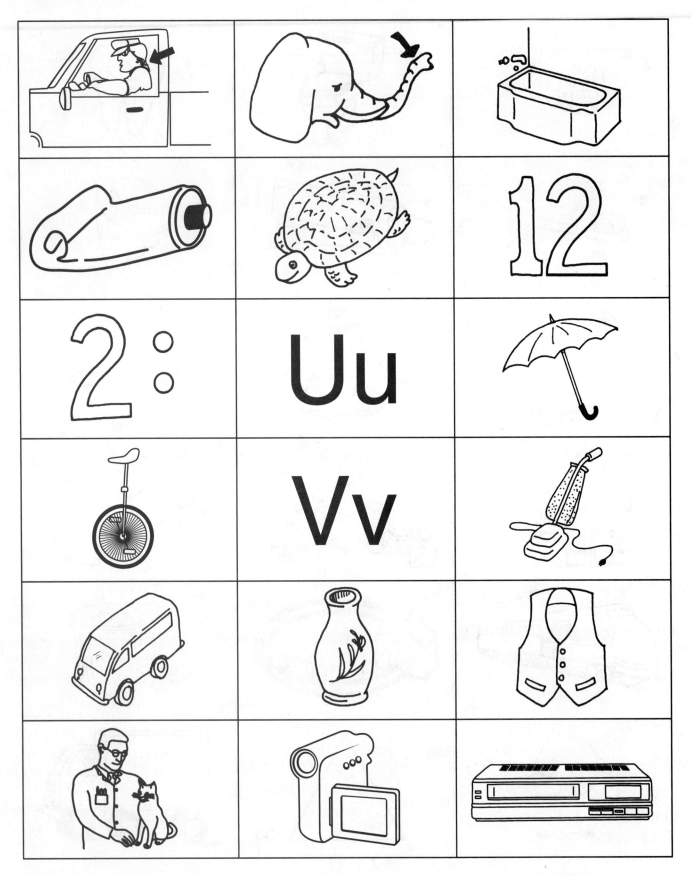

A list of the picture words and their translations into six languages is located on pages 309–330 of the Appendix.

A list of the picture words and their translations into six languages is located on pages 309–330 of the Appendix.

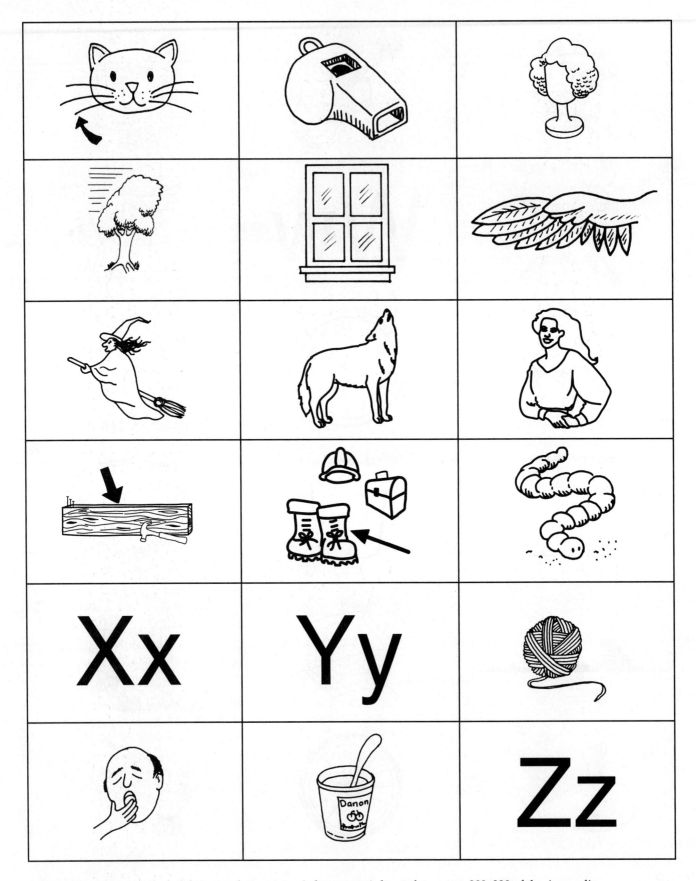

A list of the picture words and their translations into six languages is located on pages 309–330 of the Appendix.

A list of the picture words and their translations into six languages is located on pages 309–330 of the Appendix.

Sample Picture and Word Sorts

Sample Sort 1: Living Things Picture Sort

Sample Sort 2: Beginning Consonant Picture Sorts

Sample Sort 3: Introduction to Beginning Consonant Digraphs and Blends /c/, /h/, /ch/

Sample Sort 4: Final Consonant Picture Sorts
/-b/, /-m/, /-s/

-b bib	-m gum	-s bus

Sample Sort 5: Picture Sorts to Introduce Vowel Sounds /ă/, /ā/

Sample Sort 6: Same Vowel Family Picture and Word
Sorts *-at, -ad*

-at cat	-ad dad	sat
rat		
	fat	
had	hat	glad
		mad
mat	sad	pat

Sample Sort 7: Mixed Short Vowel Word Family Sorts
-ap, -ip, -op

-ap cap	-ip lip	-op top
pop	dip	rap
nap	chop	rip
mop	tap	tip
map	stop	hop
sip	zap	sap
zip	snip	hip
chip	ship	trip

Sample Sort 8: Focus on Word Sorts to Contrast Final Consonants /-g/, /-t/, /-d/

-g hug	-t net	-d bed
chat	pig	bud
nod	wig	jet
dog	sad	had
mat	bug	leg
hat	sit	pot
red	dig	log
big	mud	bat

Sample Sort 9: Beginning Consonant Digraph and Blend
Word Sorts c, h, ch

Cc cat	Hh hand	ch chin
had	cut	cup
chap	hen	chat
can	hug	cap
chest	champ	ham
hot	chip	cot
him	cub	chop
hop	hit	chick

Sample Sort 10: Community Concept Sort

Urban	Rural	Waterway
	harbor	farm
businesses	subway	cattle
port		dock
	factory	
ranch	taxi	horses
harvest		drawbridge
	skyscraper	shipping yard

Sample Sort 11: Cognate Sort

bank	music	park
train	computer	telephone
parc	telefon	muziek
tren	banco	komputer
banque	musik	treno
computator	teléfono	musique
trem	parque	música
computador	musikk	

Word Lists of Pictures in Book with Translations

ENGLISH	SPANISH	ARABIC	CHINESE	HMONG	KOREAN	VIETNAMESE
actor	actor	ممثل	演员	nkauj seev; tus poj niam ua yeeb yam	배우	nam diễn viên
add	suma	يضيف	加	ntxiv; leb ntxiv	더하기	cộng
air	aire	هواء	空氣	cua	공기	Không khí
airplane	avión	طائرة	飞机	dav hlau	비행기	máy bay
algae	algas	طحالب	海藻	ntxhuab dej	조류	Tảo
anemone	anémona	الشقائق النعمان	海葵	ib hom nroj tsuag uas tawg paj tshiab heev	아네모네	Cỏ ngỗng
ape	simio	قرد	类人猿	liab; ib hom liab loj loj	원숭이	khỉ không đuôi
apron	delantal	مريلة	围裙	ntaub npua ua hauj lwm	앞치마	tạp dề
armchair	sillón	كرسي ذات يدين	扶手椅	lub rooj zaum uas muaj chaw khuam tes	손을 놓을 수 있는 의자	ghế bành
artist	artista	فنان	画家	tus neeg mus saum hli	예술가	nghệ sỹ
astronaut	astronauta	رجل فضاء	宇航员	mos ab; me nyuam mos; mos liab	우주비 행사	phi hành gia
baby	bebé	طفل	婴儿	phau ntawv me nyuam mos	아기	em bé
baby book	libro infantil	كتاب الطفل	童书	hnab	육아일기	sách dành cho trẻ em
bag	bolsa	كيس	纸袋	lub pob	봉지	túi
ball	pelota	كرة	球	lub zais	볼	quả banh
balloon	globo	بالون	气球	ntaub nplaum lo qhov txhab	풍선	bong bóng
Band-Aid	tirita	شريط طبي لاصق للجرح	创可贴	txhab nyiaj; txhab cia nyiaj; tsev cia nyiaj	반창고	băng keo cá nhân
bank	banco	بنك	堤岸	tus neeg ua hauj lwm hauv tsev cia nyiaj	둑	Bờ
banker	banquero	مصرفي	银行家	nkoj thauj khoom	은행원	nhân viên ngân hàng
barge	barcaza	بارجة	駁船	tsev rau tsiaj los yog rau khoom tom teb	바지	Sà lan
barn	granero	زريبة	谷仓	lub pob basketball	헛간	kho thóc
basketball	baloncesto	كرة سلة	篮球	puav	농구공	bóng rổ
bat	murciélago	خفاش	蝙蝠	da dej	박쥐	con dơi
bath	baño	حمام	洗澡	ris tsho da dej	목욕	tắm
bathing suit	traje de baño	بنلة سباحة	游泳衣	hav xuab zeb ntawm ntug dej	수영복	đồ tắm
beach	playa	شاطئ	海滩		해변	bãi biển

ENGLISH	SPANISH	ARABIC	CHINESE	HMONG	KOREAN	VIETNAMESE
beach umbrella	sombrilla	مظلة شاطئ	海滩伞	kaus tiv tshav tom ntug dej	비치 파라솔	dù che ở bãi biển
bead	cuenta	خرز	珠子	hlaws	구슬	hạt (của chuỗi hạt)
beak	pico	منقار	鸟的嘴巴，鸟喙	kaus ncauj noog	부리	mỏ (chim)
bed	cama	سرير	床	txaj	침대	giường
bee	abeja	نحلة	蜜蜂	muv; ntab	벌	con ong
bell	campana	جرس	铃铛	tswb	종	cái chuông
belt	cinturón	حزام	腰带	siv tawv	벨트	dây nịt
bib	babero	مريلة الطفل	围嘴	ntaub thaiv xub ntiag	(아기)턱받이	yếm (của trẻ con)
bike	bicicleta	دراجة هوائية	自行车	tsheb kauj vab	자전거	xe đạp
bird	pájaro	طير	鸟	noog	새	con chim
blade	filo	شفرة	刀刃	hniav chais	칼날	lưỡi (dao, kiếm)
blanket	manta	بطانية	毯子	daim pam	이불	mền
blindfold	venda	معصوب العينين	蒙眼的绷带	ntaub npog qhov muag	눈가리개	dải băng bịt mắt
blink	parpadear	طرفة عين	眨眼看	ntsais muag	눈깜박임	cái chớp mắt
block	bloque	مكعب	积木	thooj ntoo	블록	dãy phố
blouse	blusa	بلوزة	（女式的）短衫	tsho poj niam	블라우스	áo sơ-mi nữ
blue	azul	أزرق	蓝色	xiav	파란색	màu xanh da trời
board game	juego de tablero	لعبة الطاولة	棋盘游戏	daim khoom ua si	보드게임	trò chơi trên bìa cứng
boat	barco	قارب	船	nkoj	배	thuyền
bone	hueso	عظم	骨头	pob txha	뼈	xương
book	libro	كتاب	书	phau ntawv	책	sách
bookmobile	biblioteca ambulante	المكتبة المتحولة	流动图书馆	tsheb thauj ntawv	이동도서관	xe thư viện lưu động
books on tape	cuentos grabados	كتب مسجلة على اشرطة	有声读物	ntawv hauv yas suab	녹음된 책	sách ghi âm
bookshelves	estantería	رفوف كتب	书架	txee rau ntawv	책장	kệ sách
boulder	canto rodado	صخر	大石头	thooj pob zeb loj loj	큰바위	tảng đá
bowl	bol	طبق	碗	tais	사발	cái chén
bowl of fruit	cuenco de fruta	طبق من الفاكهة	果盘	tais txiv	한 접시의 과일	chén đầy trái cây

ENGLISH	SPANISH	ARABIC	CHINESE	HMONG	KOREAN	VIETNAMESE
box	caja	صُندوق	盒子	thawv	상자	cái hộp
boy	niño	صبي، ولد	男孩	me nyuam tub	소년	bé trai
braid	trenza	ضفيرة	发辫，辫子	qhaib; ntxias	땋은 머리	bím tóc
bread	pan	خبز	面包	ncuav cij; khob cij	빵	bánh mì
break	romper	استراحة	折断	dam; lov	부러뜨리다	làm bể, đổ
brick	ladrillo	قرميد	砖头	pob zeb ci	벽돌	viên gạch
bride	novia	عروس	新娘	nkauj nyab	신부	cô dâu
bridge	puente	جسر	桥	choj	다리	cái cầu
broom	escoba	مكنسة	扫帚	khaub rhuab	빗자루	cây chổi
brush	cepillo	فرشاة	刷子	nplauv	솔	bàn chải
bug	insecto	حشرة	昆虫	kab	벌레	con bọ
bun	bollo	كعكة	小圆面包	lub khob cij	납작하고 단 빵	bánh mì nhỏ
bus	autobús	حافلة	公共汽车	tsheb npav	버스	xe buýt
bus driver	conductor de autobús	سائق حافلة	公车司机	neeg tsav tsheb npav	버스기사	tài xế xe buýt
cab	taxi	سيارة أجرة	出租车	tsheb ntiav	택시	xe tắc-xi
cage	jaula	قفص	笼子	pob tawb	새장	cái chuồng
cake	pastel	قالب حلوى	蛋糕	ncuav qab zib	케익	bánh ngọt
calendar	calendario	روزنامة	日历	ntawv qhia hnub hli	달력	lịch
camera	cámara	آلة تصوير	照相机	koob yees duab	카메라	máy chụp hình
can	lata	علبة	罐头	kaus poom	깡통	lon đồ hộp
candle	vela	شمعة	蜡烛	tswm ciab	초	đèn cầy
cane	bastón	عصا خيزران	拐杖	pas nrig	지팡이	cây gậy
cap	gorra	قبعة قُطنية	帽子	kaus mom	모자	nón lưỡi trai
cape	capa	عباءة	披肩	ntaub vas nraub qaum	망토	áo choàng không tay
car	coche	سيارة	汽车	tsheb	차	xe hơi
card	carta	بطاقة	纸牌	phaib	카드	cái thẻ
cargo carrier (ship)	buque de carga	حاملة البضائع	貨船	nkoj thauj khoom	화물선	Tàu chở hàng

ENGLISH	SPANISH	ARABIC	CHINESE	HMONG	KOREAN	VIETNAMESE
carrot	zanahoria	جزر	胡萝卜	zaub ntug hauv paus daj	당근	cà-rốt
cast (for broken bone)	escayola	جبس	（骨折后敷上的）石膏模	cam	기브스	băng bột (khi gãy xương)
cat	gato	قطة	猫	miv	고양이	con mèo
cave	cueva	كهف	山洞	qhov tsua	동굴	hang động
chain	cadena	سلسلة	链子	saw hlau	쇠사슬	dây xích
chair	silla	كرسي	椅子	rooj zaum	의자	cái ghế
check	marca	علامة صح	证明无误，核对无误	kos; cim	검사표시	séc
checkbook	talonario	دفتر صكوك	支票簿	phau tshev	수표첩	sổ séc
checkers	damas	رقعة الشطرنج-حجر الداما	西洋跳棋；象棋	daim das	서양장기	cờ đam
cheese	queso	جبنة	奶酪	roj mis; tshij	치즈	phô-mát
cherries	cerezas	كرز	櫻桃	txiv cherries	체리	Anh đào
chess	ajedrez	شطرنج	国际象棋	chess	체스	chơi cờ
chick	pollito	صوص	小鸡	me nyuam qaib	병아리	gà con
chimney	chimenea	مدخنة	烟道；烟囱	raj pa taws	굴뚝	ống khói
chin	barbilla	ذقن	下巴	puab tsaig	턱	cái cằm
chop	cortar	يقطع	砍劈	txiav	적다	miếng thịt sườn
clam	almeja	بطلينوس	蛤	pias deg	대합조개	con trai sò
clap	aplaudir	يصفق	拍手	npuaj teg	손뼉	tiếng vỗ tay
claw	garra	مخلب	爪，脚爪	rau taw	(동물) 발톱	móng vuốt
cliff	risco	هضبة	悬崖，哨壁	ntsa tsua; pob tsag	절벽	vách đá
climb	escalar	يتسلق	攀登	nce	오르다	sự leo trèo
clip	sujetapapeles	مشبك اوراق	回形针	tus cuam ntawv	클립	cái ghim/kẹp
clock	reloj	ساعة حائط	时钟	lub teev; moo	시계	đồng hồ treo tường
closet	ropero	خزانة	衣橱	chav rau khaub ncaws	옷장	buồng/tủ nhỏ
clothes	ropa	ملابس	衣服	khaub ncaws	옷	quần áo
clothes dryer	secadora de ropa	نشافة ثياب	烘干机	tshuab ziab khaub ncaws	건조기	máy sấy quần áo
clouds	nubes	غيوم	云	huab	구름	(những) đám mây
clown	payaso	مُهرِّج	小丑	tus neeg tas lauv	광대	chú hề

ENGLISH	SPANISH	ARABIC	CHINESE	HMONG	KOREAN	VIETNAMESE
coat	abrigo	معطف	外套	tsho tiv no	코트	áo khoác
comb	peine	مشط	梳子	zuag	빗	cây lược
comic book	libro de cómics	كتاب كوميدي	幽默连环画书	phau ntawv tas lauv	만화 책	sách truyện tranh
computer	ordenador	حاسوب	计算机, 电脑	koos pis tawj	컴퓨터	máy vi tính
cone	cucurucho	مخروط	锥面；锥体	khob zuag hau	(아이)스크림) 콘	bánh hình nón để chứa kem
construction worker	trabajador de construcción	عامل بناء	建筑工	neeg ua vaj ua tsev	공사장 인부	công nhân xây dựng
cook	cocinero	طباخ	厨子	ua noj	요리사	đầu bếp
corn	maíz	ذرة	玉米	pob kws	옥수수	bắp
cotton ball	bola de algodón	كرة قطن	棉球	paj rwb	솜뭉치	bông gòn y tế
couch	sofá	أريكة	沙发	rooj xas loos	소파	trường kỳ
cow	vaca	بقرة	奶牛	nyuj	소	con bò
coyote	coyote	ذئب	叢林狼	hma	코요테	Sói hoang
crab	cangrejo	سلطعون	蟹	roob ris	게	con cua
crackers	galletas saladas	بسكويت رقيق	薄脆饼干	ncuav kuab puab	크래커	bánh quy giòn
crane (for construction)	grúa	رافعة	起重机	tus nqa khoom	크레인, 기중기	cần trục
crayons	lápices de colores	أقلام تلوين	蜡笔	mem kob	크레용	viết chì màu
crib	cuna	مهد	有栏的小卧床	txaj me nyuam	유아침대	giường cũi
crown	corona	تاج	王冠	kaus mom huab tais; kaus mom vaj ntxwv	왕관	vương miện
crustacean	crustáceo	القشريات	甲殼綱動物	tsiaj muaj khaum hauv dej	갑각류	Loài giáp xác
cry	llorar	يبكي	哭	quaj	울다	tiếng khóc
cub	cachorro	ديسم (صغير السبع)	幼兽	me nyuam dais	동물의 새끼	con thú con
cube	cubo	مكعب	立方体：立方形	lub duab 6 sab xwm fab xwm meem	정육면체	nước đá cục
cup	taza	كوب	杯子	khob	컵	cái tách
cupboard	armario	خزانة	碗橱	txee	찬장	tủ búp phê
custodian	custodio	وصي	监护人	neeg tu tsev	관리인	người chăm sóc
cut	cortar	يقطع	剪	txiav	자르다	vết cắt
dam	dique	سد	障碍	ntswg dej; ntswg thaiv dej	댐	đập (ngăn nước)

ENGLISH	SPANISH	ARABIC	CHINESE	HMONG	KOREAN	VIETNAMESE
date	fecha	تاريخ	日期	hnub tim	날짜	ngày
deer	venado	غزال	鹿	mos lwj	사슴	con hươu/nai
desert	desierto	صحراء	沙漠	tiaj suab puam	사막	Sa mạc
desk	escritorio	مكتب	桌子	rooj sau ntawv	책상	bàn viết
dice	dados	حجر زهر	掷骰子游戏	mom khauv lauv	주사위	hột xí ngầu
digital alarm clock	despertador digital	ساعة منبه رقمية	数码闹钟	teev tawm zauv	전자자명시계	đồng hồ báo thức kỹ thuật số
dime	moneda de diez centavos	عشر سنتات	一角硬币	nyiaj npib 10 xees	10센트짜리 동전	đồng10 xu (Mỹ)
dining room chair	silla de comedor	كرسي لغرفة الطعام	餐椅	rooj zaum noj mov	식탁의자	ghế của phòng ăn
dinosaur	dinosaurio	ديناصور	恐龙	dinosaur	공룡	khủng long
dishes	vajilla	صحون	餐具	twj tais	접시	chén bát
dishwasher	lavavajillas	جلاية	洗碗机	tshuab ntxuav twj tais	설거이기계	máy rửa chén
dive	saltar de cabeza, zambullirse	يغطس	跳水	dhia dej	다이빙하다	lặn
doctor	doctor	طبيب	医生，大夫	kws kho mob	의사	bác sĩ
doctor's mask	mascarilla	قناع طبيب	医用口罩	kws kho mob daim npog qhov ncauj qhov ntswg	의사용 마스크	khẩu trang dành cho bác sĩ
dog	perro	كلب	狗	aub; dev	개	con chó
doll	muñeca	لعبة	娃娃，玩偶	me nyuam roj hmab	인형	búp bê
donkey	burro	حمار	驴子	zag	나귀	con lừa
door	puerta	باب	门	qhov rooj	문	cái cửa
doorknob	pomo	مسكة باب	球形的门把手	pob qhov rooj	문고리, 문손잡이	tay nắm cửa
dragon	dragón	تنين	龙	zaj	용	con rồng
drawing paper	papel de dibujo	ورقة رسم	画纸，图纸	ntawv kos duab	도화지	giấy vẽ
dress	vestido	فستان	连衣裙	tiab	원피스	áo đầm
drill	taladradora	مثقب كهربائي	钻孔机，钻子	tus tshau qhov	드릴	máy khoan
drip	goteo	يقطر	水滴	nrog	물방울	sự chảy nhỏ giọt
drive	conducir	يقود	驾驶	tsav	운전하기	lái xe
drum	tambor	طبلة	鼓	nruas	북	cái trống

ENGLISH	SPANISH	ARABIC	CHINESE	HMONG	KOREAN	VIETNAMESE
duck	pato	بطة	鸭子	os	오리	con vịt
egg	huevo	بيضة	卵；蛋	qe	계란	quả trứng
envelope	sobre	ظرف	信封	hnab ntawv	봉투	phong bì
Etch-a-sketch	Etch-a-sketch	حفر رسم	玩具画板	lub nraj txoj lw kab	그림그리는 장난감	đồ chơi dùng để vẽ
fall tree	árbol de otoño	شجرة خريف	秋天的树	ntoo ntuj tsaug	단풍나무	cây mùa thu
fan	ventilador	مروحة	风扇	kiv cua	선풍기	quạt máy
farmer	granjero	مزارع	农民；农场主	neeg ua teb	농부	nông dân
father	padre	اب	父亲	txiv	아버지	cha
feather	pluma	ريشة	羽毛	plaub noog	깃털	lông vũ
feet	pies	اقدام	（复数）脚	ko taw (ob txhais)	두 발	hai bàn chân
fence	cerca	سياج	栅栏	laj kab	울타리	hong rào
fin	aleta	زعنفة	鳍	tis ntses	지느러미	vây cá
fingernail clippers	cortauñas	مقص الظافر	指甲钳	txiab txiav rau tes	손톱깎이	cái bấm móng tay
fire	fuego	نار	火	hluav taws	불	ngọn lửa
firefighter	bombero	مكافح نار	消防员	neeg tua hluav taws	소방원	lính cứu hoả
fish	pez	سمك	鱼	ntses	물고기	con cá
fist	puño	قبضة يد	拳头	nrig	주먹	nắm đấm
five	cinco	خمسة	五	tsib	다섯	số 5
flag	bandera	علم	旗	chij	깃발	lá cờ
flashlight	linterna	المشعل الكهربائي	手电筒	teeb tsom	후레쉬, 회중전등	đèn pin
floss	seda dental	تنظيف الاسنان بالخيط	牙线	xov dig hniav	이빨 손질하는 끈	chỉ nha khoa
flower	flor	زهرة	花	paj	꽃	bông hoa
flute	flauta	مزمار	笛子	raj tshuab	플룻	ống sáo
fly	mosca	ذبابة	苍蝇	ya	파리	con ruồi
food	comida	طعام	食物	khoom noj	음식	thức ăn
foot	pie	قدم	脚	ko taw	발	một bàn chân
four	cuatro	اربعة	四	plaub	넷, 사	số 4
fox	zorro	ثعلب	狐狸	hma	여우	con cáo

ENGLISH	SPANISH	ARABIC	CHINESE	HMONG	KOREAN	VIETNAMESE
freeze	congelar	يُجمّد	结冰，冻结	khov; nkoog	얼다	đóng băng
freezer	congelador	ثلاجة	冰箱	lub tub yees nkoog	냉동고	tủ đá
frog	rana	ضفدعة	青蛙	qav	개구리	con ếch
fruit	fruta	فاكهة	水果	txiv; txiv hmab txiv ntoo	과일	trái cây
fruit tree	árbol frutal	شجرة فاكهة	果树	ntoo txiv	과수	cây ăn trái
galoshes	botas para la lluvia	حذاء فوق الحذاء	橡胶套鞋	khau raj tiv dej	장화	giày cao su
game	juego	لعبة	游戏	khoom ua si	게임	trò chơi
gardener	jardinero	بستاني	园丁，花匠，园艺家	tus neeg cog khoom	정원사	người làm vườn
gas	gasolina	بنزين	汽油	roj tsheb	자동차 연료	xăng
gate	puerta	بوابة	门	rooj vag	대문	cái cổng
girl	niña	بنت صغيرة	女孩	me nyuam ntxhais	소녀	bé gái
glass	vaso	زجاج	玻璃杯	khob iav	유리잔	cái ly
glasses	lentes	نظارات	眼镜	tsom iav	안경	mắt kính
globe	globo	الكرة الأرضية	地球仪	lub ntiaj teb	지구본	quả địa cầu
gloves	guantes	قفازات	手套	hnab looj tes	장갑	găng tay
glue	pegamento	صمغ	胶，胶水	kua nplaum	풀	keo
goat	cabra	ماعز	山羊	tshis	염소	con dê
goggles	gafas	نظارات تحت الماء	护目镜	iav thaiv qhov muag	잠수용 안경	mắt kính bơi
golf	golf	غولف	高尔夫球	nkov	골프	môn đánh golf
goose	ganso	وزة	鹅	os dab ntev	거위	con ngỗng
grapes	uvas	عنب	葡萄	txiv hmab	포도	(những) quả nho
graph	gráfica	رسم بياني	图	duab kab	그래프	biểu đồ
grass	hierba	حشيش، عشب	草	nyom	풀, 잔디	cỏ
grasshopper	saltamontes	جُندب	蝗虫	kooj	메뚜기	châu chấu
grill	parrilla	شواية	烧烤	qhov cub ci nqaij	석쇠	vỉ nướng
groceries	provisiones	خضار	杂货	khoom noj	식료품	tạp hóa
gum	chicle	علكة	口香糖	qhob noom ntsuas	껌	kẹo sinh-gum
gun	pistola	مُسدس	枪	phom	총	súng

ENGLISH	SPANISH	ARABIC	CHINESE	HMONG	KOREAN	VIETNAMESE
hair dryer	secador de pelo	مجفف شعر	干发用的电吹风	lub tshuab plaub hau	헤어드라이어	máy sấy tóc
hairbrush	cepillo	فرشاة شعر	发刷	zuag ntsis plaub hau	머리빗	bàn chải tóc
ham	jamón	لحم خنزير	火腿	nqaij npuas	햄	thịt xông khói
hammer	martillo	مطرقة	锤子	rauj	망치	cây búa
hand	mano	يد	手	tes	손	bàn tay
hard hat	casco de seguridad	خوذة واقية	安全帽	kaus mom tawv	안전모	nón bảo hộ
hat	sombrero	قبعة	帽子	kaus mom	모자	nón
hay	heno	قش	干草	quav nyab	건초	cỏ khô
head	cabeza	رأس	头	taub hau	머리	cái đầu
heart	corazón	قلب	心；心脏	plawv	심장, 가슴	trái tim
heel	tacón	كعب	脚跟	luj khau	구두굽	gót chân
helicopter	helicóptero	طائر مروحية	直升机	dav hlau kiv tshuab	헬리콥터	trực thăng
helium	helio	الهيليوم	氦	ib hom pa	헬륨	Khí heli
hill	colina	تل	小山	pob roob	언덕	ngọn đồi
hive	colmena	قفير خلية نحل	蜂箱，蜂房	tsev muv; zes muv	벌집	tổ ong
hook	anzuelo	خطاف صيد سمك	鱼钩	nqe lauj	갈고리	lưỡi câu
horn	cuerno	بوق	喇叭	kub	호른	cái sừng
horse	caballo	حصان	马	nees	말	con ngựa
horse and cart	caballo y carro	حصان وعربة	马车	nees thiab laub	말이 끄는 마차	xe ngựa
horse with rider	caballo con jinete	حصان مع راكب	有骑手骑在上面的马	nees nrog tus neeg caij nees	말을 타기	ngựa có người cưỡi
hose	manguera	خرطوم ماء	软管，水龙带	hlua dej	호스	vòi tưới
hospital	hospital	مستشفى	医院	tsev kho mob	병원	bệnh viện
house	casa	بيت	房子	tsev	집	căn nhà
hug	abrazo	معانقة	拥抱	puag; khawm	포옹	ôm
hut	cabaña	كوخ	小屋	tsev	오두막	túp lều
ice	hielo	ثلج	冰	dej khov; dej nkoog	얼음	nước đá
iron	plancha	حديد	熨斗	lub luam khaub ncaws	다리미	sắt
irrigation	irrigación	ري	灌溉	ciav dej ywg teb	물을 댐, 관개	thủy lợi

ENGLISH	SPANISH	ARABIC	CHINESE	HMONG	KOREAN	VIETNAMESE
jacket	chaqueta	جاكيت	夹克	tsho hnav tuaj sab nraud	자켓	áo khoác
jackrabbit	conejo del desierto	أرنب الحقل	長耳大野兔	luav loj	산토끼	Thỏ sa mạc
jacks	juego de los cantillos	فينة كهرباء	抓子游戏	ua txwv	잭게임	trò chơi đánh đũa
jar	frasco	جرة	罐，广口瓶	hwj	병	cái hũ
jeep	jeep	سيارة جيب	吉普车	tsheb ntsiv	지프차	xe jeep
jet	avión a reacción	طائرة نفاثة	喷气式飞机，喷气机	dav hlau	제트기	máy bay phản lực
jewel	joya	جوهرة	钻石	ib hom pob zeb muaj nqis	보석	nữ trang
jog	footing	هرول	慢跑	khiav	조그	Chạy chậm
juice	jugo	عصير	果汁	kua txiv	쥬스	nước trái cây
jump	saltar	قفز	跳躍	dhia	점프	Nhảy
kangaroo	canguro	حيوان الكانغارو	袋鼠	ib hom tsiaj nyob rau Auv Tas Lias uas muaj ib lub hnab ntawm plab rau me nyuam nyob	캥거루	chuột túi
ketchup	salsa de tomate	كتشاب	番茄酱	kua txiv lws	케첩	sốt cà chua
key	llave	مفتاح	钥匙	yawm sij	열쇠	chìa khóa
keyboard	teclado	لوحة مفاتيح	键盘	daim ntaus ntawv	키보드	bàn phím
kick	dar una patada	ركل	踢	ncaws	발차기	cú đá
king	rey	ملك	国王	huab tais	왕	vua
kitchen	cocina	مطبخ	厨房	tsev mov	부엌	nhà bếp
kitchen table	mesa de la cocina	طاولة مطبخ	饭桌	rooj noj mov	부엌식탁	bàn làm bếp
kite	cometa	طائرة ورقية	风筝	vauj	연	diều
kitten	gatito	هرة صغيرة	小猫	me nyuam miv	새끼고양이	mèo con
knee	rodilla	ركبة	膝盖	hauv caug	무릎	đầu gối
knife	cuchillo	سكين	小刀	riam	칼	con dao
knot	nudo	عقدة	结	pob caus	매듭	nút thắt
lake	lago	بحيرة	湖	pas dej	호수	cái hồ
lamp	lámpara	مصباح كهربائي	灯	teeb txawb	램프	đèn (để bàn)
laugh	reir	يضحك	笑	luag	웃음(n) (웃다 v)	cười
lava	lava	حمم	熔岩	kua av kub	용암	Dung nhằm

ENGLISH	SPANISH	ARABIC	CHINESE	HMONG	KOREAN	VIETNAMESE
leaf	hoja	ورقة شجر	叶，树叶	nplooj	나뭇잎	chiếc lá
leash	correa	لجام	拴狗的皮带	hlua cab tsiaj	(동물을 매는)끈	dây buộc chó
leaves	hojas	ورق الشجر	树叶	nplooj (ntau daim)	나뭇잎들	những chiếc lá
leg	pierna	ساق	腿	txhais ceg	다리	cái chân
Legos	Legos	ست من قطع بناء لعبة	乐高积木	khoom sib dhos	레고	trò chơi xây dựng (legos)
legs	piernas	ساقان	（复数）腿	txhais ceg (ob txhais)	두 다리	những cái chân
letter	carta	رسالة	信	daim ntawv	편지	lá thư
librarian	bibliotecaria	أمين مكتبة	图书管理员	kws ceev ntawv	도서관 사서	người giữ thư viện
library card	tarjeta de la biblioteca	بطاقة مكتبة	阅览证；借书证	pib qiv ntawv	도서관 카드	thẻ thư viện
lid	tapa	غطاء	盖子	lub hau	뚜껑	cái nắp
light switch	interruptor	مفتاح كهرباء	电灯开关	lub qhib thiab kaw teeb	전등스위치	công tắc đèn
lightbulb	bombilla	لمبة	灯泡	qhov muag teeb	전구	bóng đèn
lily pad	hoja flotante del nénufar	ورقة زنبق	睡莲叶子	nplooj nroj tsuag hav dej; nplooj lily	수련 잎	Lá súng
lined paper	papel de rayas	ورق مخطط	格记录纸	ntawv muaj kab	줄이그어진 종이	giấy có kẻ hàng
lion	león	أسد	狮子	tsov ntxhuav	사자	sư tử
lip	labio	شفة	嘴唇	di ncauj	한쪽입술	môi
lips	labios	شفتان	上下嘴唇，双唇	di ncauj (ob daim)	입술	đôi môi
lizard	lagartija	سحلية	蜥蜴	nab qa	도마뱀	con thằn lằn
lock	candado	قفل	锁	nruas phoo	자물쇠	ổ khóa
log	leño	جذع شجرة	原木	cav	통나무	khúc gỗ
lotion	loción	مستحضر سائل للجسم	洗液，洗剂	tshuaj tawg pleb	로션	thuốc dưỡng da
lunchbox	fiambrera, tartera	صندوق طعام	饭盒	thawv ntim su	도시락통	hộp đựng thức ăn trưa
mad	enfadado	غضب الذروة	狂怒	chim	화남	điên rồ
mail	correo	بريد	信件	ntawv	우편	thư tín
man	hombre	رجل	人；男人	txiv neej	남자	đàn ông
map	mapa	خريطة	地图	ntawv qhia chaw	지도	bản đồ
marble	canica	رخام	弹球	maj npis	구슬	đá hoa

ENGLISH	SPANISH	ARABIC	CHINESE	HMONG	KOREAN	VIETNAMESE
markers	marcadores	أقلام ذات خط عريض	（复数）记号笔	mem kob kua	마커	bút lông viết bằng trắng
mask	máscara	قناع	面具	lub looj ntsej muag	마스크	mặt nạ
mat	esterilla	بساط	垫子	ntaub pua	매트	thảm chùi chân
match	cerilla	عود ثقاب	火柴	ntais ntawv	성냥	hộp quẹt
maze	laberinto	متاهة	迷宫	kev sib chab sib chaws	미로	mê cung
measuring tape	cinta métrica	شريط قياس	卷尺	hlua ntsuas	줄자	thước đo
meat	carne	لحم	肉，肉类	nqaij	고기	thịt
medicine	medicina	دواء	药	tshuaj	약	thuốc
metropolitan	metropolitano	عاصمي	大都会	hauv nroog	도시의	người dân thủ đô
mice	ratones	فئران	老鼠	nas tsuag (ob peb tug los sis coob tshaj ntawd)	생앙쥐들	(những) con chuột
microwave	microondas	ميكروويف	微波炉	lub rhaub khoom noj	전자레인지	lò vi sóng
milk	leche	حليب	牛奶	mis nyuj	우유	sữa
mitten	mitón	قفاز صوفي	连指手套	hnab looj tes	장갑	găng tay hở ngón
mittens	mitones	قفازات صوفية	（复数）连指手套	hnab looj tes (ib khub)	장갑 한 켤레	đôi găng tay hở ngón
model plane	avión miniatura	نموذج طائرة	飞机模型	qauv dav hlau	모형비행기	mô hình máy bay
monkey	mono	قرد	猴	liab	원숭이	Khi
moo	mugido	خوار البقر	牛叫声	mod	음매 (소가 우는소리)	tiếng bò rống
moon	luna	قمر	月亮	hli	달	mặt trăng
mop	fregona	ممسحة	拖把	tus txhuam tsev	자루걸레	giẻ lau
mother	madre	أم	母亲	niam	어머니	mẹ
motorcycle	motocicleta	دراجة نارية	摩托车	maus taus	오토바이	xe gắn máy
mud	lodo	وحل	泥	av nkos	진흙	bùn
mule	mula	بغل	骡	luj txwv	노새	con la
museum	museo	متحف	博物馆	chaw ceev qub khoom	박물관	viện bảo tàng
music	música	موسيقى	音樂	suab paj nruag	음악	Nhạc
nail	clavo	مسمار ظفر	钉子	ntsia hlau	못	cây đinh
nails	clavos	مسامير،أظافر	（复数）钉子	ntsia hlau (ob peb tug los sis ib co)	못들	(những) cây đinh
nap	siesta	قيلولة	瞌睡	tso dab ntub	낮잠	giấc ngủ trưa

ENGLISH	SPANISH	ARABIC	CHINESE	HMONG	KOREAN	VIETNAMESE
neck	cuello	عُنُق	脖子；颈项	caj dab	목	cổ
needle	aguja	إبرة	针	koob	바늘	cây kim
nest	nido	عُش	巢，窝	zes	둥지	tổ
net	red	شبكة	网	hnab vij tsam	그물	lưới
news	noticias	أخبار	新闻，消息	xov xwm	뉴스	tin tức
night	noche	ليل	夜	hmo ntuj	밤	đêm
nine	nueve	تِسعة	九	cuaj	아홉, 구	số 9
nose	nariz	أنف	鼻子	taub ntswg	코	mũi
nurse	enfermera	مُمَرِّضة	护士	neeg tu mob	간호사	y tá
nut	nuez	بُندُق	坚果	txiv ntoo	견과	quả hạch
oak tree	roble	شجرة بلوط	橡树	ntoo qheb	참나무	cây sồi
page	página	صفحة	页	phab; nplooj	한 장 (쪽)	trang giấy
pail	cubo	دلو ساطل	桶	thoob	양동이	cái xô
paint	pintura	دِهان	油漆，颜料	kob	페인트	sơn
paint set	pinturas	ادوات رسم	画具	twj pleev kob	물감세트	bộ dụng cụ sơn
painter	pintor	رسّام	画家	neeg pleev kob	화가	thợ sơn
pan	cazuela	مِقلاة	平底锅	lauj kaub	냄비	cái chảo
pants	pantalones	سِروال	裤子	ris	바지	quần dài
paperclip	sujetapapeles	مشبك ورق	回形针	koob cuam ntawv	클립	kẹp giấy
park	parque	حديقة	公园	tiaj ua si	공원	Công viên
patient	paciente	مَريض	病人	neeg mob	환자	bệnh nhân
peach	melocotón	دُرّاق	桃子	txiv duaj	복숭아	quả đào
pear	pera	كُمّثرى	梨	txiv moj coos	배	quả lê
peas	guisantes	بازلاء	碗豆	taum mog	완두콩	đậu hạt
peel	cáscara	قِشرة	果皮	tev	껍질	vỏ (quả)
peg game	juego de clavijas	لعبة إبرية	类似跳棋的一种游戏	daim ntsia ua si	나무막대들 구멍에 꽂는 페그게임	trò chơi đánh chốt
pen	pluma	قلم حبر	钢笔	mem kua	펜	viết mực
pencil	lápiz	قلم رصاص	铅笔	mem qhuav	연필	viết chì

ENGLISH	SPANISH	ARABIC	CHINESE	HMONG	KOREAN	VIETNAMESE
pepper	pimienta	فلفل	胡椒粉，胡椒调料	kua txob	후추	tiêu/ớt
pet	mascota	حيوان داجن	宠物	tsiaj yug saib	애완동물	con vật yêu quý
pie	pastel	فطيرة	馅饼	ncuav qab zib	파이	bánh nướng
pig	cerdo	خنزير	猪	npua	돼지	con heo
pin	imperdible	دبوس	别针	koob khawm	핀	ghim/kẹp
pine tree	pino	شجرة صنوبر	松树	ntoo thuv	전나무	cây thông
pipe	pipa	غليون	烟斗	yeeb nkab	담배파이프	ống điếu
plant	planta	نبات	植物	nroj	식물	cây thân thảo
Play Station	Play Station	جهاز ألعاب إلكتروني (بلاي ستيشن)	游戏机	Play Station	전자오락	đầu máy chơi điện tử
pliers	alicates	كماشة	钳子	ciaj tais	뻰찌	cây kềm
plug	enchufe	قابس	插头	pob ntsaws	플러그	phích cắm điện
plum	ciruela	خوخ	李子	txiv plum	자두	quả mận
police car	coche de policia	سيارة شرطة	警车	tsheb ceev xwm	경찰차	xe cảnh sát
police officer	agente de policia	ضابط شرطة	警官	neeg ceev xwm	경찰관	cảnh sát
pond	estanque	بركة	池塘	pas dej	연못	Ao
postal worker	cartero	عامل بريد	邮递员	neeg ua hauj lwm xa ntawv	우체부	nhân viên bưu điện
pot	olla	إبريق	锅	lauj kaub	냄비	cái nồi
pretzel	galleta salada en forma de lazo	كعك مالح وحلوان	椒盐卷饼	qhob noom pretzel	프레즐과자	bánh quy xoắn (hình nút thừng)
price tag	etiqueta de precio	بطاقة سعر	价格标签	pib qhia nqi	가격표	nhãn giá tiền
printer	impresora	طابعة	复印机	lub luam ntawv	프린터기	máy in
prize	premio	جائزة	奖牌	nqi zog	상	giải thưởng
puddle	charco	بركة	泥潭	pas av	웅덩이	Vũng
puzzle	rompecabezas	لغز	拼图玩具	duab sib dhos	퍼즐	cào độ
quarter	moneda de 25 centavos	٢٥ سنت	二角五分硬币	nyiaj npib 25 xees	25센트 화폐(미)	đồng 25 xu (Mỹ)
queen	reina	ملكة	王后	poj huab tais	여왕	hoàng hậu
question mark	signo de interrogación	علامة إستفهام	问号	tus cim nug	물음표	dấu chấm hỏi

ENGLISH	SPANISH	ARABIC	CHINESE	HMONG	KOREAN	VIETNAMESE
quilt	colcha	لحاف	棉被	paj ntaub	퀼트 (누비어 꿰맨 이불)	mền có hoa văn
rabbit	conejo	أرنب	兔子	luav	토끼	con thỏ
rain	lluvia	مطر	雨	nag	비	mưa
raincoat	impermeable	معطف مطري	雨衣	tsho tiv nag	우비	áo mưa
rake	rastrillo	مجرفة لجمع أوراق الشجر	耙	tus kaus nplooj	갈고리, 갈퀴	cây cào
rat	ratón	جرذ	鼠	nas tsuag	쥐	chuột (cống)
rattle	sonajero	خشخيشة الأطفال	拨浪鼓，嘎嘎响的玩具	tus co kom nrov	딸랑이	cái lúc lắc
razor	maquinilla de afeitar	شفرة حلاقة	剃刀	tus chais	면도칼	lưỡi lam
receipt	recibo	إيصال	收据	ntawv yuav khoom	영수증	biên nhận
refrigerator	nevera	براد	冰箱	lub tub yees	냉장고	tủ lạnh
remote control	mando a distancia	تحكم عن بعد	遥控器	lub nyem nta tua	리모콘	cái điều khiển từ xa
ribbon	cinta	شريط	缎带	lub paj ribbon	리본	dây ruy băng
ring	anillo	خاتم	戒指	nplhaib	반지	chiếc nhẫn
road	carretera	طريق	路	kev	길	con đường
rock	piedra	صخرة	石头	pob zeb	돌	Đá
rocket	cohete	صاروخ	火箭	cuaj luaj	로케트	tên lửa
roof	tejado	سطح	屋顶	ru tsev	지붕	mái nhà
rope	soga	حبل	绳子	hlua	밧줄	dây (thừng)
rose	rosa	وردة	玫瑰	paj ntshua nplaim	장미	hoa hồng
rubber band	goma	مطاط	橡皮圈	roj hmab	고무밴드	dây thun
rug	alfombra	سجادة	小地毯	ntaub tiag taw	바닥깔개	thảm sàn nhà
ruler	regla	مسطرة	标尺	pas ntsuas	자	cây thước
sack	saco	كيس	袋子	lub hnab	자루	bao tải
sad	triste	حزين	忧愁的，悲哀的	tu siab	슬픔	buồn
sailboat	barco de vela	قارب إبحار	帆船	nkoj cua	돛단배	thuyền buồm
sales clerk	dependiente	موظف مبيعات	售货员	neeg luj khoom	점원	nhân viên bán hàng
salt	sal	ملح	盐	ntsev	소금	muối

ENGLISH	SPANISH	ARABIC	CHINESE	HMONG	KOREAN	VIETNAMESE
sand bucket and shovel	cubo y pala para la playa	سطل رمل وجرفة	沙桶与铲子	thoob xuab zeb thiab duav	모래 양동이와 꽃삽	xô và xẻng xúc cát
sandals	sandalias	صندل	凉鞋	khau khiab	샌달	giày có quai
sap (from a tree)	savia	نسغ	樹漿	kua ntoo	수액	Nhựa cây
sauce	salsa	صلصة	调料	kua nyeem	소스	nước xốt
saw	serrucho	منشار	锯	rab kaw	톱	cây cưa
scale	balanza	آلة قياس	台秤，秤	rab teev	저울	cái cân
scanning wand	escáner	عصا ماسح ضوئي	扫描用的象形码	pas ntsuas nqi	(마켓에서 쓰는) 가격스케너	dụng cụ scan (nhận giá hàng)
scarecrow	espantapájaros	فزاعة	稻草人	moj zeej	허수아비	bù nhìn (giữ vườn)
scarf	bufanda	وشاح	围巾	sawv hwm	스카프	khăn choàng cổ
school	escuela	مدرسة	学校	tsev kawm ntawv	학교	trường học
school bus	autobús escolar	حافلة مدرسة	校车	tsheb npav tsev kawm ntawv	학교버스	xe buýt đưa rước học sinh
scissors	tijeras	مقص	剪刀	txiab	가위	cái kéo
scoop	cucharón	مغرفة	勺子	diav daus	(아이스크림 푸는) 순가락	muỗng múc
scooter	patinete	دراجة رجل	单脚滑行车	scooter	스쿠터	xe đẩy có 2 bánh nhỏ
screw	tornillo	برغي	螺丝钉	ntsia hlau	나사	cái đinh ốc
screwdriver	destornillador	مفك براغي	螺丝刀	rab ntswj ntsia hlau	드라이버	cái tuốc-nơ-vit
seal	foca	عجل البحر (الفقا)	海豹	ntshuab	물개	hải cẩu
seven	siete	سبعة	七	xya	일곱	số 7
shampoo	champú	شامبو للشعر	洗发水	tshuaj zawv plaub hau	샴푸	dầu gội đầu
shark	tiburón	سمك قرش	鲨鱼	ib hom ntses hiav txwv uas loj thiab muaj kaus hniav ntse heev	상어	cá mập
shave	afeitar	يحلق	刮脸	chais hwj txwv	면도	sự cạo râu
shaving cream	crema de afeitar	كريم حلاقة	剃须膏	tshuaj chais hwj txwv	면도용크림	kem cạo râu
sheep	oveja	خروف	绵羊	yaj	양	con cừu
shell	concha	صدفة	贝壳	khauj khaum qwj	조가비, 껍질	con sò
shelf	balda	رف	架子	txee	선반	cái kệ
shelves	estantería	رفوف	（复数）架子	txee (ntau lub los yog ntau theem)	선반들	(những) cái kệ
ship	barco	سفينة	轮船	nkoj ntxeeg	배	tàu thuyền

ENGLISH	SPANISH	ARABIC	CHINESE	HMONG	KOREAN	VIETNAMESE
shirt	camisa	قميص	衬衫	tsho	셔츠	áo sơ-mi
shoe	zapato	حذاء	鞋	khau	신발	giày
shovel	pala	رفش	铁锨	rab duav	삽	cái xẻng
sick	enfermo	مريض	病人	mob	아프다	bệnh
silo	silo	صومعة	筒仓	tsev rau khoom	사일로	Hầm ủ
silverware	cubiertia de plata	اواني فضية	银貝	tais diav	수저	dao muỗng nĩa (bằng bạc)
sink	lavabo	مغسلة	水槽, 水池	lub dab dej	세면대	cái bồn/chậu rửa
sit	sentar	يجلس	坐	zaum	앉다	ngồi
six	seis	ستة	六	rau	여섯	số 6
skateboard	monopatín	لوحة تزلّج	溜冰板	daim txiag khau log	스케이트보드	ván trượt
skates	patines	زلّاج	冰鞋	khau log	스케이트	trượt băng
skeleton	esqueleto	هيكل عظمي	骨骼	pob txha	뼈대	bộ xương
skirt	falda	تنّورة	裙子	tiab	치마	váy
skull	calavera	جمجمة	颅骨	pob txha taub hau	두개골	cái sọ
skunk	mofeta	الظربان	黄鼠狼	puam sem	스컹크	con chồn hôi
sky	cielo	سماء	天, 天空	ntuj; nruab ntug	하늘	bầu trời
sled	trineo	مزلاج	雪橇	lub zawv zawg	썰매	xe trượt tuyết
sleeping	durmiendo	نائم	睡觉	pw	잠	ngủ
sleeve	manga	كُمّ	袖子	tes tsho	소매	tay áo
slide	tobogán	منزلق	滑梯	tus zawv zawg	미끄럼틀	trượt
slipper	zapatilla	خف	拖鞋	khau khiab	슬리퍼 (집안에서 신는 신발)	dép
smoke	humo	دخان	烟	ncho pa	연기	khói
snail	caracol	حلزون	蜗牛	qwj	달팽이	con ốc
snake	serpiente	ثعبان	蛇	nab	뱀	con rắn
snap	chasquido	طقطقة اصابع	捻手指声 (响指)	txhuam ntiv tes	손가락으로 딱 소리 내는 것	cái búng tay
snow	nieve	ثلج	雪	daus	눈	tuyết
snowman	muñeco de nieve	رجل ثلج	雪人	moj zeej daus	눈사람	người tuyết

ENGLISH	SPANISH	ARABIC	CHINESE	HMONG	KOREAN	VIETNAMESE
soap	jabón	صابون	肥皂	xab npum	비누	cục xà bông
sock	calcetín	جراب	短袜	thom khwm	양말	chiếc vớ
soldier	soldado	جندي	士兵	tub rog	병사	người lính
spear	lanza	حربة	矛	muv	창	cái giáo
spider	araña	عنكبوت	蜘蛛	kab laug sab	거미	con nhện
sponge	esponja	إسفنجة	海绵	ntaub nqus dej	스폰지	miếng bọt biển
spoon	cuchara	ملعقة	匙	diav	숟가락	cái muỗng
stage	escenario	خشبة المسرح	舞台	sam thiaj	무대	sân khấu
stairs	escaleras	سلالم	楼梯	ntaiv	층계	cầu thang
stamp	sello	طابع بريدي	邮票	daim nqi xa ntawv	우표	con tem
stapler	grapadora	كبّاسة ورق	订书机	koob tom ntawv	호치키스	cái đồ bấm (giấy)
statue	estatua	تمثال	雕像	pej thuam	동상	bức tượng
stem	tallo	جذع	茎，干	tus ko	줄기	thân (cây)
steps	escalones	خطوات	台阶	taw ntaiv	계단	(những) bậc thang/bước chân
stereo	equipo estereofónico	ستريو	立体收音器机	lub thev	스테레오	máy thu/phát âm thanh nổi
stethoscope	estetoscopio	سماعة طبيب	听诊器	lub mloog mob	청진기	ống nghe (để khám bệnh)
stick	palo	عصا	小树枝	pas	막대기	cái que
stone	piedra	حجر	石头	pob zeb	돌	đá
stool	taburete	كرسي بلا ظهر ولا ذراعين	凳子	tog	발판	ghế đẩu
stop	parar	توقّف	障碍	nres	멈춤	dừng lại
stove	estufa	فرن	炉子	qhov cub	가스레인지	cái lò
stuffed animal	animal de peluche	حيوان محشو قطن أو قماش	填充玩具	tsiaj ntim rwb	동물인형	thú nhồi bông
sub	submarino	غوّاصة	潜水艇	nkoj qab thus dej	잠수함	tàu ngầm
subtract	restar	يَنقُص	减去，扣除	rho; leb rho	뺄셈	phép trừ
subway train	metro	قطار أنفاق	地铁列车	tsheb nqaj hlau hauv qhov av	지하철	xe điện ngầm
suit	traje	بذلة	一套衣服	ris tsho xam koos	정장	bộ quần áo
sun	sol	شمس	太阳	hnub	해	mặt trời

ENGLISH	SPANISH	ARABIC	CHINESE	HMONG	KOREAN	VIETNAMESE
sunglasses	gafas de sol	نظارات شمسية	墨镜	tsom iav thaiv hnub	선글라스	kính râm/mát
sunrise	amanecer	شروق الشمس	日出	hnub tawm	해돋이	bình minh
sunscreen	loción con filtro solar	واقٍ من الشمس	遮光剂	tshuaj tiv tshav	선크림 (햇볕을 방지하는 크림)	kem thoa chống nắng
sweater	suéter	كنزة خفيفة	毛线衫	tsho sov	스웨터	áo len dài tay
sweep	barrer	يكنس	扫除	cheb	청소	sự quét
swim	nadar	يسبح	游泳	luam dej	수영	bơi lội
switch	interruptor	مفتاح تحويل	开关	chaw taws los yog tua teeb	스위치	công tắc điện
table	mesa	طاولة	桌子	rooj	식탁	cái bàn
tape	cinta adhesiva	شريط	胶带	ntaub nplaum	스카치 테이프	băng
taxi	taxi	سيارة تاكسي	出租车	tsheb ntiav	택시	xe taxi
tea	té	شاي	茶	dej tshuaj yej	차	trà
teacher	maestro	معلم-مدرّس	教师	xib fwb; xib hwb	선생님	giáo viên
teddy bear	osito de peluche	دمية دب	玩具熊	tus me nyuam dais ntim rwb	곰인형	gấu nhồi bông
teeth	dientes	اسنان	（复数）牙齿	kaus hniav	이빨들	(những) cái răng
telephone	teléfono	هاتف	电话	lub xov tooj	전화	điện thoại
television	televisión	تلفاز	电视	this vis; TV	텔레비전	ti-vi/truyền hình
ten	diez	عشرة	十	kaum	열, 십	số 10
tent	tienda de campaña	خيمة	帐篷	tsev pheeb suab	텐트	căn lều
thermometer	termómetro	ميزان حرارة	温度计	tus ntsuas kub ntsuas txias	온도계	dụng cụ đo nhiệt độ
thermos	termo	ترمس للحرارة	保温瓶	lub fwj ceev kom dej kub kub los yog txias	보온병	cái bình thủy/cái phích
thief	ladrón	لص	贼	tub sab	도둑	kẻ trộm
thirteen	trece	ثلاثة عشر	十三	kaum peb	십삼, 열 셋	số 13
thirty	treinta	ثلاثين	三十	peb caug	삼십	số 30
thread	hilo	خيط	线	xov	실	sợi chỉ
three	tres	ثلاثة	三	peb	셋, 삼	số 3
thumb	pulgar	اصبع	拇指	ntiv tes xoo	엄지손가락	ngón tay cái
tie	corbata	ربطة	领带	kas las vav	넥타이	cái cà-vạt (nơ)

ENGLISH	SPANISH	ARABIC	CHINESE	HMONG	KOREAN	VIETNAMESE
tire	neumático	عجلة	轮胎	log tsheb	타이어	lốp xe/vỏ xe
tissue	pañuelo de papel	محارم ورقية	薄纸	ntawv so ntswg	얇은 화장지	khăn giấy
toad	sapo	ضفدع الطین	蟾蜍	qav kaws	두꺼비	con cóc
toast	tostada	خبز محمص	烤面包	ci; txhiab	토스트	bánh mì nướng
toes	dedos del pie	أصابع الرجلين	脚趾	ntiv taw	발가락	(những) ngón chân
toilet	inodoro	تواليت	马桶	chaw plob	변기	nhà vệ sinh
tooth	diente	سن	牙齿	kaus hniav	이빨	cái răng
toothbrush	cepillo de dientes	فرشاة أسنان	牙刷	tus txhuam hniav	칫솔	bàn chải đánh răng
toothpaste	dentifrico	معجون أسنان	牙膏	tshuaj txhuam hniav	치약	kem đánh răng
top	peonza	نحلة	陀螺	tuj lub	팽이	chóp/đỉnh
towel	toalla	منشفة	毛巾	phuam	수건	khăn tắm
toy boat	barco de juguete	لعبة قارب	玩具船	nkoj ua si	장난감 배	chiếc thuyền đồ chơi
toy car	coche de juguete	لعبة سيارة	玩具汽车	tsheb ua si	장난감 차	xe hơi đồ chơi
toy house	casa de juguete	لعبة بيت	玩具房子	tsev ua si	장난감 집	căn nhà đồ chơi
toys	juguetes	ألعاب	玩具	twj ua si	장난감	(những) món đồ chơi
tractor	tractor	جرار	拖拉机	tsheb laij	트랙터, 견인차	xe máy cày
train	tren	قطار	火车	tsheb nqaj hlau	기차	xe lửa
train set	tren de juguete	عدة قطار	玩具电动火车组	tsheb nqaj hlau ua si	장난감 기차세트	bộ đồ chơi xe lửa
trash	basura	نفایات	垃圾	khoom pov tseg	쓰레기	rác
tree	árbol	شجرة	树	ntoo	나무	cây
triangle	triángulo	مثلث	三角形	lub duab peb ceg	삼각형	hình tam giác
truck	camión	شاحنة	卡车	tsheb thauj khoom	트럭	xe tải
truck driver	camionero	سائق شاحنة	卡车司机	neeg tsav tsheb thauj khoom	트럭운전사	tài xế xe tải
trunk	baúl	صندوق السيارة	象鼻	cov txwv	코끼리의 코	thân cây/thân người
tub	bañera	مغطس	浴盆	dab da dej	욕조	cái chậu
tube	tubo	أنبوب	装牙膏的小软管	raj	튜브	ống

ENGLISH	SPANISH	ARABIC	CHINESE	HMONG	KOREAN	VIETNAMESE
turtle	tortuga	سلحفاة	龟	vaub kib	거북이	con rùa
twelve	doce	اثنا عشر	十二	kaum ob	열둘	số 12
two	dos	اثنان	二	ob	둘	số 2
umbrella	paraguas	مظلة	伞	kaus	우산	cây dù
unicycle	uniciclo	دراجة بعجلة واحدة	单轮脚踏车	tsheb kauj vab ib lub log	외바퀴 자전거	xe đạp một bánh
vacuum	aspiradora	فراغ مكنسة كهربائية	吸尘器	tshuab nqus tsev	진공청소기	máy hút bụi
van	camioneta	عربة شحن خفيفة	货车	tsheb loj; tsheb van	밴	xe tải
vase	florero	مزهرية	花瓶	hub	화병	bình/lọ
vest	chaleco	سترة تحتية	背心	tsho khuam	조끼	áo gi-lê
veterinarian	veterinario	طبيب بيطري	兽医	kws kho tsiaj	수의사	bác sĩ thú y
video camera	videocámara	آلة تصوير فيديو	摄影机	koob yees duab mus kev	비디오 카메라	máy quay phim
video recorder/ player	aparato de video	آلة تسجيل فيديو	录像机/放像机	lub kaw dua/tso duab	비디오 녹화기	đầu máy chiếu phim/đầu máy hát đĩa
vine	viña	كرمة	藤本植物，蔓藤	hmab	넝쿨	giàn nho
violin	violín	كمان	小提琴	nkauj nog ncas	바이올린	đàn vi-ô-lông
vitamins	vitaminas	فيتامينات/مقويات	维生素	tshuaj qab los	비타민	vitamin
volcano	volcán	بركان	火山	roob hluav taws av	화산	núi lửa
wag	menear	هز الذيل	摇摆	co	꼬리 흔들기	lúc lắc/ve vẩy
wagon	carro	عربة نقل	四轮货车	laub	사륜차	xe ngựa/bò
wall clock	reloj de pared	ساعة حائط	挂钟	lub teev dai phab ntsa	벽시계	đồng hồ treo tường
washcloth	toallita	غسل ملابس	浴巾	phuam ntxuav muag	작은 얼굴수건	khăn lau mặt
washing machine	lavadora	غسالة	洗衣机	tshuab ntxhua khaub ncaws	세탁기	máy giặt
wastebasket	papelera	سلة مهملات	废纸篓	thoob rau khoom pov tseg	쓰레기통	sọt rác/sọt giấy vụn
watch	reloj de pulsera	ساعة يد	手表	lub teev	시계	đồng hồ đeo tay
wave	ola	موجة	波浪	co	파도	sóng
web	telaraña	شبكة	网	tsev kab laug sab	거미줄	mạng
well	pozo	بئر	井	qhov dej	우물	cái giếng
whale	ballena	حوت	鲸	ib hom ntses hiav txwv loj loj heev	고래	cá voi

ENGLISH	SPANISH	ARABIC	CHINESE	HMONG	KOREAN	VIETNAMESE
wheel	rueda	دولاب	轮子	log	바퀴	bánh xe
wheelbarrow	carretilla	عربة يدوية	手推车	laub thawb	외바퀴손수레	xe cút kít
whiskers	bigotes	سوالف شعر	胡须	hwj txwv	(고양이)콧수염	râu/ria (mèo)
whistle	silbato	يصفر	口哨	lub raj xuav	호루라기	cái còi
wig	peluca	شعر مستعار	假发	plaub hau cuav	가발	bộ tóc giả
wind	viento	ريح	风	cua	바람	con gió
window	ventana	شباك	窗	qhov rai	창문	cửa sổ
wing	ala	جناح	翅膀	tis	날개	cánh
witch	bruja	ساحرة	女巫，巫婆	poj dab witch	마녀	bà phù thủy
wolf	lobo	ذئب	狼	hma	늑대	chó sói
woman	mujer	إمرأة	女人	poj niam	여자	người phụ nữ
wooden beam	viga de madera	خشب للبناء - عارضة السقف	木梁	nqaj tse ntoo	대들보	xà gỗ
work boots	botas de construcción	حذاء العمل	工作靴	khau raj rau ua hauj lwm	작업용부츠	giày ống công nhân
worm	gusano	دودة	虫	cua nab	벌레 (지렁이류)	con sâu/trùng
yarn	hilo	خيط - غزل صوف	纱线，纺线	xov paj	털실	sợi/chỉ
yawn	bostezo	تثاوب	哈欠	rua lo	하품	cái ngáp
yogurt	yogur	لبن	酸奶，酸乳酪	kua mis nyeem qaub	요거트	sữa chua/da-ua
zebra	cebra	حمار وحشي	斑马	nees txaij	얼룩말	ngựa vằn
zero	cero	صفر	零	xoom	영 (0)	số 0
zigzag	zigzag	خط متعرج	之字形（线条，拐弯，物品等）	txoj kab uas nkhaus mus nkhaus los	지그재그	hình chữ chi/hình zizag
zip	cerrar con cremallera	أغلق-رفع السحاب	拉（拉链）	swb	지퍼를 잠그다	tiếng rít
zipper	cremallera	سحاب	拉链	txoj swb	지퍼	dây kéo
zoo	zoo	حديقة حيوانات	动物园	vaj tsiaj	동물원	sở thú

Templates for Sorts and Games

Template for Picture Sorts

Template for Word Sorts

Game Boards

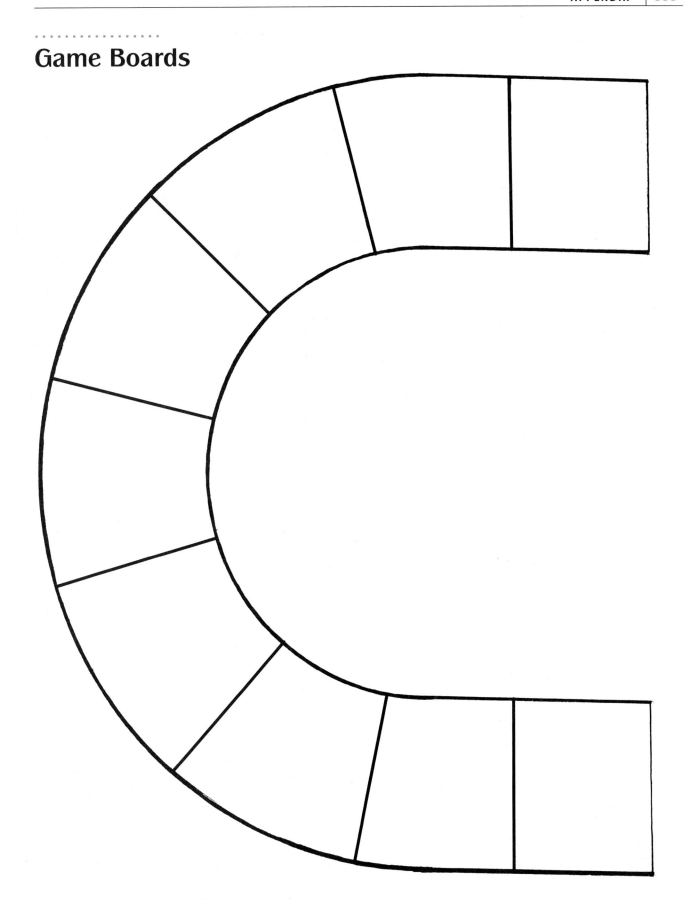

RACETRACK GAME BOARD (left and right)

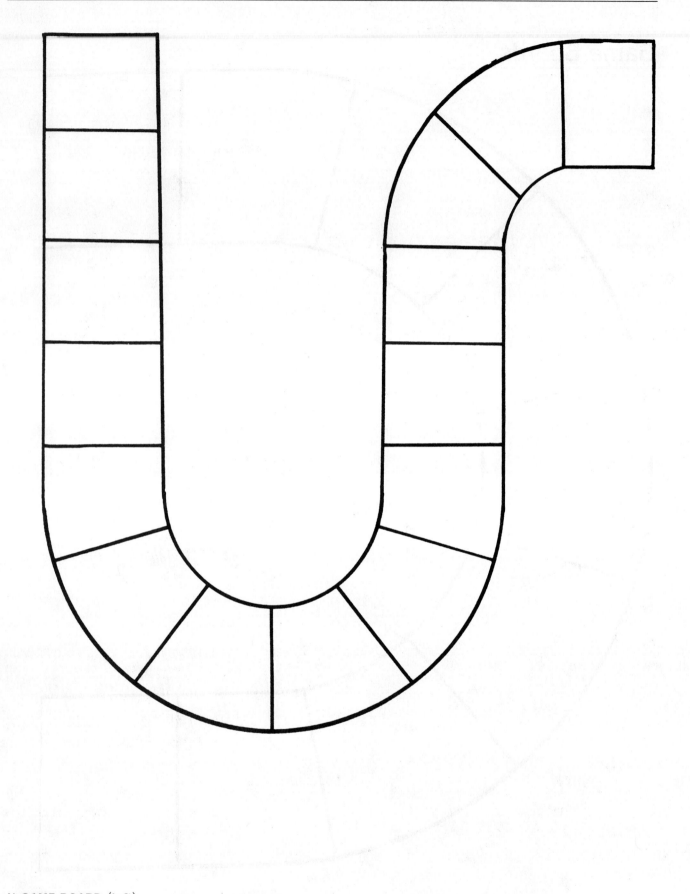

U GAME BOARD (left)

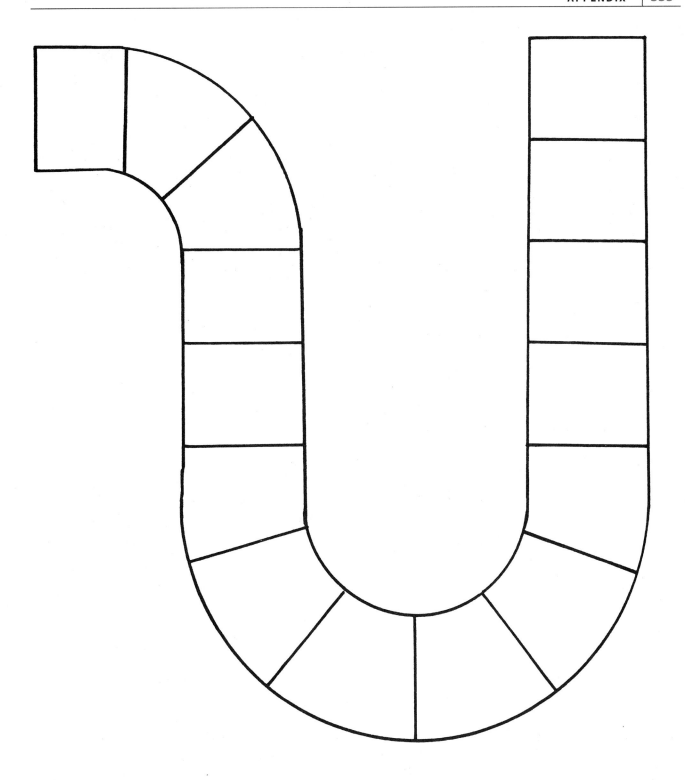

U GAME BOARD (right)

Media Guide

Chapter 3

(continued)

Chapter 4

Chapter 5

(continued)

SECTION	PAGE	GO TO PDTOOLKIT FOR *WORDS THEIR WAY*™ *WITH ENGLISH LEARNERS*
Activities for English Learners in the Letter Name–Alphabetic Stage	137	Click the Sorts & Games tab and search for "Sort 13: /s/ /m/ Beginning Consonant Picture Sorts."
Activities for English Learners in the Letter Name–Alphabetic Stage	140	Click the Sorts & Games tab and search for "Sort 33: /b/ /p/ Focused Picture Sorts to Contrast Beginning Consonants."
Activities for English Learners in the Letter Name–Alphabetic Stage	141	Click the Sorts & Games tab and search for Sorts 50–55 and Sorts 56–72.
Activities for English Learners in the Letter Name–Alphabetic Stage	142	Click the Sorts & Games tab and search for Sorts 73–86 and Sorts 87–97.
Activities for English Learners in the Letter Name–Alphabetic Stage	143	Click the Sorts & Games tab and search for Sorts 98–105 and Sorts 106–110.
Activities for English Learners in the Letter Name–Alphabetic Stage	144	Click the Sorts & Games tab and search for Sorts 111–130.
Activities for English Learners in the Letter Name–Alphabetic Stage	144	Click the Sorts & Games tab and search for Sorts 131–139.
Activities for English Learners in the Letter Name–Alphabetic Stage	146	Click the Sorts & Games tab and search for Sorts 140–147.
Activities for English Learners in the Letter Name–Alphabetic Stage	146	Click the Sorts & Games tab and search for Sorts 148–157.
Activities for English Learners in the Letter Name–Alphabetic Stage	147	Click the Sorts & Games tab and search for Sorts 158–198.
Activities for English Learners in the Letter Name–Alphabetic Stage	148	Click the Sorts & Games tab and search for Sorts 199–212.
Activities for English Learners in the Letter Name–Alphabetic Stage	148	Click the Sorts & Games tab and search for Sorts 213–227.

Additional Resources

Activities for English Learners in the Letter Name–Alphabetic Stage	127	Click the Additional Resources tab and select Template for Picture Sorts in the Templates section.
Activities for English Learners in the Letter Name–Alphabetic Stage	129	Click the Additional Resources tab and select Words in My Word Bank Chart.
Activities for English Learners in the Letter Name–Alphabetic Stage	130	Click the Additional Resources tab and search for "Sound Boards."

(continued)

SECTION	PAGE	GO TO PDTOOLKIT FOR *WORDS THEIR WAY*™ *WITH ENGLISH LEARNERS*
Activities for English Learners in the Within Word Pattern Stage	172	Click the Sorts & Games tab and search for "Sort 245: Word Sort Contrasting Spelling Patterns for Long *u* (CVCe and CVVC)."
Activities for English Learners in the Within Word Pattern Stage	173	Click the Sorts & Games tab and search for "Sort 234: Matter Concept Sort."
Activities for English Learners in the Within Word Pattern Stage	174	Click the Sorts & Games tab and search for "Sort 246: Word Sort with *a-e, ai, ay.*"
Activities for English Learners in the Within Word Pattern Stage	174	Click the Sorts & Games tab and search for "Sort 247: Word Sort with *o-e, oa, ow.*"
Activities for English Learners in the Within Word Pattern Stage	175	Click the Sorts & Games tab and search for "Sort 248: Word Sort with *u-e, ew, ue.*"
Activities for English Learners in the Within Word Pattern Stage	176	Click the Sorts & Games tab and search for "Sort 249: Word Sort with *i-e, igh, y.*"
Activities for English Learners in the Within Word Pattern Stage	176	Click the Sorts & Games tab and search for "Night Sky Game Board."
Activities for English Learners in the Within Word Pattern Stage	178	Click the Sorts & Games tab and search for "Find the Gold Game."
Activities for English Learners in the Within Word Pattern Stage	179	Click the Sorts & Games tab and search for "Sort 250: Word Sort with Long Vowel *r* Words."
Activities for English Learners in the Within Word Pattern Stage	180	Click the Sorts & Games tab and search for "Sort 251: *R*-Influenced Word Sort."
Activities for English Learners in the Within Word Pattern Stage	181	Click the Sorts & Games tab and search for "Her First Word Turn Game."
Activities for English Learners in the Within Word Pattern Stage	181	Click the Sorts & Games tab and search for "Sort 252: Word Sort with Diphthongs (*oi/oy, ou/ow*)."
Activities for English Learners in the Within Word Pattern Stage	182	Click the Sorts & Games tab and search for "Sort 253: Word Sort with Ambiguous Vowel Sounds."
Activities for English Learners in the Within Word Pattern Stage	184	Click the Sorts & Games tab and search for "Sort 254: Word Sort with *spr, str, scr.*"
Activities for English Learners in the Within Word Pattern Stage	185	Click the Sorts & Games tab and search for "Sort 255: Word Sort with *squ, thr, shr.*"
Activities for English Learners in the Within Word Pattern Stage	185	Click the Sorts & Games tab and search for "Triple Threat Racetrack Game."
Activities for English Learners in the Within Word Pattern Stage	186	Click the Sorts & Games tab and search for "Sort 256: Word Sort with Endings *dge* and *ge.*"
Activities for English Learners in the Within Word Pattern Stage	187	Click the Sorts & Games tab and search for "Sort 257: Word Sort with Endings *tch* and *ch.*"
Activities for English Learners in the Within Word Pattern Stage	187	Click the Sorts & Games tab and search for "Sort 258: Word Sort with Two-Syllable Words."
Activities for English Learners in the Within Word Pattern Stage	188	Click the Sorts & Games tab and search for "Sort 259: Word Sort with Contractions."
Activities for English Learners in the Within Word Pattern Stage	189	Click the Sorts & Games tab and search for "Sort 235: Ecosystems Concept Sort."

Chapter 7

(continued)

Chapter 8

Appendix

REFERENCES

Professional References

August, D., & Shanahan, T. (Eds.). (2006). *Developing literacy in second-language learners: Report of the National Literacy Panel on Language Minority Children and Youth.* Mahwah, NJ: Lawrence Erlbaum.

Bear, D. (1995, December). *The study of cued speech and orthographic knowledge: Implications for the understanding of articulation in orthographic knowledge.* Paper presented at the 45th Annual Meeting of the National Reading Conference, New Orleans, LA.

Bear, D., & Barone, D. (1998). *Developing literacy: An integrated approach to assessment and instruction.* Boston: Houghton Mifflin.

Bear, D., Caserta-Henry, C., & Venner, D. (2004). *Personal readers for emergent and beginning readers.* West Linn, OR: Teaching Resource Center.

Bear, D., Han, K. T., Wei, W., & DeMartini, C. (2010). *The orthographic development in English among Chinese and Korean native speakers* (Research summary). Reno: E. L. Cord Foundation Center for Learning and Literacy, University of Nevada.

Bear, D., Invernizzi, M., Johnston, F., & Templeton, S. (2009). *Words their way: Letter and picture sorts for emergent spellers* (2nd ed.). Boston: Allyn & Bacon.

Bear, D., Invernizzi, M., Templeton, S., & Johnston, F. (2008). *Words their way: Word study for phonics, vocabulary, and spelling instruction* (4th ed.). Upper Saddle River, NJ: Prentice Hall.

Bear, D., & Templeton, S. (2000). Matching development and instruction. In N. Padak, T. Rasinski, et al. (Eds.), *Distinguished educators on reading: Contributions that have shaped effective literacy instruction* (pp. 334–376). Newark, DE: International Reading Association.

Bear, D., Templeton, S., Helman, L., & Baren, T. (2003). Orthographic development and learning to read in different languages. In G. Garcia (Ed.), *English learners: Reaching the highest level of English literacy* (pp. 71–95). Newark, DE: International Reading Association.

Bear, D., Truex, P., & Barone, D. (1989). In search of meaningful diagnoses: Spelling-by-stage assessment of literacy proficiency. *Adult Literacy and Basic Education, 13*(3), 165–185.

Bialystok, E., Luk, G., & Kwan, E. (2005). Bilingualism, biliteracy, and learning to read: Interactions among languages and writing systems. *Scientific Studies of Reading, 9*, 43–61.

Bialystok, E., & McBride-Chang, C. (2005). Bilingualism, language proficiency, and learning to read in two writing systems. *Journal of Educational Psychology, 97*(4), 580–590.

Bronfenbrenner, U., & Evans, G. W. (2000). Developmental science in the 21st century: Emerging questions, theoretical models, research designs and empirical findings. *Social Development, 9*, 115–125.

Capps, R., Fix, M., Murray, J., Ost, J., Passel, J., & Herwantoro, S. (2005). *The new demography of America's schools: Immigration and the No Child Left Behind Act.* Washington, DC: The Urban Institute. Retrieved October 23, 2005, from www.urban.org.

Center for Research on Education, Diversity & Excellence (CREDE). (2004). *Research evidence: Five standards for effective pedagogy and student outcomes* (Technical Report No. G1). Santa Cruz: University of California.

Chall, J. S. (1983). *Stages of reading development.* New York: McGraw-Hill.

Chang, J. (2001). Chinese speakers. In M. Swan & B. Smith (Eds.), *Learner English: A teacher's guide to interference and other problems* (2nd ed., pp. 310–324). New York: Cambridge University Press.

Comrie, B., Matthews, S., & Polinsky, M. (1996). *The atlas of languages: The origin and development of languages throughout the world.* London: Quatro Publishing.

Corson, D. (1997). The learning and use of academic English words. *Language Learning, 47*, 671–718.

Cosentina de Cohen, C., Deterding, N., & Clewell, B. (2005). *Who's left behind? Immigrant children in high and low LEP schools.* Washington, DC: Urban Institute. (ED490 928). Retrieved October 23, 2005, from www.urban.org.

Crystal, D. (2003). *The Cambridge encyclopedia of the English language* (2nd ed.). Cambridge, UK: Cambridge University Press.

Crystal, D. (2006). *Words words words.* Oxford, UK: Oxford University Press.

Cummins, J., Chow, P., & Schecter, S. R. (2006). Community as curriculum. *Language Arts, 83*(4), 297–307.

Cunningham, A. E., & Stanovich, K. E. (1991). Tracking the unique effects of print exposure in children: Associations with vocabulary, general knowledge, and spelling. *Journal of Educational Psychology, 83,* 264–274.

Dalbor, J. B. (1997). *Spanish pronunciation: Theory and practice.* Fort Worth, TX: Harcourt Brace College Publishers.

Deese, J. (1969). Behavior and fact. *American Psychologist, 24,* 515–522.

de Jong, E. J., & Harper, C. A. (2005). Preparing mainstream teachers for English-language learners: Is being a good teacher good enough? *Teacher Education Quarterly, 32*(2), 101–124.

Del Vecchio, A. (1995). *Handbook of English language proficiency tests.* Albuquerque: Evaluation Assessment Center–West, New Mexico Highlands University.

Díaz-Rico, L. T., & Weed, K. Z. (2002). *The cross-cultural, language, and academic development handbook: A complete K–12 reference guide* (2nd ed.). Boston: Allyn & Bacon.

Dickinson, D. K., McCabe, A., & Sprague, K. (2003). Teacher Rating of Oral Language and Literacy (TROLL): Individualizing early literacy instruction with a standards-based rating tool. *The Reading Teacher, 56*(6), 554–564.

Dutro, S., & Helman, L. (2009). Explicit language instruction: A key to constructing meaning. In L. Helman (Ed.), *Literacy development with English learners: Research-based instruction in grades K–6* (pp. 40–63). New York: Guilford Press.

Echevarría, J., Vogt, M., & Short, D. J. (2008). *Making content comprehensible for English learners: The SIOP® model* (3rd ed.). Boston: Allyn & Bacon.

Echevarría, J., Vogt, M., & Short, D. J. (2010). *Making content comprehensible for elementary English learners: The SIOP® model.* Boston: Allyn & Bacon.

Ehri, L. C. (1997). Learning to read and learning to spell are one and the same, almost. In C. A. Perfetti, L. Rieben, & M. Fayol (Eds.), *Learning to spell: Research, theory, and practice across languages* (pp. 237–269). Mahwah, NJ: Lawrence Erlbaum.

Ehri, L. C. (2006). Alphabetics instruction helps children learn to read. In R. M. Joshi & P. G. Aaron (Eds.), *Handbook of orthography and literacy* (pp. 649–678). Mahwah, NJ: Lawrence Erlbaum.

Emerson, R. W. (1895). *Letters and social aims.* Boston: Houghton Mifflin.

Ferreiro, E., & Teberosky, A. (1982). *Literacy before schooling.* Portsmouth, NH: Heinemann.

Flanigan, K. (2007). A concept of word in text: A pivotal event in early reading acquisition. *Journal of Literacy Research, 39*(1), 37–70.

Flanigan, K., Hayes, T., Templeton, S., Bear, D. R., Invernizzi, M., & Johnston, F. (2011). *Words their way with struggling readers: Word study for reading, vocabulary, and spelling instruction, grades 4–12.* Boston: Allyn & Bacon.

Garcia, E. E., & Cuéllar, D. (2006). Who are these linguistically and culturally diverse students? *Teachers College Record, 108*(11), 2220–2246.

Genesee, F., Lindholm-Leary, K., Saunders, W., & Christian, D. (2005). English language learners in U.S. schools: An overview of research findings. *Journal of Education for Students Placed at Risk, 10*(4), 363–385.

Gersten, R. M., & Jiménez, R. T. (1998). *Promoting learning for culturally and linguistically diverse students.* Belmont, CA: Wadsworth Publishing Company.

Grosjean, F. (2000). Processing mixed language: Issues, findings, and models. In L. Wei (Ed.), *The bilingualism reader* (pp. 443–469). New York: Routledge.

Guerrero, M., & Del Vecchio, A. (1996). *Handbook of Spanish language proficiency tests.* Albuquerque: Evaluation Assessment Center–West, New Mexico Highlands University.

Guion, S. G., Flege, J. E., Liu, S. H., & Yeni-Komshian, G. H. (2000). Age of learning effects on the duration of sentence produced in a second language. *Applied Psycholinguistics, 21,* 205–228.

Hart, B., & Risley, T. (1995). *Meaningful differences in the everyday experience of young American children.* Baltimore: Brookes Publishing.

Helman, L. (2004). Building on the sound system of Spanish: Insights from the alphabetic spellings of English language learners. *The Reading Teacher, 57,* 452–460.

Helman, L. (2005). Spanish speakers learning to read in English: What a large-scale assessment suggests about their progress. In B. Maloch, J. Hoffman, D. Schallert, C. Fairbanks, & J. Worthy (Eds.), *54th yearbook of the National Reading Conference* (pp. 211–226). Oak Creek, WI: National Reading Conference.

Helman, L. (Ed.). (2009). *Literacy development with English learners: Research-based instruction in grades K–6.* New York: Guilford Press.

Helman, L., Bear, D. R., Invernizzi, M., Templeton, S., & Johnston, F. (2009a). *Words their way: Emergent sorts for Spanish-speaking English learners.* Boston: Allyn & Bacon.

Helman, L., Bear, D. R., Invernizzi, M., Templeton, S., & Johnston, F. (2009b). *Words their way: Letter name–alphabetic sorts for Spanish-speaking English learners.* Boston: Allyn & Bacon.

Henderson, E. H. (1990). *Teaching spelling* (2nd ed.). Boston: Houghton Mifflin.

Hiebert, E. H., & Bravo, M. (2010). Morphological knowledge and learning to read in English. In D.

Wyse, R. Andrews, & J. Hoffman (Eds.), *International handbook of English, language, and literacy teaching.* Oxford, UK: Routledge.

Hiebert, E. H., & Lubliner, S. (2008). The nature, learning, and instruction of general academic vocabulary. In A. E. Farstrup & S. J. Samuels (Eds.), *What research has to say about vocabulary* (pp. 106–129). Newark, DE: International Reading Association.

Invernizzi, M. (2002). Concepts, sounds, and the ABCs: A diet for a very young reader. In D. M. Barone & L. M. Morrow (Eds.), *Literacy and young children.* New York: Guilford Press.

Invernizzi, M., Abouzeid, M., & Gill, J. T. (1994). Using students' invented spelling as a guide for spelling instruction that emphasizes word study. *Elementary School Journal, 95,* 155–167.

Invernizzi, M., & Hayes, L. (2004). Developmental-spelling research: A systematic imperative. *Reading Research Quarterly, 39*(2), 216–228.

Invernizzi, M., Johnston, F., Bear, D. R., & Templeton, S. (2009). *Words their way: Word sorts for within word pattern spellers* (2nd ed.). Boston: Allyn & Bacon.

Invernizzi, M. A., Landrum, T. J., Howell, J. L., & Warley, H. (2005). Toward the peaceful coexistence of test developers, policymakers, and teachers in an era of accountability. *The Reading Teacher, 58,* 610–618.

Jacobson, J., Lapp, D., & Flood, J. (2007). A seven-step instructional plan for teaching English-language learners to comprehend and use homonyms, homophones, and homographs. *Journal of Adolescent and Adult Literacy, 51*(2), 98–111.

Jiménez, R., Garcia, G. E., & Pearson, P. D. (1996). The reading strategies of bilingual Latina/o students who are successful English readers: Opportunities and obstacles. *Reading Research Quarterly, 31,* 90–112.

Johnston, F., Bear, D. R., & Invernizzi, M. (2009). *Words their way: Word sorts for letter name–alphabetic spellers* (2nd ed.). Boston: Allyn & Bacon.

Johnston, F., Invernizzi, M., Bear, D. R., & Templeton, S. (2009). *Words their way: Word sorts for syllables and affixes spellers* (2nd ed.). Boston: Allyn & Bacon.

Johnston, F. R., Invernizzi, M., Juel, C., & Lewis-Wagner, D. (2009). *Book buddies: A tutoring framework for struggling readers* (2nd ed.). New York: Guilford Press.

Kenner, C., Kress, G., Al-Khatib, H., Kam, R., & Tsai, K.-C. (2004). Finding the key to biliteracy: How young children interpret different writing systems. *Language and Education, 2,* 124–144.

Koch, K. (1999). *Wishes, lies and dreams.* New York: Perennial Publishers.

Lee, L.-J. (1990). *Emergent literacy in Chinese: Print awareness of young children in Taiwan.* Unpublished doctoral dissertation, University of Arizona.

Lieberman, P. (1991). *Uniquely human: The evolution of speech, thought, and selfless behavior.* Cambridge, MA: Harvard University Press.

McCabe, A., & Bliss, L. S. (2003). *Patterns of narrative discourse: A multi-cultural, life span approach.* Boston: Allyn & Bacon.

Metsala, J. L., & Walley, A. C. (1998). Spoken vocabulary growth and the segmental restructuring of lexical representations: Precursors to phonemic awareness and early reading ability. In J. L. Metsala & L. Ehri (Eds.), *Word recognition in beginning literacy* (pp. 89–120). Mahwah, NJ: Lawrence Erlbaum.

Morris, D., Bloodgood, J. W., Lomax, R. G., & Perney, J. (2003). Developmental steps in learning to read: A longitudinal study in kindergarten and first grade. *Reading Research Quarterly, 38*(3), 302–328.

Nagy, W. E., García, G. E., Durgunoglu, A. Y., & Hancin-Bhatt, B. (1993). Spanish-English bilingual students' use of cognates in English reading. *Journal of Reading Behavior, 25*(3), 241–259.

National Clearinghouse for English Language Acquisition. (2006). *Resources about assessment and accountability for ELLs.* Washington, DC: NCELA. Retrieved June 30, 2010, from www.ncela.gwu.edu/resabout/assessment/index.html.

Nelson, O. G., & Linek, W. M. (1998). *Practical classroom applications of language experience: Looking back, looking forward.* Boston: Allyn & Bacon.

Nilsen, D. L. F., & Nilsen, A. P. (2002). *Pronunciation contrasts in English.* Long Grove, IL: Waveland Press.

Nippold, M. A. (2007). *Later language development: The school-age and adolescent years* (3rd ed.). Austin, TX: Pro-Ed.

Padak, N., Newton, E., Rasinski, T., & Newton, R. (2008). Getting to the root of word study: Teaching Latin and Greek word roots in elementary and middle grades. In A. E. Farstrup & S. J. Samuels (Eds.), *What research has to say about vocabulary instruction* (pp. 6–31). Newark, DE: International Reading Association.

Paulesu, E., Demonet, J.-F., Fazio, F., McCrory, E., Chanoine, V., Brunswick, N., et al. (2001). Dyslexia: Cultural diversity and biological unity. *Science, 291,* 2165–2167.

Perfetti, C. (2003). The universal grammar of reading. *Scientific Studies of Reading, 7*(1), 3–24.

Planty, M., Hussar, W., Snyder, T., Kena, G., Kewal Ramani, A., Kemp, J., Bianco, K., & Dinkes, R. (2009). *The condition of education 2009* (NCES 2009-081). Washington, DC: National Center for Education Statistics, Institute of Education Sciences, U.S. Department of Education.

Ransdell, S., Arecco, M. R., & Levy, C. M. (2001). Bilingual long-term working memory: The effects of working memory loads on writing quality and fluency. *Applied Psycholinguistics, 22,* 113–128.

Raphael, T. E., Pardo, L. S., & Highfield, K. (2002). *Book club: A literature-based curriculum.* Lawrence, MA: Small Plant Communications.

Read, C. (1971). Preschool children's knowledge of English phonology. *Harvard Educational Review, 41,* 1–34.

Reese, L., Garnier, H., Gallimore, R., & Goldenberg, C. (2000). Longitudinal analysis of the antecedents of emergent Spanish literacy and middle-school English reading achievement of Spanish-speaking students. *American Educational Research Journal, 37*(3), 633–662.

Rieben, L., Saada-Robert, M., & Moro, C. (1997). Word search strategies and stages of word recognition. *Learning and Instruction, 7,* 137–159.

Rivera, C., & Collum, E. (Eds.). (2006). *State assessment policy and practice for English language learners.* Mahwah, NJ: Lawrence Erlbaum.

Roberts, T. (2009). *No limits to literacy for preschool for English learners.* Thousand Oaks, CA: Corwin Press.

Ruiz-de-Velasco, J., & Fix, M. E. (2000, December). *Overlooked and underserved: Immigrant students in U.S. secondary schools.* Washington, DC: The Urban Institute. Retrieved January 3, 2010, from www.urban.org/publications/310022.html.

Saunders, W., & Goldenberg, C. (1999). *The effects of instructional conversations and literature logs on the story comprehension and thematic understanding of English proficient and limited English proficient students.* Santa Cruz: Center for Research on Education, Diversity & Excellence, University of California.

Saunders, W. M., Foorman, B. R., & Carlson, C. D. (2006). Is a separate block of time for oral English language development in programs for English learners needed? *The Elementary School Journal, 107*(2), 181–198.

Schlagal, R. C. (1992). Patterns of orthographic development into the intermediate grades. In S. Templeton & D. R. Bear (Eds.), *Development of orthographic knowledge and the foundations of literacy: A memorial Festschrift for Edmund H. Henderson* (pp. 31–52). Mahwah, NJ: Lawrence Erlbaum.

Schmitt, N., & McCarthy, M. (1997). *Vocabulary: Description, acquisition and pedagogy.* Cambridge, UK: Cambridge University Press.

Shen, H., & Bear, D. R. (2000). The development of orthographic skills in Chinese children. *Reading and Writing: An Interdisciplinary Journal, 13,* 197–236.

Slavin, R. E., & Cheung, A. (2005). A synthesis of research on language of reading instruction for English language learners. *Review of Educational Research, 75*(2), 247–284.

Spinks, J. A., Liu, Y., Perfetti, C. A., & Tan, L. H. (2000). Reading Chinese characters for meaning: The role of phonological information. *Cognition, 76,* B1–B11.

Stahl, S., & Nagy, W. (2006). *Teaching word meanings.* Mahwah, NJ: Lawrence Erlbaum.

Stauffer, R. (1980). *The language-experience approach to the teaching of reading* (2nd ed.). New York: Harper & Row.

Swan, M., & Smith, B. (2001). *Learner English: A teacher's guide to interference and other problems* (2nd ed.). New York: Cambridge University Press.

Templeton, S. (1983). Using the spelling/meaning connection to develop word knowledge in older students. *Journal of Reading, 27*(1), 8–14.

Templeton, S. (2004). The vocabulary-spelling connection: Orthographic development and morphological knowledge at the intermediate grades and beyond. In J. F. Baumann & E. J. Kame'enui (Eds.), *Vocabulary instruction: Research to practice* (pp. 118–138). New York: Guilford Press.

Templeton, S., Bear, D. R., Invernizzi, M. A., & Johnston, F. (2010). *Vocabulary their way: Word study with middle and secondary students.* Boston: Allyn & Bacon.

Templeton, S., Johnston, F., Bear, D. R., & Invernizzi, M. (2009). *Words their way: Word sorts for derivational relations spellers* (2nd ed.). Boston: Allyn & Bacon.

Thomas, W. P., & Collier, V. P. (2002). *A national study of school effectiveness for language minority students' long-term academic achievement.* Santa Cruz, CA: Center for Research on Education, Diversity & Excellence. Retrieved September 16, 2002, from www.crede.ucsc.edu/research/llaa/1.1_final.html.

Tolchinsky, L., & Teberosky, A. (1998). The development of word segmentation and writing in two scripts. *Cognitive Development, 13,* 1–24.

Townsend, D., Bear, D. R., & Templeton, S. (2009, December). The role of orthography in academic word knowledge and measures of academic achievement for middle school students. In *The orthographic knowledge of middle grade students: Academic vocabulary and spelling, and the orthographic development of struggling English learners in intervention programs.* Symposium conducted at the 59th Annual Meeting of the National Reading Conference, Albuquerque, NM.

U.S. Census Bureau. (2007). *2000 census of population and housing.* Retrieved June 30, 2010, from www.census.gov/prod/cen2000/doc/sf3.pdf.

Venezky, R. L. (1999). *The American way of spelling: The structure and origins of American English orthography.* New York: Guilford Press.

Yang, M. (2005). Development of orthographic knowledge among Korean children in grades 1 to 6 (Doctoral dissertation, University of Virginia, 2005). *Dissertation Abstracts International, 66/05,* 1697.

Zehler, A. M., Fleischman, H. L., Hopstock, P. J., Stephenson, T. G., Pendzick, M., & Sapru, S. (2003, September). *Descriptive study of services to LEP students and LEP students with disabilities: Volume I: Research report* (Contract No. ED-00-CO-0089). Office of English Language Acquisition, Language Enhancement, and Academic Achievement of Limited English Proficient Students (OELA). Retrieved January 20, 2006, from www.ncela.gwu.edu/resabout/research/descriptivestudyfiles.

Children's Literature

Ada, A. F. (2001). *Gathering the sun: An alphabet in Spanish and English.* New York: HarperCollins.

Ada, A. F., & Campoy, F. I. (2004). *Mamá Goose: A Latino nursery treasury/Un tesoro de rimas infantiles.* New York: Hyperion Books for Children. [PRS] [SPAN]

Ada, A. F., Campoy, F. I., & Schertle, A. (2003). *¡Pío peep! Rimas tradicionales en español/Traditional Spanish nursery rhymes.* New York: HarperCollins. [PRS] [SPAN]

Adelson-Goldstein, J., & Shapiro, N. (2008). *Oxford picture dictionary.* New York: Oxford University Press.

Agee, J. (2003). *Z goes home.* New York: Hyperion Books for Children. [ABC]

Aliki. (1999). *My visit to the zoo.* New York: HarperTrophy.

American Heritage (Eds.). (2009). *The American Heritage picture dictionary.* New York: Houghton Mifflin.

Andersen, H. C., & Pinkney, J. (1999). *The ugly duckling.* New York: HarperCollins.

Ayanle, N. (2005). *A Somali alphabet/Alfabeetadda Soomaaliyeed.* Portland: Maine Humanities Council. [ABC]

Bas, M. E. I. (2004). *The ugly duckling/El patito feo.* San Francisco: Chronicle Books. [SPAN]

Base, G. (1986). *Animalia.* New York: Harry N. Abrams. [ABC]

Bayer, J. E. (1992). *A my name is Alice.* New York: Penguin Putnam Books for Young Readers.

Beaton, C. (2003). *Food/La comida.* Hauppauge, NY: Barron's Educational Series. [SPAN]

Berenstain, S., & Berenstain, J. (1983). *Bears on wheels.* New York: HarperCollins.

Bornstein, R. L. (1986). *Little gorilla.* Madison, WI: Turtleback Books.

Boynton, S. (1984). *Horn to toes and in between.* New York: Little Simon.

Brett, J. (1985). *Annie and the wild animals.* New York: Houghton Mifflin.

Brown, M. W. (1993). *Four fur feet.* New York: Doubleday.

Brown, M. W. (1995). *Goodnight Moon/Buenas noches, Luna.* New York: HarperCollins. [SPAN]

Brown, R. (1998). *A dark, dark tale.* London: Mantra Publishing.

Bryan, A. (1997). *Ashley Bryan's ABC of African American poetry.* New York: Aladdin Paperbacks.

Bunting, E. (2000). *Flower garden.* Madison, WI: Turtleback Books.

Bunting, E. (2005). *That's what leprechauns do.* New York: Clarion Books.

Calmenson, S. (2002). *The teeny tiny teacher.* New York: Scholastic.

Carle, E. (1985). *The very busy spider.* New York: Philomel Books.

Carle, E. (1997). *From head to toe.* New York: HarperCollins.

Catalanotto, P. (2005). *Matthew A.B.C.* New York: Atheneum Books for Young Readers. [ABC]

Christian, C. (2005). *Where's the kitten?/Kote Ti Chat La Ye?* (English/Haitian Creole bilingual ed.). Long Island City, NY: Star Bright Books.

Cisneros, S. (1991). *The house on Mango Street.* New York: Random House.

Cleary, B. P., & Gable, B. (2005). *How much can a bare bear bear?* Fresno, CA: Millbrook Press.

Cobrera, J. (2000). *Panda Big and Panda Small.* New York: DK Publishing.

Cowley, J. (1999). *Mrs. Wishy Washy.* New York: Philomel Books.

Delacre, L. (1989). *Arroz con leche: Canciones y ritmos populares de América Latina.* New York: Scholastic. [PRS] [SPAN]

Delacre, L. (2004). *Arrorró mi niño: Latino lullabies and gentle games.* New York: Lee and Low Books. [PRS] [SPAN]

Dragonwagon, C. (1987). *Alligator arrived with apples: A potluck alphabet feast.* New York: Aladdin Books. [ABC]

Eastman, P. D. (1982). *Perro grande . . . Perro pequeño.* New York: Random House. [SPAN]

Ehlert, L. (1989). *Eating the alphabet: Fruits and vegetables from A to Z.* San Diego, CA: Harcourt Brace Jovanovich. [ABC]

Eichenberg, F. (1980). *Ape in a cape.* New York: Harcourt.

Elting, M., & Folsom, M. (2005). *Q is for duck: An alphabet guessing game.* New York: Clarion Books. [ABC]

Emberley, R. (2000). *My opposites/Mis opuestos.* New York: LB Kids. [SPAN]

Emberley, R. (2005). *My city/Mi ciudad.* New York: LB Kids. [SPAN]

Fain, K. (1995). *Handsigns.* San Francisco: Chronicle Books. [ABC]

Ganeri, A., & Oxlade, C. (2002). *First encyclopedia.* New York: Dorling Kindersley.

Glazer, T. (1973). *Eye Winker, Tom Tinker, Chin Chopper.* New York: Doubleday. [PRS]

Goldish, M. (1999). *101 science poems and songs for young learners.* New York: Scholastic. [PRS]

Gonzalez, R., & Ruiz, A. (1995). *My first book of proverbs/ Mi primer libro de dichos.* Emeryville, CA: Children's Book Press. [SPAN]

Graham, C. (1994). *Mother Goose chants.* New York: Oxford University Press. (and others) [PRS]

Griego, M. C., Bucks, B. L., Gilbert, S. S., & Kimball, L. H. (1981). *Tortillitas para Mamá and other nursery rhymes/Spanish and English.* New York: Henry Holt. [PRS] [SPAN]

Gwynne, F. (1988). *The king who rained.* New York: Aladdin Paperbacks.

Hall, N. A., & Syverson-Stork, J. (1999). *Los pollitos dicen/ The baby chicks sing.* New York: Little, Brown. [PRS] [SPAN]

Harper, C. (2008). *Charley Harper ABCs.* Los Angeles: Ammo Books. [ABC]

Hopkins, L. B. (1996). *School supplies: A book of poems.* New York: Aladdin. [PRS]

Hopkins, L. B. (1999). *Spectacular science: A book of poems.* New York: Simon & Schuster. [PRS]

Hopkins, L. B. (2003). *Alphathoughts: Alphabet poems.* Honesdale, PA: Boyds Mills Press. [ABC]

Hutchins, P. (1972). *Good night, owl!* Madison, WI: Turtleback Books.

Jaramillo, N. P. (1996). *Las nanas de abuelita/Grandmother's nursery rhymes.* New York: Henry Holt. [PRS] [SPAN]

Jenkins, S. (2004). *Actual size.* New York: Houghton Mifflin.

Jenkins, S., & Page, R. (2006). *Move!* New York: Houghton Mifflin.

Johnson, D. (1995). *Never ride your elephant to school.* New York: Henry Holt.

Johnson, S. T. (1995). *Alphabet city.* New York: Penguin Putnam. [ABC]

Jonas, A. (1997). *Watch William walk.* New York: Greenwillow Books/HarperCollins.

Jones, C. (1998). *Old MacDonald had a farm.* New York: Houghton Mifflin. [PRS]

Kalman, M. (2003). *What Pete ate from A–Z (really!).* New York: Puffin. [ABC]

Kraus, R. (1994). *Leo the late bloomer.* New York: HarperTrophy.

Krull, K. (2003). *M is for music.* New York: Harcourt. [ABC]

Lederer, R., & Morice, D. (1996). *Pun and games: Jokes, riddles, rhymes, daffynitions, tairy fales and more wordplay for kids.* Chicago: Chicago Review Press.

LeSieg, T. (1999). *The eye book.* New York: Random House.

Loewen, N. (2007). *If you were a homonym or a homophone.* Mankato, MN: Picture Window Books.

London, J. (1992). *Froggy gets dressed.* New York: Viking.

MacDonald, R. (2003). *Achoo! Bang! Crash! The noisy alphabet.* New York: Roaring Book Press. [ABC]

Martin, B. (1970). *Brown Bear, Brown Bear, what do you see?* New York: Henry Holt.

Martin, B. (1998). *Oso Pardo, Oso Pardo, que ves ahi?* New York: Henry Holt. [SPAN]

McIlwain, J. (2009). *DK children's illustrated dictionary.* New York: DK Publishing.

McPhail, D. (1990). *Pig Pig gets a job.* New York: Dutton Children's Books.

Merriam, E. (1994). *Higgle wiggle: Happy rhymes.* New York: Mulberry Books. [PRS]

Miranda, A. (2001). *Alphabet fiesta.* New York: Turtle Books. [ABC]

Molinsky, S. (2005). *Word by word.* New York: Pearson/ Longman.

Molinsky, S., & Bliss, B. (2000). *Side by side.* New York: Pearson/Longman.

Most, B. (1996). *Cock-a-doodle-moo.* Orlando, FL: Harcourt Brace.

Mullins, P. (1997). *V is for vanishing: An alphabet of endangered animals.* New York: HarperTrophy. [ABC]

Munsch, R. (2001). *Mud puddle.* Buffalo, NY: Annick Press.

Nikola-Lisa, W. (2001). *America: A book of opposites/Un libro de contrarios.* New York: Lee and Low Books. [SPAN]

Orozco, J. L. (1999). *De colores and other Latin American folksongs for children.* New York: Puffin Books. [PRS] [SPAN]

Orozco, J. L. (2002). *Diez deditos: Ten little fingers and other play rhymes and action songs from Latin America.* New York: Penguin Putnam Books. [PRS] [SPAN]

Pallota, J. (1993). *The icky bug alphabet book.* Watertown, MA: Charlesbridge Publishing. [ABC]

Parr, T. (2002). *Going places.* New York: Little, Brown.

Parry, F. H. (1995). *Day of Ahmed's secret.* New York: HarperCollins.

Payne, E. (1973). *Katy no-pocket.* New York: Houghton Mifflin.

Pearson, D. (2006). *Alphabeep: A zipping, zooming ABC.* New York: Holiday House. [ABC]

Pearson/Longman. (2008). *Longman dictionary of American English.* New York: Pearson/Longman.

Peek, M. (2006). *Mary wore her red dress and Henry wore his green sneakers.* New York: Sandpiper.

Prelutsky, J. (1983). *The Random House book of poetry for children.* New York: Random House. [PRS]

Prelutsky, J. (1986). *Read-aloud rhymes for the very young.* New York: Alfred A. Knopf. [PRS]

Priddy, R. (2002a). *My big animal book.* New York: St. Martin's Press.

Priddy, R. (2002b). *My big word book: Over 1000 essential first words and pictures.* New York: St. Martin's Press.

Raffi. (1980). *The Raffi singable songbook.* New York: Crown. [PRS]

Raffi. (1987). *Shake my sillies out.* New York: Crown. (and others) [PRS]

Raffi. (1989). *Five little ducks.* New York: Crown. [PRS]

Raschka, C. (2003). *Talk to me about the alphabet.* New York: Henry Holt. [ABC]

Ray, H. A. *Jorge el Curioso (Curious George).* Boston: Houghton Mifflin. [SPAN]

Root, B. (1993). *My first dictionary.* New York: Dorling Kindersley.

Rosa-Mendoza, G. (2001). *My family and I/Mi familia y yo.* Wheaton, IL: me+mi Publishing. [SPAN]

Sanders, M. (1995). *What's your name? From Ariel to Zoe.* New York: Holiday House. [ABC]

Scarry, R. (1999). *Richard Scarry's best word book ever.* New York: Random House.

Scheunemann, P. (2002). *The moose is in the mousse.* Minneapolis, MN: ABDO Publishing.

Sendak, M. (1988). *Where the wild things are.* New York: HarperCollins.

Sendak, M. (1990). *Alligators all around: An alphabet book.* New York: Harper & Row. [ABC]

Sendak, M. (1991a). *Chicken soup with rice.* New York: HarperTrophy. [PRS]

Sendak, M. (1991b). *Donde viven los monstruos: Where the wild things are.* New York: HarperCollins. [SPAN]

Shaskan, T. S. (2009). *If you were a contraction.* Mankato, MN: Picture Window Books.

Soto, G. (1997). *Chato's kitchen.* New York: Penguin Putnam Books for Young Readers.

Soto, G. (2004). *Chato and the party animals.* New York: Puffin Books.

Stevens, J. (1995). *Tops and bottoms.* New York: Harcourt.

Wells, R. (1973). *Noisy Nora.* New York: Penguin Press.

Westcott, N. B. (1996). *I've been working on the railroad.* New York: Scholastic. [PRS]

Wildsmith, B. (2001). *Brian Wildsmith's farm animals.* (Available in seven languages including Tagalog, Korean, Vietnamese, Spanish, and Chinese.) Long Island City, NY: Star Bright Books. [SPAN]

Williams, S. (1992). *I went walking.* New York: Harcourt.

Multilingual and Language Development Materials

American Heritage Dictionaries, Houghton Mifflin Company. Website: www.houghtonmifflinbooks.com/ahd/ dictionaries_children.shtml. Publish an extensive selection of children's and adults' dictionaries and thesauruses including the *The American Heritage Picture Dictionary* (2009).

Barron's Educational Series, Inc. 250 Wireless Blvd., Hauppauge, NY 11788. 800-645-3476. Website: www.barrons.com. Publish ESL materials and children's books in many languages.

Benchmark Education Co., 629 Fifth Ave., Pelham, NY 10803. Website: www.benchmarkeducation.com. Publish ESL materials and books in Spanish and English leveled for reading and language level.

Butte Publications, Inc. PO Box 1328, Hillsboro, OR 97123. 866-312-8883. Website: www.buttepublications .com. Picture dictionaries and workbooks, photograph libraries, and other language support products.

ChinaSprout, Inc. 110 W 32nd St., Fl. 6, New York, NY 10001. 212-868-8488. Website: www.chinasprout .com. Chinese and English bilingual books.

Cinco Puntos Press. 701 Texas, El Paso, TX 79901. Website: www.cincopuntos.com. Literary press specializing in publishing the literature of the U.S./Mexico border, Mexico, and the American Southwest.

Colorín Colorado. Website: www.colorincolorado.org. Articles, resources, and book lists for teaching English learners—in English or Spanish.

Culture for Kids. 4480 Lake Forest Dr. #302, Cincinnati, OH 45242. 800-765-5885. Website: www.culture forkids.com. Bilingual and multilingual materials in over 30 languages and cultural studies on hundreds of countries.

DK Publishing. 375 Hudson St., New York, NY 10014. 646-674-4020. Website: www.dk.com. Picture dictionaries and encyclopedias with photographs.

ESLgold. Website: www.eslgold.net. Provides resources for students who are learning English vocabulary and grammar and for the teachers who serve them. Materials are organized by proficiency level and include color photos of numerous vocabulary words.

Groundwood Books/Libros Tigrillo. 110 Spadina Ave., Suite 801, Toronto, Ontario, Canada M5V 2K4. Website: www.groundwoodbooks.com. Multicultural books including for teens, Spanish language materials.

Hmong Arts, Books, and Crafts (ABC). 298 University Ave. W., St. Paul, MN 55103. 651-293-0019. Website: www.hmongabc.com. Large selection of Hmong books and resource materials.

Independent Publishers Group. 814 North Franklin St., Chicago, IL 60610. 312-337-0747. Website: www .ipgbook.com. Extensive catalog of children's books and books in Spanish.

International Children's Digital Library Foundation. Website: http://en.childrenslibrary.org. Access scanned books in many languages.

Kaplan Early Learning Company. 1310 Lewisville Clemmons Rd., Lewisville, NC 27023. 800-334-2014. Website: www.kaplanco.com. Hands-on materials for language learning and bilingual resources.

Lakeshore Learning Materials. 2695 E. Dominguez St., Carson, CA 90895. 800-428-4414. Website: www.lakeshorelearning.com. Hands-on materials for language learning and bilingual resources.

Language Lizard, PO Box 421, Basking Ridge, NJ 07920. Website: www.languagelizard.com. A resource for bilingual children's books and other products in over 40 languages.

Learning Props. PO Box 774, Racine, WI 53401. 877-776-7750. Website: www.learningprops.com. Games, books, and curriculum kits for bilingual preschool learning.

Learning Resources. 380 North Fairway Dr., Vernon Hills, IL 60061. 888-489-9388. Website: www.learningresources.com. Cards, games, and books for language learning.

Lee & Low Books. 95 Madison Ave., Suite #1205, New York, NY 10016. Website: www.leeandlow.com. Multicultural books with many translations into Spanish. Leveled books that focus on diverse characters and experiences.

Mama Lisa's World. Website: www.mamalisa.com/world/atoz.html. Links to nursery rhymes and songs from around the world.

MantraLingua. 1005 N. Commons Dr., Aurora, IL 60504. 630-851-2111. Website: www.mantralingua.com. Bilingual books in 46 languages, posters, CDs, games, etc.

Master Communications, 4480 Lake Forest Dr. #302, Cincinnati, OH 45242-3753. 513-563-3100. Website: www.master-comm.com. Bilingual books, classroom materials, and electronic resources that promote global understanding.

me+mi publishing, inc. 128 S. County Farm Rd., Suite E, Wheaton, IL 60187. 888-251-1444. Website: www.memima.com. Bilingual concept books in English and Spanish.

Merriam-Webster, Inc. 47 Federal St., PO Box 281, Springfield, MA 01102. 800-828-1880. Website: www.WordCentral.com. Children's dictionaries and resource materials.

Milet Publishing. 333 North Michigan Ave., Suite 530, Chicago, IL 60601. 312-920-1828. Website: www.milet.com. Bilingual books in over 25 languages, world literature, and bilingual picture dictionaries.

Minnesota Humanities Commission/Bilingual and Heritage Language Programs. 987 E. Ivy Ave., St. Paul, MN 55106. 651-772-4246. Website: www.minnesotahumanities.org. Literacy and parent education resources available in numerous languages such as Spanish, Somali, and Hmong.

Multicultural Books and Videos. 28880 Southfield Rd. #183, Lathrop Village, MI 48076. 248-559-2676. Website: www.multiculturalbooksandvideos.com. Books, audio, and video materials in heritage languages and bilingual versions.

National Geographic School Publishing/Hampton-Brown. PO Box 4002865, Des Moines, IA 50340. 888-915-3276. Website: www.ngsp.com. Instructional materials for language, literacy, and content areas in English and Spanish.

Oxford University Press. 198 Madison Ave., New York, NY 10016. 212-726-6000. Website: www.oup.com. Publisher of Oxford Picture Dictionaries and bilingual picture dictionaries in many languages.

Pan Asian Publications. Website: www.panap.com. Children's books and electronic resources in Chinese, Korean, Spanish, Vietnamese, Russian, and more.

Peppercorn Books & Press, Inc. PO Box 693, Snow Camp, NC 27349. 877-574-1634. Website: www.peppercornbooks.com. Books and materials for children and adult English learners, including bilingual materials in numerous heritage languages.

Priddy Books, St. Martin's Press, Macmillan Publishing. Website: http://us.macmillan.com/author/rogerpriddy. A series of simple expository books from illustrated word books through early reference titles for older students.

ProLingua Associates. 74 Cotton Mill Hill, Suite 315A, Brattleboro, VT 05301. Website: www.prolinguaassociates.com. Interactive language teaching products for secondary and adult levels.

Resources for Reading, Inc. 130 East Grand Ave., South San Francisco, CA 94080. 800-278-7323. Website: www.abcstuff.com. Materials and supplies for reading teachers, including literacy materials in Spanish.

Saint Paul Public Schools English Language Learner Program, 360 Colborne St., Saint Paul, MN 55102. 651-767-8320. Website: http://ell.spps.org/ELL_On-line_Store.html. Glossaries, handbooks, literacy support materials, and curriculum kits in multiple languages including Hmong and Somali.

Salina Bookshelf, Inc. 1254 W. University Ave., Suite 130, Flagstaff, AZ 86001. 877-527-0700. Website: www.salinabookshelf.com. A Navajo language publishing company.

Scholastic, Inc. 524 Broadway, Fl. 9, New York, NY 10012. 212-965-7965. Bilingual and Spanish-language books.

Star Bright Books. The Star Building, 42-26 28th St., Suite 2B, Long Island City, NY 11101. 800-788-4439. Website: www.starbrightbooks.org. Publish children's books in 20 languages.

Trabalenguas. PO Box 286, LaGrange, IL 60525. 708-352-3502. Website: www.spanishspeech.com. Phonological awareness games and vocabulary cards in Spanish.

University of California, Los Angeles. (2010). *Language Materials Project*. Website: www.lmp.ucla.edu/Profile.aspx?menu=004. Teaching resources for less commonly taught languages. Includes background information, authentic teaching materials, language profiles, and related resource sites for almost 100 language groups.

INDEX